CATHOLIC HOME SCHOOLING

Mary Kay Clark, Ph.D.

God bless you
and your family.

Seton Press
Front Royal, Virginia

The Cover

The cover is a photograph of Our Mother of Good Counsel, freely donated by Mr. Joao S. Cla Dias, a photographer and author of the beautifully illustrated book *The Mother of Good Counsel of Genazzano*. I thank him for his generosity.

Many years ago, I learned about this miraculous fresco and have had a special devotion to the Blessed Virgin Mother under this title ever since. It seems especially appropriate for home schooling mothers or prospective home schooling mothers to ask for her counsel as they make decisions about their family life.

The miraculous fresco is located in the little town of Genazzano, Italy. Many miracles in relation to the fresco have been reported.

The fresco, of unidentifiable materials, has been suspended in the air for the past five centuries. It has been venerated over the centuries by popes and saints.

Amazingly, miracles have been associated not only with the original, but also with copies of the original. It is my prayer that Our Mother of Good Counsel will work miracles in the hearts of Catholic parents who read this book and direct them to do what is best for their families to live the authentic Catholic family life.

—Dr. Mary Kay Clark, Ph.D.

Catholic Home Schooling

A Handbook for Parents

By Dr. Mary Kay Clark, Ph.D.
DIRECTOR OF SETON HOME STUDY SCHOOL

"Suffer the little children to come unto me, and
forbid them not." – Mark 10:14

Seton Press

Front Royal, Virginia

Third Edition.

Library of Congress Card Catalog No.: 93-60757

ISBN: 978-1-60704-138-2

Requests for permission to make copies of any part of the work should be mailed to:

Seton Home Study School
Permissions Department
1350 Progress Drive
Front Royal, VA 22630

Printed and bound in the United States of America.

Seton Press
Seton Home Study School
1350 Progress Drive
Front Royal, VA 22630
2014

This book is dedicated to the Sacred Heart of Jesus,
and to His Blessed Mother under her title,
"Our Mother of Good Counsel."

Contents

Acknowledgments

I wish to thank my parents, John and Jacqueline Lynch of Cleveland, Ohio, for my Catholic upbringing, which led me to teach my children at home and eventually to write this book.

I thank those who have helped me write this book, especially my sons Kevin and John.

In addition, I gratefully thank those who have donated chapters: Dr. Mark Lowery, home schooling father and professor of Moral Theology; Ginny Seuffert, a home schooling mother of twelve children who has many years of home schooling experience; Kenneth Clark, my oldest son and Seton's home schooling attorney; Cathy Gould, a certified LD (Learning Disability) counselor for Seton; and Cathy Rich, a home schooling mother with an LD child.

I also thank my husband Bruce, and my seven sons, Kenneth, Kevin, Daniel, Paul, John, Jim, and Timothy, for their cooperation over the years which has helped me to grow spiritually, and allowed me to spend so much time working with home schooling families.

In addition, I am grateful to Father John Hardon, Father Charles Fiore, Father Paul Marx, and Father Robert Fox, all now deceased. I thank Father Matthew Habiger. I also thank Father Constantine Belisarius, who is a counselor at Seton. All these priests have been very supportive of Catholic home schooling and my work.

I thank all the staff at Seton Home Study School who work together so cooperatively to make home schooling possible for many Catholic families.

Finally, I thank all the Seton Home Study School families who have allowed me the privilege of being part of their home schooling experience.

Foreword

by Father Robert J. Fox

Parents, if any of you are inclined to think the content of this book, *Catholic Home Schooling,* is out of focus or extreme, let me, as a pastor, share some experiences with you.

I know what it is to serve the same parish as assistant priest and later as pastor, in both cases teaching grades one through twelve each week. I know what it is to teach in a Catholic school where children were taught the basics of the Catholic Faith, only to return years later after the Second Vatican Council and discover that children in the same school now knew almost nothing about Catholicism.

I know what it is to be assigned as pastor to a parish where, when I arrived, teenagers in the high school CCD program saw no difference between Catholicism and the "great world religions" of Islam, Buddhism, and Hinduism. I know what it is to be assigned to still another parish where the CCD teachers thought it was "ecumenism" not to teach that the Catholic Church is the True Church. I know what it is to give a two-day workshop to parish priests on the religious education of youth at one of the most prestigious Catholic universities in the United States and have someone from the university staff tell me I had no right to insist that young people be taught that the Catholic Church is the True Church.

Since ordination, I have taught in my parish grades one through twelve each week of the school year. As the bishop is the primary teacher of the Faith in the diocese, so as pastor I am the primary teacher in the total parish, and I want to know what is going on in our classrooms. I was ordained when everything was in place: Catholic schools were CATHOLIC schools. Children and teenagers knew the basics of the Faith.

Twelve years after being transferred from the parish where I first served, I was reassigned there as pastor. I discovered that the children in the full-time Catholic grade school now did not know the basics of the Faith. Catholic students in the local high school, most of whom had gone through the local parish grade school, had no idea that in Holy

Communion we receive the Body, Blood, Soul, and Divinity of Jesus Christ. They had no idea that the Mass re-enacts throughout all time the Sacrifice of the Cross. They had no concept of sin as mortal or venial or the obligation of Sunday Mass. What is more, their parents were ignorant of the fact that their children knew almost nothing about the Faith. They had completely entrusted their own primary duty as educators and formers of their children to others. They did not bother to check if their children were being taught the Faith. They assumed others were doing it for them.

When I was a newly ordained priest, my greatest love, after offering the Holy Sacrifice of the Mass and administering the sacraments as acts of Jesus Christ extended in time and space, was the education and formation of children and teenagers. After all these years in Christ's holy priesthood, my priorities remain the same. I consider my work in educating and forming children as auxiliary to the primary task of parents and as an extension of my duty to preach the Gospel of Jesus Christ.

Writing for the Catholic press, I know what it is to receive thousands of letters from Catholic parents in every part of the United States. During the past 25 years, these parents often discovered too late that their children were not being taught Catholicism, but were being taught heresy. To give a few examples:

"We have eight children. They robbed our first five children of the True Faith in Catholic grade and high school. They'll not get our remaining three. We are teaching them at home ourselves." Or, "Father, in our local school, children are being taught in the name of the Catholic Church things that we know are contrary to Catholicism. Will we be sinning if we take them out of that school?" My answer: "You are asking the wrong question. You should ask, 'What is my responsibility if I leave them in?'"

Often I have heard this in reply: "But the alternative in the public school is even worse. No discipline, no morals, etc....What can I possibly do?"

Now I can answer that question with, "Read the book *Catholic Home Schooling* by Dr. Mary Kay Clark, and you will know what you are seriously bound to do."

The Second Vatican Council was not responsible for the abuses so rampant today. An Ecumenical Council is guided by the Holy Spirit. Also, there are some notable exceptions to what I wrote above, concerning the failure to teach the Faith in Catholic schools. There are some good Catholic schools remaining. The number is not great. There are good informed pastors. There are also pastors who do not know what is going on in their CCD programs or local Catholic schools. They have too often entrusted everything to others, just as parents have.

Some pastors simply do not understand the obligations of parents to teach their children. "We don't want that magazine on our parish rack. It promotes home schooling." That is what one pastor said of the family magazine for which I am editor. "Those people are a bit odd. They home school their children. They are hindering development of their children by home schooling them."

These kinds of statements—made by laity, religious, and priests— are contrary to authentic Catholic Faith. Even some pastors display their ignorance of Church teachings and the documents of the Second Vatican Council by failing to recognize the validity and importance of home schooling.

The Declaration on Christian Education of Vatican II makes it very clear:

> As it is parents who have given life to their children, on them lies the gravest obligation of education. They must therefore be recognized as being primarily and principally responsible for their education. The role of parents in education is of such importance that it is almost impossible to provide an adequate substitute.

When the present book, *Catholic Home Schooling,* fell into my hands, and after reading the Introduction, which I considered an accurate assessment of the problems we face today, the first chapter I looked at was "The Father's Role in Home Schooling." When I addressed the International Symposium for the 75th anniversary of Fatima—where Our Lady came as a catechist and Mother of Evangelization—I laid much of the responsibility for the crisis in faith today on the fathers of our families. The crisis of faith is something that has been escalating for several centuries, reaching back to the Protestant Revolt and to the causes which led up to it. Catholic fathers have frequently relinquished their roles, while mothers have all too often fallen for the Feminist Movement.

The next chapter I could not wait to get at was "The Socialization Issue." This is the first objection I hear to home schooling. Strange, in having led multiple hundreds of youth for many years from every part of the United States and Canada to Fatima for four weeks each summer, I have noticed no social problems with home schooled youth. I have found that those who are home schooled possess a maturity I have not witnessed in other youth.

Next my eyes fell on the chapter "Discipline in the Catholic Home Schooling Family." I have noticed on the youth pilgrimages to Europe that those best in possession of self-discipline, who immediately grasp why we are in Mary's land and what I am attempting to accomplish, are often those who are home schooled. They are always (I say "*always*") the youth who know their Faith in some depth and can discuss it intelligently. They are motivated youth from motivated parents. They come motivated to experience the Church as One, Holy, Universal, and Apostolic.

Observing the modernists, the dissenters within the Church, and growing secularism invading our parish churches—having succeeded quite well in our schools—Fulton J. Sheen said, "It is the laity who will save the Church." I can say, in my own work as pastor and journalist these 25 years past, that what has helped me remain quite optimistic that truth will prevail and that the Sacred Heart of Jesus and the Immaculate Heart of Mary will triumph has been the thousands of good parents from coast to coast who have contacted me. They have been gravely concerned that their children be educated and formed in true Catholicism.

Young people on "Youth for Fatima" pilgrimages often conclude their two weeks by saying, "Now I am not alone. Now I know there are many other youth across the United States whose parents are teaching them the same Catholic values of faith and morals as my parents have been doing for me."

Parents, in home schooling you are not alone! I have been writing for the last 30 years on Catholic education and formation, on the duty of parents as the primary educators of their children, and on the need for faithfulness to the Magisterium. About a quarter of a century ago, a Catholic parent encouraged me to give up my apostolates in order to form Catholic home schooling programs. It would have meant giving up my assignment as pastor of a parish also. She and some other Catholic parents, in desperation because there were no good Catholic or public schools locally, were using home schooling programs such as those produced by Baptists. They attempted to supply the Catholic doctrine to the essentially

Protestant programs. I thought this practice risky at best. But now we have our own Catholic home schooling. And it is logical that such came from the laity.

We are still in the infancy of home schooling for our modern times. But home schooling in itself is as old as the Church. There was a time when the Divine Liturgy and the home were the chief and only educators in the Faith. If our Catholic schools, which made such a noble contribution in the past, failed in any special area, it was the failure to communicate to parents that *they* are the primary educators and formers of their children in the fullness of True Faith and that it is virtually impossible to provide an adequate substitute.

Father Robert J. Fox, *Fatima Family Apostolate*

Preface

by Thomas A. Nelson

"Does home schooling make sense academically, and if so, can I do it?" These two questions are undoubtedly uppermost in the minds of many parents who are considering home schooling. Dr. Mary Kay Clark has written *Catholic Home Schooling* in large part to answer these two extremely important questions—as well as, of course, to give the spiritual reasons for home schooling.

The purpose of this Preface is to add an exclamation mark to what Dr. Clark says in her book and to answer a resounding "Yes" to both of the above questions.

First of all, why does it make excellent sense academically? As a former teacher with a Master's Degree in Education who has taught self-contained sixth grade twice, once in Catholic, once in public school (for two years each), public high school English for two years, and junior college philosophy for two years; as someone who has seen good, bad, and mediocre teachers; who has seen good and bad things done in the name of education; who has enjoyed some success as the fruit of hard work and intelligent planning; who has seen every mistake in the book committed and gotten away with by state "certified" teachers; who has had to mop up students academically after they spent years under poor instruction; having these credentials I believe I can say, with a certain amount of authority, that home schooling makes sense academically, and this for eight basic reasons:

1. You do not waste the students' time. In a junior or senior high school setting, about one hour 40 minutes per day are spent among a) home room b) traveling between classes and c) getting ready to leave class and settling down in the new class. Added to this, between one-half hour and one hour, average, are spent going to and coming from school. This amounts to more than two hours wasted during the day, not to mention classroom time ill-spent, wasted by an unprepared or poor teacher or

waiting for unprepared and/or poor students to respond or be dealt with by the teacher.

2. You do not re-teach what the student already knows. Since the parent-teacher knows intimately what has been covered in the previous days, weeks, months, and years, she does not have to go back and cover that ground all over again, other than to make a general review. It is axiomatic academically that the larger the context the less gets taught. During the 1960s one of the last of the one-room school houses in the United States closed. Almost every student who attended eight years of school there went on to win a National Merit Scholarship after high school. The reason was simple: the school had an excellent teacher who knew all the children and did not re-teach them what they already knew, but kept them growing and growing. About the same time, there was a study done on the schools of Finland which showed that those children that came from the northern hinterlands where most schools had only two teachers—one for the first four years of grade school and one for the second four years—did much better academically than children from the larger towns and cities, where there was a different teacher for every year. The reason deduced by those conducting the study was that the teachers in these small schools knew their students well and did not re-teach what had already been learned.

3. You can give your own children more individualized attention. Even if you are a mother with a large family, you can still give far more, and far faster, individual attention to each of your children than a teacher in a classroom with 25 to 30 students. You do not have to take attendance, deal as much with naughty children, or handle administrative details. You can get right to work and your children are not waiting for help.

4. You can gear the work to a pace your children can handle and that will keep them interested. One of the chief reasons for failure in school, or failure of students to do well in school, is the slow (sometimes snail-paced) speed of the class.

5. You can (and should) eliminate the option to fail! Not adopting this simple academic principle is much of the reason why public schools do not succeed academically with all students. After all, the opposite of failure is success. If the teachers in public schools, along with the administrations, all swore themselves not to fail with any child and to do whatever it takes to succeed with every child, then every child would go forth a success, academically speaking, even from our public schools.

Despite lack of support from the administration, I was always able to achieve this objective in both public and Catholic schools. The idea is not hard. Applying it is. It means lots of work. The school bus leaves, the children must be on it (or so everyone thinks), the teachers shrug their shoulders and mollify their consciences with, "If the parents don't care, what can I do?" and take their unearned paychecks and let tomorrow's generation slip through their academic fingers irreparably unprepared for life. And the country has another batch of the uneducated to help after they leave school and to try to bootstrap up into something productive once they enter the work force. Or, it sends them on to college to learn finally what should have been taught in grade school and high school.

6. You can build in automatic consequences for failure to perform. This reason is actually an extension of number 5 above, but it is covered separately because of its importance. Building into your home school regimen automatic consequences for failure to perform a) on time, b) with work completely done, c) with work done correctly, and d) with it executed well (i.e. neat, clean, well written and well punctuated) will ensure academic excellence. Because we are all subject to Original Sin, we tend not to want to do what we should, especially if it is hard. To inculcate a spirit of virtue in your children, therefore, it is imperative always "to hold the stick" as a consequence for failure to perform, to perform on time, to perform completely and well. If your children know that automatically they will receive extra schoolwork in those areas where they are weak, PLUS a nice little essay (well executed, now!) on why they should have their work done properly and on time, every time they fail to perform, believe me, they will start to perform! It may take a week or two or three of this routine to break bad habits, but the extra work load, plus being deprived of some of their free time, will eventually send a message that the avenue of failure is no longer open. Within a short time you will, by this method, channel a balky student into the path of success, which is a pleasant experience, and he or she then becomes self-motivated, and that battle is won.

7. You can emphasize reading. Ninety-nine percent of academics hinges upon reading. I used to require a book a week, on top of all other English curriculum—or in self-contained sixth grade, on top of all other work. There were cries and moans for two weeks or so, but because I would allow the students to read anything they wanted, as long as it was

a decent book, the idea was easy to sell. Reporting was easy, always done on 3 x 5 cards handed in at the end of each month. Occasionally, reports were given orally to others in the class, and about once a month a book report was given as the topic of the weekly essay. Extra credit was given for extra books read. The average student can easily read more than one book per week in addition to other work. The results of this practice are incredible: up goes vocabulary, up goes reading comprehension, up goes interest in school, up goes the ability to write good sentences, up goes the psychosomatic ability to read faster and faster with more and more understanding, up goes the fund of knowledge acquired, up goes the ability to spell, up goes the interest in all sorts of things, and up goes student confidence that they can achieve academically. You can achieve amazing results with your children, and if you implement the "book a week" reading program—even if you are the world's worst possible teacher—your children will far out-pace whatever they could have achieved in the very best of formal schools. Make this simple reading program "the academic safety net" of your home schooling effort and you cannot miss success.

8. Home schooling eliminates the silliness and nonsense picked up from peers. Rather than your children modeling themselves on some cool goof, they will continue to model themselves on you as they have since infancy, and their behavioral education will continue to be formed by an adult. The net result is that you will have adult-acting children, especially if you continue to speak to them intelligently on intelligent topics and expect intelligent conversation from them.

Other reasons could be elicited, and Mary Kay Clark does so, but these eight reasons should be enough to convince you that home schooling is a sound concept academically. Now we must address the second important question: "Can I do it?"

Why not? You are presumably a person of at least reasonable intelligence—and certainly a person of uncommon common sense if you have gone to the effort to begin reading this book and possibly even to the expense of buying it. That much shows you realize that something is very wrong with education today, and you would like to do something about it for your children.

Let me assure you, as a teacher who taught in six different situations—in grade school, high school, and college—teachers are human beings, just like you and me. There are good ones and bad ones, well educated ones and poorly educated ones, effective ones and ineffective ones, energetic ones and lazy ones. Just keeping your children from the bad influence of bad teachers is a tremendous plus.

Probably what bothers you is the nagging question "Can I teach?" "Can I actually do it?" I answer, again, "Why not?" Thousands of incompetents are teaching in our schools; are you going to be any worse? The old time nuns that made the Catholic educational system the model and marvel of our country were basically high school educated ladies. Granted, their orders helped them with instructions in how to teach, but you can get that sort of information in "how to" books and from other home schoolers. Plus, the course work from the home school suppliers— and even the text books themselves—hold your hand through the work. Teaching is largely a question of getting in and starting to swim.

In home schooling your own children, nobody is asking you to do anything horribly difficult. I learned partially by doing, but especially by the guidance of a fellow sixth-grade teacher. You too can call on others who are home schooling to help you, just as this teacher helped me.

The Roman writer Tacitus said, "*Omne ignotum, pro magnifico,*" which translates roughly, "Everything unknown is taken for wonderful." Right now, if you are apprehensive about home schooling, you are operating under the typical human syndrome of taking as wonderful that which is unknown. Let's face it, once you do it, it won't be unknown any more, and your fear of teaching your children at home will disappear. All you have to do is get in and do it. If you get over your head in some area, call upon other home schoolers for help with your problems. And, of course, Dr. Clark addresses a great many of these problems in this tremendous book.

If, in any way, I can be an added voice of encouragement to that of Dr. Clark, let me say that you do not need to have a college degree to become an excellent teacher, but you do have to work at it. You don't have to have extraordinary intelligence to teach your children; you mainly have to want them to excel. You do not need many fancy courses in teaching to know how to teach, but it does help to ask other teachers (home schoolers or otherwise) for advice on particular points. In short, what I would like to say to you mothers and fathers is this: "You can do it!" Even if you have only a high school education (or less), "You can do it!"

A simple principle exists in all education. The teacher always learns more than the student. You are going to learn the subjects that you teach your children. That will make you a better you. It will also give you a great deal in common with your children. And it will help to make your home a little university of human knowledge. Rather than shirk from this role, you should embrace it as a wonderful learning experience. Not only can home schooling work for your children, it has a far better chance of working than any other alternatives available. So what are you waiting for?

Pray for guidance—especially to Our Lady of Good Counsel, through the Holy Rosary—read this book, talk with those who are home schooling, and then step out there with confidence.

Introduction

The story of how I came to be the Director of Seton Home Study School is, in many ways, the story of a typical Catholic family seeking the authentic Catholic family lifestyle in confusing times. In my travels to various cities, I have been surprised by the similarities of stories among Catholic families struggling to keep the Faith.

The oldest of a family of nine children, I grew up in the forties and fifties in Bethesda, Maryland, a suburb of Washington, D.C. My parents were active politically in the Republican Party and often campaigned for better legislation, usually concerning education and family issues. They were concerned about the local public schools and better education; once my father ran for the local school board. They were active in the Church and involved with the parish school. Mom and Dad fought against pornography in the fifties, giving lectures to parent groups.

While in high school in Cleveland, Ohio, I met Bruce, my future husband, but went on to a Catholic college for four years. Bruce and I were married the month I graduated from college, but I continued my education at Western Reserve University and at Catholic University to obtain my Master's degree. My husband was in the army while I was in college, and later, after we were married, he was recalled for the Berlin Crisis. My first baby, Kenneth, was born almost exactly a year after we were married.

During the early sixties, though I was married, pregnant, working as a librarian and going to Western Reserve library graduate school, I was still involved with my mother in Church and political activities. The encyclical *Pacem in Terris* was published, and we both attended conferences to hear "Catholics" proclaim that we should accommodate Socialists and Communists. We attended lectures where "Catholic" women gave their own version of what it meant to be a modern Catholic woman.

In the sixties, the first immediate disturbance to an ordinary family's faith came with the "new" religion texts in schools and parish programs. The publishers' names became household words, as parents across the country compared notes with relatives and friends. My mother started

Concerned Catholic Parents of Cleveland, a group dedicated to fighting the new religion being promoted in the Catholic schools. During this battle, I moved to Columbus, Ohio, with Bruce and our three young children. I was asked by parents in Columbus to analyze a catechism series. I spent hours in a seminary library researching the teachings of the Church and became convinced that the "new" religion texts were not presenting Catholic truths.

The basic problem with the new religion texts back in the sixties was their failure to teach the Ten Commandments, Original Sin, actual sin, Confession, the Holy Sacrifice of the Mass as a re-enactment of Christ's Sacrifice on Calvary, and so on. The emphasis was on deciding for oneself what was best; truth was subjective. Children were not taught that the Catholic Church is the True Church, nor that the pope is the vicar of Jesus Christ on Earth. Church truths, if mentioned at all, were presented as just another viewpoint among many from which to choose.

Catholics United for the Faith was started during this turbulent period, evaluating religion texts being used around the country. *The Wanderer* became very popular as a support for all of us who thought we were alone.

The Catholic parents in Columbus, as in other cities throughout the country, were not willing to sit by quietly. Our first enterprise was to print the questionable quotes from the new religion texts on flyers and distribute them to every Catholic Church at all Masses on a particular weekend.

This activity caused quite a stir, which resulted in the formation of a city-wide organization, Catholic Parents of Columbus. Membership quickly included parents from all over the state. We printed a monthly newsletter and met with pastors and parish committees, as well as with the diocesan board of education, and even with the bishop. We sponsored a weekly radio program to teach the truths of the Faith.

After a year or so, not only had no changes been made by the diocesan authorities or educators, but updated versions of the new religion texts were proceeding further from the official teachings. A second "parking-lot apostolate" project encompassed the whole Columbus area, extending well into the suburbs. After a couple of years, our parking-lot apostolate struck for a third time.

More years passed, and though parents continued to complain and actively tried to seek a return to the teachings of the Church, things became continually worse. In fact, by the late sixties the first sex education program appeared in the Catholic schools: the "Becoming a Person" series from Benziger Publishers.

Our organization fought back again. We published a flyer with exact quotes from the "Becoming a Person" program and distributed it one weekend in every parish parking lot at every Mass at every church in the greater Columbus area. The result? Complaints were made by parents about the pornography we were putting on the windshields, even though the explicit sexual quotes were directly from the textbooks their own children were using in the schools! Nearby Protestant churchgoers were terribly upset when their cars were accidentally covered with "Catholic" pornography.

Diocesan authorities were upset about the parents' movement against their new and "relevant" changes! We had a meeting with the diocesan school board to complain officially, but to no avail. We had meetings with pastors and with parents in various parishes. We even met with the bishop.

Like a steamroller, the Catholic schools continued to push toward a confused new religion which parents could not recognize, to implement secular humanism in other subject areas, especially social studies, and to teach explicit sexual material fraudulently titled "Family Life Education." We felt pulled into the sewer of discussing explicit sexual perversions.

By 1971, we in the Catholic Parents of Columbus organization felt our energies were being wasted in trying to change the schools and/ or the educators. So the organization changed its approach completely. We decided to form our own Catholic school, Mater Dei Academy, in Columbus, Ohio.

Through the 1970s, Mater Dei was a tremendous success. It is still in existence. Parents in other cities around the country began similar schools. Philosophy professor Dr. William Marra founded "Holy Innocents" schools. *Wanderer* columnist Frank Morris began a school in Denver. Anne Carroll, wife of Dr. Warren Carroll, the founder of Christendom College, started Seton School outside Washington, D.C. Similar schools sprang up in Cincinnati, Cleveland, Detroit, Denver, New York City, Dallas, Los Angeles, and other areas around the country. Some are still going.

At one point, I think there may have been about 200 small parent-operated Catholic schools in the country. After helping various parent groups in nearby states, a group of us sponsored a convention in Cleveland to help start parent-operated schools and to help with home schooling. Parent-operated schools had names like Agnus Dei, Mater Dei, Our Lady of Fatima, and Rosary Academy. The names reflected parents' love for the Blessed Mother, the Rosary, and the use of Latin in Catholic culture.

Though some of these schools continue to this day, by the 1980's most parents were overwhelmed by the tremendous difficulties of raising a family and running a school at the same time. By 1985, more and more Catholic families were starting to teach their children at home.

In 1982, Seton Home Study School was founded by Anne Carroll as a division of Seton School in Manassas, Virginia. Our family moved to Front Royal, Virginia, to be near Christendom College, where my two oldest sons were attending college. In 1983, I joined Seton Home Study as the assistant director. There were about 50 students in the home study division and about 100 students in the day school. Today the day school has about 350 students, whereas the home study school has approximately 11,000 students. By 1991, the home study division had grown so large that Seton Home Study School officially separated as a legal entity from the day school. In 1981, the home study division was run from one room in the Seton School building. Today, our building totals about 40,000 square feet. We have 75 full-time employees, and another 75 part-time, many off-premises and several seasonal employees.

Meeting with families around the country, I have seen a pattern repeated. Families first start complaining to Church authorities, hoping for understanding and a return to the teachings of the Church. Parents discover their complaints are not heeded. Then, after a few years, many parents form a school or simply start schooling with another family or two—or start home schooling just one or two children or enroll in a home study school. The means may be different, but the emphasis is the same: parents become the teachers; students learn from parents.

What the new breed of Catholic educators and catechists did not count on is that today's parents are better informed and mothers are more sure of themselves and their ability to educate their own children. At first, Catholic educators were able to intimidate parents regarding the religion texts, making parents doubt their own understanding of their faith learned in childhood. But Catholic educators could not fool Catholic parents about sex education programs.

Some people in the Church minimize the abuses in Catholic education and counsel patience, but parents cannot wait for a better day at the expense of their own children's souls. Children are being formed, one way or another, with every passing day, and parents rightly feel pressured to take action. The Church can wait decades to deal with issues, but children have only a few short years in which they will either become good Catholics or be lost to the Church, to the Faith, to eternal salvation.

When I speak with some older parents or with grandparents, tears come to their eyes as they admit they have lost their older children. "My children don't want children" is a fairly common remark. Young parents, however, are discovering, through the grace of God, their deep privilege and grave obligation to be the primary educators of their children. Even parents who are not aware of the depth of the Catholic teachings are determined to keep their families strong in traditional values. They have a love for Jesus and Mary and refuse to keep their children in schools which reject the teachings of the Church, or even simple moral truths.

Parents are pulling their children out of Catholic schools because they cannot find a single Catholic textbook. They bring their children home because teachers say parents who pray the Rosary are old-fashioned. Mothers do not want their children subjected to laughter and verbal abuse from teachers and peers who think wearing a scapular is silly. Finally, parents do not want their children to experience the degradation of sex education programs.

Mothers who are home schooling are giving their children love and stability, a spiritual way of life, a habit of looking to Jesus and Mary for answers and of making the sacramental life real and active in the home.

Families who are home schooling are joining with other home schooling families whenever possible to attend Mass, to say the Rosary, to visit Marian shrines, to make Advent wreaths, to decorate May altars, and in general to make the traditional beliefs, faith, and customs of the Catholic heritage an integral part of their lifestyle. With their philosophy and activities, home schooling families are preserving the Catholic Faith and are becoming a faithful remnant in difficult times. Home schooling families are fostering vocations to the priesthood and religious life. Above all, however, they are planting the seeds—through the formation of their children—for a new springtime of the Catholic Faith.

Parents today realize they are living in a pagan society in which Christian values, particularly those related to family life, are being destroyed through the media and through government policies. They also realize our Catholic children are losing the Faith through the Catholic schools they once trusted and which were built through the sweat and money of their parents and grandparents.

Parents see that the time has come for them to stop depending on others to transmit the Faith to their children. The time has come to stop looking to Catholic schools for the solutions to their problems. They do not doubt that the Church will survive, as Christ promised. However, these parents are discovering that part of Our Lord's promise is the grace offered to revitalize the Church through strong Catholic families. These home schooling parents are responding to that grace.

Chapter 1:
Why Catholic Home Schooling?

The reasons why Catholic families choose home schooling are as varied as the families themselves. While each family might give varying explanations of its reasons, we can see some trends. Many highly-educated parents simply believe that they can do a better job educating their children than schools could do. Many parents are devoted to the welfare of their children, and they are willing to take the momentous step of assuming complete control of their children's education. Many parents see home schooling as a way to strengthen their family life and hold their family together during a time when half of the marriages in this country end in divorce.

Other parents are dissatisfied with the available schools, whether public, private, or Catholic. Sometimes they see in the schools an anti-family social agenda which is pushed at the children through the teachers and textbooks. Homosexuality and "same sex marriages" are being discussed in many schools as an optional alternative. We see parents turning to home schooling because of the guns and knives, the beatings, the physical abuse and attacks that are part of the daily scene in many schools today. When any major violence occurs at a school, some parents decide that that is the last straw and turn to home schooling.

Some parents are dissatisfied because they see the schools as simply another over-regulated bureaucracy. Instead of making sure that each child learns, some schools seem more focused on keeping up the school's test scores. This can put a great deal of pressure on both teachers and children.

It is a sad fact that many Catholic home schooling families recognize the deficiencies in their local Catholic school. The Catholic parochial school system in the United States has had a wonderful reputation for many years. It is generally accepted by Catholics and non-Catholics that the parochial school system is able to keep out troublemakers and, with a religious base, the discipline problems are not as great and the educational progress is better. There is no doubt that this was and is true. The work of many parochial schools, especially in the inner cities, is nothing short of heroic. They offer many children an escape from an unrelentingly hostile public school system.

However, even though they are much better than public schools, Catholic schools are often not all that they should be. Many Catholic parochial schools started changing in the 1970s when the catechisms started changing: doctrine was watered down, some doctrines were not even taught. By the 1980s, parents were rebelling in greater numbers. While parents were unhappy with the fluff that was being taught in the new catechisms, the worst nightmare for parents was the sex education programs. As parents started complaining and withdrawing, as parents started their own small schools, the parochial school tuition started climbing, fewer parents sent their children, and schools began to close.

On the other hand, the very success of Catholic schools has led to another problem. Many non-Catholics now attend the schools and many Catholic schools have non-Catholic teachers, even non-Catholic principals, and parents find it impossible to discuss what is being taught with such teachers. This has led to a lessening of the Catholic identity of some schools. At one school on the East Coast, a Protestant teacher was encouraging Catholic students to attend a Protestant worship service. Parents complained, the pastor let her go, but the local bishop insisted (probably for reasons related to labor laws) that the Protestant teacher be kept. This reinforces the point that schools have many constituencies to please. The rights of Catholic parents and students may actually be far down on the list.

At this time in the life of the Church, of course, we have the whole situation regarding the sexual abuse of children, and the resulting programs directed toward children in the schools. These "safe environment" programs are not what parents want their children to be learning at such a young age. Parents are now complaining that the solution, which is indoctrinating thousands of young children about child sexual abuse, and warning kids about the danger of "good touching and bad touching" of relatives and friends, is doing more harm than good, and is not solving the problem. The problem is not the children's education, but those inside the Church who have rejected traditional doctrine. According to figures from the National Catholic Education Assocation, from 2000 to 2004, Catholic school enrollment in the U.S. dropped from 2.6 million to 2.4

million. Whether that is because of the abuse scandals, or because of the programs instituted in reaction to those scandals, no one knows.

Years ago, some parents were frightened to try home schooling, worried about the responsibility and about their own ability to educate their children. They were afraid they did not have the skills or the education to teach their children. However, with the numbers of friends and relatives who are doing it, and with the numerous Catholic home school support groups available, parents know help is available for embarking on this adventure. In addition, home schooling programs such as Seton Home Study School are available with counselors to help in each subject area and grade level.

We have all heard the stories, the miserable situations that families have to deal with in the schools. We see kids being beaten up, sexually abused, drugged, sometimes by fellow students, sometimes by teachers. *Education Week* reported that eight percent of children in the public schools have been sexually abused or harassed by school teachers and employees. We have read about the episodes in the school bathrooms where kids are beaten or killed, the incidents in empty classrooms or unprotected corners in the school, the dangers on the streets as children walk to school, the beatings and sexual incidents on the school buses.

To move through this blackboard jungle is not only dangerous to a child's spiritual, physical, and emotional health and safety, but on top of it all, few are getting an education. The statistics of the low test scores are so commonplace, showing the lack of educational progress, that no one even suggests it could be otherwise.

Recently a book was published called *Uncle Sam's Plantation*, a black woman's testimony about the government agenda in the public schools and in urban renewal programs. She believes that the poor, especially in the black community, are slaves to the government agenda and welfare programs. Worst of all, the children of inner-city families are taught not to worry, the government will provide all their needs, and they should not worry about any consequences to any kind of activity in which they feel like indulging. Abortions, robberies, drugs—it makes no difference. Do it if it feels good at the time.

Catholic schools are influenced and affected by the public school agenda. In fact, there are practically no publishers of Catholic textbooks, that is, history books, spellers, or English books.

Instead of asking why parents choose home schooling, perhaps we should ask whether any parents would choose public school if they thought they had a real choice. Do parents really make a free choice to send their child to a public school, or are they pressured by the law and the high cost of private or parochial school education?

The majority of parents who want to find another solution, and who have made the decision to home school, have done so because they have met home schooling families with good children. The children are not on drugs, they are clean and tend to be innocent, and to dress simply and modestly. They do not speak rudely and with a dirty mouth. They are not accepting the latest ideas regarding sexual activity and gay "marriages." Home schoolers tend to be obedient, and they can speak with some amount of knowledge about something. Sometimes, these home schooling students even speak clearly about the teachings of the Church, which many parents have not heard even from the pulpit in recent history.

Sex education

More and more parents are choosing home schooling because of explicit "sex education" which is really not just sex education but a political promotion of the homosexual agenda, promoting civil unions instead of marriage, as well as full recognition under the law of these immoral lifestyles. One must assume that, when homosexual marriages are declared legal in a state, as has happened already in a few states, the sex education curriculum in the schools will have to be modified to include homosexual practices. One wonders how many people who now support "equal marriage rights" will not be so supportive when equality mandates that gay and lesbian sexual practices must be taught in the classroom.

The promotion of homosexuality in school is part of the pattern of attacking traditional Judeo-Christian beliefs about sexuality. Another part of the attack is the condom brigades, which have invaded practically every school in the country to peddle their wares. Sadly, even in Catholic schools, parents have discovered that teachers are instructing the students on how to use condoms because they assume, they say, that the kids are going to be sexually active. I have heard from mothers who have removed their children from Catholic high schools after Planned Parenthood was invited to speak to the students.

Some Catholic mothers learn about the sex education programs as they become involved in crisis pregnancy centers, in helping girls who have become pregnant, and as they become active in the pro-life movement. Mothers have learned that public schools not only have "health clinics" which give the students condoms and abortifacients, but give the girls a day of the week in which they can obtain permission slips from the school nurse to visit the community health clinic for abortion referral service if they "need" it—all this without parental knowledge or consent.

The AIDS crisis has brought into many schools demonic new curricula which include homosexuality. Under the guise of teaching non-violence, civil rights, and non-discrimination toward ethnic groups, the curricula teach young children that homosexuality is a morally acceptable practice which should not be discriminated against or spoken against in a "hateful" way.

A mother wrote this several years ago. Today it is not news:

> Most recently, the public school system in New Jersey, New York, and Connecticut, announced that they will be introducing three new books in the first grade: *Daddy's Roommate*, *Heather Has Two Mommies*, and *Gloria Goes to Gay Pride*. All these books deal with the topic of homosexuality and "alternative" lifestyles. In our opinion, this is immoral and blasphemous. We couldn't believe we were witnessing this. They removed prayer in the school, only to drill this kind of literature down the throats of our impressionable children.

In the FIRST GRADE! The more mothers learn about the sex education programs and the promotion of the homosexual agenda, the more likely they are to home school their children.

Many so-called health classes also teach that children are a burden. They require students to carry five-pound sacks of flour, or eggs, with them wherever they go. They are forced to treat the objects like newborn babies; so for example, they can not go to the rest room unless a friend agrees to "watch the baby." Some schools even have specially manufactured dolls that cry uncontrollably and exhibit other difficult behavior patterns. Other schools make the children wear heavy weights on their chests and abdomens to simulate the discomfort of pregnancy. Students are indoctrinated with all the negatives of pregnancy and child rearing. While this is intended to prevent teen pregnancy, it reinforces the message that children are a problem to be avoided, not a gift to be appreciated.

Character formation

Some parents have started home schooling because of the broad range of false and immoral ideas propagated by books, teachers, classroom discussions, and peer pressure in schools. Many parents first learn of these immoral ideas through the books assigned to their children for book reports. The stories in these books often present young people involved in early sexual activities, with no comment that this is immoral conduct. The books teach the children that fornication is normal behavior, having sex on dates is routine, and that "taking the pill" is as common as wearing tight jeans.

An eighth grade girl was supposed to do a book report on a story about a woman who consulted a voodoo witch and whose husband had committed adultery with the witch. When the mother complained about the book, the teacher declared that the children like reading these books. When the mother went to the principal, he told her that her concern was "just her opinion," and he did not think he could do anything even if she wrote a formal complaint. Parents have asked that their children be allowed to read different books for their reports, but most teachers are very insistent that the children read these "X-rated" type books.

One mother pulled her high school daughter out of the Catholic high school in her junior year. She said that her daughter was daily arguing in class against the students and against the teacher, standing up for pro-life values mainly, as well as many other traditional Catholic doctrines. She felt her daughter was so upset all the time that she could not concentrate on her studies.

One father enrolled his daughter in home study after visiting her Catholic high school classroom when the students were having a debate about Presidents Clinton and Bush. When abortion was mentioned, the teacher said that was a subject which could not be part of the debate. Later, the debate teacher allowed the pro-Clinton students to chant "pro-choice" over and over while the pro-Bush students were speaking.

Academics

Some parents have chosen home education because of the lack of academics being taught in the schools. Parents are upset that their children receive A's on report cards, or are even classified as gifted, and then they discover how little they have learned. One mother wrote this:

Time allotted for systematic instruction in basic subjects seems to be spent discussing strategies for achieving New Age goals, or personal "decision making" based on a poll of the peer group. "Creativity" is the current god of education, created to cover the glaring deficiencies of thirty years of mismanagement. On a general basis, the only area in which personal discipline and endeavor are demanded so as to reach the highest standard of excellence is that of sports.

The main problem heard from parents regarding academics is that children are not learning to read. Instead of phonics, a proven method of teaching reading, most schools use the look-say method, or the current fad, the whole language method. No matter which method is currently in vogue, or what they call it, if it is not phonics, children will not learn to decode sounds to read words. While other methods may work for a few years, by the fifth or sixth grade, the method will break down. Of course, if a child cannot read, grades in all subjects will plummet quickly.

The United States is currently 49th among the nations of the world in educational achievement, 39th in literacy. One out of every four students will never reach high school; one out of every four who reaches high school will never graduate. The U.S. Department of Education, based on a National Literacy Survey, estimated in 1993 that between 40 and 44 million adults in the United States are functionally illiterate.

Beyond the failures of the education in the school systems, the high profile successes of home schoolers have been very good advertising for home schooling. With the success of home schooling children in national spelling, geography, and essay contests, parents are not as hesitant to try it themselves. Although home schooled students make up perhaps only 2% of the school age population, they are often 10% or more of the Scripps-Howard National Spelling Bee finalists. In 2004, home schoolers made up 13.2% of the spellers. According to Paige Kimble, director of the National Bee, "I think there's a certain sense of astonishment. And frankly, I think there's also a sense of respect and jealousy."

When parents see home schoolers winning spelling bees or geography bees, it becomes clear that home schooling is a viable option for academic excellence. Michael Smith of the Home School Legal Defense Association, says that these high-profile successes make home schooling "credible to many people who were thinking before that this is just done by a bunch of weirdos who want to go in the back woods and isolate their children."

Parents are meeting leaders in all fields, even in Congress, who are home schooling their children. Consequently, home schooling does not appear as weird or something strange and unusual any more. Since home schooling is more acceptable, and since more parents are obviously successful, other parents are not as reluctant as they once were to consider home schooling their children.

As far back as the Reagan Administration, national leaders have recognized the failure of the American school system to teach even basic skills. Federal programs and entitlements, like "No Child Left Behind," are an attempt by the federal government to address this failure. While citizens can hope that failing schools will turn around, change will come slowly, if at all. Home schooling families wish institutional schools well, but recognize that parents have only one, unrepeatable opportunity to educate each child.

Even those parents whose children excel in institutional schools, and who are somewhat happy with the schools they have chosen, are complaining. A growing minority of students exhibits out-of-control behavior, and stressed teachers are typically spending huge amounts of time on so-called "classroom management." The current policy of putting severely handicapped children into regular classrooms, while laudable in theory, has placed more stress on teachers and other students. The need to control the classroom has resulted in more and more little boys being medicated to help them to sit still. In the midst of classroom chaos, intelligent, cooperative children are often ignored. Good students often are assigned to tutor their underachieving peers. Parents who have carefully raised their children to be morally upright and academically ready feel that their students are being cheated out of the education they deserve.

Weep for your children...

When Jesus spoke these words to mothers, He was not referring to children who lose their physical lives, but to those children who lose their spiritual lives, their souls.

Jesus once said to His Apostles, "I say to you, my friends, do not be afraid of those who kill the body but cannot kill the soul. But rather be afraid of him who is able to destroy both soul and body in Hell."

As director of Seton Home Study School, I receive many phone calls from parents each day. The calls in which the parents tell me of the physical abuse of their children are distressing. But the most distressing calls are the calls from parents who say, "I sent five of my children to public schools, and they have all lost the faith. I only have my youngest at home now, and I want to home school to try to save her."

The souls of babies cannot be destroyed by the abortionist, but the souls of children can be destroyed in the school.

Hearing the horror stories about public schools from parents day in and day out, it is hard not to reach the conclusion that the public schools of this nation are the enemy of this nation, and the enemy of each American child. The schools and their promotion of drugs through the drug programs, their promotion of illiteracy through erroneous non-phonetic reading programs, their neutral presentation of contraception and abortion, their neutral "alternative" lifestyle presentation of homosexuality and gay marriage, their presentation of depressing and inappropriate concepts that can lead to psychological disorders and even suicide, are the training camps of the enemies of Jesus Christ and His Church.

The Charter of the Rights of the Family, issued by Pope John Paul II in 1982, declares that parents have the right to keep their children out of any school which sets itself against their moral and religious convictions.

Well, what do you do when *every available school* goes against your Catholic moral and religious convictions?

We are in spiritual warfare. Give all the speeches you want, but children will not listen after being in the training camp of the enemy. Write all the books you want, but Catholics will not read them after being in the training camp of the enemy. Take to court all the constitutional cases you want, but the judges and juries will have been trained in the enemy's camp, and they will not understand the issues.

Our spiritual enemies are being trained in the schools! The future lies in the children, as our enemies well know. The children are being trained in the camp of the enemy!

As long as your children or your grandchildren, your nephews or nieces, or your neighbor's children, are being trained in the camp of the enemy, our spiritual enemies could not care less about your books and your speeches. They have the children. They have the Future in their camp.

Unless we bring our children home to the family, and teach them the truths of the Catholic Faith, the leaders of tomorrow will not hear, they will not listen, they will not understand the Truth. They will be imbued with secular humanism. They will be deadened to the Truth.

Perhaps our American secular culture has gone so far that there is little hope for change. Secular humanists sit as judges and jurists, as educators and school superintendents, as lawyers and as legislators, as textbook authors and teachers. The secularists miss no chance to impose their values upon us, while judging our moral standards to be "un-Constitutional." Their values are "open-mindedness," while our values are "bigotry." While sending Martha Stewart to jail for lying about her stock trading, the same week brought us legal "gay marriage" in Massachusetts.

But there is hope in the next generation of home schooled adults. We can place great hope in a generation trained and living the Catholic life, one which is better educated than those taught in the schools, not influenced by peers or perverse lifestyles, but a generation acting by God's Truths.

Home schoolers are independent thinkers. They are not pressured to agree with the group (there is no classroom group) or with an authority other than God and His representatives, their parents, who are teaching the Catholic Faith, and living the Catholic Faith.

Catholic children trained at home in a complete family catechetical program can be, and will be, effective leaders in restoring the nation and the Catholic Church. It is not too late. It is never too late.

Raising "Cradle Catholics"

What parents quickly discover once they start teaching their children is that home schooling is a very special way of living. Most of us have come to love this lifestyle so much that even if the best Catholic school were next door, we would not send our children there.

In recent decades, some families founded and supported excellent private Catholic schools. Some failed, but even where they thrived, parents learned that operating a school is not beneficial to family life. Because they lack parish support, tuition is frequently very high, literally impoverishing some families. Often these schools are a great distance from the home, and September to June becomes a never-ending nightmare of loading and unloading children in and out of automobiles. Parents with several children are leaving their children with babysitters to "volunteer" at school functions and often selling candy bars and gift-wrap. Home schooling families enjoy a peace and serenity unknown to these over-stressed private school families.

To the casual observer, home schooling means teaching one's children all the academic subjects at home. To Catholic home schooling parents, it means teaching about God and His Word, teaching about living the Catholic life through example as well as books, and teaching the academic subjects through the perspective of the Truths of Jesus Christ.

The main purpose of Catholic home schooling is to raise saints. The reason to take on the responsibility of Catholic home schooling is to raise cradle Catholics. A cradle Catholic is a person born into a Catholic family who is taught the culture, the traditions, and the faith of the Catholic Church by words, actions, songs, sacraments, and sacramentals. This teaching is given primarily by parents, but also by other family members. Many Catholic home schooling parents these days are converts, or reverts, to the Faith. Although these parents may not have been raised in a strong Catholic environment, they can still provide that environment for their children.

In this modern, confused pagan society, we need to raise a generation of cradle Catholics. These children will be a small minority among many who have accepted the anti-Christian teachings of our society. Our children will need the strength and the graces which come from a lifetime of living the Faith. Growing up Catholic—in an atmosphere of love as well as sacrifice and reparation—is necessary in order to loyally defend the Faith and to proclaim it courageously in a post-Christian world.

Raising children as Catholics in a strong and stable Catholic home filled with Catholic culture and traditions should produce Catholics who both understand the Catholic Faith and live the Catholic lifestyle.

Historically, many born and bred cradle Catholics may not have been able to score high on a theology quiz, but they knew in their hearts, in their souls, and in their very bones, what *being Catholic* is all about. They had a *sensus fidei*, a sense of the faith. Their devotion to daily Mass, their love for the Blessed Mother and the Rosary, their prayers and lighting of candles—all these indicate the authentic Catholic lifestyle, a deep love and understanding of Jesus and His Church.

Today, the best defense, and often the best offense, against heresy and other deviations from Catholic truths, are the common people—the laity—living the authentically Catholic lifestyle throughout the liturgical year.

It should come as no surprise that sacramentals and the sacramental life have been systematically attacked. The simple devotions of the Catholic people—the Rosary, the scapular, the Stations of the Cross, the Advent wreath—give structure and substance to the Faith. The symbolism of these devotions helps the faithful to understand the profound mysteries of life which they represent.

In our current pagan society, where the Catholic schools have been using secular textbooks since the 1960s, where Catholic parents have trusted the Catholic schools to pass on the Faith and the culture, many of the Catholic treasures have been lost to millions. The sacramental life in the home carried the Irish through hundreds of years of persecutions, and sacramentals carried Japanese Catholics through hundreds of years with no priests. But the sacramental life and sacramentals are now completely unknown to a whole generation of Catholics.

It is not an overstatement to say, as the beloved Catholic professor, the late Dr. William Marra, has said, that a generation of children today has been deprived of their Catholic inheritance—the treasures not only of the knowledge of the graces and supernatural helps of the Church, but of the Catholic cultural heritage.

Certainly the laity have reacted: the Traditional Mass Society, the *Una Voce* organization asking for a traditional ordinariate, Mother Angelica's Eternal Word Television Network, and Catholics United for the Faith. The parent-operated schools started in the Sixties have now organized with an Association. Christendom College, Magdalen College, Thomas Aquinas College, Ave Maria University, Southern Catholic College, and more—all these are among the innumerable organizations that have been started by the laity to restore the Church, defend the Faith, and protect the family and the unborn.

Catholic home schooling is a natural and logical part of the ongoing restoration of the Church. Catholic home schooling is a family apostolate in the forefront of the spiritual battle to preserve the Catholic Faith and the Catholic culture and traditions. Unless the changes occur within the basic unit of society, the family, changes will not happen in the Church and in the nation.

The continuing attacks on the family have been devastating to our Church and society. As always, it has been the children who have suffered the most from the breakdown of family bonds. The shattering of families has shattered the hearts and lives of innumerable children.

It is precisely because the family has been so assaulted, and nearly destroyed, that many members of the Catholic Church and our American society have lost Christian values. When homosexuality and gay "marriages," a direct attack against family and children, is accepted and legal as an alternative lifestyle in America, one no longer can pretend to live in a Christian nation.

The necessity of home schooling

The only answer for Catholic families is to bring the children home, keep them close, and teach them in the inner sanctum of the domestic church, our Catholic homes. Many of us Catholic home schooling parents have chosen to keep our children away from the influences of the pagan society right from the cradle. At the same time, we want to keep our children aware of society's problems, and prepare them for the fight ahead of them.

Some well-meaning Catholic parents believe that their children should be promoting good Catholic ideas in the public schools. Some pro-lifers believe that other children need to hear the message of respect for life which their children bring to the school. While sympathizing with the concept and applauding the efforts their children are making, we home schooling parents strongly disagree with the premise that children should be trying to evangelize in the schools.

There is nothing Biblical or remotely Catholic in the idea that *children* should be placed for six hours a day, five days a week, in an environment which continually savages their beliefs. *All* the secular texts are permeated with anti-Christian values, New Age ideas, and feminist views. But worst of all, they are permeated with a mentality that everything is relative, that truth is not absolute, that God is irrelevant, and that every idea is as good as every other.

Home schooling parents are disgusted at the horrors that are perpetrated on children in the name of education. Children are learning filthy language and filthy ideas from their textbooks! Children in schools are acquiring all kinds of sexual information, and consequently accepting perverse activities as acceptable behavior. Little girls are encouraged by peers to have boyfriends, which, combined with sex education, has been emotionally devastating to some young children.

In such an environment, even children of committed Catholics will pick up some modern secular values and attitudes. It would be impossible not to! They are certainly learning terminology and information which is inappropriate, not only for their age level, but for any decent Christian.

Catholic children—even from the best of families—are human beings and likely to be influenced by the constant barrage of anti-Catholic and immoral ideas which are promulgated for hours and hours every day, by the textbooks, by the teachers, and by the other students. This is supplemented even more graphically by movies and television, by video and computer games, by the Internet, by youth "music" and sports "heroes" championing immoral lifestyles.

What chance does a Catholic parent have, who spends perhaps a few minutes a day talking about the Catholic position on population control, on true compassion, or on the gift of life? Generally, the school supervises the children for more hours than the parent. How is the parent to undo, in a short time in the evening, all the damage that has been done by the school for the five to seven hours a day?

Why not send children to a parent-operated school?

The time, money, and energy involved in running a parent-operated school is huge. I helped to establish one in Columbus, Ohio, and was the principal during the 1970s.

A parent-operated school needs to be run by someone whose children are grown, or by someone whose career is taking care of the school. Mothers who are having children are the ones who want such a school, but they cannot give the proper amount of time to their own children and families if they run a school.

The constant problem of raising enough money to pay the rent and the salaries can be emotionally and physically draining. In addition, there is a problem finding good Catholic textbooks. Many Catholic parent-operated schools, even some private Catholic schools operated by religious orders, do not have Catholic textbooks. Seton Home Study School now produces Catholic textbooks which are being purchased by many parent-operated schools.

Some parent-operated schools are successful, but many are not. Most parent-operated schools have a short life span. Many do not make it through the first year due to financial pressures, leadership problems, personality differences of the board members, children with learning problems, and parents whose ideas differ about various aspects of the school.

Let's assume that you could find a Catholic school that is run by totally committed lay Catholics, that enforces good Christian discipline, and that uses Catholic textbooks. Perhaps the teachers even take the children to Mass every week, and encourage frequent Confession. And, as an added bonus, let's assume the tuition is reasonable.

The fact is, however, that ANY school takes children away from the parents and out of the home. No matter how good the school itself, it may take away from the stability and strength of the family. Time spent in school is time not spent forming lasting bonds in the family. The best teacher is not going to be around for the child years into the future, but parents and siblings will be.

Other benefits of home schooling for the Catholic family

There are many, many benefits of home schooling for the Catholic family. There are benefits to each individual member as well as to the whole family, the Church, and the nation.

For the student

The benefits to the individual student are obvious. The spiritual and moral development which the parents can shape according to Catholic values is the most important and long-lasting benefit. In the home environment, there is no challenge to the parental influence, either by peers, textbooks, or secular-thinking teachers. Home schooled children tend to be innocent and mature at a natural pace without being thrown into sex-ed classroom and playground conversations and discussions beyond their natural interests and maturity level.

Personal development is natural, not adversely affected, as children grow up in a stable family situation. The home schooler's personality is shaped by the family, the basic and natural unit of society, rather than by hours of interaction with others at the same level of immaturity. Because of the breakup of so many families, children from original-parents families are often in a minority in the classroom. Children from families living the Christian lifestyle of sacrifice rather than materialistic pursuit find themselves an oddity in the classroom.

Another area of benefit is in keeping the child away from the rampant materialism which is drummed into children at an early age, especially by aggressive advertising. The pressure to have the latest and greatest of everything, from clothing to cell phones, starts before the age of ten. This pressure ties a child's self-worth to his possessions rather than his character, and ill-prepares a child for the sacrifices necessary later in life.

Academic development is decidedly superior for the home schooled student. It has become almost a self-evident proposition in America that the school is not a place for learning. When the U.S. Department of Education researched the academic situation in the nation's schools in 1983, they wrote the pamphlet "A Nation at Risk." They pointed out that such a terrible disaster has happened in American schools that our nation is at risk of losing its freedom. The authors, educational bureaucrats who believe in the system after all, went so far as to say that if a foreign power had done to this country what the educational establishment has done, we Americans would consider it an act of war!

Socialization

Another benefit for the home schooled student is social development. The papal documents repeatedly stress the value and importance of children learning at home, from parents and other members of the family. One pope pointed out that each member of the family represents a microcosm of different groups in society. Thus children learn about the needs and interests of the elderly from grandparents. In a Catholic family, they are likely to learn about the helplessness of babies and their need for protection. They learn to forgive those who disregard their possessions as they deal patiently with little brothers and sisters. Home schooled children learn to serve others as they help younger siblings with their studies or chores. Obedience and respect for authority are learned as parents respect grandparents, as children respect parents.

The interaction of children with members of the family at different stages of maturity is far more beneficial to healthy social development than the interaction with children in the same grade level in the schools.

In most schools, there is an almost visible line separating the students by grade level.

Many children in the schools, often from broken homes, have parents whom they see so seldom that they have little opportunity to learn from adult role models. School children tend to follow their peers. Classroom teachers are so dedicated to promoting individual "freedom" that they do not provide the moral, social, or personal leadership they once did.

For the mother

Catholic home schooling provides benefits for the Catholic mother. Home schooling provides the Catholic mother the opportunity to fulfill her responsibility in her marriage vocation to educate her children. It provides a maturing process for a young mother as she dedicates herself in service to youngsters who look up to her with loving eyes for direction. It causes the young mother to want to learn Truth, and to pass it on to those trusting souls who have full confidence in her ability and knowledge.

When a young lady marries, she may be inexperienced in matters of sacrificing for others. But as the children arrive, as she takes the responsibility to get up in the middle of the night to care for crying babies or sick children, as she surrenders her own self to serve the helpless, a young mother's maturing process is obvious. Home schooling provides a continuation of that maturing process, a process that encompasses academic development, social development, personal development, and spiritual development.

But if Catholic women could express their emotions in earthly words, feminists would be surprised at the ultimate pleasure and joy mothers experience as they teach their children. Home schooling mothers know in their hearts the inexpressible personal reward of working, teaching, learning, and praying with their own children.

Many a mother cries in happiness as her baby gives a first smile, a first word, a first laugh. Such inexpressible moments happen as she nurses her baby, as she teaches him to take his first steps, as she teaches him the Sign of the Cross. This continues as she teaches him the catechism, his addition and subtraction, his geography and his Catholic history, his spelling words and his essay writing.

When her baby becomes a teenager, she finds joy in his ability to discuss ideas, in his ability to stretch his mind to understand the Faith, in his ability to take pleasure in a twist of words in a poem. She sees her youngster reading a novel for the first time, and takes delight in having a discussion with him about the characters in the story.

Many home schooling mothers have told me that their education was wasted on them when they were young, but now they are enjoying relearning everything from how to diagram a sentence to learning about the Earth to discussing the French Revolution.

For the father

There are benefits for the father in the Catholic home schooling family. Father can see, provide, and protect his family in his home. The children are not scattered around in different schools during the day, scattered at dinnertime at different school-sponsored sports events, scattered after dinner with school friends or social activities away from home.

Fathers work hard these days to provide for their family, yet they are often deprived of the joy of time spent with the children. In the home schooling family, the father can share in the very joys for which he is providing. In a way, it seems cruel for dads to miss that joy because of school-related activities. While fathers who have their children in school may be able to spend time with their children, home schooling fathers have many more opportunities since the children's schedule can be adapted so easily.

When the children are at home in the evening with their father, or if the children are engaged in activities with their father, he is establishing and living out the Church teaching that family and children relationships are important. Somehow, children seem to have a natural built-in respect for the authority of Father. If Father thinks that being at home with the children is important, that value will be conveyed in the living of it. You can bet that these children will be at-home parents with their children someday.

Fathers in the home schooling family are likely to become more deeply aware of their responsibilities as head of the family as they are surrounded with their "responsibilities" almost continually. And they will become more aware of the consequences of their decisions and how they affect individual members of the family as well as the family as a whole.

Father will lead, but also respect, and even depend on the support of his own children, especially as they grow into young adults.

The Catholic father will grow in his own understanding of what fatherhood means as he sees the dependency of his home schooled children who look to him for guidance and direction, for wisdom and faith. The Catholic home schooling father is likely to grow in his own spiritual life as he directs his children in the Faith. Many mothers have phoned to tell me that when their husbands became involved in the Catholic home schooling lessons, and when they heard their children asking questions about the Catholic Faith, they themselves began to study and learn more about the Faith. Several mothers have told me that their non-Catholic husbands converted after being involved in Catholic home schooling.

About twenty years ago, a priest who had been visiting in Rome told me that Pope John Paul II favored home schooling because he believed that it will benefit the whole family to learn more about their faith. The pope believed that home schooling is of special benefit for parents to learn more about their faith as they teach it to their children. When I first heard the pope's remark, I thought it seemed like a strange comment, but as the years have gone by, more and more parents call and tell me that they have learned more about their faith, and have grown in their faith through teaching their own children.

For the family

In addition to the benefits of home schooling for individual members of the family, there are benefits to the family as a whole. Home schooling can strengthen internal family relationships as members help each other in the learning process. As members of the family work and learn together, and come to understand the strengths and weaknesses of each other, they develop Christian virtues which help them to live together peaceably. They learn to work out problems together, and to stand as a unit against outside influences or pressures.

Some have advised me not to idealize the home schooling situation so greatly. Consequently, I will say this: not every home schooling family is perfectly happy. Like all families, we have our struggles. At the same time, I believe it is possible for a family with children in school to be a happy, healthy, united family. However, from all the phone calls I have received over the past twenty years, my conclusion is that families teaching children at home are much happier, in spite of the struggles, than families with children in schools, even "good" schools.

For the community

Home schooled children benefit the community because their values are not shaped by peers but by parents who instruct their children about the Church teachings on current problems in our society. These young people grow up being activists on social issues, especially issues such as abortion. Home schoolers are more likely to picket abortion clinics and attend pro-life rallies. This "hands-on" Catholic social action will result ultimately in a generation of Catholic leaders, educated and dedicated, willing and anxious to be involved in changing our society. Even now, graduates of home schooling are leaders in their community.

These observations are based on my experiences attending Human Life International and other pro-family or pro-life conferences. Home schooled students and graduates are often present. Students attending schools are not only absent, but parents even remark to me that their children do not agree with them and have been influenced by the schools to reject their pro-life values. Sadly, some have even said that their married children refuse to have children, or that their children are living in sinful lifestyles.

For the Church

The Catholic Church is already reaping the benefits of home schooling families. As parents teach their children at home, many come to a greater understanding and realization of the joy of children. Home schooling families are responding to God's Will to be open and charitable regarding having children. And their children and their children's children are likely to do the same if they continue home schooling.

The pope is constantly encouraging evangelization. But the most effective evangelization is from parents to children. When I was growing up, it was considered a goal to convert at least one person to the Catholic Faith. Every Catholic parent has the opportunity to convert his children to the Catholic Faith. Just as in converting friends and neighbors, however, good example is the best means for the conversion of our children. As home schooling parents, we have more opportunities to give good example in living the authentic Catholic life as our children are at home with us every day.

The Catholic home schooling family benefits the local Catholic parish community, especially other home schooling families, or families struggling to maintain traditional Catholic values. The Catholic home schooling family gives witness to Catholic truths, the main truth being that, with God's grace, the authentic Catholic family life *can* be lived.

Seeing the vocations from home schooling families, one Midwest bishop has made a special invitation for home schoolers to visit his diocese and attend his seminary. He understands that the home schooling family is supportive of vocations. We have heard this from vocations directors of several growing seminaries. They say that home schooled young seminarians know their catechism and respect the special vocation of the priesthood.

At Seton Home Study School, we hear often of students going on to religious life. In fact, Justin Ferguson, a former Seton student, while he was studying in a seminary in Rome, received the great honor of giving one of the readings at Pope Benedict XVI's installation Mass.

For the nation

The shortcomings of public education have been repeatedly exposed. Although many people have pushed more parental choice in education as a way out of the problem, the educational bureaucracy in this country will not allow true parental choice. The only choice that the educrats favor is choice which lets parents choose among public schools which are 99% the same. Even charter schools, which are still public schools but with some of the layers of bureaucracy removed, have been relentlessly attacked by the teachers' unions.

It is ironic that we are constantly being told of the benefits of diversity, but the education bureaucracy ruthlessly enforces complete conformity. Diane Ravitch, an historian of education and Research Professor of Education at New York University, recently published a book called *The Language Police,* in which she cites example after example of words being deleted from textbooks by publishers because educational bureaucrats have decided that certain words and ideas are politically incorrect. According to an article by the publisher, this book "documents the existence of an elaborate and well-established protocol of beneficent censorship…. Women cannot be depicted as caregivers or doing household chores. Men cannot be lawyers or doctors or plumbers."

Phyllis Schlafly, a Catholic leader who frequently speaks at educational and Catholic conferences, who founded Eagle Forum some years ago to encourage women to become informed and politically active, has been writing and publishing the *Education Reporter* newsletter for many years. Her newsletter informs parents about the terrible and ridiculous events going on in the schools. She encourages parents to fight back. In the January 2004 issue of her newsletter, she reported that an eighth grade class in New York had not had a math teacher all year, so the kids watched movies during that class time. A teacher in Washington, D.C., insisted the kids repeat over and over again various words of profanity to desensitize them to the books he was requiring them to read. A Los Angeles school gave extra credit to students studying Islam when they "fasted" for three days during Ramadan. Other items are unprintable.

For those of us who love our country and want to restore it to Christ, we see our home schooling family as a means to help our nation grow in the love of God, and consequently return to Christian values and Christian civilization. Our Catholic home schooling families are training leaders dedicated to Christian moral values, families who will help return the nation to Christian common sense. Our home schooling families, now and in the future, will help our nation to find itself, to understand its purpose, to seek Christian heroes, and to take direction from Christian precepts. The specific virtues which Catholic home schooling families are developing, and which will benefit our nation, are loyalty, patriotism, honesty, clear thinking, obedience to authority, respect for the law, respect for life, respect for the elderly, responsibility, dedication to work and the value of work, self-discipline, justice, charitable works, and mercy. These are virtues without which no nation can long survive. Most importantly, Catholic home schooling families are passing on the true Catholic Faith, which will be crucial to any Christian restoration of our beloved country.

With so many benefits of home schooling for children and parents, for families, for the Church, and for the nation, I hope parents soon realize that the reason they should teach their children at home is not because of the problems in our society and in our schools, but because it is the best way to live the authentic Catholic family life.

Chapter 2:
What Is Catholic Home Schooling?

As I travel around the country to home schooling conventions, meeting parents, students, as well as priests and others in religious life, I have come to realize that most people don't know what is meant by Catholic home schooling. Simply put, Catholic home schooling means that the directives from the Church and the Bible given for education are put into effect in the family. At the same time, the family is living the Catholic family life as the "domestic church," the church of the home.

There is a basic misunderstanding about Catholic education. Most people think that education is something that ought to be done in a school with certified teachers during a set number of hours each day. According to the Bible and Church documents, "education" primarily means formation by parents in the home, and it is something that is going on all the time. This parent formation includes religious education, and all other education which should be taught from a Catholic viewpoint.

Why did the Church start Catholic schools? In the beginning, they were to be a supplement only, not to replace parents. In the United States, there was a movement in the early 1800s for compulsory education of children. This meant that children between the ages of perhaps 7 and 16 were required by law to attend a school every day. Since the vast majority of the population of the United States was Protestant, the schools were heavily influenced by Protestant thinking. The Catholic parochial school system was started because the Catholic children were receiving a Protestant education in public schools. However, the existence of the Catholic schools does not take away the rights and duties of parents to pass along the Faith to their children.

Catholic teaching and culture are wonderful treasures that have been stored up for us for thousands of years. The Catholic Faith and lifestyle is quite distinctive from either a secular or Protestant way of life. Catholic home schooling should be just as distinctive, and should embrace the particular riches of Catholicism.

What is a *Catholic curriculum*?

The word curriculum comes from the Latin words for "running course." In English, a curriculum is a course or plan of study. The Latin base for the word captures the two parts of a curriculum very well: a curriculum is a plan that requires action. A Catholic curriculum is one in which every subject taught is permeated with the truths of the Catholic Faith. A Catholic curriculum is not a standard curriculum that simply includes a religion class. Every class is to incorporate Christ's teachings. Indeed, the whole action of learning is seen as a progression toward Christ. How else can we follow the direction of St. Paul to "restore all things in Christ"?

Some of us may remember the old Catholic publishing company, the Bruce Publishing Company. They were a publisher you could trust. In 1956, the company published a book titled *A Catholic Philosophy of Education*. This book was written by two Fordham University professors with doctorates in education. They wrote what all the Catholic educational books were stating at that time, and which followed the teachings of the Church.

In the chapter titled "Religious Education," the authors wrote the following statement: "Religious education is the primary function, the *raison d'etre*, of the Catholic school. It not only transmits to the pupil divine truths of which the Church is the guardian, but also teaches conformity to the way of life exemplified by Jesus Christ, who in His own words states, 'I am the way, and the truth and the life' (John 14:6), and codified in the eternal tenets of the moral law. Only by conduct in conformity to these truths and this way of life can man fulfill the purpose of his creation. Religion must, of necessity, permeate all life and education. Its teachings constitute the very core and foundation upon which all education for the true, the good, and the beautiful must be founded."

Some people think that what we are doing in Catholic home schooling is some sort of new idea. In fact, Catholic home schoolers are, or should be, following the directives of the Church by permeating all life and education with our Catholic Faith and values.

In past generations, education was seen as intimately connected with religion. It was generally understood that the two could hardly be separated. However, our modern society has advanced the view that education can and should be separated from religion. Putting them back together is now a radical concept, and parents often ask me how it can be done. In this chapter, I will explain how Seton Home Study School helps parents to accomplish that goal by using a Catholic home schooling program. (I use Seton only as an example. Other home schools or families not using a program will do things somewhat differently.)

Arithmetic

People laugh when we speak about making our math courses Catholic. But we do it anyway. No subject can be divorced from God because God is Truth, indeed the Creator of Truth. Therefore, He is the Creator of math. We need to make this clear to our children on a frequent basis.

When we started Seton Home Study School in 1980, we started with a Protestant math series since no Catholic series was available. Recently, we have published our own Catholic math books for kindergarten through fourth grade. We also use the Saxon series, which has been acclaimed nationally for helping students to dramatically improve their math scores.

If we use math in our daily life, and if our daily life is to be lived with Jesus Christ, then our math must be impacted by our Christian values. It can be and should be. For instance, we need to be honest and accurate in our financial dealings with others.

In schools, students are given math word problems so that they may learn to apply abstract concepts to real situations. In the secular texts, the real-life situations involve classroom or school situations, and kids doing things together, usually without family members, with little mention of parents or brothers and sisters. In the Catholic home schooling families, the real-life situations involve visiting shrines as a family, going to Mass together, playing with other home schoolers, enjoying family activities, field trips with home school support groups, and picketing abortion clinics with friends. Consequently, the aim of our math series is to reflect the real-life situations of a Catholic home schooling family. Problems relate to real-life Catholic family situations, involving real people. Problems relate to gas mileage on the way to a rosary rally, measuring a floor width at the parish church, working in a Catholic bookstore, and so on. We hope these math word problems help our children to realize the importance of honest and accurate math in the Christian life.

Some may say that it is "overkill" to try to Catholicize even math word problems. *The Wall Street Journal* recently ran an article explaining how the public schools are using all means at their disposal to turn children into militant environmentalists, especially by scaring them about global warming. The schools incorporate the idea into their curriculum, and school plays, and activity books for the children to take home to their parents. The goal is to convince the children to pressure their parents into changing the family lifestyle. Regardless of the merits of the information, the people who run the schools understand that what they consider important must be reinforced throughout the curriculum. They do not limit it to a few lessons in science class. The secular humanists who run the public schools promote their agenda in all subject areas. We Catholics, as directed by our Church, must promote Jesus Christ and the Christian life in all subject areas.

Art

There is no reason why the majority, if not all, of the art projects in the Catholic home cannot be related to our Faith and the liturgical year. Even simple drawings of trees and flowers remind us of God's goodness and generosity. The liturgical year is so rich in the celebration of saints and religious events that there are almost unlimited possibilities in the area of creative art projects.

At Seton, we give ideas and some directions for arts and crafts projects. In our sixth grade book, the children learn to draw using a grid. They draw a picture of St. Michael slaying the dragon, and another of a guardian angel. The students learn about the color wheel and then design stained glass windows. The students learn about the shields of knights, especially the shield of St. Joan of Arc, and learn to draw the insignia for shields for known crusaders. For the feast of the Sacred Heart, the children learn to make a stuffed red-velvet heart, starting with construction paper and a pattern. They are encouraged to place their heart on the family altar.

Internationally known artists H. Reed Armstrong and his wife Roxolana were kind enough to write an arts and crafts book for Seton. Mrs. Armstrong worked with a Catholic religion teacher to produce a second Seton arts and crafts book. While these books teach techniques, the children are learning about Catholic Faith, Catholic art, and culture at the same time.

In addition, because of the lack of Catholic religious art available, some years ago Seton started reproducing great Catholic religious art in art appreciation books for our students. For grade five, the Seton art appreciation book is based on the mysteries of the Rosary. For grade seven, the book focuses on the religious art of James Tissot, especially known for his details and accuracy of the Holy Land and his depiction of the Passion. For grade eight, great religious art is taught in chronological order, depicting art by such luminaries as Fra Angelico, Leonardo da Vinci, Raphael, and Michelangelo.

Beyond the art books, the front and back covers of all of Seton's textbooks feature great Catholic art and architecture. Great pieces of religious art are also often featured inside the books.

English

Catholics who attended the Catholic schools before 1960 are familiar with the Loyola University Catholic English series. The Loyola series represented what can be done to permeate the curriculum with Catholic values. Unquestionably, these books were excellent teaching tools for grammar and composition. Catholics have always stressed these areas because we recognize their importance to our spiritual goals. Consequently, God blessed the Catholic graduates with an unusual ability not only to write concisely and accurately, but also to think logically.

Seton is now producing a Catholic English series following the directives of the Church. In a lesson on contractions, the student will read "Hasn't he read about St. Elizabeth?" In a lesson on verb endings, the student will read, "St. Joan of Arc was winning the battle." In a lesson on adverbs, the student will read, "The nobleman sincerely repented of his sins." Composition assignments relate to stories in the Bible as well as to the lives of the saints and of the Holy Family.

English should teach our children an appreciation for the Catholic Faith and the practice of the Faith, as well as for high standards in grammar and composition.

Handwriting

In the secular handwriting texts, the students practice their letters by writing sentences or paragraphs which often promote secular humanist values.

In Seton's Catholic handwriting workbooks, we not only have many religious pictures or paintings, but the selections the students write are about the saints, Catholic culture, or from the Bible. For the letter "V" in third grade, students practice by writing the sentence: Veronica's Veil is a precious relic of the Vatican. For the letter "D," they write: David, the shepherd boy, slew the giant Goliath. In fourth grade, the students practice writing selections from the Bible, a beautiful selection about the Brown Scapular, and a paragraph about St. Margaret Mary. These are just a few selections from a book filled with such items.

In the Handwriting Five book, in the grade in which the students are learning American History, students write a paragraph in their handwriting book about a shrine located in each state, such as Our Lady of the Prairies in North Dakota and the Sorrowful Mother shrine near Portland, Oregon. One paragraph they write is: "Catholic history abounds in Emmitsburg. St. Elizabeth Ann Seton, America's first native-born saint, opened the nation's first Catholic school here. Mount St. Mary's Seminary housed Mother Seton's sisters after their arrival. The shrine of St. Elizabeth Ann Seton, named a minor basilica by Pope John Paul II, contains her relics."

History

Our history books recognize that the central event in history is the Incarnation of Jesus Christ, and that those who followed Christ in His footsteps were instrumental in shaping the history of the world and the culture of their times.

In first grade, in *American History for Young Catholics*, children learn about Christopher Columbus, the first Thanksgiving, Kateri Tekakwitha, Junipero Serra, Rose Philippine Duchesne, Mother Cabrini, and other saints who influenced American history. In second grade, in *Great Saints in World History*, the children learn about patron saints of countries around the world and how they influenced the culture of those countries. They learn about St. Thomas the Apostle, St. Denis of France, St. Nicholas, St. Patrick, St. Boniface, St. Stephen, and many others. In third grade, our children read *The Catholic Faith Comes to the Americas*. The children learn about St. Martin de Porres and St. Rose of Lima, about the North American martyrs, about Father Francisco Kino and Father Antonio Margil, about Catholics in the War for Independence, missionaries to the Indians, nuns who worked as nurses, and so on.

In the fourth grade, children read *The Catholic Faith Comes to the New World*, which focuses on the three hundred years between Columbus' discovery and the end of the War for Independence. In fifth grade, the text is *America's Catholic Heritage*. Students learn about our country's history following the War for Independence, especially the men and women who helped build this great nation.

In sixth grade, using the text *Our Catholic Legacy, Vol. 1*, the students learn world history from pre-history to the Age of Discovery. The Crusades and the Middle Ages are covered from a Catholic perspective. Students learn that Western Civilization was shaped by the Catholic Church. In seventh grade, with *Our Catholic Legacy, Vol. II*, students continue with world history, covering the Age of Discovery up through the modern War on Terrorism.

In eighth grade, the students are presented with more advanced concepts about America, and the importance of Catholics and Catholic concepts in American life and government. Contents of *The History of the United States* include colonial history, the struggle for the continent, disputes with England, the War for Independence, the Constitution, the Church in early America, the settlement of the West, Jacksonian democracy, the two World Wars, the cold war, President Kennedy and Catholic issues, Vietnam, and President Reagan.

Our two high school history texts, *Christ the King, Lord of History* and *Christ and the Americas*, emphasize not only the role of Catholics, but also Catholic ideas about government and political events.

We consider history to be one of the most important subjects for home schooling families. Living in a post-Christian society, our children need to learn from the past in order to make the necessary changes in the future to bring Christ back to the center of life in our nation, and in the world.

Music

Music is important for children as a means of learning the Christian message, as well as giving children the opportunity to express Catholic beliefs in song.

Our texts follow the liturgical year, offering songs not only for Christmas and Easter, but also for St. Patrick's Day, St. Joseph's feast day, and other special days. Books at the older grade levels teach Gregorian Chant.

Catholic culture is rich in art and music. We need to teach our children about these spiritual treasures. Much of the art and music of our modern society is without beauty. Our children should have the opportunity to learn about, see, and hear great Catholic art and music.

Phonics

Seton has published several books in a Catholic phonics series, teaching phonics along with Catholic culture. Our kindergarten book follows a thoroughly phonetic system, the best method for learning to read. Our own artist worked tirelessly to produce pictures for letters and sounds, such as a priest saying Mass for M, a drawing of a nun for N, a picture of a pope for the P sound, and Jesus standing next to a lake with the Apostles in a boat for a J sound. In addition, a wonderful Catholic alphabet rhyme is included. At the end of each chapter, a Catholic poem is included for parents to read to the children so they can hear the rhyming sounds. The pictures show children going to Mass and Communion, standing in line for Confession, and lighting candles beside a statue of an angel kneeling in adoration.

Phonics 1 for Young Catholics is a two-book set and, like the kindergarten book, has many Catholic pictures. Our second grade phonics book includes an image of Mary, the Mother of Jesus, for students to say and write the letter M. *Phonics 3 for Young Catholics* is filled with Catholic lessons along with phonics and word study. One exercise has the student read sentences, filling in the blanks with the correct "sh" words. One of the sentences is "In Confession, our sins are _____ away." The student is to supply the word "washed." In the fourth grade phonics book, a sentence for which the student must find a suffix is "The nuns remained active for many years, teaching and nursing." And another: "We carried a beautiful statue of the Blessed Mother in the procession."

Phonics 5 for Young Catholics includes the following sentences to teach Catholic Faith and culture: "It is a sin to tell a lie" [ie sound]. "While we should recoil from sin, we should always love the sinner" [oi sound]. "Our faith is an irreplaceable gift from God" [prefixes]. "The grandfather taught his grandchildren how to say their prayers" [compound words].

It takes more time and effort, but what a joy it is to teach our children our Catholic Faith and family values, "in season and out of season," as the Bible teaches.

Physical Education

This is another area where people laugh at the idea that sports could be "Catholic." Actually, the popes, especially Pope John Paul II who was so athletic in his youth, have written often about sports and how such activities can be spiritual lessons for us. The popes have compared the self-discipline in sports with the self-discipline required in the spiritual life. In fact, St. Paul compared the spiritual life to running a race.

So while we give lessons for specific individual exercises, we relate these to the spiritual life, following the direction of St. Paul and the popes. In second grade, the children are told after an exercise that "This should help you to stand straight the way God wants you to stand." And again: "This will help strengthen the stomach muscles God gave you." And again: "Even while having fun, we must thank Jesus for giving us good health so we can exercise." This kind of teaching helps us all to appreciate our health and to realize that God expects us to take care of our bodies, the temples of the Holy Spirit.

Reading

In the area of reading, there are many Catholic materials we can give to our children. The regular curriculum at Seton uses the *Faith and Freedom* reading series, which emphasizes Catholic family life in the younger grade levels. In the upper grades, the stories teach the children about the values of Catholic immigrant families in the various parts of the new American nation. In sixth grade, the stories are about Catholic people in Europe in times past, relating it to the study of Old World History.

At least two book reports a year are to be biographies of saints. For other book reports, we recommend other books which emphasize Catholic values.

In addition to readers, Seton has written *Reading for Comprehension* and *Reading-Thinking Skills* workbooks which promote Catholic values, usually through the stories of saints. The fourth grade books contain a variety of stories of the saints and a variety of articles on Catholic culture.

The fifth grade *Reading-Thinking Skills* workbook contains a variety of thinking activities, such as word classification, chronology list and cycles, word meaning analysis, and so on. However, throughout the book is the continuing story of St. Thérèse, the Little Flower, during her childhood years.

The fifth grade *Reading for Comprehension* workbook consists of a long story about a Jewish boy and an Egyptian boy during the time of Moses. The student learns about life during that period and how the Jews lived in Old Testament times. Here is a selection from the book as the Jewish people follow Moses in the desert:

> They drove their animals down onto the dry bed of the sea. They stared nervously at the rippling walls of water, at the same time marveling at the works of the Lord God. The waves of the sea high above their heads clashed like cymbals as they hurled themselves together, loudly objecting to their strange displacement.
>
> Jacob and Seti kept their families near the watery walls, fearing the press of anxious people in the middle of the great throng. The two fathers kept themselves between their families and the hastening people, the mothers and small children being between the fathers and the big boys. Thus, Joe and Pepi found themselves moving fast next to the wall of water on the right side.
>
> Joe and Pepi were not the only ones to find it irresistible to stick their hands into the water of the walls! Joe put his hand into the water up to his elbow, splashing himself all over as he moved along—and so did Pepi! The wall kept its vertical position. The boys showed their fathers their wet hands.
>
> Jacob said, "The Lord God is mighty—His strength past our comprehension—keeping the sea away from us!"
>
> "Amen!" said Seti.

The *Reading 6 for Comprehension* contains objective and some interpretation questions for short selections on various saints, such as St. Vincent Ferrer, St. George, St. Helena, St. Blaise, and St. Lucy. The whole *Reading 6-Thinking Skills* contains the story of the exciting missionary adventures of St. Francis Xavier.

The *Reading 7 for Comprehension* objective and interpretive questions are based on thirty-six short selections on a variety of Catholic topics, such as articles on St. Bridget of Sweden and the prayers given to her by Our Lord in several visions; the story of the Wedding at Cana; angels and guardian angels; St. Catherine Labouré and the Miraculous Medal; and the Seven Last Words of Jesus.

The *Reading 8 for Comprehension* objective and interpretive questions are based on thirty-six short selections on the lives of saints primarily, but also contain an article the Divine Mercy image, an article on the Stigmata of St. Francis, an article by St. Augustine on lying, and the words of Jesus on love.

Reading 7-Thinking Skills is based on the life of St. Joan of Arc. *Reading 8-Thinking Skills* is based on the life of St. Margaret Mary.

Here is a selection from *Reading 8 for Comprehension*, Lesson 44: The Stigmata of St. Francis:

> "Do you know," said Christ, "what I have done to you? I have given you the Stigmata, which are the marks of My Passion, so that you may be My Standard-Bearer. And as I descended into Limbo on the day of My death, and delivered all the souls there by the merits of My Stigmata, so do I grant you each year on the anniversary of your death, to visit Purgatory, and by the virtue of your Stigmata, you shall release all the souls whom you shall find there belonging to your three Orders — namely Friars Minor, Sisters, and Penitents — as well as others who have had great devotion to you, and you shall lead them to the glory of Paradise."

Questions which follow the *Reading for Comprehension* selections are of three kinds: some are objective questions, some are interpretive, and some are application questions. These latter questions are to help the children to think about the application of the ideas, such as a particular virtue of a saint, and how they might apply the virtue in their own lives.

Religion

Religion is the heart of Catholic education. Our core text is the *Baltimore Catechism*, which, as Father Bourque declared on Eternal Word Television Network, is contained within the pages of the *Catechism of the Catholic Church*. The *Baltimore Catechism*, St. Joseph edition, covers all basic doctrines: the Creed, the Ten Commandments, the sacraments, and prayer. It includes questions and answers for study, fill-in exercises, and Bible references.

Other books are included in each grade. Bible Story books are included, except in eighth grade where we have a Church History text.

Seton has written a text-workbook supplemental religion series, each with an *imprimatur* (an approval from a bishop that a book is free from doctrinal errors). These are further explanations of the lessons in *The Baltimore Catechism*, which include the opportunity for students to answer questions in the book. These books contain numerous religious paintings.

Science

Catholic science textbooks in the past were very minimally Catholic. Sometimes the only thing "Catholic" was the author's name. We have been working to produce Catholic science textbooks which truly reflect Catholic thinking or some aspect which relates to our Faith.

In grade one, for example, we teach the children about the heart and blood. We conclude the chapter with information about the Eucharistic miracle of Lanciano: "The blood is real blood. The flesh is real flesh. The flesh is muscular tissue from the heart. The blood is type AB. There is no explanation as to how flesh could be kept without decaying for 1200 years. What we know by faith, science has also found!"

In grade two, in teaching about multi-colored butterfly wings, children read, "It is amazing how God makes the patterns on butterflies' wings so colorful and so varied." In discussing the compass, our science book declares that "This is another example of God's goodness. Without the compass, sailors in the past could never have found their way through the oceans."

In the fourth grade Catholic science text, written by a Catholic home schooling father and Ph.D. college physics professor, students read: "The wind reminds us of the Holy Spirit, the third Person of the Blessed Trinity. Remember the wind blowing on Pentecost Sunday? Remember it was the way God chose to reveal Himself to the Prophet Elijah in the Old Testament? Can you find the story in your Bible?"

The books are filled with science about the constellations, the Earth, moon, and space; the oceans and the weather; liquids, solids, and gases; machines and magnetism and electricity; plants and insects; cells and bones and food groups; safety and fighting disease. But they are also filled with the Author of science.

The grade seven science book focuses on geology, rockets, energy and force, and chemistry. Included are many relevant Biblical references. While studying light, for instance, several Scripture passages are pointed out. The following is a quote which teaches the importance of accurate scientific observations:

> Our faith in Jesus Christ and His Church is supported by many facts that were carefully described and handed down to us by the Apostles and their successors. The importance of a faithful record of these facts helped to make Christians careful observers and describers of the physical world and paved the way for the great scientific discoveries of the past two thousand years.

It is essential when teaching about the physical universe that we recognize and praise the Creator of the physical universe, as well as learn more about Him through His creation.

Spelling

Secular spellers include the words to be studied, the spelling rule, and a selection to be read in which the spelling words are used. The selections may be sentences or paragraphs which promote a politically correct agenda or reflect the thinking of the secular culture in some way.

The *Spelling for Young Catholics* series composed by Seton may teach the same spelling words plus some words from our Catholic culture, but includes reading selections which promote Catholic values. In the grade two speller, for example, while children learn to spell words with the sound of short "o," they read a paragraph about St. Bernadette. In the grade three speller, while learning to spell words with the letter "e," they read sentences such as "Jesus is really present in the Holy Eucharist."

The speller in grade four includes stories from the Bible about Abraham, the Ark and the Tabernacle, King Saul, David, and Solomon. The speller for grade five includes stories about St. Nicholas of Tolentino, St. Edward the Confessor, St. Isidore the Farmer, St. Hugh of Lincoln, St. Mary Magdalen de Pazzi, Blessed Margaret of Castello, St. Clare of Montefalco, St. Zita, St. Rita, and many more.

The speller in grade eight teaches the students about St. Joan of Arc, Cardinal John Henry Newman, the Black Madonna of Czestochowa, the University of Paris, and St. Lawrence.

Vocabulary

We have recently completed our *Vocabulary for Young Catholics* series. These workbooks include sentences based on the catechism, Bible stories, sacramentals, lives of the saints, and general Catholic culture.

In grade four, for example, some of the vocabulary sentences are "Father Peters told Tom he said all the Mass responses *correctly*." "Mom said it is *possible* that we can attend early Mass on Easter."

In the seventh grade, our students learn "Preaching the Word of God to the world was an ambitious *endeavor*." "After Pentecost, the apostles were *conscientious* about the mission Our Lord had given them."

Conclusion

In summary, a truly Catholic curriculum is possible. Not only is it possible, but it is also necessary if we want to be thoroughly and authentically Catholic, and, frankly, if we want Christianity to survive. There are some who say that having Catholic materials is not especially important, since parents can add Catholic content, or advise their children about problematic areas. They say that as long as materials are true and good, they do not need to be Catholic.

I must disagree with this view. It is true that many good secular materials are available, and they should not be shunned entirely. However, the point of Catholic home schooling is to pass on the Faith. Is it not something of a contradiction to say that the Faith is so important that parents are going to the trouble of home schooling their children, and then say that Catholic materials are not important? The first mark of any Catholic home school ought to be its Catholic identity. It is difficult to maintain a Catholic identity if the books being used are uniformly secular.

Catholic home schooling is for all families who want to live the Faith every day as Jesus has instructed us, and who want to be sure that their children remain practicing Catholics as well. Catholic home schooling is for all families who realize that without strong Christian families, the future of our world is bleak indeed.

Chapter 3:
Church Teachings on Marriage and Education

Since the education of children is an essential part of the vocation of marriage, it is important to understand the Catholic Church's teachings regarding marriage and education.

The clear and absolute teaching of the Catholic Church is that marriage was raised to the level of a sacrament by Jesus Christ. This is based on the Gospel of St. Matthew, Chapter 19, verses 4 to 9:

> Have ye not read that he who made man from the beginning, made them male and female? And he said: For this cause shall a man leave father and mother, and shall cleave to his wife, and they two shall be in one flesh. Therefore now they are not two, but one flesh. What therefore God hath joined together, let no man put asunder.

The same words by Jesus were repeated in Mark's Gospel, Chapter 10, verses 2 to 12. Interestingly, in both Gospels, these words of Jesus are followed by the incident of little children gathering around Jesus. "Little children were presented to Him … and the disciples rebuked them that brought them." It is not a coincidence that children, the primary purpose of marriage, were presented to Jesus immediately following His teachings on marriage. Parents bring their children to Jesus for His blessing.

It is obvious that Jesus wants parents to have children and to bring them TO Him not just physically, but also spiritually—which is where our marriage vocation to educate our children has its foundation.

It was not a coincidence that Jesus scheduled His first public miracle at a wedding ceremony, nor that the miracle was specifically requested by His own Mother. Jesus wants us to understand that marriage is a sacred vocation and a sacrament, and if we fulfill His Will regarding the responsibilities of marriage, we will receive an abundance of graces and blessings, many through the intercession of His Blessed Mother.

According to the Catholic Church, the primary purpose of marriage consists of two co-equal responsibilities: the procreation of children and the education of children.

They are co-equal responsibilities.

They are equally important.

The educating of children by parents is a duty, a serious responsibility of the vocation of the Sacrament of Matrimony. From the many statements of the popes, we know that this education includes the daily "formation" of children by their parents to be good Catholics, but also includes parents' responsibility to ensure that in their children's academic schooling, either at home or in a school, the Catholic Faith "permeates every branch of knowledge." This is what home schooling is all about.

Home schooling is a re-affirmation of the marriage of the husband and wife. Indeed, home schooling can bring about many changes for the better in marriages where the spouses have drifted apart.

This seems like an incredible statement, but it is absolutely true. It is true because, as husbands and wives use their sacramental graces to fulfill their marriage vocation to teach their children, they obtain more graces, both sanctifying grace and actual graces. These graces enable a husband and a wife to understand and to live out an authentic Catholic marriage and authentic Catholic family life. They come to better understand their own Catholic beliefs and values as they home school.

The commitment and daily sacrifice on the part of parents as they home school their children can help them to grow spiritually as well as in the practice of the authentically Catholic family lifestyle. Educating one's children is intimately entwined with the purposes of marriage. The more we teach our children, the more we understand our vocation. The more we understand our vocation, the more successful will be the results of home schooling our children.

A public statement

Every Catholic marriage is a public statement that we are honoring Christ's commands concerning marriage. Each baby born into a Catholic family is a public statement to our pagan society that we are obeying God's command to increase and multiply, to provide souls for His kingdom. Every Catholic home schooling family is making a statement that we are going to take the responsibility given to us by God, and we are going to take it seriously.

Just as Jesus is faithful to His Church, His bride, and will be faithful to each one of us as members of His Church, so we are to be faithful to Him by being obedient to His commands. Consequently, following Christ means being faithful to our spouse in marriage, and being faithful to our children in their Catholic education.

Sadly today, affected by our over-materialistic society, young adult Catholics often look on love and marriage with a humanistic view. Even some Pre-Cana conferences deal more with how the prospective spouses can get along together and with how to prevent babies rather than with the Church teachings about the responsibilities of the vocation of marriage.

In the current American society, most parents, Catholic and non-Catholic, will never learn about the vocation and responsibilities of the Sacrament of Matrimony. If families become involved with home schooling or pro-life activities, they may find Catholics who will give them a good example. Hopefully, this will propel them to read and learn about their vocation of marriage.

For those who want to learn the teachings of the Catholic Church about marriage, there is no lack of material. The Catholic Church, knowing the importance of marriage and family, has constantly given her children guidance in this area. Perhaps the most important encyclical written for married Catholics is *Casti Connubii* (On Christian Marriage). It is the basic document all married Catholics and Catholics considering marriage should read and study.

Casti Connubii

In this encyclical, Pope Pius XI, inspired by the Holy Spirit, instructed Christian couples about the graces which we receive from the Sacrament of Matrimony to help us live out our duties in the vocation of marriage.

These graces help us to fulfill the duties of the married state: the first duty to cooperate with God in having children, and the second duty to educate our children in the Christian virtuous life.

Pope Pius XI declared that:

> ... the faithful can ... open up for themselves a treasury of
> sacramental grace from which they draw supernatural power for the
> fulfilling of their rights and duties faithfully, holily, perseveringly,
> even unto death. Hence this sacrament not only increases sanctifying
> grace ... but also adds particular gifts, dispositions, seeds of grace, by
> elevating and perfecting the natural powers.

Thus the Catholic Church teaches that we can have a *treasury of
sacramental grace* from the Sacrament of Matrimony. From this treasury,
we can draw *supernatural power*. This power will help us to fulfill the *rights
and duties* of the married state. We will be able to fulfill them faithfully.
We can fulfill them in a holy manner. We will be able to persevere as we
fulfill our duties. With our matrimonial graces, we will be able to persevere
even unto death!

The Catholic Church teaches that we merit more sanctifying grace
as we fulfill our duties, and can merit even extra gifts, such as certain
dispositions or graces, to elevate and perfect some natural powers we
already have. The natural abilities, in every area, seem to increase as home
schooling mothers and fathers dedicate themselves to their children in
fulfilling these responsibilities.

Pius XI continues:

> By these gifts the parties are assisted not only in understanding,
> but in knowing intimately, in adhering to firmly, in willing effectively,
> and in successfully putting into practice, those things which pertain
> to the marriage state, its aims and *duties*, giving them a right to the
> actual assistance of grace, whensoever they need it for fulfilling the
> *duties* of their state. (Emphasis added)

The Catholic Church declares that we will obtain the grace from
God *whenever* we need it for fulfilling the duties of the married state. If we
believe Jesus, if we believe in His Church, if we believe in the infallibility
of the pope as the Vicar of Jesus Christ, how can we doubt for a minute
that we will have the graces and ability to educate our own children?

Some parents say they lack confidence in their ability to teach their
children. But we are not supposed to have confidence in our own ability.
We are supposed to have confidence in Jesus Christ! We are supposed to
have confidence in His Word in the Bible and in the infallible documents
of the Church as proclaimed by the Vicar of Christ. We are supposed to

have confidence in the graces which He has given us and continues to give us as we teach our children, as we fulfill the duties of the vocation of the Sacrament of Matrimony.

Why some parents are not successful

Pius XI goes on to explain why some parents may not be successful in fulfilling their responsibilities:

> Nevertheless, since it is a law of Divine Providence in the supernatural order that men do not reap the full fruit of the sacraments ... *unless they cooperate with grace*, the grace of matrimony will remain for the most part an unused talent, hidden in the field, unless the parties exercise these supernatural powers, and cultivate and develop the seeds of grace they have received.
>
> If however, doing all that lies within their power, they cooperate diligently, they will be able with ease to bear the burdens of their state and to fulfill their duties. By such a sacrament, they will be strengthened, sanctified, and, in a manner, consecrated. (Emphasis added)

The power to educate

Continuing in the encyclical letter, *Casti Connubii*, Pope Pius XI repeats the long-standing teaching of the Church:

> The blessing of offspring, however, is not completed by the mere begetting of them, but something else must be added, namely the proper education of the offspring. For the wise God would have failed to make sufficient provision for children that had been born ... if He had not given to those to whom He had entrusted the power and right to beget them, the power also and the right to educate them.
>
> Now it is certain that both by the law of nature and of God, this right and duty of educating their offspring belongs in the first place to those who began the work of nature by giving them birth, and they are indeed forbidden to leave unfinished this work.... In matrimony, provision has been made in the best possible way for this education of children.

And then Pius XI quotes again from the Code of Canon Law of 1917, "The primary end of marriage is the procreation and the education of children."

Education: the long-term duty

In our child-abusing and pro-abortion society, it is important that the emphasis today among good Catholics be on recognizing that children are a gift from God, and that we remain open to life in the marriage union. The fact is that the long-term obligation for parents, the day-to-day, minute-by-minute obligation over a period of many, many years is not procreating, but educating.

For some reason, Pre-Cana conferences spend much of the class time on the physical aspects of marriage, and whether this or that birth control method is okay or not. It is a serious omission in these classes that the graces of the sacrament, as well as the long-term process of spiritual growth of the family members through education, is ignored.

Father Hardon on marriage

In the summer of 1991, Father John Hardon, who was an outstanding Catholic theologian, gave a summer course at Christendom College on the Sacrament of Matrimony. He taught the basic principles of Christ concerning marriage. His exposition on the sacrament was so beautiful that all those hearing it were filled with gratitude to God for this great gift.

Father Hardon's first message was that it is a Divine Law that every marriage must be monogamous, that a man may have only one wife, and a woman only one husband, until one of them dies. And every marriage between baptized persons is intrinsically indissoluble. No matter what non-Christians, Eastern Orthodox, Protestants, or Catholic writers urge, there cannot and will not ever be a change in this Divine Law. The unity and the indissolubility of marriage has always been the universal teaching of the Church of Jesus Christ.

This foundation for marriage means that parents need to work out their family problems, seek solutions together, and not run from their spouses. This means the family will be stable for the children, and will provide a solid environment for educating them at home.

A mother unhappy with her marriage can and will find solace in the daily teaching interaction with her children. She cannot dwell on her personal problems as she daily teaches her children, by prayer and good example, as well as by more formal methods.

Graces

Especially interesting for home schoolers was Father Hardon's lesson on graces of Christian marriage. We know from our catechism that we receive sanctifying grace as well as a sacramental grace when we receive each sacrament.

What most of us did not realize is that this single one-syllable word, *grace*, has so much meaning to our vocation of marriage. The special sacramental grace of each sacrament, as the catechism teaches, helps our intellects to know what is God's Will, and to understand better how to carry out God's Will in responding to certain events in our lives. It helps our will to carry out God's Will. The sacramental grace of Matrimony helps us to apply our intellect and will to the situations related to our vocation of marriage.

Father pointed out that while we need these graces to help our intellect and will, the primary purpose of these graces is to help each spouse to be an instrument of grace to the other spouse! The husband's primary duty as husband is to be a channel of grace to his wife, to help sanctify her; the wife's primary duty as wife is to be a channel of grace to her husband, to help sanctify him.

In addition, parents have special sacramental graces from the Sacrament of Matrimony by which they are to serve as channels of grace to their children. And from experience, many of us have come to realize that our children serve as channels of grace to us parents.

Certainly the directives of God to Moses, that parents are to teach their children and be an example to their children, sitting and walking, rising and resting, clearly show us that we are to be "channels" for teaching the Ten Commandments. With the institution of the Sacrament of Matrimony by Jesus, this responsibility can be more easily fulfilled because of the special sacramental graces. And the responsibility extends beyond the Ten Commandments. It includes an authentic Catholic family lifestyle.

The responsibility to help save the souls of our family members is an awesome responsibility. It is an overwhelming responsibility. Obviously, without the abundance of sacramental graces, this would be impossible.

The bottom line is that we must be good. We must be obedient, not only because we love God, not only to save our own soul, but

also because we need to serve as an example for our spouse and for
our children.

> Then after he had washed their feet, and taken his garments, being
> set down again, he said to them: "Know you what I have done to you?
> You call me Master, and Lord; and you say well, for so I am. If then
> I being your Lord and Master, have washed your feet; you also ought
> to wash one another's feet. For I have given you an example, that as
> I have done to you, so you do also." (John 13:12-15)

Cooperate with grace

While we received these graces at the Sacrament of Matrimony, we
must constantly work to use these graces. Nothing beats that combination
for personal fortification against the continual daily onslaughts of the
spiritual enemy: daily prayer, especially the Rosary, daily Mass if possible,
and Confession at least once a month.

As we cooperate with grace, we will be able to go beyond the strict
duties of our vocation, not only to recognize what else we must do, but
to carry out these responsibilities beyond the strict duty. Grace helps us
to "be apostolic," says Father Hardon, to our spouse, to our children, and
even to other families.

Edouard Cardinal Gagnon from the Pontifical Council on the
Family told me at a Philadelphia conference that American parents need
to evangelize in their own families. The cardinal believes that home
schooling is vital for evangelizing from one generation to the next. It is
because parents neglected their duties in the past to educate their children
themselves and relied on the schools that we have suffered the loss of faith
among Catholics today, the cardinal stated.

Marriage is permanent

No human authority can dissolve a valid, sacramental, consummated
marriage. This principle deserves special attention, due to the almost
universal breakdown of marriage and the family in "materially
superdeveloped countries," as Father Hardon says. Current attitudes about
individual freedom have made many people think that marriage is merely
a relationship of convenience, not a covenant made with a spouse and
God. Consequently, there is a loss of commitment by millions of people
to their marriage and to their families.

Home schooling is a complete reversal of these modern trends. Home schooling parents are willing to make God-ordained commitments, commitments to family, commitments to their spouse as they teach together, and commitments to their children, serious commitments involving time and energy and sacrifice.

Marriage strengthens society

Many home schooling parents understand that strengthening marriage and family also strengthens society. Home schooling parents' commitment to raise Catholic children means their Catholic values will ultimately "rule the world." Home schooling parents see clearly that the eternal rewards offer ultimate freedom for themselves and for their children. With the home schooling families, the national trend toward divorce and remarriage will be considerably slowed down, in this generation and in the generation to come.

Jesus became Man to redeem the human race, not only individual persons but also human societies, especially the basic unit of human society, the family. Families are called to become holy as families, and Jesus "merited the graces they need to become holy in this life," as Father Hardon taught. It is a "theme running through the New Testament that Christ has redeemed the human race, not only individually but collectively, not only personally but socially."

It is part of our Catholic tradition that God has ordained certain angels as guardians of cities and towns, of churches and city halls, of nations and peoples. Consequently, it is not too difficult to imagine that if families are called to be holy, if Christ died to redeem families as families, each family must have a family guardian angel.

In the Catholic Byzantine Rite marriage ceremony, the bride and groom each wear a crown, symbolizing the beginning of a new "kingdom" for God. From each family, living the Christian life, not only will their children come to populate Christ's kingdom, but a second generation will come to Christ, and then a third. This reflects the instructions in Exodus, in which Moses told the people to teach God's Commandments to their children, and their children's children.

My parents have nine living children. Eight are married and there are 43 living grandchildren, and many great-grandchildren. Now that's what I call a family kingdom!

Superhuman charity

Jesus makes "superhuman demands" of married people and their families, especially demanding a superhuman charity towards one another, says Father Hardon. It is superhuman to, day after day, put up with the faults of your spouse. It is superhuman especially in today's society when all of us are so influenced by the media propaganda telling us to "do your own thing," to "be yourself," and as Frank Sinatra sings, to do everything "MY way."

"Be true to yourself" has a new meaning today. It means "Me first!" So to remain faithful to someone for a lifetime, to put up with another's faults for a lifetime, to give up our own personal wants and desires for the good of our spouse, for the good of our family, for the glory of God, demands superhuman effort. These superhuman demands by God can be met only with the "superhuman light and strength made available by Christ's redemptive death on Calvary." These superhuman personal sacrifices of self can be met only with sanctifying grace, sacramental grace, and actual graces, all coming to us from the Sacrament of Matrimony and the other sacraments.

In practical terms

Married people thoroughly understand the tremendous difficulty in obeying Christ's command to "turn the other cheek." It is not our enemies who are so difficult to forgive. It is our spouse who is so difficult to forgive! And sometimes our children!

Father Hardon declared that the secret for a peaceful and happy marriage and family life is to realize that our spouses, our children, our parents, and our other family members are all potential vehicles of grace for us. No other creatures are as close, as constant, and as providential. No matter how difficult or demanding, our family members are a gift from God, a gift of His loving Providence, an opportunity for us to grow spiritually.

However, to see what God wants us to do, for us to choose what God wants, requires constant daily prayer.

Father Hardon reminded us that in addition to living a holy lifestyle in our vocation of Catholic marriage and family, our family is to be a witness in our pagan society to Christ and to His teachings. In a world that has "abandoned Christ, ignores Him, and even openly opposes Him," we and our family must be a source of grace in our society which is "literally struggling for survival." We must have a family-to-family evangelizing apostolate.

Humanae Vitae

In the encyclical letter of Pope Paul VI, *Humanae Vitae* (Of Human Life), the teachings of the Catholic Church regarding marriage and the procreation of children are carefully explained. In this encyclical, the pope repeats the teachings of the Church regarding the importance of education as essential to the vocation of marriage. He writes about collaborating with God "in the generation and education of new lives." And again, "Marriage and conjugal love are by their nature ordained toward the begetting and educating of children."

Pope Paul VI declared that:

> Christian married couples … must remember that their Christian vocation … is reinforced by the sacrament of matrimony. By it, husband and wife are strengthened and as it were consecrated for the faithful accomplishment of their proper duties, for the carrying out of their proper vocation even to perfection, and the Christian witness which is proper to them before the whole world.

Notice again that the pope is stressing that husbands and wives who have received the Sacrament of Matrimony are *consecrated* in order for them to accomplish the proper purposes of the married state.

The vocation of parents to educate

In the 1960s and 1970s, Catholic parents started home schooling because they believed it was the only option to protect their children. Parents began to investigate the Scriptures and the teachings of the Church to determine if home schooling is approved by the Church.

Historically, traditionally, and doctrinally, the Catholic Church strongly promotes, not just supports, parents teaching their own children.

In 1875, the Vatican sent "Instructions" to the bishops of the United States in regard to Catholic children attending the public schools.

Instructions of the Holy Office to the Bishops of the U.S.,

November 24, 1875

> To the Sacred Congregation, this method (of public education) has appeared intrinsically dangerous and absolutely contrary to Catholicism. Indeed because the special program adopted by these schools excludes all religious instruction, the pupils cannot grasp the elements of the faith, nor are they instructed in the precepts of the Church, and therefore they are deprived of that which is most essential for man to know and without which it is impossible to live in a Christian manner....
>
> [O]n July 14, 1864, [Pope Pius IX] wrote to the Archbishop of Fribourg: "In all places, in every country where this pernicious plan to deprive the Church of its authority over schools is formulated, and worse still, put into effect, with the result that the young will be exposed to the danger of losing their faith, it is the duty of the Church to make every effort not only to take steps to obtain the essential instruction and religious training for youth, but even more so to warn the faithful, and to make it clear to them that they cannot frequent such schools which are set up against the Catholic Church."
>
> These words, founded on the natural and divine law, state definitely a general principle, have a universal bearing, and apply to all countries where this injurious method of instructing youth will unfortunately be introduced.
>
> It is, therefore, absolutely necessary that all bishops should make every effort to see to it that the flock entrusted to them may avoid every contact with the public schools.

If the public schools of the nineteenth century were morally unacceptable, how much more so does this condemnation apply to today's schools?

The Instruction goes on:

> This instruction and this necessary Christian education of their children is often neglected by those parents who allow their children to frequent schools where it is impossible to avoid the loss of souls or who, notwithstanding the existence of a well-organized neighboring Catholic school or the possibility of having their children educated elsewhere in a Catholic school, entrust them to the public schools without sufficient reason and without having taken the necessary precautions to avoid the danger of perversion; it is a well-known fact that, according to Catholic moral teaching, such parents, should they

persist in their attitude, cannot receive absolution in the Sacrament of Penance.

There are even some schools which call themselves "Catholic" that do not proclaim the fullness of Catholic truth. Parents must not assume that the word "Catholic" on a school's letterhead or front entrance ensures faithfulness to Church teaching.

If it had not been for the problems in the schools, Catholic parents would probably not have even thought about teaching their children at home, and would not have discovered the joys of the authentic Catholic family lifestyle. They would not have realized the blessings of living the Catholic Faith daily in every aspect of their lives.

Government schools

When the government public schools began after the Civil War, there was no Protestant "religion" class in these government schools. But the Protestant philosophy or values permeated the textbooks and curriculum, teachers were Protestant, and Catholic children were being influenced by them.

In the *Blumenfeld Education Letter* of September, 1990, Mr. Blumenfeld quoted a Catholic of the 1800s regarding the American public schools:

> So far as Catholics are concerned, the system of Common Schools in this country is a monstrous engine of injustice and tyranny. Practically, it operates a gigantic scheme for proselytism.... the faith of our children is gradually undermined.... In general, so far as it professes to be religious, it is anti-Catholic, and so far as it is secular, it is pagan.

Today, many Catholic children attend the government schools or "Catholic" schools and imbibe the secular values. The traditional parish one-hour-a-week CCD program, even if it presents traditional Catholic ideas, cannot compete with the seven hours a day, five days a week the Catholic children spend in the camp of the enemy of the Catholic Church. The schools are turning the souls of the children away from love of God, away from love of family, away from love of country, away from the love of our Catholic Faith.

In the following encyclical, Pope Leo XIII declared that the heads of families are commanded to keep their children away from schools where there is a lack of devotion and reverence for God.

Encyclical *Sapientiae Christianae*, January 10, 1890

This is a suitable moment for Us to exhort especially heads of families to govern their households according to these precepts, and to educate their children from their earliest years. The family may be regarded as the cradle of civil society, and it is in great measure within the circle of family life that the destiny of the State is fostered. Consequently they who would break away from Christian discipline are working to corrupt family life and to destroy it utterly, root and branch. From such an unholy purpose they are not deterred by the fact that they are inflicting a cruel outrage on parents, who have the right from nature to educate those whom they begot, a right to which is joined the duty of harmonizing instruction and education with the end for which they were given their children by the goodness of God.

It is then incumbent upon parents to make every effort to resist attacks on this point and to vindicate at any cost the right to direct the education of their offspring, as it is fitting, in a Christian manner; and first and foremost to keep them away from schools where there is risk of their being imbued with the poison of impiety.

Where the right education of youth is concerned, no amount of trouble and labor is too much. In this matter there are many Catholics of various nations who deserve to be praised and who incur great expense and exhibit much zeal in opening schools for the education of children. It is desirable that this noble example be followed according to the needs of the times.

However, let everyone be firmly convinced, first of all, that the minds of children are best trained above all by the teaching they receive at home. If in their growing years they find in their homes the rule of an upright life and the exercise of Christian virtue, the salvation of society will be in great part assured.

The total curriculum must be Godly

In 1897, in the encyclical *Militantis Ecclesiae*, by Pope Leo XIII, the pope teaches that the total educational program is to be permeated with "the sense of Christian piety," with the sense of devotion and reverence toward God and the doctrines taught by Jesus Christ.

Encyclical *Militantis Ecclesiae*, August 1, 1897

In this matter special care must be paid to these points. First of all, Catholics should not frequent "mixed" schools [those for Catholics and non-Catholics], especially those for little children. They should everywhere have their own schools and should choose excellent, trustworthy teachers. An education which contains religious errors or which bans all religion, is full of dangers: and this often happens in the schools we have called "mixed." Let nobody easily persuade himself that piety can be separated from instruction with impunity.

In fact, in no period of life, whether in public or in private affairs, can religion be dispensed with, much less can that inexperienced age, full of life, yet surrounded by so many corrupt temptations, be excused from religious obligations.

Whosoever, therefore, organizes education so as to neglect any point of contact with religion is destroying beauty and honesty at their very roots, and instead of helping the country, is preparing for the deterioration and destruction of the human race. For, once God is eliminated, who can make young people realize their duties or redeem those who have deviated from the right path of virtue and fallen into the abyss of vice?

Religion must not be taught to youth only during certain hours, but the entire system of education must be permeated with the sense of Christian piety. If this is lacking, if this holy spirit does not penetrate and inflame the souls of teacher and pupil, small benefit will be derived from any other sort of education; instead damage will be done.

Almost every sort of training has its dangers, and only with difficulty will these be averted from growing youth, especially if the divine controls are lacking which restrain their minds and wills. Great care must therefore be taken so that what is essential, namely, the pursuit of justice and piety, may not be relegated to a second place, confining youth to the visible world and thus leaving their vital potentiality for virtue to rot; so that, again, while teachers, with painful exertion, drill on boring subjects and analyze syllable and accent, they may not neglect that true wisdom, whose beginning is the fear of the Lord and whose precepts demand obedience in every circumstance of life.

A wide knowledge should go hand in hand with care for spiritual progress; *religion must permeate and direct every branch of knowledge* whatever be its nature, and by its sweetness and majesty must make so great an impression on the minds of youth as to be an incitement to better things.

Since it has always been the Church's intention that *every branch of study be of great service in the religious formation of youth*, this particular subject matter not only must have its place, and the principal place at that, but nobody should be entrusted with so important a teaching role who has not first been declared suitable for the purpose in the judgment and by the authority of the Church.

On Christian Education of Youth

Another great Catholic encyclical is On Christian Education of Youth or, in Latin, *Divini Illius Magistri*, published in 1929, by Pope Pius XI.

This encyclical letter is the most powerful Catholic Church document commanding parental responsibility in the education of children. Pius XI quotes the Code of Canon Law of 1917, Canon 1113:

> Parents are under a grave obligation to see to the religious and moral education of their children, as well as to their physical and civic training, as far as they can, and moreover to provide for their temporal well-being.

Leo XIII is quoted extensively in this encyclical:

> By nature, parents have a right to the training of their children, but with the added *duty* that the education and instruction of the child be in accord with the end for which by God's blessing it was begotten. Therefore, it is the *duty* of parents to make every effort to prevent any invasion of their rights in this matter, and to make absolutely sure that the education of their children remains under their own control in keeping with their Christian *duty*, and above all to refuse to send them to those schools in which there is danger of imbibing the deadly poison of impiety. (Emphasis added)

Pope Pius XI continues to quote Pope Leo XIII: "...the *obligation* of the family to bring up children includes not only religious and moral education, but physical and civic education as well, principally insofar as it touches upon religion and morality." This is an important quote for parents to remember, for it reminds us that the sacramental graces will help parent-teachers in all academic areas.

Family education

Pope Pius XI continues in *Divini Illius Magistri*:

> We wish to call your attention in a special manner to the present-day lamentable decline in family education … for the fundamental *duty* and *obligation* of educating their children, many parents have little or no preparation, immersed as they are in temporal cares. The declining influence of domestic environment is further weakened by another tendency … which … causes children to be more and more frequently sent away from home, even in their tenderest years. And there is a country where the children are actually being torn from the bosom of the family to be formed (or to speak more accurately, to be deformed and depraved), in godless schools and associations, to irreligion and hatred … thus is renewed in a real and more terrible manner the slaughter of the Innocents. (Emphasis added)

These were strong words from the pope. When children are deformed and depraved in godless schools, this is a more real and more terrible slaughter of the Innocents than in the Biblical slaughter of the Innocents, says the pope. And this was long before children were being taught in 5th grade to practice putting condoms on bananas in the classroom.

The next several pages of quotes are from this same encyclical by Pope Pius XI.

> It is therefore as important to make no mistake in education, as it is to make no mistake in the pursuit of the last goal, with which the whole work of education is intimately and necessarily connected. In fact, since education consists essentially in preparing man for what he must be and for what he must do here below, in order to attain the sublime goal for which he was created, it is clear that there can be no true education which is not wholly directed to man's last end, and that in the present order of Providence, since God has revealed Himself to us in the Person of His only-begotten Son, Who alone is "the Way, the Truth and the Life," there can be no ideally perfect education which is not Christian education.

Christian education is necessary for human society

> Hence the supreme importance of Christian education, is not merely for each individual, but for families and for the whole of human society. The unsurpassed excellence of the work of Christian

education becomes manifest and clear; for after all it aims at securing the Supreme Good, that is, God, for the souls of those who are being educated, and the maximum of well-being possible here below for human society. And this it does as efficaciously as man is capable of doing it, namely by cooperating with God in the perfecting of individuals and society, inasmuch as education imprints upon the soul the first, the most powerful and lasting impression for life, according to the well-known saying of the Wise Man: "Raise up a child in the way he should go, and even when he is old, he will not depart from it."

The family has prior educational rights over the civil society

Education is essentially a social and not merely an individual activity. Now there are three essential societies, distinct one from the other and yet harmoniously combined by God, into which man is born: of these, two, namely the family and civil society, belong to the natural order. In the first place comes the family, instituted directly by God for its particular purpose, the procreation and the formation of offspring; for this reason it has priority of nature, and therefore of rights, over civil society.

All actions must be done in light of the supernatural

This is clearly set forth by Pius X, of saintly memory: "Whatever a Christian does, even in the order of earthly things, he may not overlook the supernatural; indeed he must, according to the teaching of Christian wisdom, direct all things towards the supreme good as to his last end; all his actions, besides, insofar as they are good or evil in the order of morality, that is, in keeping or not with the natural or divine law, fall under the judgment and jurisdiction of the Church."

Family rights in education cannot be violated

The family holds, therefore, directly from the Creator the mission, and hence the right, to educate the young, a right inalienable because inseparably joined to a strict obligation, a right anterior to any right whatever of civil society and the State, and therefore inviolable on the part of any power on earth.

That this right is inviolable St. Thomas proves as follows: "The child is naturally something of the father ... so by natural right the child, before reaching the use of reason, is under the father's care. Hence it would be contrary to natural justice if the child, before arriving at the use of reason, were removed from the care of its parents, or if any arrangement were made concerning him against the will of the parents." And as this duty on the part of the parents continues up to the time when the child is in a position to provide for itself, this same inviolable parental right of education also endures. "Nature intends not merely the generation of offspring, but also its development and advancement to the perfection of man considered as man, that is, to the state of virtue" as St. Thomas himself says.

Children belong to the family

On this point the common sense of mankind is in such complete accord, that they would be in open contradiction with those who dared to maintain that the children belong to the State before they belong to the family, and that the State has an absolute right over their education. Untenable is the reason they adduce, namely that man is born a citizen and hence belongs primarily to the State, not bearing in mind that before being a citizen, man must exist; and existence does not come from the State, but from the parents, as Leo XIII wisely declared: "The children are something of the father, and as it were an extension of the person of the father; and, to be perfectly accurate, they enter into and become part of civil society, not directly by themselves, but through the family in which they were born."

"And therefore," says the same Leo XIII, "the father's power is of such a nature that it cannot be destroyed or absorbed by the State; for it has the same origin as human life itself."

Education must be in accord with the purpose of man's existence

It does not, however, follow from this that the parents' right to educate their children is absolute and despotic; for it is necessarily subordinated to the last end, and to natural and divine law, as Leo XIII declares in another memorable encyclical, where he sums up the rights and duties of parents: "By nature parents have a right to the training of their children, but with this added duty: that the education and instruction of the child be in accord with the end for which, by God's blessing, it was begotten."

State laws should protect family educational rights

Consequently, in the matter of education, it is the right, or to speak more correctly, it is the duty of the State to protect by means of its legislation, the prior rights, already described, of the family as regards the Christian education of its offspring, and consequently also to respect the supernatural rights of the Church in this same realm of Christian education.

Christian education concerns the whole man

It should never be forgotten that the subject of Christian education concerns man as a whole, soul united to body by nature, together with all his faculties, natural and supernatural, such as right reason and revelation show him to be; man, therefore, fallen from his original estate, but redeemed by Christ and restored to the supernatural condition of adopted son of God, though without the preternatural privileges of bodily immortality or perfect control of appetite. There remain, therefore, in human nature the effects of original sin, the chief of which are weakness of will and disorderly inclinations.

The mind must be enlightened, the will strengthened

"Folly is bound up in the heart of a child and the rod of correction shall drive it away." Disorderly inclinations then must be corrected, good tendencies encouraged and regulated from the tender age of childhood, and above all the mind must be enlightened and the will strengthened by supernatural truth and by the means of grace, without which it is impossible to control evil impulse, impossible to attain the complete and full perfection of education intended by the Church, which Christ has endowed so richly with divine doctrine and with the Sacraments, the efficacious means of grace.

Sex education in the schools a grave danger

Another very grave danger is that naturalism which nowadays invades the field of education in that most delicate matter of purity of morals. Far too common is the error of those who with dangerous assurance and under an ugly term propagate a so-called sex-education, erroneously imagining that they can arm youths against the dangers of sensuality by purely natural means, such as foolhardy initiation and precautionary instruction for all indiscriminately, even in public;

and, worse still, by exposing them at an early age to the opportunity, in order to accustom them, so it is argued, and as it were to harden them against such dangers.

Evil results from weakness of the will

Such persons grievously err in refusing to recognize the inborn weakness of human nature, and the law of which the Apostle speaks, warring against the law of the mind; and also in ignoring what is taught by facts, from which it is clear that, particularly in young people, evil practices are the effect not so much of ignorance of intellect as of weakness of a will exposed to dangerous occasions, and deprived of the means of grace.

Education in the family more effective and lasting

The first natural and necessary element in this environment, as regards education, is the family, and this precisely because it is so ordained by the Creator Himself. Accordingly, that education which is received in a well-ordered and well-disciplined Christian family will, as a rule, be more effective and lasting, and more efficacious in proportion to the clear and constant good example set, first by the parents, and then by the other members of the household.

The lamentable decline in family education

Nevertheless, Venerable Brethren, and beloved children, We wish to call your attention in a special manner to the present-day lamentable decline in family education. The offices and professions of a transitory and earthly life which are certainly of far less importance, are prepared for by long and careful study; whereas for the fundamental duty and obligation of educating their children, many parents have little or no preparation, immersed as they are in earthly cares.

Pastors should help parents teach their children

For the love of Our Savior Jesus Christ, therefore, We implore pastors of souls, by every means in their power, by instructions and by catechisms, by word of mouth and by widely distributed written articles, to warn Christian parents of their grave obligations. And this should be done not merely in a theoretical and general way, but with practical and specific application to the various responsibilities of parents touching the religious, moral and civil training of their children, and with an indication of the methods best adapted to make their training most effective, in addition to the influence of their own exemplary lives.

Fathers, be patient, yet discipline your children

The Apostle of the Gentiles did not hesitate to descend to such details of practical instruction in his epistles, especially in his Epistle to the Ephesians, where among other things he gives this advice: "And you, fathers, provoke not your children to anger." This fault is the result not so much of excessive severity, as of impatience and of ignorance of the means best calculated to effect the desired correction; it is also due to the all-too-common relaxation of parental discipline which fails to check the growth of evil passions in the hearts of the younger generation.

Parents are vicars, or representatives, of God

Parents, therefore, and all who take their place in the work of education, should be careful to make right use of the authority given them by God, whose vicars in a true sense they are. This authority is not given for their own advantage, but for the proper upbringing of their children in a holy and filial "fear of God, the beginning of wisdom," on which foundation alone all respect for authority can rest securely; and without which, order, tranquility and prosperity, whether in the family or in society, will be impossible.

Parents are forbidden to send their children to irreligious schools

From this it follows that the so-called "neutral" or "lay" school, from which religion is excluded, is contrary to the fundamental principles of education. Such a school moreover, cannot exist in practice; it is bound to become irreligious. There is no need to repeat what Our Predecessors have declared on this point, especially Pius IX and Leo XIII, at times when laicism was beginning in a special manner to infest public schools.

We renew and confirm their declarations [in 1864, 1880, 1884, 1886, 1887, and 1894], as well as the Sacred Canons, in which the frequenting of non-Catholic schools, whether neutral or mixed, those namely which are open to Catholics and non-Catholics alike, is forbidden to Catholic children, or at the most is tolerated, on the approval of the Ordinary [bishop] alone, under determined circumstances of place and time, and with special precautions. Neither can Catholics allow that other type of mixed schools, where the students are provided with separate religious instruction, but receive other lessons in common with non-Catholic pupils from non-Catholic teachers.

Note: Canon 798 of the 1983 *Code of Canon Law* states, "Parents are to entrust their children to those schools which provide a Catholic education. If they are unable to do this, they are obliged to take care that suitable Catholic education is provided for their children outside the schools."

The definition of an authentic Catholic school

The mere fact that a school gives some religious instruction (often extremely stinted), does not bring it into line with the rights of the Church and of the Christian family, or make it a fit place for Catholic students. To be this, it is necessary that all the teaching and the whole organization of the school, its teachers, syllabus and textbooks of every kind, be regulated by the Christian spirit, under the direction and maternal supervision of the Church; so that religion may be in very truth the foundation and the crown of youth's entire training; and this applies to every grade of school, not only the elementary, but the intermediate and the high institutions of learning as well.

To use the words of Leo XIII: "It is necessary not only that religious instruction be given to the young at certain fixed times, but also that every other subject taught be permeated with Christian piety. If this be wanting, if this sacred atmosphere does not pervade and warm the hearts of masters and scholars alike, little good can be expected from any kind of learning, and considerable harm will often be the consequence."

The supernatural man is the product of Christian education

The proper and immediate aim of Christian education is to cooperate with divine grace in forming the true and perfect Christian … For the true Christian must live a supernatural life in Christ: "Christ Who is your life," and display it in all his actions … For precisely this reason, Christian education takes in the whole of human life, physical and spiritual, intellectual and moral, individual, domestic, and social ...

Hence the true Christian, a product of Christian education, is the supernatural man who thinks, judges, and acts constantly and consistently in accordance with right reason illumined by the supernatural light of the example and teaching of Christ.

The Catholic man perfects the natural with the supernatural

The authentic Christian does not renounce the activities of this life, he does not stunt his natural faculties; but he develops and perfects them, by coordinating them with the supernatural. He thus ennobles what is merely natural in life ...

Christian education ennobles and benefits human society

This fact is proved by the whole history of Christianity and its institutions, which is nothing else but the history of true civilization and progress up to the present day. It stands out conspicuously in the lives of the numerous saints, whom the Church and she alone, produces; in whom is perfectly realized the purpose of Christian education, and who have in every way ennobled and benefited human society.

Christian education has benefited all social institutions

What of the founders of so many charitable and social institutions, of the vast numbers of saintly educators, men and women, who have perpetuated and multiplied their life work, by leaving behind them prolific institutions of Christian education, in aid of families and for the inestimable advantage of nations?

Such are the fruits of Christian education. Their price and value are derived from the supernatural virtue and life in Christ which Christian education forms and develops in man. Of this life and virtue Christ Our Lord and Master is the source and dispenser. By His example, He is at the same time the universal model, accessible to all, especially to the young, in the period of his Hidden life, a life of labor and obedience, adorned with all virtues, personal, domestic and social, before God and men.

The teachings still stand

The content of the encyclical On Christian Education of Youth has been taught over and over in encyclicals and papal documents, right up to the present time. In 1955, in a papal letter to the cardinal of Malines, Pope Pius XII wrote about this encyclical:

> The inviolable principles which this document lays down regarding the Church, family, and State in the matter of education, are based on the very nature of things and on revealed truth. They cannot be shaken by the ebb and flow of events. As for the fundamental rules which it prescribes, these too are not subject to the wear and tear of time, since they are only the faithful echo of the Divine Master, Whose words shall never pass away. The encyclical is a real Magna Carta of Christian education, "outside which no education is complete and perfect."

Later in the same letter, the pope repeated the teaching that the family has a "priority of right over the State in the matter of education." But the Church has the right and duty to teach "the highest truths and laws of the religious and moral life." And the pope concludes:

> The State therefore has the duty to respect the prior rights of the family and of the church in the matter of education, and even protect these rights. If the State were to "monopolize education," this would violate the rights of individuals, of the family, and of the Church.

The divine responsibility

In the encyclical *Mit Brennender Sorge* in 1937, Pope Pius XI wrote strong words for those pretending to have Catholic schools:

> The formal preservation of religious instruction, especially when controlled and shackled by incompetent people, in the atmosphere of a school which, in the teaching of other subjects, works systematically and invidiously against religion, can never be a justification for a believing Christian to give his free approval to such a school that aims at destroying religion.

> … keep this in mind: no earthly power can release you from the divine responsibility which unites you to your children. None of those who today are suppressing your right in the matter of education, and pretending to free you from your duty in this matter, will be able to reply for you to God Almighty when He asks: "Where are those whom

I have entrusted to you?" Let each one of you be able to reply: "I have not lost any of those whom You have entrusted to me." (John 18:9)

Summi Pontificatus, October 20, 1939

The charge laid by God on parents, to provide for the material and spiritual well-being of their offspring and to procure for them a suitable training, imbued with the true spirit of religion, cannot be wrested from them without grave violation of their rights.

Undoubtedly, that formation should aim as well at preparing youth to fulfill with intelligence, conscientiousness, and pride those duties of noble patriotism, which gives to one's earthly fatherland all due measure of love, self-devotion, and service. On the other hand, a formation which forgets, or worse still, deliberately fails to direct the gaze and desire of youth to their heavenly fatherland, would be an injustice to youth, an injustice to the inalienable duties and rights of the Christian family ...

The souls of children, given to their parents by God and consecrated in Baptism with the royal character of Christ, are a sacred charge over which the jealous love of God watches. The same Christ Who pronounced the words "Suffer the little children to come unto Me" has, for all His mercy and goodness, threatened with fearful evils those who offend the ones so dear to His Heart.

Of all that exists on the face of the earth, only the soul is immortal. A system of education that did not respect the sacred precincts of the Christian family protected by God's holy law, that attacked its foundations, barred to the young the way to Christ ... that considered apostasy from Christ and the Church as a proof of fidelity to the people or to a particular class, would pronounce its own condemnation ...

Speech to teachers

In a speech to secondary teachers in 1949, Pope Pius XII declared that the "Chair of Peter" has always dedicated itself to standing for parental rights. He wrote:

> [The Chair of Peter] will never consent to let the Church, which received this right [to guard the welfare of souls] by divine mandate, or the family, which claims it through natural justice, be deprived of the effective exercise of the natural right.

Second Vatican Council

In the Declaration on Christian Education of the Second Vatican Council, October, 1965, many of the above quotes are repeated, re-emphasizing and supporting the traditional teachings of the Church. In fact, the words of this Council are even stronger than previous documents:

> Since parents have given life to their children, they are bound by a *grave obligation* to educate their offspring, and so must be regarded as their primary and principal educators. Their role in education is of such importance that where it is missing, its place can scarcely be supplied. For it is the parents' task to create the kind of family atmosphere, inspired by love, and by devotion toward God and men, that is favorable to the complete personal and social education of their children.

> The family is therefore, the principal school of the social virtues which are necessary to every society. It is therefore above all in the Christian family, inspired by the grace and the responsibility of the sacrament of matrimony that children should be taught to know and worship God, and to love their neighbor ... In the family, they will have their first experience of a well-balanced human society.... Parents should appreciate how important a role the truly Christian family plays in the life and progress of the whole people of God. (Emphasis added)

In the Decree on the Apostolate of Lay People, the pope and bishops teach, in Paragraph 11:

> [Christian parents] are the first to pass on the Faith to their children and to educate them in it. By word and example they form them to a Christian and apostolic life.... [they] assert with vigor the right and duty of parents and guardians to give their children a Christian upbringing.

> The mission of being the primary vital cell of society has been given to the family by God Himself. This mission will be accomplished if the family, by the mutual affection of its members and by family prayer, presents itself as a domestic sanctuary of the Church ["domestic church" is another translation]; if the whole family takes its part in the Church's liturgical worship; if it offers active hospitality and practices justice and other good works for the benefit of all those suffering from want.

Christian families bear a very valuable witness to Christ before the world when all their life they remain attached to the Gospel and hold up the example of Christian marriage.

In the Decree on the Pastoral Constitution on the Church, the Council declared:

> ... by its very nature the institution of marriage and married love is ordered to the procreation and education of the offspring ... When they are given the dignity and role of fatherhood and motherhood, [parents] will eagerly carry out their duties of education, especially religious education, which devolves primarily on them. (No. 48)

> Marriage and married love are by nature ordered to the procreation and education of children ... Married couples should regard it as their proper mission to transmit human life and to educate their children. (No. 50)

Pope Paul VI, in an address before the Committee for the Family in 1974, spoke about the virtues which the family should be promoting:

> ... the home is the privileged place of love, of the deep communion of persons, of apprenticeship in the continual and progressive self-giving of husband and wife to each other.... This love necessarily presupposes tenderness, self-control, patient understanding, faithfulness and generosity ...

And again: "conjugal love must not only master instinct, but it must overcome selfishness incessantly."

Catechesi Tradendae

In *Catechesi Tradendae* (Catechesis in Our Time), an apostolic exhortation promulgated in 1979, Pope John Paul II reminds us of the traditional teachings of the Church regarding teaching of the catechism:

> The family's catechetical activity has a special character, which is in a sense irreplaceable. This special character has been rightly stressed by the Church, particularly by the Second Vatican Council.

The footnotes to this statement point out that councils of the Church have "insisted on the responsibility of parents in regard to education in the faith." Cited are the Sixth Council of Arles, Council of Mainz, Sixth Council of Paris, documents of Pius XI, the "many discourses and messages of Pius XII," and several documents of the Second Vatican Council.

Here is the quote from *Catechesi Tradendae* which explains why Catholic home schooling works:

> Education in the faith by parents, which should begin from the children's tenderest age, is already being given when the members of a family help each other to grow in faith through the witness of their Christian lives, a witness that is often without words but which perseveres throughout a day-to-day life lived in accordance with the Gospel. This catechesis is more incisive when, in the course of family events (such as the reception of the sacraments, the celebration of great liturgical feasts, the birth of a child, a bereavement) care is taken to explain in the home the Christian or religious content of these events.

Pope John Paul II goes on to say:

> [In places] where widespread unbelief or invasive secularism makes real religious growth practically impossible, "the church of the home" remains the one place where children and young people can receive an authentic catechesis. Thus there cannot be too great an effort on the part of Christian parents to prepare for this ministry of being their own children's catechists, and to carry it out with tireless zeal.

Notice the phrase "church of the home," which is similar to the previous papal phrases "domestic church" and "sanctuary of the home."

Code of Canon Law

The 1983 Code of Canon Law speaks strongly about parents' rights and responsibilities in the education of their children, in all subjects, and especially in religious education and in the preparation of their children for the reception of the sacraments:

Canon 226.2:

> Parents, because they have given life to their children, are bound by the most grave obligation and enjoy the right of educating them; therefore, it is first for the Christian parents to take care for the Christian education of their children according to the teaching handed on by the Church.

Canon 774.2:

> Before all others, parents are bound by the obligation of forming their children by word and example in the faith and the practice of the Christian life …

Canon 776 proclaims: "The pastor is to promote and foster the role of parents in the family catechesis mentioned in Canon 774.2."

Canon 793.1 states:

> Parents and those who hold their place (such as guardians) are *bound by the obligation* and enjoy the right of educating their children; Catholic parents also have the *duty* and the right of selecting those means and institutes by which, in the light of local circumstances, they can better provide for the Catholic education of their children. (Emphasis added)

Canon 835.4:

> … parents share in a special way in this office of sanctification through their conjugal life in the Christian spirit, and in taking care for the Christian education of their children.

Canon 1055.1 declares: "The matrimonial covenant … is by its nature ordered toward the good of the spouses and the procreation and education of children …"

Canon 1134 declares: "… in Christian marriage, moreover, spouses are strengthened and, as it were, consecrated by this special sacrament for the duties and dignity of their state."

Canon 1136, from the section "The Effects of Marriage":

> Parents have a most grave *duty* and enjoy the primary right of educating to the very best of their ability, their children physically, socially, and culturally and morally and religiously as well. (Emphasis added)

Canon 1366 declares: "Parents, or those holding the place of parents, who hand over their children to be baptized or educated in a non-Catholic religion are to be punished by censure or other just penalty."

In *Home Schooling and the New Code of Canon Law*, canon lawyer Edward N. Peters writes:

> The canonical rights of parents over the education of their children are strongly affirmed in the 1983 Code of Canon Law. Therefore, any attempt, whether by proper ecclesiastical authorities or otherwise, to restrict the prudent exercise of these educational rights (including, as we shall argue shortly, the parental decision to home-school a child) must by canon law be strictly scrutinized lest the exercise of those

rights be unjustly impeded.... What is important to realize, however, is that questions concerning the practice of home schooling affect not just the child's right to an education, but ultimately the sacramental identity and mission of the family and each of its respective members.

Pope John Paul II's *Familiaris Consortio*

Perhaps the most important modern document for home schooling families is the apostolic exhortation The Role of the Christian Family in the Modern World, or *Familiaris Consortio*, published in 1981. This encyclical should serve as a basis for greater study by Catholic home schooling parents as we grow in a deeper understanding of the Sacrament of Matrimony and the graces and duties of the married state.

Pope John Paul II proclaims:

> The task of giving education is rooted in the primary vocation of married couples to participate in God's creative activity: by begetting in love and for love a new person who has within himself or herself the vocation to growth and development, parents by that very fact take on the task of helping that person effectively to live a fully human life.... the family is the first school of those social virtues which every society needs. The right and duty of parents to give education is essential, since it is connected with the transmission of human life; it is original and primary with regard to the educational role of others ... it is irreplaceable and inalienable, and therefore incapable of being entirely delegated to others or usurped by others. In addition to these characteristics, it cannot be forgotten that the most basic element, so basic that it qualifies the educational role of parents, is parental love, which finds fulfillment in the task of education ... as well as being a source, the parents' love is also the animating principle and therefore the norm inspiring and guiding all concrete educational activity, enriching it with the values of kindness, constancy, goodness, service, disinterestedness and self-sacrifice that are the most precious fruit of love.

It is obvious that home schooling parents need to be sure that they themselves are developing these Christian virtues, and that their children are developing them also. In this way, we can bring these virtues to our society as well. Pope John Paul II continued in this exhortation to emphasize the educational priority of the parents by calling it a "mission."

For Christian parents the mission to educate ... has a new specific source in the sacrament of marriage, which consecrates them for the strictly Christian education of their children.... it enriches them with wisdom, counsel, fortitude, and all the other gifts of the Holy Spirit in order to help the children in their growth as human beings and as Christians.

The sacrament of marriage gives to the educational role the dignity and vocation of being really and truly a "ministry" of the Church, at the service of building up her members. So great and splendid is the educational ministry of Christian parents that Saint Thomas [Aquinas] has no hesitation in comparing it with the ministry of priests.

A vivid and attentive awareness of the *mission* that they have received with the sacrament of marriage will help Christian parents to place themselves at the service of their children's education with great serenity and trustfulness, and also with a sense of responsibility before God.

Charter of the Rights of the Family

In 1983, Pope John Paul II published the Charter of the Rights of the Family, mainly to support parents in their right to oppose sex education programs in the schools. The pope re-emphasizes the irreplaceable role of the family as having primary rights in the education of children.

The family constitutes much more than a mere juridical, social, and economic unit, a community of love and solidarity which is uniquely suited to teach and transmit cultural, ethical, social, spiritual, and religious values, essential for the development and well-being of its own members and of society.

The family is the place where different generations come together and help one another to grow in human wisdom and to harmonize the right of individuals with other demands of social life....

Since they [parents] have conferred life on their children, parents have the original, primary, and inalienable right to educate them; hence they must be acknowledged as the first and foremost educators of their children.

Parents have the right to educate their children in conformity with their moral and religious convictions, taking into account the cultural traditions of the family....

Parents have the right to choose freely schools or other means necessary to educate their children in keeping with their convictions.

Parents have the right to ensure that their children are not compelled to attend classes which are not in agreement with their own moral and religious convictions.

The rights of parents are violated when a compulsory system of education is imposed by the state from which all religious formation is excluded.

It is obvious that God's plan for Christian families is for parents to dedicate themselves to educating their children. This is not a haphazard mission, but a full-time mission, a duty and a command, to be fulfilled on a daily basis. It encompasses primarily religious education and preparation for the sacraments, but it includes making sure that education is imbued with a spirit of piety.

Some parents decide to home school for academic reasons, and often find the struggle too difficult. But those who are committed to the Faith and to authentic Catholic family values are able to undergo tremendous pressures and crosses, even from family members.

Pastors, bishops, and other religious should encourage parents who are willing to make the difficult sacrifices to fulfill their mission and duty by teaching their children at home. Pope John Paul I, in September of 1978, when speaking to a group of U.S. archbishops and bishops, remarked about the importance of family prayer. He declared that the church of the home, through family prayer, could bring about a renewal of the Church and a transformation of the world. "A most relevant apostolate" for the twentieth century, he believed, is parental teaching of God's love and parental support of the Faith by good example.

In conclusion, Pope John Paul I pleaded with the American bishops:

> Dear brothers, we want you to know where our priorities lie. Let us do everything we can for the Christian family, so that our people may fulfill their great vocation in Christian joy and share intimately and effectively in the Church's mission—Christ's mission—of salvation.

Letter to Families

Pope John Paul II declared 1994 as the Year of the Family and began the year with his Letter to Families. In this document, the pope repeats the long-standing teachings about the rights and responsibilities of parents and children. He begins by writing, "The celebration of the Year of the Family gives me a welcome opportunity to knock at the door of your home, eager to greet you with deep affection and to spend time with you." The pope emphasizes that God gave His Only-Begotten Son to the world, but that He chose to have Him enter "into human history through the family.... The divine mystery of the Incarnation of the Word thus has an intimate connection with the human family."

The first section of this document is important in teaching again what marriage means, why God instituted the Sacrament of Matrimony. Under the heading "The Civilization of Love," the pope speaks of The Marital Covenant, The Unity of the Two, The Common Good of Marriage and the Family, The Sincere Gift of Self, Responsible Fatherhood and Motherhood, and Love is Demanding.

At the end of this section (section 16), the pope writes about education in the family. The pope points out that parents, in the process of educating their children, are giving themselves to their children.

> 16. *What is involved in raising children?* In answering this question, two fundamental truths should be kept in mind: first, that man is called to live in truth and love; and second, that everyone finds fulfillment through the sincere gift of self. This is true both for the educator and for the one being educated. Education is thus a unique process for which the mutual communion of persons has immense importance. The educator is a person who *"begets" in a spiritual sense.* From this point of view, raising children can be considered a genuine apostolate. It is a living means of communication, which not only creates a profound relationship between the educator and the one being educated, but also makes them both sharers in truth and love, that final goal to which everyone is called by God the Father, Son, and Holy Spirit.

What a consolation and privilege for parents to realize that the Church recognizes their work of educating their children as a genuine apostolate!

After a few paragraphs about education being a gift of self, and stating that "Education then is before all else a reciprocal 'offering' on the part of both parents," the pope writes:

> With good reason, then, the Church asks during the Rite of Marriage: "Will you accept children lovingly from God, and bring them up according to the law of Christ and His Church?" In the raising of children, conjugal love is expressed as authentic parental

love. The "communion of persons," expressed as conjugal love at the beginning of the family, is thus completed and brought to fulfillment in the raising of children. Every individual born and raised in a family constitutes a potential treasure which must be responsibly accepted, so that it will not be diminished or lost, but will rather come to an ever more mature humanity. This too is a process of exchange in which the parents-educators are in turn to a certain degree educated themselves. While they are teachers of humanity for their own children, they learn humanity from them. All this clearly brings out the organic structure of the family, and reveals the fundamental meaning of the fourth commandment.

The Church recognizes that in the process of teaching our children, we mature ourselves, we learn from our children. How many of us have seen things differently because of a comment from one of our young children?

If it is true that by giving life parents share in God's creative work, it is also true that by raising their children *they become sharers in His paternal and at the same time maternal way of teaching.* According to Saint Paul, God's fatherhood is the primordial model of all fatherhood and motherhood in the universe (cf. Eph 3:14-15), and of human motherhood and fatherhood in particular. We have been completely instructed in God's own way of teaching by the eternal Word of the Father who, by becoming man, revealed to man the authentic and integral greatness of his humanity, that is, being a child of God. In this way, He also revealed the true meaning of human education.

Through Christ, all education, within the family and outside of it, *becomes part of God's own saving pedagogy,* which is addressed to individuals and families and culminates in the paschal mystery of the Lord's death and resurrection. The "heart of our redemption" is the starting point of every process of Christian education, which is likewise always an education to a full humanity.

We parents are part of God's plan for educating our children to attain eternal happiness with Him in Heaven. From having the children whom God created and then raising them for the purpose of attaining eternity with Him, flow graces which make us qualified to teach our children what they need to know for eternal salvation.

Parents are the first and most important educators of their own children, and they also possess a *fundamental competence* in this area: they are *educators because they are parents.* They share their educational mission with other individuals or institutions, such as the Church and the state.

But the mission of education must always be carried out in accordance with a proper application of the *principle of subsidiarity*. This implies the legitimacy and indeed the need of giving assistance to the parents, but finds its intrinsic and absolute limit in *their prevailing right* and their actual capabilities. The principle of subsidiarity is thus at the service of parental love, meeting the good of the family unit.

For parents by themselves are not capable of satisfying every requirement of the whole process of raising children, especially in matters concerning their schooling and the entire gamut of socialization. Subsidiarity thus complements paternal and maternal love and confirms its fundamental nature, inasmuch as all other participants in the process of education are only able to carry out their responsibilities *in the name of the parents, with their consent* and, to a certain degree, *with their authorization*.

The family is called to carry out its task of education *in the Church*, thus sharing in her life and mission. The Church wishes to carry out her educational mission above all *through families* who are made capable of undertaking this task by the sacrament of matrimony, through the "grace of state" which follows from it and the specific "charism" proper to the entire family community.

How reassuring to see that the Church wants parents to carry out the task of education for their children! The Church recognizes that by the Sacrament of Matrimony, parents are made capable of teaching their children.

Certainly one area in which the family has an irreplaceable role is that of *religious education*, which enables the family to grow as a "domestic church." Religious education and the catechesis of children make the family a true *subject of evangelization and the apostolate* within the Church. We are speaking of a right intrinsically linked to the *principle of* religious *liberty*. Families and more specifically parents, are free to choose for their children a particular kind of religious and moral education consonant with their own convictions. Even when they entrust these responsibilities to ecclesiastical institutions or to schools administered by religious personnel, their educational presence ought to continue to be *constant and active*....

Religious education classes are fine for parents who want to use them, but parents are "free to choose" for their children a local church or school, or even their own home religious education program, as long as it is in line, of course, with Church teachings.

> The *gospel of love* is the inexhaustible source of all that nourishes the human family as a "communion of persons." In love the whole educational process finds its support and definitive meaning as the mature fruit of the parents' mutual gift. Through the efforts, sufferings, and disappointments which are part of every person's education, love is constantly being put to the test. To pass the test, a source of spiritual strength is necessary. This is only found in the One who "loved to the end" (Jn 13:1). Thus *education is fully a part of the "civilization of love."* It [education] depends on the civilization of love and, in great measure, contributes to its upbuilding.

> The Church's constant and trusting prayer during the Year of the Family is *for the education of man* so that families will persevere in their task of education with courage, trust, and hope, in spite of difficulties, occasionally so serious as to appear insuperable. The Church prays that the forces of the "civilization of love" which have their source in the love of God, will be triumphant. These are forces which the Church ceaselessly expends for the good of the whole human family.

The Truth and Meaning of Human Sexuality

The Pontifical Council for the Family issued this document in 1995 with the subheading "Guidelines for Education within the Family." It is specifically addressed to parents, as noted in the introductory commentary by Cardinal Trujillo who headed up the Pontifical Council for the Family. While the emphasis by the cardinal is on teaching children about human sexuality, the document also emphasizes parents' rights in all education. In an article explaining why the Council issued the document, Cardinal Trujillo wrote:

> The parents' right to be the first educators of their children, especially during childhood and adolescence, is a requirement of the natural order and represents a constant high point in the teaching of the Church. In the Letter to Families ... The recently published document comments, "... parents are rich in an educative potential which no one else possesses. In a unique way, they know their own children; they know them in their unrepeatable identity, and by experience, they possess the secrets and the resources of true love" (n.7).

Of course, the Pontifical Council for the Family realizes that not all families are fully aware of this right and duty that is their own and irreplaceable, under normal circumstances. Families sometimes leave this task to silence, to the indirect but often unhealthy influence of chance, the television, or the school … In this way, a kind of *expropriation* has taken place by the schools, or rather by personnel who are not in harmony with the parents, who act using methods not in accord with the parents, and who are concerned often only with promoting their own pragmatic or ideological conceptions …

Moreover, we must not overlook the fact in this situation that the organizations promoting *family planning* and guided by the precept of anti-natalism, have found ways of inserting themselves into the "education" of adolescents and of taking the place of families.

In *Truth and Meaning*, Chapter IV on "Father and Mother as Educators" is key to showing once again that the Church regards parents as the primary educators and the decision-makers for their children's education, especially in such important areas as human sexuality.

As spouses, parents, and ministers of the sacramental grace of marriage, they are sustained from day to day by special spiritual energies, received from Jesus Christ who loves and nurtures His Bride, the Church.

… the Sacrament of Marriage, which consecrates them for the strictly Christian education of their children: that is to say, it calls upon them to *share in the very authority* and love of God the Father and Christ the Shepherd, and in the motherly love of the Church, and it enriches them with wisdom, counsel, fortitude, and all the other gifts of the Holy Spirit in order to help the children in their growth as human beings and as Christians (n.37).…

Parents must never feel alone in this task. The Church supports and encourages them, confident they can carry out this function better than anyone else (n.40).…

[I]t is extremely important for parents to be aware of their *rights and duties,* particularly in the face of a state or a school that tends to take up the initiative in the area of sex education.

The Holy Father John Paul II reaffirms this in *Familiaris Consortio:* "The right and duty of parents to give education is *essential* … it is *original and primary* … and it is irreplaceable and *inalienable.*"(n.41)

This doctrine is based on the teaching of the Second Vatican Council and is also proclaimed by the *Charter of the Rights of the Family:* "Since they have conferred life on their children, parents have the original, primary, and inalienable right to educate them; hence they have ... the right to educate their children in conformity with their moral and religious convictions (n.42) ...

No one is capable of giving moral education in this delicate area better than duly prepared parents (n.43).

This right also implies *an educational duty*. If in fact parents do not give adequate formation in chastity, they are failing in their precise duty. Likewise, they would also be guilty were they to tolerate immoral or inadequate formation being given to their children outside the home (n.44)....

Therefore, through this document, the Church holds that it is her duty to give parents back confidence in their own capabilities and help them to carry out their task (n.47).

In conclusion, the documents of the Church fully encourage and support parents in home schooling their children.

Chapter 4:
How to Begin Catholic Home Schooling

Before you begin Catholic home schooling, you must be convinced it is what you want and be committed to doing it.

Home schooling is not like buying a new coat. Catholic home schooling is a way of life. It should be something you have already attempted in some small way with your children, by teaching religion, by teaching about the sacraments, by turning off the TV once in a while, and trying to be an authentic Catholic family.

Catholic home schooling is not easy or simple. It is primarily a commitment to God, and secondarily a commitment to family. Once you have decided you want to make this commitment, you should try to prepare yourself.

Begin by making a novena, that is, nine days of special prayers. Start by going to Confession. Then, take nine days to pray to the Blessed Mother or to the Sacred Heart. Go to Mass each day. Pray to your guardian angel and to the children's guardian angels, asking them to pray for you. Ask your patron saint to help you. Say the Rosary every day if possible. Ask for the grace to know what you should do, for the courage to make the right decision, for the strength to carry it out. Have your spouse join you as much as possible in these nine days of prayer. You will need at least a minimum of support from him or her. This is, after all, a responsibility of the vocation of marriage.

If you finally decide after nine days of prayer that you should home school, but your spouse remains against it, ask if he or she would allow you just one year as a trial. After all, considering the reputation of the schools these days, the children would not lose out much academically by staying out of school for a year, even if they did not learn anything in that time.

Despite all of the above, don't put off home schooling until everything is perfect, and you have no doubts about the project. You will always have doubts, and things will never be perfect. At some point, if you think it's what God is calling you to do, take the plunge! John Paul the Great used to use the phrase "Step out into the deep." This is what Our Lord meant when He called St. Peter to come to Him on the Sea of Galilee, and Peter stepped out of the boat and onto the water. Everyone who starts home schooling is, in some sense, stepping out into the deep.

How to tell your husband

Since ninety percent of the time it is mothers who want to teach their children at home, this section is directed to mothers. However, if you are a father who wants to home school your children, these ideas will help you also.

Some husbands think that home schooling is some sort of underground movement, a kind of "Mother Earth" fad. Show your husband as much home schooling literature as possible. We have information on Seton online at www.setonhome.org. Your husband can learn about Seton, as well as home schooling in general, by listening on our website to audio speeches by various speakers from home schooling conferences. Besides Seton's website, there are scores of other websites on home schooling in general and Catholic home schooling in particular. Just go to any search engine and type in "Catholic home schooling."

A good source for statistics about home schooling is the National Home Education Research Institute (NHERI). They offer several quick-fact sheets giving statistics on numbers of children being educated at home, levels of achievement, demographics, and social and emotional adjustment. They can be found online at www.nheri.org.

If you are considering Seton, tell your husband that Seton is accredited. Accreditation is important in many professional organizations, and husbands understand that.

If more is needed, there are videos, cassette tapes, and books available from Seton conferences. Ask your husband to read this book, or read passages to him. Other materials are available from us or from your local Catholic home schooling organization. If you can take your husband to one of the Catholic home schooling conventions, he will see hundreds of people who are home schooling or who are considering home schooling. It will not seem like such a strange idea when he sees good Catholic people who teach their children at home.

If your husband is willing, take him to your local support group meetings, particularly when you know that other fathers will be present. This will be an opportunity for him to ask questions of other fathers.

Visit your local library or Catholic bookstore and look over the home schooling books available. Many more, of course, are available at the state Catholic home schooling conventions. Encourage your husband to read a few books and become more informed about home schooling. If he won't read them, then you should read them yourself and discuss the ideas with him.

Some fathers are concerned that home schooling will turn their children into weird anti-social misfits. Ginny Seuffert suggests that if your husband thinks the children will be weird, take him to the local mall. Look around for the most strangely dressed teenagers—ones with purple hair, tattoos, and piercings—and ask them if they are home schooled.

The chapter in this book by Dr. Mark Lowery, a home schooling father of a large family, might help your husband.

Statement of philosophy

Before you start home schooling, write out the reasons why you want to teach your children at home. This will help you to clarify your own goals. Try to express yourself clearly and specifically, as this will refine your thinking and strengthen your resolve. You need to fully understand your own reasons for making this decision which, after all, you may have to defend to relatives, in-laws, fellow parishioners, and friends.

Be sure to discuss this thoroughly with your spouse if possible. He (or she) should completely understand your perspective. Take the time, if your children are older, to have a family conference. You and your spouse should explain to your children exactly why you believe so strongly that you should teach them at home. Including the children early in the discussions may head off complaining and bitterness later.

Once you have a statement of philosophy about your reasons for home schooling, and what you want to accomplish with your home schooling, post the statement in a prominent place in your home. You will need to refer to this on the days when the going "gets tough." It will serve as a frequent reminder to everyone in the house.

Statement of goals

In addition to your statement of philosophy, write a list of specific goals or objectives. For instance, some religious goals might be that everyone goes to Mass every day, that you and the family go to Confession once a month, that at least once a week certain activities should relate to the liturgical calendar. Character-building goals might be that little Susie learns to say "please" and "thank you," that Johnny might learn to be gentle and not irritate his younger brother, that George might begin to appreciate his parents, and so on.

Academic goals might be, if you are in an enrolled program, that the children finish a grade in nine months, or that no matter what, little Sally is going to learn her multiplication tables this summer. Seton has produced a "Scope and Sequence" series which sets out academic curriculum goals for each subject in each grade level. While you may want to reshape these, they can give you an idea about writing your own. In some states, parents are asked to submit a curriculum guide every year for each child. In any case, setting goals will both give you a guide for your work and give you a sense of achievement when the goals are reached.

For an example of academic goals, you can go online and search for "Virginia Standards of Learning." You can click on a particular subject and a specific grade level, and you will see a list of goals which the Virginia public schools have set for their students. These can give you an excellent picture of what is expected academically at each grade level. Keep in mind that the goals listed are not necessarily achieved by most public schools. While they are happy to write "standards," a fairly large percentage of public schools do not meet those written lists of standards.

Having specific goals keeps you and your children on track. Even if you do not accomplish your goals exactly as planned, unless you have written goals, you will never reach any goals. With more and more parents turning to home schooling, we are starting to see some parents allowing too much to "fall through the cracks." Unless you write down your goals, then, like an unwritten budget, the daily steps toward the goal are forgotten, and soon lessons are not accomplished. You begin to feel frustrated and wonder why you ever started this anyway. You may even feel guilty, or start to lose confidence in yourself.

Post a reminder

Most parents choose home schooling for both positive and negative reasons. These negative reasons are usually dissatisfaction with the schools the children were attending. So, it can be helpful to make a list of the disadvantages of having your children in school. These can be a list of just phrases, but it is important because they are personal and meaningful to *you*. You do not need these as much for the children as for yourself. You can work with your children and have them make a list for themselves, assuming they are old enough to understand.

Some mothers seem to forget after a couple of years exactly what the problems were when the children were in a school. They begin to think that maybe it was not really that bad in the first place. Some children are returned to school because of frustration or difficulties, but many children beg to return home after a semester of misery and shock at the rather crude, barbaric, and base culture in the school. Parents who think that the schools are okay for any child have not spent a full day in a school for a number of years. Just walk around to the classrooms, walk around the halls between classes, visit the playground, attend a class for a while. Spend just one full day in a school and then ask yourself, "Would I want my child to spend 180 days a year in this place?"

Sometimes mothers will call Seton Home Study School with the most terrible stories of emotional and psychological abuse of their children. After a year or two at home, they think maybe the next year will not be so bad. So little Susie goes back to school. Within two weeks, little Susie is listening to bad language and repeating sleeping-around stories, and wants to wear immodest clothes to match the girls at school. She wants a boyfriend, a weird haircut, a tongue piercing, a tattoo, etc., etc. Hopefully, as often happens, thank God, this will not happen. Rather, Susie will see the pathologies rampant in the school and ask Mom to let her come home again.

The stories we hear are so outrageous that we think most parents do not hear about them or do not believe them because they are so incredible. It is the same with abortion. It is so evil that our minds cannot comprehend the horror of it.

Parents who are home schooling their youngest children should make notes about the effects of school on their older children. Even good parents have had children who have left the Church, who have married outside the Church, who have divorced, who have had children out of wedlock, or who have lived with boyfriends or girlfriends without the benefit of marriage. Remind yourself of these problems from which you want to spare your remaining children.

We need to face hard facts. We are living in a pagan society. The Catholic philosopher Alice von Hildebrand has remarked that it is even worse than a pagan society because the pagans at least believed in some gods. Our society seems to believe in almost nothing at all beyond immediate gratification.

Schools are physically dangerous places for children. It is not unusual to read about boys being picked up by police for having a loaded gun in school. In fact, in a study done by the U.S. Department of Health and Human Services, it was estimated that *1 out of every 20 students carries a gun to school at least once a month*. Having guns and knives in the public schools has become so common, that one of the debates among administrators these days is about the most effective machine to detect the weapons as children enter the building. In 1999, the year of the Columbine shootings, twelve other school shootings were reported during an eighteen month period. Schools are trying to enforce gun-free zones as well as drug-free school zones.

The media has in the last few years focused on sexual abuse of children by priests. That is a horrible problem, but the media tends to ignore sexual abuse of children in public schools by faculty and staff. A recent study found that nearly 10% of students report being victims of sexual misconduct from teachers or support personnel in their school. (*Hostile Hallways*, American Association of University Women, 2001)

Of course, the more serious danger in schools is the spiritual danger. Father Hardon used to point out that when you have educators who are supportive of mothers' "rights" in the killing of innocent unborn babies, or who even think that abortion, fornication, or homosexuality can be justified alternatives, how can you morally allow these people to teach your children about anything at all, spiritually or academically? What we are headed for now, with legal homosexual "marriages," is not only a school curriculum which must teach these legal alternatives as moral alternatives, but also if anyone speaks openly against such activities, they will be charged with "hate crimes."

In fact, as time goes on, there will be fewer and fewer "good teachers" as teachers are forced to promote immoral lifestyles to their students. Godly teachers will more and more feel that they cannot be a part of a system which requires them to teach lies and immorality. This will leave only the teachers who agree with the immorality.

Grandparents

One of the problems you need to face before you begin home schooling is what your own parents or in-laws will think. What will they say? Will they support you or oppose you? Will they criticize you in front of the children? Try to do your best to explain to them why you are home schooling, since they do have a legitimate interest in the welfare of your children.

Most grandparents are not aware of just how bad the schools have become. If they think the schools aren't so bad, ask them to spend a day in a local school. They should be aware of the low academic standards since the television and newspaper reporters, as well as the governors and the president of the United States have acknowledged it. You can certainly point out to them that most schools do not offer children a quality education. That will be hard to dispute.

Besides offering the negatives about schools, explain the positive reasons why you are home schooling. Explain the teachings of the Church, and that you believe as the Church teaches, that you have the graces to make this decision, and that God will give you the graces to carry out this responsibility. Let them understand your spiritual reasons. They should respect you for that.

If possible, consider asking your parents or in-laws to help. Some families have reported that grandparents make wonderful teachers. They love their grandchildren, are patient, and many have the time. Grandparents come to understand and to see the positive benefits of home schooling as they themselves participate in some way.

When grandparents are opposed to home schooling, often it is because they think the children will not be properly socialized. Give them the information contained in the chapter in this book, "The Socialization Issue," as well as the information from the NHERI website. Also, point out the many opportunities for good socialization which your children will have through home schooling groups, through sports, through music lessons, through church or church youth groups, or through clubs.

Some grandparents think that home schooled children will not be able to go to college. Such thinking is certainly not keeping up with the times. Thousands of home schooled students are currently attending college. Private colleges are looking for high SAT or ACT test scores. Most are not concerned about where or how the students obtained their knowledge. In fact, private colleges often look to create a diverse student body, and being a home schooled student may actually help a student's chances of being admitted.

State colleges usually require only the G.E.D. test by home schoolers. However, some states may require other specific documentation.

Traditional Catholic colleges have been very pleased with home schooled students. Many Seton graduates are offered scholarships every year from Catholic colleges such as Christendom, Magdalen, Thomas Aquinas, Ave Maria, and Franciscan University of Steubenville. After all, home schooled students are self-motivated, self-disciplined, are not on drugs, and tend to have traditional Catholic and family values. They are exactly what good Catholic colleges want.

Also adding to the acceptance of home schooling by colleges is that many colleges now offer home degree programs themselves. These have become very successful and well-attended, especially with the use of online courses, interactive media, and CD-ROM, as well as more traditional television-based courses. Besides the Discovery Channel and the Learning Channel, secondary and college students can tune in Mind Extension University and Oklahoma State courses. These are becoming more fine-tuned as some people are obtaining Master's degrees and even Ph.D.s in Curriculum Development for online courses! Colleges cannot simultaneously run their own home degree programs and tell home schooled students that they aren't qualified for admittance.

If grandparents remain opposed, tell them you would like to try home schooling for a year and see how it works. During the year, have them visit occasionally while you teach, or have your children read for them, or recite their multiplication tables for them.

Sometimes, however, grandparents actually work to turn the children against home schooling and cause a serious problem for the family.

Some have gone so far as to call local authorities and complain that their grandchildren are not being educated. This is a difficult situation, but we need to remember that they are being sincere in their beliefs, even if they are inaccurate. Parents may need to make grandparents realize that the family will not be able to visit them if the problem continues. Some parents believe the grandparents cannot be told about their home schooling because of the potentially very unpleasant situation. This decision needs to be prayed about. Please be cautious, wise as serpents, gentle as doves.

The pastor

After you have firmed up your commitment to home schooling, after you have had some discussions and come to an agreement with your spouse, after you have talked with your parents and in-laws and other relatives, the next concern is your pastor and the parishioners.

Of course, you are under no general obligation to inform your pastor of what you are doing. However, it does tend to come up, especially if you take the children to weekday Masses. In such cases, the pastor is going to ask you why the children are not in school. You also may want to prepare your children for the sacraments yourself, rather than have the children attend the parish classes. In such a case, you will need to explain to the pastor that you are home schooling and are teaching religion at home.

From the documents of the Catholic Church, many quotes of which are contained in this book, you should have a pretty good grasp of Church teachings, knowing that it is not only your right but your responsibility to teach your children.

However, many pastors are not aware of the Catholic Church's teachings in these documents which apply to the rights and responsibility of parents in the matter of educating their children. In seminaries, home schooling is not even discussed. So your approach needs to be cautious.

These days, there are probably few parishes in which the pastor is not aware of at least one or two home schooling families. So, if you are a new home schooling family, you probably won't be breaking any new ground. However, since priests are reassigned with some frequency, you might end up with a new priest who doesn't know about home schooling. In that case, it might be a good idea to get together a few home schooling families and meet with the pastor to explain what you are doing.

The fact that priests are reassigned from time to time is actually a good reason to start a parish-based home schooling support group. If there is a quasi-official home schooling group already in the parish, and if customs and traditions have already been in practice for years, it will be more difficult for a new pastor to come in and cause any difficulties for home schoolers.

Fellow parishioners and neighbors

The most common reason why home schooling families have problems with local school authorities is because of unfriendly neighbors. Before you begin home schooling, contact your local support group. Find out how neighbors in your community are reacting to home schooling. If they are not friendly, you have two choices. You can stay in the neighborhood and try to work to establish understanding or tolerance, or you can move. Both options need to be seriously considered.

We are living in a strange period of American history in which child abuse has become a big business! People are aware that they can make anonymous phone calls to local social service agencies and complain about people they do not like without any possible recriminations. The cry "Child abuse!" can begin a terrible series of events for a family. Be aware of the dangers, and keep alert. Also, keep in touch with other home schooling families. Don't ostracize yourself from friends. In fact, if there are any pro-life candidates running in a local election, help in their campaigns. Having local officials as friends can be of great help in time of persecution from neighbors or teachers.

In the past, home schooling parents often decided to keep their children indoors during school hours. However, home schooling is much more common and much more accepted now. Unless there is a specific problem with a specific neighbor, letting the children go outdoors during the day should not be controversial.

You should choose your neighbors carefully. There are areas where home schooling is strong. You should be looking for Catholic people who want to strengthen family values. Hopefully, you can find a location where other Catholic home schooling families are located. Many of us had ancestors who, at great personal sacrifice, moved to America because of religious intolerance elsewhere. It is because of our religious and family values that we have decided to teach our children at home.

If your neighbors are deep-down intolerant, see if you have some of that determination from your ancestors to make a move for your family.

If you are considering a move and have options of where to move, check with other home schoolers first. The Internet, especially the message boards, are great for finding out information about different communities.

State or local home schooling associations

Become a dues-paying member of your Catholic state home schooling association. They likely publish a monthly or bi-monthly newsletter which keeps you informed about proposed state legislation which can affect home schooling families. They announce statewide or regional home schooling meetings or conventions. They keep you informed about activities which are of interest to Catholic home schooling families.

Join your local Catholic home schooling support group. If one has not been started, start one yourself, even if with only one other Catholic home schooling family. It is a beginning. And you can give each other the support you need. Eventually, more families will be encouraged to start home schooling because you have a "group" to help them, and then they will join your group to find help and eventually to help others. Isn't this evangelization?

Home School Legal Defense Association

Many home schooling parents enroll in the Home School Legal Defense Association (HSLDA). This is a Christian legal insurance corporation which, for a reasonable yearly fee, will give legal counseling to home schooling families who have any problems with local or state authorities. HSLDA has lawyers in each state, familiar with the state laws and how local school districts are interpreting state legislation. We recommend that Catholic home schooling families join HSLDA each year, even if the home schooling situation is running smoothly in your state. If you do not use the services, your fee will be put to good use defending the rights of home schooling families across the nation.

Historically, home schoolers could not have the favorable legislation they have today if it had not been for HSLDA working to defend home schooling families in court and working for better legislation.

We encourage Catholic home schooling parents to take advantage of the legal expertise and insurance of having attorneys in their own state who are knowledgeable about the state laws. However, we highly recommend that Catholic parents keep informed about current laws and pending legislation. You can go to the HSLDA website to find the latest updates and any relevant cases.

State regulations

Learn about the home schooling laws and regulations in your state. While home schooling is legal in every state, you will want to be familiar with your own particular state laws and regulations. You can obtain them from your state home schooling association or on the HSLDA website. If you join HSLDA, they will answer your questions also.

It is appropriate that we are concerned about educating ourselves about the state and local laws and regulations. If you really want to delve into it, read the home schooling court cases in your state. It is interesting material! However, we highly recommend that you do not follow any regulations which go against your conscience. If you feel uncomfortable about any regulations, call an attorney at your state home schooling association, or call a Catholic attorney. Also, if your superintendent asks for any information beyond the state requirements, please call a home schooling attorney.

Be aware of the fact that many school districts tend to interpret the state laws as they would like the laws to be, rather than as the laws actually are. For example, a school district might send out a letter saying that all home schoolers must follow a certain regulation. But the law itself might say that home schoolers can follow any one of three or four options. Be sure to inform yourself about the law and your rights when dealing with local school districts. After all, your right to home school your own children comes from God, not from state legislators, or from local school districts.

Program or no program

Decide if you want to enroll in a Catholic home study program, or if you want to try to do it yourself. If you are an experienced teacher, you probably have more self-confidence, have an idea about where to obtain materials, and possibly have a good grasp of the scope of the concepts which should be learned at various grade levels.

If you want to hear about the advantages of not being enrolled in a program, contact families who are doing it on their own. Each family has its own unique goals, ideas, methods, and materials, so you should talk to several home schooling mothers, and take the ideas which you like best. You can check out Catholic home schooling websites or Catholic home schooling mailing lists for more information or commentaries from families who home school on their own.

If you do not enroll in a program, your first major objective will be to find Catholic textbooks. Twenty years ago, you could go to a St. Vincent de Paul shop, or local garage sale and purchase used Catholic textbooks. Now they are practically non-existent. If you are not living in a predominantly Catholic community, it will be nearly impossible to locate old Catholic textbooks.

Catholic publishers

When the Catholic schools decided to take state and/or federal funds, they were not allowed to use these funds for anything religious. As a consequence, the publishers of Catholic materials stopped publishing. This has been true since the 1970s.

There are some publishers of Catholic books for children but it is difficult to recommend most of them as textbooks. The old Vision books, a series of saints' biographies, are being reprinted by Ignatius Press. TAN Publishers is printing saints' biographies. Bethlehem Books is publishing stories of Catholic heroes. These are good reading for book reports. Nevertheless, it would take a mother a good deal of time to use something like this for vocabulary development, reading comprehension, and analytical thinking skills, skills which should be included in a good educational curriculum.

Seton offers several series of Catholic texts and workbooks, which are available for sale generally through Seton Educational Media (www. setonbooks.com). You do not need to be enrolled in the Seton program in order to use these books.

The big controversy

If you are going independent and not enrolling in a Catholic program, there is a controversy about whether it is better to have Protestant or secular texts when no Catholic texts are available.

If you absolutely cannot find a Catholic or Christian textbook, then you need to turn to a secular text. This should be your last resort, however. The reason is that not only is God totally ignored, but all the modern secular attitudes and values, and current politically correct ideas, are usually presented throughout the text, even if they do not relate to the topic. The secular textbooks today are literally filled with un-Christian ideas, and sometimes these are difficult to recognize because we have all become somewhat affected by the pagan society in which we live. Many of these un-Christian ideas relate to social values, feminism, life issues, government principles, and so on.

At Seton, while we are writing Catholic textbooks as quickly as we can and constantly are looking for good Catholic textbooks, we reluctantly use a few secular texts along with Catholic and Christian textbooks. However, we present the Catholic viewpoint in the lesson plans and tests.

Some Catholics believe they should not give money to a fundamentalist Protestant publisher. Please remember that the Christian fundamentalists believe in the Bible and the Ten Commandments, and are opposed to abortion, homosexuality, witchcraft, and other occult activities. At secular publishing houses, in which the employees are likely to be a reflection of the community in general, you can find all these things being practiced.

In our pagan society, when you go shopping for anything any place, some of your money is going for the support of persons who do not agree with you on abortion, homosexual "marriages," and other basic anti-Christian practices. The question is whether you would rather your money go to buy books which may contain some small amount of anti-Catholic material, or whether you want your money to go to buy books which are pervasively anti-Christian.

Catholic home study schools

There are many advantages and benefits to having children enrolled in a Catholic home schooling program. If you are not an experienced teacher, or if you have been a teacher but do not have the time to work on all the details of setting up daily lessons, you will probably want to enroll in a program. If you want Catholic textbooks, you should enroll in a Catholic home study school, though most are now selling their books. If you want counseling, grading, a report card, and other school services, you will want to enroll in a program.

Besides traditional correspondence schools, there are also some Catholic home schooling programs that offer their courses online, such as Regina Coeli Academy (www.reginacoeli.org).

Just as there is no single car that is best for everyone, just as people have different needs and are looking for different qualities in a car, the same is true of a home study school. There is no one Catholic home study school that is best for everyone. A family needs to look at what each home study school offers to decide which is best for them and for their children's needs.

Remember that none of the Catholic home study programs will be detrimental or dangerous to your child, as are most secular schools. With home schooling you are in control each minute of each day. You can make changes as you go along. If you start with one program, and it does not quite meet your needs, you can change the following year. While it is an important decision, do not feel that you are locked into it permanently.

Some Catholic home schoolers recommend that you use a non-Catholic program, such as the Calvert program. The logic behind this is difficult to understand. If you are going to the trouble of home schooling in order to instill Catholic values in your children, why would you choose a program which does not affirm those values and the Faith? Some might reply that you don't need to limit your home schooling to the use of only Catholic materials. True, but if you use a non-Catholic program, which is supplying most or all of the materials you use, you are effectively limiting your home schooling to using only non-Catholic materials. And with the number of Catholic programs available, it is hard to believe that parents cannot find a Catholic home school that suits their family.

Flexibility

Some home schooling parents believe that if they enroll in a program, they will not have the flexibility they could have otherwise. This depends on how much flexibility you want, versus a certain amount of structure to help keep you on schedule. I assume all programs encourage flexibility, but I can only speak directly about Seton. Our motto at Seton is "Adjust the program to fit the child, not the child to fit the program."

Seton requires parents to submit tests for their children if they want a grade on a report card. If they do not want a report card, or want to compile their own grades, they need not submit tests to Seton. No matter what the lessons suggest or recommend, parents are entirely free to teach as they wish. However, grades on the Seton report card are based on the average of the tests or work graded by the parents and the average of the tests graded by the Seton graders. What parents teach to prepare the children for the tests, or how they teach, or at what pace they teach, is entirely up to them.

Some home study programs have a calendar, some do not. At Seton, there is no calendar, so parents and students are not under pressure to submit tests by a certain date, which certainly allows flexibility. Also, Seton and other Catholic home study programs should be able to customize the materials, sending higher level books in one or more subjects, or sending lower level books when a student needs more remedial work. Seton also offers customized service for children with special learning needs through a certified LD teacher and others who can help determine the specific needs of a child.

Lesson plans

Enrollment in a Catholic program is the easiest way to home school. Programs such as Seton contain complete materials and ready-to-go daily lesson plans. Lesson plans can provide not only daily assignments, but also tips for teaching, diagrams, supplemental information, enrichment activities, Internet links, graphics, and so on. The Seton English lesson plans for a year for high school tend to run a couple of hundred pages because of the appendices related to book analyses, and because of detailed explanations for reading assignments and paragraph writing. The home schooling parent, or student, can use whatever information is needed and skim over information not needed.

A home schooling mother whose children are enrolled in a program has the advantage of having an objective person helping to evaluate the schoolwork and/or tests. The teachers do not simply grade the student's work, but add comments to help the student as well as give encouragement. Stickers and stamps, many religious, are given for work well done. Certificates of Achievement for excellent work are offered to encourage children. The children themselves can benefit from the knowledge that their family is part of a Catholic school—and that their work is evaluated by a teacher familiar with the same grade level.

Another advantage of enrollment is the counseling service by teachers. Catholic counseling service is and should be an integral part of the home schooling service. Some schools, such as Seton, have specialists in learning disabilities, as well as high school teachers certified in specific subject areas, many of whom have advanced degrees or are practicing college professors. Other schools may offer similar services which may be useful to you.

Counseling is available at Seton and probably by other schools not only by mail and by phone but also by fax, by Message Boards over the Internet, and by e-mail. The current technology provides quick and sometimes instant service for students.

Enrollment in a program, especially for parents without college degrees, often helps in keeping local school authorities such as school boards, superintendents, or principals, from bothering home schooling families. In general, local school authorities do not like parents to take the responsibility of home schooling their children. However, when parents enroll their children in a home school program, they are less likely to bother the parents because they realize that there is a third party overseeing the student's work.

Accreditation

Seton Home Study School is accredited by the Southern Association of Colleges and Schools, as well as the Commission on International and Trans-Regional Accreditation. Mother of Divine Grace is accredited by the Western Association of Schools and Colleges. These are accrediting agencies which are recognized by the U. S. Department of Education. (Some other home schools are accredited by agencies not recognized by the U. S. Department of Education. For more information on different types of accreditation, see Chapter 15.)

To confer accreditation, the association's accreditation committee reviews the curriculum materials to see if there are sufficient daily lessons or guidelines for a student to learn on his own. There are no "philosophy of content" guidelines. They evaluate home study programs based on business methods, efficiency, and staff qualifications. In addition, they send a survey to the "client families" to see if there are any problems and determine if the school fulfils its contractual obligations.

Accreditation helps school district superintendents to know that a home school program has been objectively evaluated by professional educators and has passed certain criteria. They can be assured that it is in fact an honest business operation, using professional business methods, and not a fly-by-night organization.

Many school superintendents want home study schools to be evaluated by the state department of education of the state in which the school is located. They believe that this department takes a closer look and has better knowledge about the school than an out-of-state accreditation committee. In fact, when the accreditation committee visits Seton, a representative from the Virginia Department of Education also visits.

Some states, such as Virginia and Nevada, have official lists of approved home schools. Enrollment in these schools can exempt families from some state legal requirements otherwise imposed. Consequently, to make it easier for parents, Seton has worked to be approved as a home study school in these states.

It is not strictly necessary that a home school program be accredited or be on an approved list of providers maintained by a state. However, these two things do tend to minimize problems from local school officials. So, if you decide to use a program, you will need to decide how important accreditation is to your family.

Withdrawing from the local school

When you decide to home school, if your child has been attending a local school, try to make the change at the beginning of a school year, at the semester break, or during a long vacation, such as at Christmas or Easter. It makes little difference academically for children in the elementary grades to change schools at any time of the year, but it would be easier emotionally for the children to do it at a clean break. However, at the high school level, a student could lose credits by withdrawing before the semester ends. Nevertheless, often a situation is so serious that parents must pull their children out of school immediately.

It is best not to have your children talk about leaving a school while they are still attending. Teachers, principals, parents, and students sometimes react in unpleasant ways when they know a student is leaving to be home schooled. Many truly believe that anyone taught at home cannot obtain a good education. Sometimes public school officials become upset because each student lost represents state funding they do not receive.

Once you are ready to start home schooling, notify your school principal in writing, unless you have good personal relationship with the school personnel. A short letter, sent by certified mail, should state simply that you have decided to enroll your child in a private Catholic school, and the request for records will be sent to them shortly from the new school. This last statement is important because it signifies to them that, in fact, you are enrolling in a school. The former school is less likely to contact you if they expect a request for school records.

Students are sometimes withdrawn from a school after some ill-will between the parents and school officials. There may be a temptation to "tell off" school officials. If so, resist the urge. No good can possibly come of it, and no one needs to make more enemies.

The home study school should send parents a form, such as a "Request for Transfer of Records," which needs to be signed by parents and returned to the home study school. This is then mailed to the previous school. Most schools do not like parents to personally bring in the Request form, but want to receive it from the new school, thus giving evidence of the student being enrolled somewhere else.

If home schooling parents do not want the student records requested, or want a delay on the request, that should be no problem. Parents may request that such forms not be sent to the previous school. In fact, only the high school records are absolutely necessary for transferal. However, the former school will be less concerned about a student's whereabouts if the student's records are out of their filing cabinet, so seriously consider requesting the transcript file be sent to the home school even if you choose not to get a diploma from the home study school.

Questions from the previous school

Keep in mind that a) home schooling is legal in every state but b) local school authorities do not like home schooling. School principals or superintendents may harass home schooling parents. They usually get away with it when parents are uninformed and want to avoid confrontation or unpleasantness. In recent years, we have seen schools make some kind of arrangement, whether it be charter schools or simply students attending a single class, so that the school may claim that the student is enrolled and thus the school can obtain state and federal money. This makes schools a little friendlier.

Whenever the local school principal or teachers ask why you are home schooling, be sure to present the positive reasons. Talk about the benefits of your family learning together, the individualized instruction, the flexibility, unifying family experiences, and that you want to do more with teaching your children your Catholic values. If local Catholic school teachers are upset, simply say that you are going to try this home schooling "alternative" for a year and see how it works out.

Whenever possible, avoid unpleasant discussions with public or Catholic school personnel. Unexpected and unpredictable repercussions may hurt your child, your husband and his job, your family, and/or your home schooling.

It is important to stress the positive benefits of home schooling for your family and your child, and not to mention any negatives regarding the former school.

Placement tests

Most home study programs have an evaluation or "screening" procedure for grade placement. Placement tests are sent to the parents to administer to the children. The tests tend to be low in grade level because they are geared for the public school students. However, don't purchase a higher level test unless it is for your own benefit. Some states have laws about reaching a certain level on the test, so you don't want a test that is too advanced for your child. (However, if your child has a learning disability, the state is not allowed to force these tests on such children. Children with learning problems are protected by federal laws.)

While the scores will present an objective picture of a student's achievement level, it is only one factor. Parents' observation and evaluation are more important in determining the grade level. The home study program should defer to the parents' decision in this matter since the parents know their own child and his learning level. However, parents should be careful not to push a child into a higher grade level unless there is full confidence a child will do well. More times than not, a child who skips a grade suffers consequences later, mostly due to immaturity in dealing with analysis-type questions. A student that is able to read the words on a page is not necessarily mature enough to understand those words.

The curriculum

If you are Catholic, you will naturally want your teaching to reflect your faith. This follows the directives of Rome, which are contained in many encyclicals and other documents. The Church clearly states that the curriculum should be permeated with Catholic values.

This presents something of a problem because it is difficult to find Catholic textbooks. This situation has improved in recent years because Seton has produced over one hundred Catholic books. Not even Seton can yet offer 100% Catholic texts. However, in addition to publishing more Catholic textbooks, we are also in the process of producing Catholic online courses and tutorials, chiefly for high school.

As mentioned earlier in this chapter, Catholic parents are often faced with the question of whether to use Protestant or secular books in some subjects. If you use Protestant books, some basic errors which occur include editorial slants regarding historical events, or mistranslations or misinterpretations of the Bible. Certainly anything regarding the Blessed Mother, Catholic Europe, Christopher Columbus, Galileo, Catholic saints, and the Rosary, is going to be presented in an unfavorable light. In addition, sometimes there is outward prejudice expressed in words such as "Romanism" or "papists."

Catholic home schooling parents should obtain at least one of two books explaining the most common doctrinal errors in Protestantism. *Catholicism and Fundamentalism* by Karl Keating is available from Ignatius Press. *Protestant Fundamentalism and the Born Again Catholic* by Father Robert Fox is available from the Fatima Family Apostolate. If you are using Protestant texts, these will alert you to the typical errors in Protestant thinking.

Secular books are not good for Catholic children. In fact, secular books are worse than Protestant texts. Secular authors simply ignore the fact that God exists and that there are absolute moral values. They also follow whatever the current politically correct fad happens to be, while glorifying popular culture—a culture that is all too often not appropriate for children to emulate. At this date, there are simply not enough Catholic textbooks to provide a totally Catholic program. If you create your own curriculum, you will need to decide on a case by case basis what is the best book for your child.

How much time?

One of the most common questions mothers ask before they start home schooling is "How much time will it take each day?"

There is no simple answer. A little girl in first grade who is anxious to learn is obviously going to take less time than a little boy who is not interested in school and wants to spend his day playing outdoors. A boy starting in sixth grade who cannot read is going to take longer than a boy who started home schooling in first grade. Students with less motivation and fewer study skills will take longer than those who have them. Children with learning problems will take longer to learn.

Your educational philosophy has a great deal to do with how much time you will be teaching. For instance, many parents feel that the important subjects can be finished up by noon, with some fun activities scheduled in the afternoon. If you intend for your children to go on to college, on the other hand, you may want to take more time on academics, especially in high school.

Our Seton program gives a suggested time for each subject, but that obviously would vary from child to child. Math and reading should be scheduled for about an hour a day, while spelling and vocabulary can usually be done in 20 minutes for each. English, religion, history, and science are usually 30 to 40 minute classes. High school classes require about 50 minutes each for most students. This would not include reading for book reports.

With this said, we could state that most children in the primary grades (one to three) could probably finish most of their work in about three hours, although those hours should be broken up throughout the day. Students in the intermediate and junior high grades could finish the major work in four hours, but extra reading for book reports, for instance, might take another hour in the evening.

High school students should plan on 45 minutes to an hour a day per subject, with perhaps an extra hour in the evenings or weekends for extra reading or research. Students who wish to attend very selective colleges will probably want to take more time for specific subjects or specific projects. For example, students may wish to spend extra time learning a foreign language or in honing their musical skills.

While we have talked about the time involved for the teaching or learning periods, there is also a certain amount of time parents need for preparation. This also varies. Usually with the primary grades, no preparation is necessary, as you can just move along with the lessons as the child learns. However, with the other grades, a certain amount of preparation is necessary as you may need to do more teaching. You should figure an hour to two hours a week to look over what you need to do for the following week.

At the high school level, the time required to help your children depends on whether they have been home schooling in the earlier grades. Most students coming out of schools do not have good study skills and need more parental help. Students who have been home schooling for several years can do practically all their high school assignments without help. However, it is important for parents to involve their high school students in discussions about their schoolwork, especially religion, literature, and history, in order to convey the proper Catholic perspective. If you are learning a high school course, such as math, along with your student, this can take a substantial amount of time.

Un-Schooling

A topic which is closely related to the amount of time spent is the concept of un-schooling. While this approach may vary from family to family, un-schooling can be generally defined as a philosophy of learning without set lessons and assignments. At one extreme, this can mean absolutely no "book-learning." In a modified version, this might mean children work in their math book, for everything else they simply read whatever fiction or non-fiction books interest them.

Un-schooling can be related to the "unit study" approach in which the student focuses on one topic and learns everything about that. Unit study can be very rigorous, but in the un-schooling approach, the unit study would be informal with the student choosing what to study and when he or she will study.

Un-schooling can be very attractive, especially because it does not require any formal work from parents or students. If the only schoolwork that a student does is simply going through his day picking up whatever he happens to learn, then there are very few demands on either parent or child. Since getting children to do any work is often difficult for parents, an un-schooling approach can be a quick path to a more peaceful and relaxed family life.

Complete un-schooling is probably done primarily at the lower grade levels. As the grade levels increase, and a child begins to prepare for college, there will be specific areas of knowledge that the child will need to know. Colleges will want to see math credits and language credits and science credits, and a student who is completely lacking in any of these areas would find difficulty being admitted to college.

Catholic mother Suzie Andres has written a book called *Homeschooling with Gentleness* which discusses how she has used un-schooling in her family. From her account, her son Joseph seems to have benefited from this approach. Mrs. Andres is careful to stress, however, that this is not an approach that she advocates for everyone.

Everyone needs to decide the approach that is best for their family, but un-schooling would seem to have a few drawbacks as well as advantages. For one, it seems best suited for families and children who are committed readers. Even though there is not a formal program, if the children are reading all the time, they are still learning. If children are not good readers or not enthusiastic readers, un-schooling may lead to very little learning of anything.

If families choose un-schooling because they feel it is pedagogically best for their child, it is understandable. But if families choose un-schooling for discipline reasons (because the kids just won't do their schoolwork), one has to wonder whether this is really helpful to the children and family. If kids won't do their schoolwork, they probably won't do housework, and they probably won't learn their catechism. So what message is being sent when kids simply don't have to do something if they don't feel like it?

There is a larger societal issue, too, with un-schooling. For years, the education establishment has been accusing home schoolers of not really being committed to education. They have said that home schooling is not good education. Home schoolers have combated this charge by demonstrating that their children are exceptionally well-educated, and they have the test scores to prove it.

However, if large numbers of home schoolers ever adopted the un-schooling approach, then test scores would likely drop, at least in the lower grades. The scores would drop because many students would wait until they were older than normal to learn reading and math. One un-schooling website reports, "… it isn't unusual to find unschoolers who are barely eight-years-old studying astronomy or who are ten-years-old and just learning to read." This might have no ill effects in the long-run, but obviously a ten-year-old just learning to read will not score well on standardized tests. If the test scores of home schoolers were to fall, the education establishment would have an easier time passing restrictive regulations. So, while un-schooling may work for particular families, it could have negative consequences for home schooling in general.

Arranging the home

Home schooling is a way of life, involving all members of the family, and probably involving most of the living space. If at all possible, you should have some specific area of your house set up for schooling. Some families create a classroom in the basement, putting in colorful panels and bookcases for all the schoolbooks, with lots of good lighting. In some homes, the family room is the classroom. Some families convert the garage into the classroom. One family converted a small building on the property into a classroom.

It is difficult to use the dining room or the living room as the main classroom. There needs to be a permanent place where books, globes, encyclopedias, and desks can be kept. If you use a general use room for schooling, you will be constantly moving books and materials in and out of the area.

Because your time will be spent teaching, you will be spending less time doing housework, cooking, and cleaning. We advise having a gigantic spring cleaning before you begin to home school. Throw out everything you possibly can, and then throw out a little more! Limit the number of items, especially dishes and glasses, in the kitchen. You will need room for books and other learning materials, for such things as science projects and art projects. In another chapter, we will deal more specifically with the housework. We know that this is a real sacrifice for those women who want to keep their homes in "apple pie" order, but we also know that these ladies are willing to make this sacrifice for their children.

Home schooling is a lifestyle. The home will be redecorated eventually. Maps will be put up on the walls, and a globe or telescope or a model of a heart will appear. If presently there is no altar or place for prayer, this should be added. Also, prepare places to post drawings and samples of schoolwork well done.

You should decide whether it would be easier to teach the children all together in one room, or have the children work in different rooms. Most families end up with a combination, with children doing math and English, for instance, in separate rooms, but coming together for other classes, such as religion and music. This can be changed back and forth as you proceed through the year. More details about grouping the children for learning are contained in the chapter "Home Schooling in the Large Family."

When the materials arrive

Children often do not like school, but they like learning. What comes as a surprise to most parents is how eagerly the children look through the textbooks when they arrive. Sometimes the kids just start going through the materials, reading the stories and filling in the first few pages of workbooks.

When a family chooses a home schooling program, parents and children need to take time to examine the home school materials, locate the answer keys, see the pattern of the assignments in each subject, notice the schedule and kinds of tests, and in general become familiar with the overall program.

It is important to involve the children in some of the decision-making. Work with the children, for instance, on the schedule. Most children like the most difficult subjects in the morning, with the easier subjects in the afternoon. Ask the children to use colored pencils or pens and outline their weekly schedule, and to post it near their desks.

One thing that schools do that families sometimes don't think about is having fire drills. This is something that every family, home schooling or not, should do. The family should discuss the fire exits, and practice fire drills. It is a good beginning-of-the-year project for the children to chart a diagram for a fire exit for each room. They should draw the room and, in a colored pen, trace the exit route. This should be posted in each room. Make sure the children understand fire safety, and what they should do in case of fire.

By the way, do not forget to purchase several fire extinguishers. Show older children how they work. Also, have a field trip to the fire station, and ask a fireman to demonstrate the different kinds of extinguishers. He can explain when you need a new one. Encourage your children later in the year to submit a poster for the local fire safety contest.

I enrolled my boys in local First Aid and CPR classes sponsored by the Red Cross. Most hospitals offer such classes. If you are going to have your children at home all the time, you and they need to be prepared to take care of emergencies. You may be surprised how calm your children can be in an emergency when you yourself might be "losing it." Having your children help could save the life of someone in your family.

Other supplies

Before you begin to home school, purchase whatever you need to set up a schooling or learning area. Purchase not only the normal school supplies, such as notebooks, pens and pencils, and a pencil sharpener, but other supplies which give you and your children a psychological help to prepare yourself for the job ahead. For instance, buy a chalkboard or find a piece of plywood and help your children paint it with special chalkboard paint. Having the children help with the school equipment encourages them and motivates them toward doing the work, toward writing on the board they helped to paint.

Consider repainting or repapering the walls for the "classroom." Locate a special table or desks at a garage sale. Some children want a school desk; it just seems more like school. Of course, if you prefer *not* to have a classroom atmosphere, that is up to you. Try to be creative to obtain an environment which helps you and your children to become motivated and excited about learning at home.

Visit other home schooling families in your area and see how they arrange their home schooling area to give you some ideas. Do not hesitate to emphasize those hobbies or special gifts or talents which predominate in your family.

Conclusion

Many home schooling families have found that the special times we have with our children as we pray, work, and learn together can never be equaled for the joy they bring us. Though there are quite a few things which must be accomplished even before you begin, once you do begin, you will believe it was all worth it.

Beginning is a big first step toward trusting in Jesus to provide you with the graces to fulfill His commandment to teach your children.

Remember that as a member of the Mystical Body of Christ, you are entitled to many graces. Just ask for them.

Chapter 5:
Home Schooling in the Large Family

Most people become a little overwhelmed at the idea of teaching a large number of children at home. Home schooling in a large family, however, is not more difficult. It is less difficult—still difficult, but less difficult because now you have help from your older children.

The basic reason why home schooling in a large family is less difficult is that there are so many people to help you to do the chores around the house, to help with the schoolwork, to help even with disciplining. In addition, older children who have been trained in the past now can set a standard or pattern for the younger ones to follow.

God's overall plan

Home schooling is easier if we understand how important our home schooling family is in God's overall plan for our salvation, for the Church, and for our society. It is easier to persevere in spite of great difficulties if we realize that the final goal or victory is so great.

We may think our own life and the lives of our particular family members are not important in God's overall total plan for humanity. But each one of us is vital in God's plan.

In the encyclical *Humanae Vitae*, Pope Paul VI asks that Catholic married couples evangelize other married couples about God's teachings regarding birth control. Our very lifestyle, our daily example, is a kind of evangelization. Because we are following God's commands when we teach our children, we are representing something unusual in our society, and we are going to cause other parents to investigate, and perhaps to convert to living the authentic Catholic family life. One of the best examples we can give in today's pagan society is to have children and to take on personally the responsibility to educate our children rather than hand them over to government schools.

Furthermore, our home schooling is important as we learn and practice our Catholic Faith, not only for our own salvation, and for the salvation of our immediate family, but also for the salvation of our future grandchildren, and great-grandchildren.

Our home schooling family can have many consequences in God's overall plan for the salvation of souls in our parish, in our neighborhood, and extending beyond that as God wills. Like St. Francis, we home schooling parents are called not simply to repair our local church, or in this case, our own domestic church. We are also called to evangelize all of Christendom by giving an example of the authentic Catholic family life.

The secular society encourages people to practice perversions openly, to "come out of the closet." We Catholics need to be open ourselves, perhaps not aggressively promoting home schooling, but certainly not being fearful to tell others about home schooling in response to inquiries.

The large family promotes the virtuous life

The large family is especially important in God's plan for the fullest development of a virtuous individual, a virtuous family, and a virtuous society. The Catholic family of whatever size is, as the Catholic Church teaches, a domestic church. But the large family provides the opportunities for training children in practicing more virtues, more often, and more deeply. The larger the family, the more aspects of the general society the family members tend to represent. In a large family, children have more opportunities for interrelating, and thus the members of the family have more opportunities to practice Christian virtues, such as kindness, patience, generosity, sharing with others, doing things for others before being asked, sympathizing with members of the family who are sick or elderly, and taking care of babies. In general, the larger the family, the more demands there are for the individual child.

Most large families are required to practice the virtue of poverty. This is not to say that the families live in actual poverty. It means that large families must do without a lot of "extras" to which other families are accustomed. According to figures from the U.S. Department of Agriculture, the average family will spend $235,000 to raise a child born in 2003. And that does not include college costs. Of course, the more children you have, the less you will spend on each. But even if a family were to spend half the average on six children, that would come to $705,000. That is $705,000 that is not available for new cars and vacations.

Now, while less money may be an external fact, it can be an internalized virtue as parents and children grow in understanding how unimportant material things are in comparison to people and values. As Catholic parents repeatedly "choose life," the message is clear to the children as they sacrifice to make room for more.

The virtue of quick obedience is vital to sanity and order in a large family. The large family needs to have obedience and respect for authority, or, when times of crisis arise, the members of the family will not remain steady but will go in too many different directions for the good of the whole family. A large family, where children are required to be obedient not only to parents but often to older children in the family, provides more opportunities to explain and live the Fourth Commandment, which directs us to obey all proper authority.

Unacceptable behavior cannot continue long in a large family because so many people in the family will not put up with it. Pressure would be on Mom and Dad from other siblings if parents put up with misbehavior by a single child, or if parents did not sufficiently punish disobedience. In fact, older children will mete out the punishment if parents do not. It is readily recognized in a large family how the practice of virtue is necessary for the good of each member of the family as well as the family as a whole. Individual members have learned in the large family how to practice virtue in the larger society, such as at the workplace, in the marketplace, in the parish, in the neighborhood, in civic and political life.

We all realize the necessity of living the virtuous life for the purpose of saving our immortal souls. But it is also part of God's plan for us to evangelize others in our society. Catholic home schooling families are part of that plan. We need to humbly accept the fact that God has chosen our own family to fit into that plan by performing an important task in evangelization. This should inspire us to be the very best Catholic family we can be.

Steve Wood, a former Protestant minister who has been active in the pro-life movement for several years, once visited Front Royal. He had a very large family of eight children at that time. He made the remark, to which all of us can testify, that whenever the whole family goes anywhere, their very presence is a witness to Christian values. People know that this family has given up material things for the sake of having a large family. Once they were in a restaurant with all the children, and a woman came up to his wife and said, "You are religious, aren't you?" His wife answered, "Yes." Then the lady said, "Catholic, right?" And, though they had been converts only three days, his wife answered, "Yes, Catholic."

The large family is a symbol of the internal life of faith, a symbol recognized even by those who have rejected such a life. The large family is a public rejection of the prevailing secular values of materialism and the self-fulfillment goals without personal sacrifice promoted by the contraceptive mentality, the feminists and homosexuals, and abortionists.

So the first tip for home schooling successfully in the large family is understanding what we are about and why. Then, write it down and tape it on a wall and refer to it often, on good days as well as bad.

The second tip for home schooling successfully in the large family is for the teaching mother to evaluate herself, her own emotional and spiritual life, to understand herself and her strengths and weaknesses, and to discipline herself to be an authentic Catholic wife and mother.

The teaching mother

There is no question about the importance of disciplining our children, but what about our own self-discipline? Home schooling mothers must have self-discipline. We need to ask ourselves questions, such as, "Am I able to control myself so I don't use angry words with the children? Or with my husband in front of the children? Do I discipline the children when I should, or is it just too difficult to bother with it?"

We should pray to Our Mother of Good Counsel to give us the virtues of patience and understanding, as well as good judgment and perseverance. We need to be consistent in administering correction, yet be sensitive to special needs. We must pray for the courage and emotional strength to train our children to choose to be obedient.

In the first year of home schooling, our household routine will be changed, to put it mildly. We need to be ready to accept these changes and to learn to accept sacrifices related to material things.

Discipline yourself to keep going. Do not hesitate to enlist the help of other good Catholic home schooling mothers who will certainly be happy to help you with your current problems. Seeing how other home schooling Catholics resolved a problem often makes a seemingly intractable situation become less difficult to handle. And, of course, depend on the Blessed

Mother—the best of all home schooling mothers—to bring you through the tough times, as well as those blessed moments of smooth sailing.

Many saints are examples for us. St. Elizabeth Ann Seton continued to teach her own children through many difficulties. She taught while her husband was extremely ill and needed her attention. She taught after her husband died, while she was in Italy. She taught her own and other children in Emmitsburg, Maryland, when she established a little school. Through it all, she kept her children with her, even after she became a nun. The first convent was very cold and primitive, and she became sick with tuberculosis, but she kept her children around her through all these tough times. Home schooling means keeping your children around you, no matter what, because problems can only be solved when your family is together, when you work together, when you pray together, when you sacrifice together.

Discipline yourself to keep going when the problems seem overwhelming: an alcoholic spouse, an unfaithful spouse, death or serious illness, too small a house, an uncontrollable budget, living with in-laws. These are situations when children need you more than ever; in school, children turn to drugs, sex, and immature peers for answers to these problems. Be there for your children.

The times of trouble are exactly the times to keep your children close to you, to Jesus, to the stable Catholic family home schooling lifestyle. In times of trouble, your children will be channels of grace to you, and you will be channels of grace to your spouse and your children. Home schooling provides the opportunity and time for this flow of grace. Trust in God to provide you with the time and space through Catholic home schooling.

God gave you the graces to understand the need for home schooling, now have faith He will give the graces to help you continue. He *will* give you the graces to discipline yourself, and to consistently discipline your children.

Remember that the highest manifestation of love is giving and sacrificing, as Jesus did by suffering and dying for us. Home schooling is a continuing act of giving and sacrificing for the most important people in your life—your own children. Train yourself, discipline yourself, to give and to sacrifice.

When suffering comes, we must remember that suffering is a gift from God. It teaches us humility. It teaches us the true meaning of love as we sacrifice and give for others though we may seem unappreciated. God permits suffering so that we draw closer to Him. He told this to Sister Josefa, as explained in *The Way of Divine Love*. He told her that He must allow illness and problems so that people will turn to Him in their distress because so many of us completely forget about Him when things are going well.

On Eternal Word Television Network, Mother Angelica often interviewed people with problems—medical problems or problems with children on drugs, an alcoholic spouse, or teens as unwed mothers, and so on. Their stories are ones of spiritual growth! That is why God allows suffering.

We need to understand that home schooling—especially in a large family where the trials and tribulations, the aggravations and frustrations continue for many years—is a special blessing! What you will discover is that you can be truly happy, even with daily frustrations.

St. Paul gives us encouragement in the First Letter to the Corinthians: "My beloved brethren, be ye steadfast and unmovable, always abounding in the work of the Lord, knowing that your labor is not in vain." Again, St. Paul wrote to the Philippians: "I can do all things in Him Who strengthens me."

We must be like the Blessed Mother, who had faith and trust in Him. At Cana, she said to the waiters, "Do as He tells you!" She had faith that He would provide what was needed because He had already demonstrated it at their home.

Trust in Jesus and His Blessed Mother. Whether you have a large family or a small family, whether you have a single parent or a two-parent family, be motivated, be disciplined, trust in His word, and believe: "I can do all things in Him Who strengthens me."

Group teaching

To be successful in home schooling, especially in the large family, parents need to group the children according to subject matter or ability. The general principle is to combine the children in classes whenever possible. And secondly, remember that the greatest "educational resource" in your family is the other members of the family.

Let us use these principles in a quite large family. The "Kelly" family has a baby, a toddler, and children in kindergarten, second grade, fifth, sixth, ninth, and tenth grade. How should they organize their home schooling?

Art, Music, Physical Education

In general, all the children, except the baby, may take art, music, and physical education together. In art, the children's work may be at different levels, but the children certainly can all be assigned to, for instance, make Easter cards. One child may be cutting and pasting, another may be drawing original artwork, another may concentrate on an Easter poem for his card.

In music, the family may sing together, listen to liturgical chants, visit a music store and learn about musical instruments, attend a local high school or church musical production, or even join a local musical dramatic group.

Physical education is certainly easy. In my family of seven boys, they all played baseball, football, and other sports together. Children about the same age may join a gymnastic class or fencing class, as my boys did, or other local sports activities.

If you enroll your children in any art, music, or sports activity, be sure to monitor at least the first three or four classes or practices, and more if you have time.

Fifth and sixth graders

Looking at the grade levels of the Kelly family, it is obvious that the fifth and sixth graders could easily be combined in some classes. Mothers have found that, in general, girls often can be moved up in reading, spelling, and vocabulary, while boys can be moved up in math and science. (Of course, this is a general rule open to variation.)

The easiest classes for group teaching are religion, science, and history. The lower-level child could move up with the older, but it would not hurt an older child to review or work on the same topic as the younger child's assignments. After working with the children for a couple of weeks, a mother can usually evaluate which child should be moved up or down a level, subject by subject.

With both children reading the assignments by alternating paragraphs, the younger child should be able to keep up. In addition, the children learn to work together, hopefully to become friends, and to come to some understanding about God's various gifts to each individual person. They are learning also to practice the virtues of charity, patience, and understanding as they work and learn together.

In a large family, when you may not be able to give as much time to each child, be sure each one is at the level where he feels comfortable. Be sure each child does not need a great deal of help. Better to start a little lower and have your child be able to do the work rather than starting a little higher, where he would need more daily help and you and he both may feel frustrated.

Another advantage to children working together is that they will tend to keep each other progressing in their work so mother does not have to supervise them as closely. She will, of course, need to be available to explain new concepts, to explain instructions if necessary, to listen to reading pronunciation at least twice a week, and to discuss the studies in religion. At the fifth grade level and above, the students can help grade each other's, or their own, daily work.

Kindergarten and second grader

The kindergarten child and the second grader will take more of a parent's time since they are just beginning their schooling. However, if mother assigns the second grader to be a "teacher's aide" sometimes for the kindergarten child, she will find it not only gives her more time, it also strengthens the phonics or math skills for the older child.

When a child is having difficulty in a subject area, he could become a teacher's aide in the same subject with a younger child. Teaching the lower level skills or concepts will reinforce the foundation and thus strengthen the subject area for the older child.

In addition, the older child learns to be patient and kind to his younger brother or sister, thus practicing the greatest of the virtues, charity. The younger child learns (eventually) to appreciate help from a family member, learns to be humble in receiving, and learns the value of older brothers and sisters. The virtues of humility and trust are thus learned early.

Both the kindergarten child and the second grader can help with the toddler, perhaps playing "school" and teaching letters and numbers to the toddler. Emphasis on service starting with young children will result in charitable acts of mercy later on in life. Remind your children of the words of Christ when He washed the feet of the Apostles, "I have given you an example, that as I have done to you, so you do also."

Some mothers like to teach a young child to read during the summer. By concentrating on the child's reading during the summer, less time needs to be spent during the regular year when there are more demands from other children as well.

Sometimes mothers would like to move a younger child up with an older child, but believe it is too much of a jump. Consider working over the summer with a child in a lower grade, such as in reading, spelling, or vocabulary, so in the fall, the child may be able to move up with an older sibling. At these lowest levels, children may need much more than a summer, however, to absorb abstract concepts.

High school

Some parents are nervous about teaching high school subjects because they are concerned that they may not be qualified. They sometimes ask, "How can I teach geometry or chemistry when I do not understand these subjects myself?"

There are several answers to this problem. First, if you have access to a computer, consider buying educational software for the particular subject. There are so many excellent programs available now for such a wide variety of topics, you should have no problem finding one that fits your child's needs.

Second, look for a tutor who could come in once a week to teach the subject.

Third, try enrolling in community college courses for advanced math, advanced science, and advanced foreign languages. Taking only a single course limits social interaction with the other students, but gives your child access to all the resources of the college.

Fourth, some home schooling families pool their resources and meet together with someone in the community who has expertise in a particular subject area. For instance, I know one group of students which has a class with a research chemist. Another group is meeting with a teacher from

France who enjoys helping home schooling children learn French. There are many other examples.

The important thing to remember is that Catholic home schooling is not primarily about geometry or chemistry; it is about living the virtuous Catholic life. It is primarily about raising saints, not scholars. If the choice is between my child never mastering geometry because I cannot teach it and my child being daily taught to accept pagan values, the choice is obvious.

Ninth and tenth graders

The ninth grader in our imaginary Kelly family should be able to do a good amount of work on his own. If students are home schooled for the elementary years, they are usually independent learners at the high school level. Mine kept saying, "Mom, I can do it myself!"

At the high school level, mothers need to keep aware of the progress, and to be involved in discussions of religion, and of other subjects if necessary. Subjects which would require more discussion would be English, in relation to the books read and analyzed, history, and sometimes geography. Algebra and geometry are usually not difficult if children have been home schooled previously. Otherwise, we encourage fathers or older siblings to help out. Most of the time, however, high schoolers are able to move ahead with their assignments without too much supervision.

You do have to be careful, however, that students keep up in *all* subjects. Sometimes a student will especially like one subject, and not like another. When that happens, the student tends to spend much more time on the one and neglect the other. You want to make sure that students keep up with everything they need to do on a daily basis.

However, if the child is *starting* home schooling in ninth grade, problems sometimes arise because the student does not have the academic background, study skills, or motivation. In addition, school teachers may not have demanded that he work up to his potential.

Some children in the schools are pressured by their peers not to appear to be bright or to do well. In these cases, Mother may have to work with the ninth grader more than she anticipated.

The home schooling mother must keep in mind that one of her aims is to teach the student to develop study skills so that he may continue his schooling more on his own. At Seton, we have written a mini-study skills course which we send to our students in grades seven through twelve. In fact, it is freely available on the home page of our website at www.setonhome.org. We give advice about setting up a place and time to study, having books and other study materials at hand, how to avoid distractions, and so on.

The mini-study skills course explains about taking notes, outlining a chapter, studying important details, and remembering facts. Once these skills are mastered, a student will learn more easily.

Hopefully by tenth grade, Mother needs only to supervise in a few subjects, though we encourage parents to be involved in discussions.

Ninth and tenth continued

The ninth and tenth grade students should be able to take several courses together, especially courses that need not be taken in any order. History, geography, religion, literature survey courses, and science courses usually can be taken by students at different grade levels because they do not build on concepts from the previous year. A foreign language could be started early by the younger student in order to work with an older brother or sister.

Obviously, the ninth grader will not be able to take algebra 2 or geometry with the older student. It is likely that the English course will not be able to be taken together because certain rules of writing, analysis, composition, and grammar are assumed to have been learned in ninth grade. However, if a student is ambitious, a younger student could take one subject, such as algebra 1, over the summer, intensively, in order to take a more advanced course with an older brother or sister during the regular school year.

A rebellious teenager

One of the banes of modern existence is the rebellious teenager. If parents start a teenager in home schooling, there may be some problems. If a teenager is rebellious, the first year of home schooling may be mainly a program to teach Catholic family values and attitudes, including self-discipline. It may take up to two years to finish the academics.

Some parents pull their children out of the public or Catholic high school as late as twelfth grade. We know it is difficult, but the idea of "better late than never" is an important admonition here. Even at this late date, if parents realize the dangers of the school environment to their child's soul, they can take these last months to teach as much as they can as fast as they can.

Some parents, when realizing the dangers to their children, as well as their child's lack of good Catholic values, will start their children over with the high school subjects, especially religion, history, and literature. Some students start the whole high school curriculum over again to obtain the Catholic perspective. Much of the material can be learned quickly because it is review, yet it has an entirely different perspective. The politically correct concepts learned in geography classes, for instance, can be corrected through a Catholic perspective. Catholic lesson plans for geography might include a variety of topics presented with the Catholic viewpoint—topics such as multi-culturalism and globalism, population growth and Communism.

Part-time grouping

We have discussed grouping two children together in a class, moving an older down or a younger up in a subject where they can both benefit from taking a single class together. But there is another kind of grouping which can work also, called part-time grouping.

For instance, suppose you have children in grades four, five, and seven, and you do not want to teach three different levels of religion, science, or history, but you feel the ability differences are such that you cannot combine them in their daily work assignments. A way to handle this would be to group all the children together for a discussion or explanation of a particular topic. Your presentation would be geared to the middle child most likely, using the middle child's textbook or lessons. But later, or the next day, each child could do his own textbook assignment at his own level. Thus, the fourth grader may be working on memorizing the catechism facts on the Fourth Commandment, the fifth grader may be answering factual questions, and the seventh grader may be writing a paragraph on a more complex situation of a young teen who is disobedient to his parents or another authority figure.

Other family members

While the family members you most rely on to help teach the children are usually the other children themselves, your husband should be helping also. (This is covered more specifically in the chapter on the father's role.)

Other family members who might help are grandparents. They often have the time and energy to help by babysitting or by teaching. Encourage even reluctant grandparents to help because, in most cases, the more they learn about home schooling, the more supportive they become.

Grandparents can be really great teachers for your children. They have so much experience, knowledge, and wisdom about living the Catholic life. They are a veritable treasure for your children. They tend to be very patient, sensitive, understanding, and loving toward their grandchildren. This wonderful, often cuddly, security for your children is a healthy environment for growing spiritually as well as intellectually.

Grandparents are wonderful teachers for the younger children, but their wisdom and experience can be a deep learning experience for teenagers, who tend to think they know everything. In a pagan society which is accepting euthanasia and promoting the value of usefulness over the value of living a holy life, grandparents in the home schooling family teach priceless lessons. This multi-generational teaching is something which children in schools never experience.

High school and college level children are great at helping younger siblings, especially in math and English. Another favorite helper among home schoolers is a retired teacher or a retired nun, who might help on a once-a-week basis to review math or English work.

Consider having older children spend time, taking turns, maybe one-half hour per day with your preschoolers. The older children can play with them or babysit, or teach them their letters or numbers. This is important interaction among the children, benefiting both the younger and the older child.

Do not neglect allowing the preschoolers to be involved in the home schooling situation. They should not feel left out. They can be playing on the floor or sitting in someone's lap, or have their own "schoolbook" or be writing with chalk on a blackboard. Involving preschoolers will mean fewer discipline problems. In addition, these children start picking up the lessons early, are better students as they unconsciously adopt learning skills, and anticipate their home schooling with eagerness as a sign of growing up.

Flexibility

To be successful in your home schooling in the large family, you must be flexible. That's a terrific understatement! The biggest academic benefit in home schooling is the individualized curriculum. If you do not gear the material and pace to your child's individual learning strengths and weaknesses, you are missing out on a great benefit.

At Seton, we always encourage flexibility. Our motto is: "Adjust the program to fit the child, not the child to fit the program." This means that while there might be specific mathematical facts which need to be learned in a particular grade level, we recommend that you teach the daily lessons at a pace and with a method that is best for the student.

An individual child may be able to do two lessons in one day, or at another time, he may need to take two days to do one lesson. Some young boys and girls in the warm months will need to have several short lessons so they can go outside and play more often.

At Seton, while we provide day-to-day lessons and recommendations, these are to serve as a guideline. If you want to follow them exactly, you certainly may. Many parents do. On the other hand, if you wish, you may adjust them, giving more oral assignments rather than written, or shortening an assignment because your child learned the concepts quickly. You might want to enrich a lesson in reading, for instance, by doing more research in an encyclopedia about an artist mentioned in a reader.

Enrichment

Be flexible in your daily lessons whenever possible by utilizing supplemental materials to enrich the lessons. Go over the lessons for the following week on the previous weekend. If you have the Internet, try to find websites with material appropriate for your child. The Internet has changed learning forever by providing an incredible amount of information at your fingertips. Finding exactly what you want on the Internet can be difficult, so you want to become as familiar as possible with Internet search engines. When you find good online resources, bookmark the pages so you can use them over again. Browsers let you organize bookmarks into categories, so you could have your favorite places for science, for history, for religion, etc.

Some families don't want to have Internet access for fear of allowing bad influences into their home. That is understandable, and it is a judgment call each family will need to make. In general, the Internet is a tool, and like any other powerful tool, it can be used for good or evil. Once you have it, it is hard to believe that you ever did without it.

If you can, visit the library for books, pamphlets, CDs, DVDs, and reference books which relate to the upcoming lessons. Ask the librarian for an explanation of all the features or materials they offer. Ask about borrowing books from other libraries through inter-library loan. Most libraries have circulating reference books, usually older editions of encyclopedias. Also, ask your librarian if she might be selling the library's older copy of the encyclopedia. You should be able to purchase the whole set for about $25. You can also try buying an encyclopedia set on eBay. Even if you use the encyclopedia on the Internet, students still like books. Books are still essential to learning. Lots of kids like to just leaf through encyclopedias to learn about different topics, which you can't do with a software encyclopedia.

Ask the librarian about other sources where you can obtain information and study materials. Local and state governments offer loads of free materials. Check garage sales for used encyclopedias and other reference books, such as illustrated science encyclopedias.

School teachers, limited because of space, time, location, and overload of student problems, cannot begin to offer children the almost unlimited resources available to the home schooling family.

Scheduling

Scheduling can be very tricky for the large family. Some mothers like all the children to be taking the same subject at the same time. Thus all the children have math from 9:00 to 10:00. The advantage to this is that as you move from child to child, you may find it easier yourself in your teaching. Also, if a child needs to help another child, their studies are on the same subject at the same time.

On the other hand, some mothers need to hear the children read their stories every day, so they stagger the reading classes. Some mothers find that they can concentrate on the older children and their assignments in the early morning, while helping the younger children later in the day. Some mothers schedule working with a child on his weak subject at the same time another child is working on a subject in which he needs no help.

Most mothers try to cover the more difficult subjects in the morning, when the children are fresh, while saving the workbook-type assignments in the afternoon. Of course, if you have a baby who naps in the afternoon, that is a good time to listen to reading or to help a child on a more complex subject such as English. Many mothers prefer the children to take one subject with Dad in the evening or on Saturdays.

While it is important to be prepared to be flexible in case something changes, it is better to start the year with a definite schedule and to try to stick with it for a few weeks or months if you can, before making changes. Structure provides stability and discipline, which children want and need.

Children need routine. They want to know when it is time for dinner, when it is time to go to bed, when they can play, when they have to do the math or English, when it is time to pray or go to Mass. Routine gives them security, and they are more willing to do WHAT they should do WHEN they should do it. In a large family, things can easily become chaotic without a schedule.

Children often are more motivated to keep to a schedule if they have some input in making out the schedule. Ask them if they want their easiest subject first or their most difficult subject first. You may not always be able to accommodate, but try to whenever possible.

When you have worked out the schedule together, have each child write out his schedule, and then decorate it artistically with colored pens or crayons. The schedules can be put on the wall of the room where they do most of their school work. With this kind of personal attention to their schedule, they are more likely to follow it.

While parents are encouraged to adjust their plans to the needs and abilities of their children, having a written schedule as a guideline makes them and their children feel better. They have a road map. They know where they are going, even if they do not keep the exact pace, or even if they make changes now and then.

Starting the year

With a large family, it is important to start the school year a little slowly. The public schools schedule 180 days of school, but not all the children are actually in attendance 180 days. They are out sick, or have field trips, or there are training days for teachers. Many times children have little schooling when they have substitute teachers or when some all-school event is going on. Schools have an abundance of study halls and movies. So do not worry if you do not have exactly 180 days of school. It is better to start slowly and establish good procedures for the year.

Start the oldest child, or if you are grouping, the oldest two children, for the first week, but do not teach the other children that week. Take that first week to make the schedule, locate the answer keys, see how often tests are scheduled, become familiar with the pattern of the assignments, and so on. If your oldest is in high school, be sure he becomes familiar with the materials and how to use them. During that week, the pattern can be set for the weeks to come.

In the second week, teach the next oldest, or two, and work without interruptions from the other children as much as possible. You can teach all the children this way when you start each new school year. Some mothers like to do this before the Labor Day weekend so the full-fledged program can begin in September.

Be sure each child knows what to do if Mother is not available at the time needed. He may be told to a) continue with the current assignment as best as possible by going on to other problems; or b) read for a book report; or c) do an assignment for another course. Do not allow your children to waste time waiting for you to be available. You may need to institute a "wait and waste" punishment until they understand the value of time.

Fridays

Some large families find it very difficult to have home schooling for five days a week because they need a day for other things. They schedule only four days a week, allowing a fifth day for catching up with anything not finished on the first four days, or for doing housework, or scheduling doctor appointments. When there is a Holy Day during the week, some families like to have either no classes or fewer classes. In my family, we omitted a couple of subjects on Holy Days to give us extra Mass and prayer time.

Some families use Friday primarily for the whole family to clean up the house. In a large family, have teams for the chores, with one older child working with a younger child. That way, the younger one is learning from the older, and the older one cannot daydream because he is in charge of supervising the younger one. The chore is done faster and more thoroughly.

Unique but typical day

Prospective home schooling mothers often call and ask what a typical home schooling day is like. They are worried about just how much demand there is going to be on their time.

As most of us have learned, there is no typical home schooling schedule. It is unique for each family because each family is unique. How much "demand" on the mother is unpredictable. Boys are often more demanding. Younger children are more demanding than older ones. Older children just starting are more demanding than younger ones just starting. In some families English takes more time, and in other families math takes more time. In some families, science goes quickly and composition takes forever.

In one family, the mother is totally devoted to her family and their needs. Everything is organized down to the last cup. She has her children trained to work in certain places, to study at certain times, to do each day's work exactly as written in their lesson plans. The girls read and read, and obtain very high scores on tests. They love learning, and eat it up like candy as Mother devotes each minute of the school day to making the lessons exciting.

In another family, Mother does not have time to take off her bathrobe. She is on the phone with the needs of the pregnancy center, but she keeps the lessons going as her children work in the living room. She checks on their lessons between her calls. She has a large family, and the older children often help the younger ones. She gives help when it is needed. She and her husband are professionals, and the house is like a library. The children spend much time reading many books.

Another mother has several children but only one child old enough for formal schooling. She sits the baby on her lap while her boy reads and the toddlers play on the floor. Sometimes she listens to the math facts while she puts the clothes in the washing machine. Sometimes her son goes to his room where it is quieter to study his phonics. Her husband teaches new math concepts to her son every morning before he goes to work.

One family lives on a farm, and the children need to help Dad during certain seasons of the year. During the off season, the children work hard on their schooling, and Dad helps them. During the farming season, the children do not do as much schoolwork except in the evening, as they are busy helping Dad during the day. The children have projects of their own with 4-H. They even raise and market their own crop.

Another family does their home schooling between their music lessons, since Dad is a professional musician and wants them to practice often. They love to play in the local orchestra. They really do not like math and have a tutor come once a week to help out.

A family with several children in high school has joined with two other home schooling families with high school students. They hired a tutor to review the high school science and math assignments, while Mother continues to teach the younger children.

One family has high school children active in drama, and the lessons are often done in the theater. In another family, the high school girls are active in volunteering at a local hospital, and schoolwork is arranged around their schedule. In many families, pro-life activity is an important part of the Catholic social work.

In another family, two high schoolers are being paid as they serve as apprentices, the girl in office and bookkeeping, the boy in welding and machine work.

In one family, the boys work several hours a week with the local priest, helping around the church and rectory. A high school boy in another family helps out as a teacher's aide at a school for children with special needs.

In most families, home schooling methods change as children grow older. Methods and scheduling change with different children. While one child did well working in his own bedroom in quiet, another child seems to work better at the dining room table with sounds all around him.

Time causes us to change, and time causes our children to change. Dads may be more or less available for helping with the home schooling as they change jobs.

As is obvious, a typical day for any one family is not a typical day with any other family. Each family is unique in its gifts and talents, in its weaknesses and interests, and these things shape the home schooling schedule. It is also shaped by the occupations of the parents. Some children learn farming and animal husbandry, others learn to program the computer, while still others learn to knit sweaters and sew beautiful dresses.

My own family

People often ask me how my seven boys were home schooled. So here is my typical but unique story. This is presented only as an example of what one family has done. It may give you some thoughts about your own situation, but it is certainly not presented as an ideal for you or any other family.

When I first started home schooling, I was working as an elementary school principal for a private parent-operated Catholic school which I founded along with some other Catholic parents. My younger children attended. (Later, I home schooled all my children.) My three oldest boys were in high school at this time. They worked at their studies, each on his own grade level, while I was away. When I came home at four o'clock, I looked over their work, asked them questions, or they asked me questions. On Sundays, I would spend the afternoon grading and writing out their assignments for the week.

My sons did a great deal of school work. They worked the regular school hours, and were able to read extra books from the library or do extra reading in the encyclopedia. They read literature and political works since these are my main interests. We went to the library every week.

A few years later, in another house, I had left my job as principal and was home schooling full time with all my children, except for my oldest who was in college. We had one large room where most of the boys had their own tables and scheduled assignments. They worked on their own grade levels, and I would rotate my time with them.

A younger boy was in a separate room with a neighbor boy in the same grade level. I taught them both, with some help from a friend on occasion. My youngest simply played wherever I was.

In a third house, the boys were older and helped a great deal with household chores. I was going back to work, by this time, on a limited basis. Two and then three of the boys were in college. Much of my professional work was done at home in the evenings. I continued to have each boy work on his own grade level most of the time, but did have them work together on science projects.

My husband up to this point had helped only occasionally, but now he began to spend more time helping the boys in math and history. The older boys began to help the younger boys, especially in math.

The schooling schedule was very similar in all three situations. We started the day with prayer: Morning Offering, Litany of the Sacred Heart, and a reading of the life of the saint for the day. Our first class was always religion, with math always the second subject. Subjects the children needed me for, such as English and reading, always followed in the morning. For English, I often used a blackboard for diagramming, which made it more fun for my boys. I listened to the boys read each day, if only for 15 minutes, up to eighth grade. Proper pronunciation and inflection seems important to determine a degree of comprehension. The assignments in the readers at the end of the selections I considered very important.

Phonics, spelling, and vocabulary were done in the late morning or early afternoon. My boys tended to do these easily, though they were often careless with spelling. They needed more practice with their handwriting, so the spelling and vocabulary were handwriting lessons also.

In the early years, we said the daily Rosary in the evening, but I realized the children were too tired. So we decided to say the Rosary at 11:00 AM, and whoever was home (from college) would join in. After lunch, we would say more prayers, the Angelus and the Act of Contrition especially. While we tried to say prayers at the end of the school day, this did not work out as the children often finished at different times.

The boys did science and history on their own in the afternoon, though further supplemental reading was done regularly in the encyclopedia and with library books. Dad would occasionally take the children to a museum or historical area.

When I lived near a library with films, we would obtain films every week, mostly on science topics. I really missed this once we moved to a small town.

Afternoons were spent doing easy workbook-type assignments. Physical education was a subject integrated throughout the day, since my boys were active between classes, jumping rope being a favorite. My boys became experts at jump rope tricks. Though the boys went outdoors during lunchtime, they otherwise were not allowed in the yard until after three o'clock. I felt more comfortable without questions being asked by neighbors.

Some of my children had piano lessons, which was the music curriculum. Otherwise, it was not regular, though my husband is a semi-professional musician. They daily heard good music on the piano. Art was more of an inspirational topic; they did it when they or we were inspired. We always did projects related to the important holidays and liturgical feasts: Thanksgiving hats, Christmas decorations, Easter posters.

No matter what the arrangement for the home school assignments, we always had daily prayer, scheduled at regular times of the day. I myself attended Mass frequently, almost daily. My boys did not attend daily Mass with me, though they went on occasion. This was because the Mass was fairly late and caused too much disruption with the home schooling, and because I did not want my children being outside during school hours.

My situation many years ago was unusual. My last two children, ages fourteen and seventeen at that time, had been doing their home schooling in my office. That year, some of us local parents were teaching our high schoolers together for some subjects. I taught American literature, one father taught math and science, my husband taught history, a college-age brother taught Latin, and a priest taught religion. In a couple of classes, it was mostly a supervisory situation. In other classes, we did more teaching.

It is obvious from my own experience, and from the many experiences that have been shared with me by home schooling mothers, that there are many ways to home school successfully. There is no typical home schooling situation, or even best home schooling situation. It is important that parents work out the schedule, methods, or programs that are best for their children.

As the year progresses

In some subjects, the children can quickly learn the pattern for a week, which remains the same for every week of the year. This is often true for vocabulary, spelling, and handwriting. After a couple of weeks, the child knows the daily assignments, and should not need too much help. This is a help for the mother in the large family.

After you have been home schooling for a while, if you have a child who seems to dawdle or fool around or dreams away the time, you might consider scheduling the classes around meals and snacks. This is especially effective with boys. For instance, you can schedule a one-half hour math class before breakfast, two or three classes before a morning snack, two or three classes before lunch, and so on. Meals or snacks are not eaten until the assignment is done.

Of course, whether you have a small or large family, when you are making out your schedule, plan morning and afternoon prayer, the Rosary, and whatever other religious activities are appropriate according to the liturgical year. Daily Mass attendance is something toward which we should all strive.

Short classes

It is best for younger children to keep lessons short. Usually, more math will be learned in three 20-minute classes than a one hour class. Reading class can be divided up into a reading session, then a workbook or written assignment.

Do not have too long a school day. Home schooling is far more intensive learning than in a classroom, so do not go past five or six hours total. For primary age children, many can do the work in a few hours. It would be better to work on a Saturday morning, or to make your school year longer, than to have children work a very long day. After a certain amount of formal class time, children simply cannot absorb any more, so continuing becomes pointless. You certainly might include more hands-on learning to add variety. Using kitchen measurements, for instance, will help diversify the learning process for math, as a child helps with cooking a meal.

Integrate your housework

When you are making out your schedule, consider doing housework and home schooling at the same time. For instance, I used to listen to my children read or listen to their math facts while I washed the dishes or wiped off the kitchen counters. I would have the children working in the kitchen while I cooked. Admittedly, I have never been much of a housekeeper, but the boys helped with the housework.

By the way, after having my babies, I would often help my older children with their studies while I lay in bed nursing my baby. Just think of home schooling as an integral part of the normal Catholic family life.

Integrate their chores

Include household chores for the children in the daily home school schedule. This is especially important in the large family where there is so much to do and mothers will become exhausted if they try to do all the housework. Even a two-year-old child can feel important by doing some sort of job.

In my family, I found that my boys did not like chores after school hours. They preferred chores along with the schoolwork, between the subjects to break up their schoolwork, and also because when the school day was done, their chores were finished.

Another reason for having chores between classes is that studies have shown that children perform better mentally when physical exercise is interspersed with the lessons. A study reported in *Prevention* magazine showed that children's grades improved when short daily exercises were included between classes right in the classroom.

Potential interruptions

Many mothers of large families are very busy, and working pro-life or other activities into the busy schedule is fairly common. However, work outside the home should be kept to a minimum until the children are older. Of course, activities *with* the children, such as picketing abortion clinics or helping the needy, are important to teach Catholic values by example.

Do not let phone calls and other people's problems keep you from fulfilling your own priorities with your own children. Too many mothers spend so much time helping others that their own children suffer. Charity DOES begin at home!

You should try to minimize the interruptions for your children as well. Especially when children reach an age where they can babysit, change diapers, and help with many other jobs, it is easy to pull them away from their schoolwork to have them help around the house. Helping is important, and can be educational and assist in developing virtue, but it can't become so frequent that a student falls behind in schoolwork. Students need blocks of time to concentrate on their work. Many interruptions, even if only for a few minutes at a time, can be extremely detrimental to studying.

Older children return home

Another situation happening with large families is that older children in their twenties, some even older and married with children, tend to come back home when they have problems. While this is fine, they must understand that you have responsibilities first with the younger children still needing guidance. If older children come back home and move in, they should be helping the whole family situation, not making more demands on you. Schedule them to help, either with classes or errands or housework, which is really a minimal request.

Location, location, location

Some families add an extra room to the house, or make a classroom from a family room, a garage, or a basement room. Some families use another building on the property, such as a garage or tool shed. The children along with the parents can work to make this their special place for home schooling. It is very motivational for the children to do their schoolwork in the room or building which they worked so hard to make their own by decorating it themselves.

In locations such as a barn or family room, the children often work together; but keep in mind that children do need quiet time for some of their courses. For the large family, a basement recreation room or something similar is ideal, a room where the formal schoolwork is done during the day.

As many families have told us, home schooling is very adaptable to changes in location. Many families take the children with their books and lessons on vacations, or visits to elderly or sick family members, or on business trips. Lessons can be done even while waiting in a doctor's office.

Grading

Parents sometimes complain about the time it takes to grade their children's work. A way to cut down on this time is to encourage your children to grade their own papers immediately after they have done their assignment. The advantage to this is that children can recall their thought processes when they answered their questions or problems, and thus can learn from their grading. In addition, self-grading develops honesty and usually accuracy. For the mother in a large family, it really cuts down on paperwork time.

A tip for saving time is for the children to mark off assignments in their plan book after they are done, corrected from the answer key, and then graded. This does not mean that Mother should not check the work, but answers can be spot-checked or randomly double-checked.

Home library

For the large family, it is especially useful to build up a family library, especially of Catholic books. With a large family and the many varied interests and demands, you will need your own library sooner or later. Purchase used books from the public library book sales, even encyclopedias and other reference books. Check for used books at thrift shops, at home schooling conventions, and at St. Vincent de Paul shops. Also, especially in Catholic areas, comb the garage sales for old but good Catholic books. Sometimes you can even find old textbooks, as well as saints' biographies.

Dictionaries are very important for children to learn to use at a very young age. You can buy beginning, intermediate, and advanced dictionaries, often used, at libraries and garage sales. Be sure there are plenty of dictionaries in the house, and insist that the children use them. Sometimes I think we should give prizes to the child who uses the dictionary the most often.

Look for other used items, such as globes, atlases, microscopes, aquariums, bird cages, book cases, historical photographs or paintings, any educational equipment or games. Buy lamps, desks, and study tables at thrift stores. Of course, you can get all of these things on eBay for a pretty good price, but sometimes the shipping charges make it better to look locally.

Local activities

Do not rush to enroll children in local activities. Some are fine, but many families register children in too many, to the point where the activities control family life. In a large family especially, formal outside social activities are not as necessary, or not necessary at all.

Don't feel like you must always have your children enrolled in some class or sports activity. Even with families of only two or three children, these activities can quickly begin to take over the family. Having four or five or six children all in soccer or gymnastics or dance will become too hectic to bear after a while.

We have this modern idea that parents must provide supervised activities all the time for children. Before this idea came along, there was something that children managed to do on their own without much input from adults. It was called "play."

Further enrichment

In a large family, where Mother cannot listen to all the children read every day, or hear the answers for all the questions, have children use the tape recorder for reading, for proper inflection and pronunciation, for recording words for future tests in spelling and vocabulary, and for answering questions.

If parents attend home schooling conferences, usually CDs are made of the speeches or workshops. It may be helpful for children to listen to some of these tapes, especially if they cover ideas about learning subject matter, such as science.

In a large family, when you cannot spend the money for music lessons for everyone, spend the money to teach one child a musical instrument, then have that child teach some of the younger children. You could have one child take an arts and crafts class, and then come home and teach the other children his lessons.

If your children watch a television show, ask them to look up at least one thing in the encyclopedia which relates to the TV program, and share it with the family at dinnertime. This encourages the children to analyze the programs they watch for educational content.

A large family often does not have the money for field trips, or because of the busy schedule, it is seldom possible to find the time. In that case, consider mini-field trips to local businesses in town, such as to the bakery, print shop, or welding shop. Take the children to visit the post office when you need to purchase stamps, or the local upholstery shop when you buy fabric. Look for local, no-cost, but educational field trips just in your regular travels around town.

Consider everything you do as a possible opportunity to teach your children.

And then there is the computer

For the large or small home schooling family, there is nothing like a computer to make home schooling easier. Purchase a computer, even if old and used. These are wonderful helps for the children. Word processing is valuable especially for boys who think faster than they can write. Boys will see better results and be happier to do schoolwork when they see good work on paper.

The computer is also good for storing a record of work done and for getting copies of things back later. Along those lines, be sure to make backup copies of the work on the computer. It is really not a question of whether your computer will crash, but when. If you don't have a CD or DVD recorder, it's a good investment. One DVD or CD could hold all the schoolwork the children did for a whole year, and it is a lot more convenient than saving reams of paper.

Structure versus non-structure

One of the topics buzzing around home schooling groups is the issue of structure versus non-structure in home schooling families. Looking through the home schooling literature, it seems that some programs advertise freedom and independence, others advertise high academics, some advertise character education, some the unit approach, some basic skills and content. Some of this might also be characterized as an un-schooling approach, which was discussed in the previous chapter.

The programs which are unstructured, or using the unit approach, claim that structured programs are trying to bring the classroom into the living room. Those promoting programs which are structured are heard to say that the lack of structure could result in basic skills or areas of knowledge "falling through the cracks."

Often, the unstructured programs or unit approach programs revolve the various subject lessons around an idea or concept. Christian programs, for instance, will take a concept of a virtue, such as patriotism or loyalty, and start with characters from the Bible who practice this virtue. Historical characters are studied who may demonstrate this virtue. Spelling words, vocabulary words, and historical readings may be taken from the Bible. Grammar lessons, such as the study of nouns, would be based on sentences from the Bible or historical readings.

Proponents of this approach believe that children's interest level and motivation is high because the program is more child-directed. Because the motivation is high, even the spelling, vocabulary, and English are learned more thoroughly, they say, than in a structured approach.

Obviously, in an unstructured program in which the studies are more child-directed or child-initiated, the child will be more motivated because he is more interested, assuming that he is interested in some particular topic. The conclusion is that a consequence of the high motivation is a good education. If mothers are highly involved to make sure that all the skills are covered, this could be true. However, there is no question that many children have received excellent educations through the structured programs as well.

Certain home schoolers and home school leaders believe that the "burnout" experienced by some home schooling mothers is due to structured programs or the structured classroom approach. This is too simplistic. Burnout can be caused by lack of organization, lack of discipline, lack of support by the spouse, antagonism by family and friends, and personal and family problems. It also can be caused by the amount of work required by parents for an unstructured program.

Sometimes families begin on a structured program, then go off the structure for a year, then return to the structure because they feel it is too difficult without the daily lessons. One mother, a well-educated professional, admitted she liked the accountability aspect of a structured program, which helped her to keep on track. She also found that her children were more motivated, especially the junior high and high school students, when they received papers back with grades and comments from a teacher.

It is my contention, however, that there is no one curriculum or method of curriculum for every student, for every family, or for every mother. A basic premise of home education is that the best education is one tailored to the needs and abilities of the child. So the structure or no structure debate must be resolved by each family.

Catholic educational history

There are advantages to both the structured and unstructured approaches that we Catholics should not forget. Formalized Catholic education was begun by the Catholic Church with the cathedral schools in Europe. From those schools came such great scholars as St. Albert and St. Thomas Aquinas. It would be a denial of history, a denial of the achievements of the Western World, in fact, to deny the great education provided by the structured curricula of the Catholic schools and universities.

However, within the structure of the programs was an encouragement of creativity, creative thinking, and flexibility of methods.

Consider the *Summa Theologica* of St. Thomas Aquinas. St. Thomas had certain truths to teach, but he encouraged his students to ask questions. He first restated the questions, then he gave his basic teaching, such as the proofs for the existence of God, then he answered the questions. He encouraged questions and discussion among the students.

Think about the excellent convent schools in the United States. From the convent schools came great Catholic women leaders, women who volunteered their services for the community, in schools and in hospitals, established Catholic charities for the poor, the sick, and the elderly. Some became doctors and lawyers. The schools which taught them facts also taught them thinking skills, how to be creative, how to initiate projects, strong writing skills, and perhaps most important, how to serve their neighbor.

Patrick Buchanan and William Bennett, two well-known Catholic political thinkers, are products of the superior Catholic school system. They attended structured Catholic schools. In fact, they both attended Gonzaga High School in Washington, D.C. Neither friend nor enemy could say that they are not deep thinkers, are not creative, are not well-educated and articulate speakers and writers. Yet they learned English using Loyola University's structured *Voyages in English* series, which promotes a high level of understanding of the English language as well as composition exercises. Within the composition exercises in that structured series, creativity and original thought are fostered.

So what is the answer?

The answer is a balance between structure and non-structure. But this balance must be reached after a consideration of various factors. These factors include the age of the student, learning ability, the best learning style for the student, the teacher-parent's ability, and the subject matter itself.

Older children need more structure because certain skills and basic content must be learned. Each day, the student should be reading, practicing his handwriting, doing his phonics and math drills. Nearly every day, spelling and vocabulary should be studied. English grammar needs to proceed more cautiously according to the maturity of the student, since this involves a higher degree of logical thinking. Composition exercises, however, should be started as early as first grade, with creative sentences and even short creative paragraphs. The amount of time spent and the time of day for the composition exercises should be regular.

Children want a certain amount of structure. It gives them stability and a sense of things being in order. How would we feel if some days Father had Mass at 8:00, sometimes 9:00, sometimes 10:00. We would quickly become frustrated and stop attending Mass. In the same way, children need to get up at a certain time, to eat at a certain time, to rest at a certain time. This promotes mental and physical health, comfort, confidence, and security.

Structure regarding the time *of* a class, the amount of time *for* the class, and possibly even a routine for the class, such as for the study of spelling and vocabulary, will result in security and healthy progress in learning the material.

On the other hand, some classes lend themselves naturally to flexibility, such as science and history. In these subjects, the lessons may be closely followed, or there may be more creativity and ingenuity. The science program at Seton, for instance, has daily and weekly lessons with the textbook, but projects and experiments are encouraged.

While our history courses include a textbook and daily lesson assignments, field trips to historical museums or famous battlefields are encouraged. Historical or biographical films or videos or Internet resources, even tours at battlefields, are available. Such activities can enrich and supplement the courses.

In religion, especially with the large family, we encourage flexibility by having two or more children learn the same subject matter at the same time, but do individual assignments at their own level, or do a project together as the parent decides is best. The children may all discuss the Seventh Commandment with Mother or Father, but perhaps the older children should read more details in their text, while the youngest may draw a colorful picture of a child returning his library book on time, and the middle child may need to work on memorizing a catechism answer.

Testing and grades

One aspect which parents do not like about a structured program is what they consider an emphasis on testing and grades. There are advantages and disadvantages with testing and grades. Advantages include helping mothers and students stay on a fairly regular schedule, and having a "proof" of consistent progress. In some states, formal testing and a report card are either required, or serve as a protection against harassment by local or state education authorities. The advantage of no testing and grades is a lack of pressure on mothers and students to perform in a certain way or by a certain time.

After high school

If a parent chooses not to enroll in a program for the high school years, the parent should become fully informed about what is expected by the college or vocational school which the student is likely to attend. The college should be asked what they expect, not only in the way of curriculum but also for report cards and standardized testing.

Some state colleges have a written policy to accept students who come from non-accredited schools on a first semester probationary trial basis. They can regard home schoolers who are not enrolled in a school as drop-outs. While this is unfair, this is the policy with some state colleges. Some colleges may be changing this policy, but you need to find out from the college to which you intend to send your child. Private colleges, of course, can make their own rules, and tend to be more accepting of students based on SAT scores.

Eternal Word Television Network

Many families do not have televisions, but I do recommend it if you can get EWTN, Mother Angelica's Catholic station. Some of these programs can be scheduled into your home schooling day. If you cannot obtain this excellent Catholic station in your area, we encourage you to purchase a satellite dish. The station is on 24 hours a day, seven days a week. You can have your satellite fixed so that only EWTN will come in. It brings into your home the very finest Catholic people to encourage you and your children to live the Catholic life.

For the home schooling family, the people on EWTN make the Catholic Faith alive, vibrant, meaningful, and relevant for our children. These programs support the faith and culture which we are trying to convey, but which often seem foreign or "weird" in the midst of a pagan society.

Conclusion

If I could say that anything is typical about home schooling families, it is that most are doing their best to keep up a strong prayer life. Most have scheduled prayer; many attend Mass during the week. As I visit families in my travels, I am impressed by the humble lifestyles and fervent dedication to their children, to God, and to their Church.

Just remember that family prayer is essential not only for successful home schooling, but also to survive as a Catholic family. Pray every day with your children. Teach them formal prayers and informal "conversation" with God.

We all need to respect other families and their methods. At the same time, in our own family, we need to adjust to the different personalities as well as the needs and abilities of each child. Ultimately, this will result in a generation of Catholic adults who see the value of individualizing the learning process, and the value of each individual as a child of God. This will result in a better Christian society, both academically and spiritually.

Chapter 6:
The Sacramental Life

The most important key for success in home schooling is living the authentic Catholic sacramental life in the family. The sacramental life means not only the regular reception of the Sacraments of the Holy Eucharist and Penance, but also the daily practice of using sacramentals to help live the life of prayer and to celebrate the feasts of the liturgical year.

The Catholic home has been termed the "domestic church" by the Second Vatican Council and many Church documents. If our home is to be truly a "domestic church," then using sacramentals and revolving our family activities around the liturgical year is not only appropriate but the best plan for a family to live the authentic Catholic family life.

The Church dispenses the seven sacraments as a direct means for its individual members to receive sanctifying grace from God. This sanctifying grace is necessary for each member of the home schooling family. We can receive graces also through the sacramentals, which are approved by the Church, but which we can use in our own home.

The Holy Eucharist

I believe that daily reception of Jesus in the Sacrament of the Holy Eucharist is most important for the Catholic home schooling family. If you want to be successful in your Catholic home schooling, attend Mass every day, and receive the Holy Eucharist, preferably with your children.

If you cannot attend Mass every day, then attend when you can. Start by going one extra day a week, perhaps on Friday.

On days when you cannot attend Mass, say the Mass prayers at home with your children. Ask Our Lord to come to you and your children in a Spiritual Communion. It is the teaching of the Church, based on Galatians 5:6, "Faith that worketh by charity," that those who greatly desire to receive Jesus in the Holy Eucharist do benefit and profit to some degree by the sacrament. The Council of Trent declared that the faithful can receive from a Spiritual Communion "if not the entire, at least very great benefits." On Eternal Word Television Network, when the Mass from the Monastery of the Angels is televised every day, Sister encourages the viewers to receive Jesus spiritually, and leads the viewers in a Spiritual Communion prayer.

We Catholic home schooling families are in the forefront of the spiritual battle to save souls, the Church, and the nation. We need Jesus with us every day in this battle against the spiritual forces of evil.

The graces from the Sacrament of the Holy Eucharist help us deal with the daily worries and frustrations of every family. Many of us have learned that it is not so much a big crisis that wears us down but the constant little aggravations. Many of us are called to be saints by dealing with small but constant daily problems.

Jesus wants us to show our love for Him by visiting Him and having Him come to us every day. Jesus did not establish the Sacrament of the Holy Eucharist only to have His friends ignore Him in this sacrament He has so lovingly given us. Coming to us in Holy Communion, Jesus shows His extreme love for us as He wants to be with us, as He wants to give Himself to us, and we should show Him our gratitude by receiving Him as often as possible.

The most important event that is happening in your town each day is the coming of the Son of God, Jesus Christ, in the Blessed Sacrament. How can we not be there? How can we not be there to receive the Son of God?

For those of us who are able to attend Mass every day, we need to pray for all our fellow home schooling families. As members of the Mystical Body of Christ, they can utilize our prayers and the resulting graces. This kind of charity on our part will obtain great favors from Jesus and Mary for our own home schooling.

With our society drowning in its own immorality, the command by Jesus to be a light and leaven in society takes on new meaning. We simply cannot survive and promote the Faith without the DAILY help of Jesus Christ Himself present within us. As Father John Hardon so often remarked, for Catholic families to survive, we need to make extraordinary efforts to live holy lives.

We must take our children to daily Mass, and teach them about the meaning of the Mass. The closer we bring our children to Jesus, and teach them about His death for our sake, the more they will love Him and obey

His commands, and obey our commands. With obedient and respectful children, we will have successful home schooling.

Home schooling burnout, much talked about at state home schooling conferences, results when children are difficult, either in the training of the will or the learning of the academics. It also occurs because mothers struggle to meet the many demands of home schooling, housework, cooking, and taking care of the needs of their husbands. But if the home schooling mother can develop her spiritual life by receiving Jesus daily, and the home schooling children can come to know and to love Jesus more by receiving Him in the Blessed Sacrament, burnout is much less likely to happen.

As we teach our children about the Sacrament of the Holy Eucharist, we need to relate it to their home schooling. We can better understand Jesus and the world which God created as we study our books and become educated. The more we know about God, the more we can love Him and serve Him properly. Once our children understand the relationship between learning from our Catholic books and learning about God, there should be fewer conflicts in the home schooling of our children.

The more we love Jesus, the more worthily we can receive Him in Holy Communion. As we receive Him more worthily, He will give us the graces to learn even more about Him, to love Him more deeply, and thus to do better in our schoolwork, in our chores, and in our relationship with the other members of the family.

It is a theological principle that the more we utilize the graces we receive, the more graces we will be given. So the more graces we receive from the daily reception of the Holy Eucharist, the more graces we will obtain to fulfill our teaching duties. The more graces our children receive, the more graces they will obtain to be good students and good children, thus ensuring successful home schooling.

Home schooling for the Catholic family is most successful because of reception of the Holy Eucharist by parents and children. In the Catholic home filled with Jesus daily, the atmosphere of love and spiritual growth will permeate both home schooling and the whole domestic environment.

Penance

The Sacrament of Penance is one of our biggest helps in living the Catholic life on a daily basis. Some people want to do only the minimum required by the Church, going to Confession once a year if one is in mortal sin. Some Catholics try to go to Confession at least once a month.

Many years ago, I decided to go to Confession every week during Lent. It changed my life. I discovered how many imperfections I had been overlooking. When you examine your conscience each night, and add them up each Saturday, you really have a pretty good list of careless faults. You begin to realize your unkind and unnecessary remarks, unkind thoughts, and moments of impatience, not to mention distractions during prayer. With only a monthly Confession, you tend to overlook the small faults. The bottom line is that we are all called to be saints, to be perfect, as Our Lord Himself commanded. If we want to be serious about trying to live the perfect life, we should seriously consider whether we are sufficiently examining our conscience and using the Sacrament of Penance frequently enough.

If we are really aiming to be the best possible Catholic family, a goal might be to try to go to Confession each week, all year long. Because of the paganism of our environment, we are likely to become desensitized to sin. Receiving the Sacrament of Penance every week will help us and our children to concentrate on strengthening our virtues and ultimately on improving our Catholic family life. As everyone in the family is working together to improve, as we discuss the imperfections with the children at bedtime, or in the car on the way to Confession, we help each other in a calm way to become saints.

St. Francis de Sales taught that if you are trying to rid yourself of a fault, you need to practice the opposite virtue, and in an extraordinary way. For instance, if your fault is that you tend to say unkind things about a person, then you should make a point first, not to say unkind things, but second, to say especially kind things even when it is not necessary.

In a way, home schooling is following the directive of St. Francis de Sales. When we know that what our children are learning in school is detrimental to their spiritual welfare, it is not sufficient to simply take them out of the sex education class. We need to do everything we possibly can to give our children the very best Catholic education. We know it is wrong to expose our children to anti-Catholic values five days a week. But it is a matter of heroic virtue to take on the total responsibility of teaching our children at home to be sure that they receive the very best Catholic education we can provide.

We need to relate our home schooling to the Sacrament of Penance. Our children need to understand first, that it is our duty as parents to teach them, and second, that it is their duty as children to obey us and learn more about obeying God. If the children do not obey us in their studies or in their daily chores, then they have committed a sin. When you help your children review their sins for Confession, help them see that refusing to do their work, complaining or whining while doing their work, doing their work in a sloppy or careless manner, not applying themselves, and daydreaming do not please God and are shirking of their responsibility.

As we proceed through each day, we should be reminding our children when they commit a sin to be sorry and to tell it in Confession. When a child hits a brother, we must remind him to be sorry and confess it. When a child is disobedient about doing a chore, we need to remind him to be sorry and to confess it. When a child refuses to do his math, we need to remind him to be sorry and to confess it. In the evening at prayer time, sins could be reviewed with each child, appropriate to his age, and there could be a discussion about how to avoid the same sin again. This should not be a constant nagging, but a spiritual uplift.

Some parents believe that while the child should be corrected at the time of the offense, a discussion about the religious implications should take place later when the child is not upset about the wrongdoing. Whenever the discussion seems suitable, spiritual writers have always encouraged a nightly examination of conscience and Act of Contrition. This is a good habit for all of us, adults and children.

Home schooling will be successful in a Catholic family pursuing the virtuous life through a daily examination of conscience and weekly or biweekly Confession.

Baptism

If you are having babies every other year, your children should be attending the rite of the Sacrament of Baptism fairly often. If not, be sure to take your children to the parish church when a Baptism is scheduled, and teach them about this essential sacrament. Explain the sacrament, going over the words of the rite:

> You have asked to have your child baptized. In doing so, you are accepting
> the responsibility of training him (her) in the practice of the Faith. It will be
> your duty to bring him (her) up to keep God's Commandments as Christ
> taught us, by loving God and our neighbor.

It is clear that home schooling is an acceptance in the deepest way
of the responsibility given to parents at the baptism of their children.

The priest in the Sacrament of Baptism prays that the parents and
godparents serve as good examples of faith for the child being baptized.
Explain to your children that the best way for parents to serve as good
examples is to spend time with their children. Home schooling is the best
method of education because it gives parents the most time to be good
examples to their children. A Baptism is an excellent occasion to review
the Catholic truths on Adam and Eve and on Original Sin, which is now
to be washed off the soul of the little brother or sister. Teach your children
about their godparents and their important role in your family.

After reading about the various times when God used water for the
benefit of His people, the priest continues the Rite of Baptism with the
Renunciation of Sin and Profession of Faith. The parents and godparents
are told:

> You must make it your *constant* care to bring him (her) up in the practice
> of the Faith. See that the divine life which God gives him (her) is kept safe
> from the poison of sin, to grow always stronger in his (her) heart.

It strikes me that constant care means home schooling. There is little
opportunity for constant care if a child leaves the house on a school bus
at 7:30 in the morning and returns at 4:00 o'clock in the afternoon, too
tired to discuss anything at all, least of all religion.

Certainly one has only to turn on the television or visit a school to
see the nearby "poison of sin." Notice that we parents are admonished not
only to keep our child away from sin, but, in agreement with St. Francis
de Sales, we are to do something positively good to make the practice of
the Faith as well as divine life "grow always stronger." This is the purpose
of Catholic home schooling.

After you have discussed all this with your children, the whole
family can participate in a special ceremony, either on a birthday, or on an
anniversary of a Baptism, or at a Baptism of a baby, or whenever it seems

appropriate, to have a renewal of Baptismal vows. Father could repeat the questions and the rest of the family could answer.

Do you reject Satan?
I do.
And all his works?
I do.
And all his empty promises?
I do.
Do you believe in God, the Father Almighty, Creator of Heaven and Earth?
I do.
Do you believe in Jesus Christ, His only Son, Our Lord, Who was born of the Virgin Mary, was crucified, died, and was buried, rose from the dead, and is now seated at the right hand of the Father?
I do.
Do you believe in the Holy Spirit, the holy Catholic Church, the communion of saints, the forgiveness of sins, the resurrection of the body, and life everlasting?
I do.

As you go over the words of the sacrament, explain how Baptism, Catholic family life, and home schooling are related. For instance, if we Catholics renounce the devil and enter God's family at Baptism, then we must avoid sin and perform virtuous acts as we grow up, and, as our catechism says, live according to the teachings of the Church. As our children see their admission into the Church family through the Sacrament of Baptism, they more clearly understand their role and obligation in regard to learning more about their Catholic Faith through home schooling.

Confirmation

In Confirmation, the baptized young person receives the Holy Spirit in a deeper way, is strengthened in grace, and "sealed" or marked as a soldier of Jesus Christ. Most children respond eagerly to the idea that they are made soldiers of Christ at Confirmation. Teach your children about St. Francis of Assisi, who thought he wanted to be a soldier of his city, but soon learned how to be a soldier of Christ. Teach your children about St. Ignatius of Loyola, who was a soldier until he was thirty years old and then put on the armor of poverty and humility. Teach your children about St. George, a young soldier who advanced in the army but who rebuked the emperor for persecuting the Christians, and then became a soldier of Christ.

Explain that Confirmation strengthens virtues that help youth become soldiers of Christ, such as courage, loyalty, moral strength, and strength against temptations. Use a catechism and explain how each virtue can help in their studies and how they can grow in each one through their studies.

Teach your children that while the seeds of the seven gifts of the Holy Spirit are infused at Baptism, they are made fully operative in the Sacrament of Confirmation with their cooperation. These gifts are wisdom, understanding, counsel, fortitude, knowledge, piety, and fear of the Lord. If these gifts are explained to your children each year, and how they relate to home schooling, the children will be more inclined toward home schooling.

Point out that home schooling is in some respects like boot camp, employing weapons both for the mind to learn about God and the will to love and obey God. My boys took this very seriously. One of my boys investigated the possibility of joining one of the orders of knighthood. He thought there should still be an order of knights to fight evil around the world, and was disappointed to discover that none still exists which actually does battle! In light of recent developments in Iraq and in other countries in that part of the world, maybe a Catholic home schooler needs to revive one of the orders of knights to give spiritual help to Christians suffering in the Middle East.

Another one of my sons became a Marine because of his concern to fight for Christian values and against atheistic Communism. He lobbied for the Afghan freedom fighters, and on his own, visited them on the front line of war in Afghanistan. He discussed with them the concept of hating the sin but loving the sinner, or at least praying for the sinner's conversion. They were sure he was crazy! Later, he served in Desert Storm, and took part in the ground assault and the battle for the airport in Kuwait City. While working on a doctorate in philosophy, he was a lobbyist for the Bosnians in Washington, D.C. He sees all these activities as part of being a soldier of Christ.

One of the favorite movies around my house is *Cyrano de Bergerac*. It is the story of a soldier who fights for honor, an actor and writer who defends virtue and traditional values, a man who sacrifices his own happiness for the happiness of the girl he loves and a friend he cares about. Cyrano is a Christian gentleman, whose white plume represents his desire to live the highest standards of the virtuous life. A movie like this is great for discussing Confirmation.

Take the children to see a Confirmation at your church. If the bishop gives the symbolic slap on the cheek, explain the symbolism as a reminder that we soldiers of Christ must expect to suffer for Christ as we fight for His truths. Most bishops are not giving this symbolic slap anymore, but you can certainly talk about it with your children. This can be related to any current pro-life efforts which you and your family may be undertaking, as well as to home schooling as a preparation for life as a soldier of Christ.

Marriage

Explain the Sacrament of Matrimony to your children. In accord with its primary purpose, marriage gives a couple two equal responsibilities: to have children and to educate their children. Explain to your children that if they are disobedient or do not do their home schooling, it is difficult for you to fulfill your marriage duty. Some of the papal documents on marriage, which faithfully expound on the responsibilities of teaching and training children, could be explained to the children.

Take the children to see a wedding at the parish church at a time when you can explain the ceremony. Impress on them the formality and seriousness of the sacrament. Let them understand the duty you have before God, from the Sacrament of Matrimony, to educate them: that you have made a solemn promise before God and the Church to be responsible for educating the children whom God gives you.

Extreme Unction, or Anointing of the Sick

Extreme Unction or Anointing of the Sick should be explained to your children for many reasons, but each year it should be related to the home schooling effort. This sacrament helps us to focus on eternity. This is a good time to discuss the shortness of life and this temporal abode. Emphasize that our ultimate aim is to be happy with Jesus in Heaven. Such a discussion can easily be led into home schooling and our emphasis on the eternal truths, versus the schools, whose usual and main emphasis is on this world and its measures of success.

Holy Orders

Home schooling gives children the opportunity to grow spiritually in the Faith without being pressured by teachers or fellow students to conform to current social values. More than one mother has told me that because of the home schooling, a very young son, still in primary grades, began to talk about becoming a priest. More than one parent has told me about a son who wants to learn Latin, or who practices saying the Mass, or who wants to dress like a priest. It is not unusual in a Catholic home schooling family for boys in elementary or junior high levels to avidly read biographies of saints.

Boys and girls can be taught the value of the priesthood and religious life. The best way is to read about and discuss the lives of the saints. Even while they are growing up, our children should be concerned about bringing the knowledge of Jesus Christ to others. Our home schooling way of life can help each family member to grow spiritually so that, whether or not a child enters religious life, he or she can still help others to come to know and love Jesus, and even convert them to the Catholic Faith.

Catholic home schooling families are to build up Christ in the domestic church and bring Him to society through their children. Therefore, we parents need to discuss the catechism and the Bible with our children to emphasize that only priests can offer the Mass and administer the wonderful gifts of the Sacrament of Penance and the Holy Eucharist.

As we highlight the value of service to others in the priesthood and religious life, our high school children should be encouraged to help at local rest homes for the aged and other similar places. Home schooling gives the flexibility for our children to choose these special, valuable, charitable works. We often hear from parents that they believe that home schooling was instrumental in helping their son or daughter choose the religious life.

There is no question that all seven sacraments should be meaningful in the lives of our children. As they understand the meaning of each of these sacraments, as they regularly attend Mass, receive Holy Communion daily or frequently, and go to Confession each week or every other week, such good families, struggling to be authentically Catholic, will not be disappointed in the abundant graces bestowed by God.

The Sacramentals

While the sacramental life means frequent reception of the sacraments, the sacramental life also means the daily use of sacramentals.

Sacramentals are a part of our authentically Catholic cultural heritage which have, unfortunately, fallen out of favor in the modern world. Yet sacramentals are an important supplement for the practice of our Catholic life and, in some cases, may be the only way for families to maintain the sacramental life during the week between Sunday Masses.

The Catechism of the Catholic Church says of sacramentals, "These are sacred signs which bear a resemblance to the sacraments. They signify effects, particularly of a spiritual nature, which are obtained through the intercession of the Church. By them men are disposed to receive the chief effect of the sacraments, and various occasions in life are rendered holy." (1667)

Sacramentals are signs reminding us of God, of the saints, and of Catholic truths. While sacraments were instituted by Jesus Christ as a direct means of obtaining sanctifying and sacramental graces, sacramentals were instituted by the Church to obtain graces for us indirectly. The chief benefits from the sacramentals are actual graces, the forgiveness of venial sins, the remission of temporal punishment, health of body and material blessings, and protection from evil spirits.

Catholic home schooling parents should begin using sacramentals with their children if they are not using them now. It is humbling to realize that God, standing behind the declarations of His Church, is willing to forgive venial sins and remit temporal punishment due to sin through the use of sacramentals. This is a fantastic gift which needs to be taught to our children and used by them for their own spiritual benefit.

The *Catechism* explains that the chief sacramentals are blessings by priests and bishops, exorcisms, and blessed objects of devotion. The most popular blessed objects of devotion are the rosary and the scapular. Other blessed objects are holy water, candles, ashes, palms, crucifixes, medals, relics, images or statues of Our Lord, the Blessed Mother, and the saints. A church building, benediction, novenas, and the Stations of the Cross are also considered sacramentals. The *Catechism* says, "There is scarcely any proper use of material things which cannot be thus directed toward the sanctification of men and the praise of God."

Take the time to read about these blessed objects in *The Catholic Encyclopedia* or other books. The history of the Rosary, the Blessed Mother's appearances, and the many miraculous events in history due to the Rosary are all fantastic teaching opportunities to impress on our children the value of an authentic Catholic sacramental life. *The Catholic Encyclopedia* lists all the various types of scapulars, with their many colors and associations with various religious orders, not to mention the miraculous events that have occurred as a result of people wearing scapulars. (A version of the Catholic encyclopedia is available online at www.newadvent.org/cathen.)

No one can guarantee that Catholic home schooled children will be perfect because they say a daily Rosary and wear a scapular. However, from my own experience and from what I hear from parents on the phone, children living the sacramental life are more likely to be good and obedient children. In fact, several parents have admitted to me that the spiritual growth of their young children has been a humbling experience. Some of us Catholic home schooling parents have come to a new understanding, though admittedly inadequate, of the spiritual life of very young saints, such as St. Therese, the Little Flower.

Sacramentals help us to create the domestic church in our home. We need to redecorate our home with sacramentals to make it a Catholic home. The Catholic Church has traditionally wanted families to surround themselves with reminders of the Faith. This goes back to the time when Moses spoke to the Jewish people about obeying the Ten Commandments. Moses said that God wanted signs of their faith on the doorposts, on the doors, on the entrances to the house. They were to wear signs on their foreheads and on their wrists. These physical signs, like our sacramentals, were to be not only a witness to belief in His truths, they also served as a moment-to-moment reminder that God belongs in our daily household activities and thoughts.

Living the authentic Catholic life means not only receiving the sacraments, but surrounding ourselves in our homes with sacramentals as reminders of our Faith, as continual opportunities to immerse ourselves in Jesus and His Blessed Mother, in His saints, and in His doctrinal and moral truths. St. Francis de Sales said that if one wishes to lead a devout life, things and events of our daily life should lead us to think about God and His attributes. If our surroundings encourage us, we and our children will more easily be led to such admirable thoughts.

An example

Let me briefly mention my own home as an example, since I am sometimes asked, of a home with religious articles. In the living room, I have used the fireplace mantle as our "altar" where I have two sculptured Stations of the Cross which were removed from a parish church that was being remodeled. Relics and holy pictures are there also, including a cross, the type to be used when someone needs to receive Extreme Unction or Anointing of the Sick. An original painting of the Blessed Mother, a large antique painting of St. Rita, and a three-paneled painting of Our Lady of Perpetual Help are on my living room walls.

Every room in my home has religious statues, pictures, and relics. Both my china cabinets are filled with religious statues, primarily of the Blessed Mother. The dining room table centerpiece is a statue of the Baby Jesus with an angel kneeling over Him. An angel sits over my stove, and a statue of the Sacred Heart near my kitchen sink.

My collection is the result of years of visiting garage sales, St. Vincent de Paul shops, parish church sales, religious goods stores, and every conceivable place to purchase religious items. My mother always had her home filled with religious statues, pictures, and relics. Now my sons bring me religious items. My son Paul brought religious statues from Spain. Friends and Seton families send religious gifts from around the country; these are placed around the Seton offices.

If our homes are not clearly identifiable as Catholic to anyone walking into the living room, we are not following the directives of God to His people. The Catholic environment of our home will help all the family members to be good and virtuous. On more than one occasion, I can remember saying, "Don't say that in front of the picture of the Blessed Mother. Do you want her to feel bad?"

Father John Hardon, who often spoke about Catholic family life, encouraged our families to have statues, pictures, and medals of the Blessed Mother in our homes. He also recommended that family members join the Association of the Miraculous Medal. The Miraculous Medal received its name because so many miracles have happened for those who wear the medal. The design of the medal was given by the Blessed Mother to St. Catherine Labouré in 1830 in France. The medal reads, "O Mary, conceived without sin, pray for us who have recourse to thee."

The Enthronement

Catholic home schooling families are rediscovering an old tradition: consecration of the family to the Sacred Heart through an enthronement ceremony. This is a family devotion and ceremony growing out of the promises of the Sacred Heart of Jesus to St. Margaret Mary. The purpose is to have the family recognize the reign of the Sacred Heart in their home, to be detached from worldly goods, and to try to imitate the virtues of the Holy Family. A picture or a statue of the Sacred Heart is to have a special place of honor. A priest usually comes to the home, and blesses the statue or picture as the Sacred Heart is officially enthroned as King of the family. The words of consecration and the ceremony are approved by the popes, who have granted a partial indulgence, with a plenary indulgence under the usual conditions of having been to Confession and Holy Communion and prayed for the intentions of the Holy Father (at least one Our Father and one Hail Mary) within several days, before or after the enthronement.

Usually the enthronement ceremony is done on the Feast of the Sacred Heart or of Christ the King, or on a First Friday, or on the occasion of a First Communion. It is usually done after a Mass at the parish church. While the act of consecration is the necessary part of the ceremony, families often say the Litany of the Sacred Heart and sing appropriate hymns. Some families invite relatives and friends, and have a little social gathering afterwards.

The liturgical year

Many sacramentals with appropriate prayers should be used in conjunction with the liturgical year. The liturgical year, starting with Advent, takes us through the history of mankind awaiting Jesus our Redeemer, and then through the life of Jesus Christ. This is a wonderful way for us to grow spiritually, but best of all, a joyful way to teach our children how to live and practice authentic Catholic family life through the year.

In our Seton lesson plans for art classes, we suggest many arts and crafts activities through the liturgical year which relate to the feast days. We especially encourage murals or mobiles or other arts and crafts projects which all the children can work on together.

Advent

Certain traditional Catholic practices can be started and maintained over the years to help us better understand and love our Catholic Faith. During Advent, the making of the Advent wreath is a very special event. It can be made one year, and simply added to or refreshed in the following years. Making these traditional items as a family, and then using them the following years brings back memories, and is a unique treasure for each family. You can start out with something simple, but as the years go by, add more purple velvet ribbons, and bunches of wheat and grapes, real or otherwise, to the wreath.

The nightly lighting of the candles on the wreath and saying the Advent prayers make the home seem more like the domestic church! If you miss Mass any of the days, you may want to recite the appropriate Mass prayers for the day. In addition, the Daughters of St. Paul sell Advent calendars which include daily Bible readings or illustrations. These little calendars, with doors which are to be opened each day of Advent, are especially exciting for the little children.

Many families start a Christmas Crib for Baby Jesus, which is empty at the beginning of Advent, but every day each member of the family adds a piece of straw, representing a very small secret sacrifice, a gift which the person makes in preparation for Christmas. By Christmas morning, the Crib is filled with straw and ready for the Baby Jesus.

Father Charles Fiore, now deceased, often spoke at Catholic home schooling conferences. He told us about a family who takes the statue of the Baby Jesus at the beginning of Advent and puts it at a distance, outside the house. Each day of Advent, the Baby Jesus is moved a little closer to the Christmas Crib by one of the children until, on Christmas morning, He reaches the Crib. These projects are hands-on learning experiences to help the children understand the real meaning of Advent and Christmas.

Shortly after Advent starts, the Feast of St. Nicholas is celebrated. In the Byzantine Rite, this feast is celebrated with a party for the children at the parish hall, with "St. Nicholas" giving out gifts to the children. In our domestic church, it needs to be a meaningful occasion, emphasizing the joy of giving of which St. Nicholas was such a good example. It can be a time for each member of the family to exchange a very small gift, or donate to the parish poor box.

Similar creative activities may be done for the Feast of the Immaculate Conception, and the Feast of Our Lady of Guadalupe. These feasts can be preceded by a novena, as well as by the Litany of the Blessed Virgin Mary. Eternal Word Television Network broadcasts the Mass on December 8 from the National Shrine of the Immaculate Conception.

Be sure to impress on your children the meaning of the Feast of the Immaculate Conception. The current popular reference to an unborn baby as a "fetus" may be "politically correct" terminology but should not be accepted by us. Our babies are people from the moment they are conceived. The use of the word "fetus" is an attempt to dehumanize our babies.

Visit shrines on the feast days. The *Catholic Almanac* lists the Catholic shrines by states. Find out which ones are near enough to visit, and take the whole family. If a shrine is not nearby, visit a parish church which is unfamiliar to the children. Teach your children about the Faith from the statues, pictures, and stained glass windows. Take a camera so you can remember your visit later and discuss the events depicted in the windows. A video camera would be great because it can adjust to the light coming through the stained glass. When you go on vacations or travel to other cities, visit shrines and historic churches.

As you celebrate liturgical feasts, precede them with a novena. A novena is nine days of prayer, usually specific prayers said in relation to a saint or feast day. Sometimes these can be found at shrine bookstores or in older prayer books, but they also can be original prayers. TAN publishes an inexpensive booklet called *30 Favorite Novenas*. This includes novenas to the Blessed Mother, St. Joseph, St. Michael, and St. Anne.

A novena in preparation for Christmas should be started on December 16. At the start of the nine days, you could put up a Jesse Tree, or a Christmas tree. On this tree, for nine days, the children can hang items to represent symbolically various Old Testament characters or events preceding the birth of Jesus. For instance, a fragment of an apple may represent Adam and Eve's original sin, which eventually led to the Incarnation. The slingshot of the boy David as he fought and killed Goliath and the burning bush which Moses saw are favorite themes for children to draw for the tree.

After Christmas

Other days which can be celebrated with religious activities or projects are the Twelve Days after Christmas, the Feasts of St. Stephen, of the Holy Family, of Good King Wenceslaus, of St. John the Evangelist, of the Holy Innocents, and of St. Elizabeth Ann Seton. While you want to celebrate the major liturgical feasts every year, some of the smaller feast days could be celebrated every few years.

There are some specific things the family can do in relation to each feast, but the family may celebrate all of them with the reading of the Biblical event or of the biography of the saint. The family can act out scenes from a saint's life, or write a play, or put on a puppet show. Asking a religious sister to dinner, or a priest to come for a special blessing adds to the reverence of the celebration. Include the Rosary, the use of holy water, singing or listening to some hymns, or watching a video of the saint's life.

Epiphany

The Feast of the Epiphany is a high holy day, especially in the Byzantine Rite. On the days from Christmas to the Epiphany, the Three Kings, plus their camels, slowly make the trip around the base of the Christmas tree, approaching the stable in which resides the Holy Family.

On the Feast of the Epiphany, some Catholic families exchange one small gift with another member of the family, to represent the gift giving of the Three Kings. Gifts could be given to a poor family with a new baby, or to the elderly at a nursing home. Other families celebrate by having the children dress like the Kings and act out the journey. Each year, as the family grows, the costumes become more elaborate.

This feast day would be an opportune time to discuss with your older children the reign of Christ the King, not only in our home but also in our country. Teach your children that just as the Three Kings bowed down to Christ the King, so the leaders of our country, and of all countries, need to bow down and obey the Laws of God. Explain to your children that unless laws are in conformity to God's Laws, they are not just, even if the majority of the people vote for them.

Feasts of February

If your parish church does not have a procession on February 2, the Feast of the Presentation of Our Lord in the Temple, have one in your domestic church. Candlemas Day, as this is often called, should include the blessing of candles, but you may obtain previously blessed candles. Read the Bible story of the Presentation. Try to obtain a meditation or reading on the Presentation from a book about the mysteries of the Rosary.

The Blessing of Throats with crossed blessed candles on the Feast of St. Blaise, February 3, is a beautiful sacramental for Catholics and non-Catholics in order to obtain good health and relief from sore throats or other throat problems and protection from evils. Mothers have traditionally considered this blessing important for their babies.

On February 11, the Feast of Our Lady of Lourdes, try to visit a Lourdes shrine, or write to a shrine and ask how they celebrate the feast day. Some of the prayers and activities could be re-enacted in your domestic church. By the way, many Marian shrines have replicas of the Lourdes shrine or of St. Bernadette, though it may not be advertised. Devotion to Our Lady of Lourdes was once very popular in this country. Encourage your children to read the biography of St. Bernadette and to see the movie. After Fatima, this was Our Blessed Mother's greatest and most miraculous appearance.

Ash Wednesday

Ash Wednesday is the first day of Lent. Everyone should attend Mass on Ash Wednesday. Explain the meaning of Father's words as he blesses foreheads with the ashes: "Remember, man, that thou art dust, and unto dust thou shalt return." Be sure to discuss the rules of fast and abstinence with your children. In our home, we have stressed the meaning of abstaining from meat on Fridays, but we also have abstained from meat on Wednesdays of Lent which is additionally recommended in the Byzantine Rite. In the Byzantine Rite, no meat or dairy products may be taken on the day of the Great Fast, the first Monday of Lent, or on Good Friday.

The Mass on Ash Wednesday sets the tone for Lent, and graphically illustrates the meaning of life and death. The family should discuss the lesson of Ash Wednesday and the Lenten sacrifices each member of the family intends to make. In addition to small daily sacrifices, we need to encourage our children in positive acts of prayer or generosity or instant obedience. I told my kids, "What's the point of giving up candy for Lent if you have arguments or tease a brother or say something unkind?"

Fasting has become unpopular in America, but the meaning and value of fasting needs to be taught to our children. Lent is a reminder of the forty days of the fast of Jesus in the desert. While Mother and Father may restrict their diet considerably, children should be encouraged to abstain from desserts or sweets.

Various references to fasts in the Bible could be explained several times during Lent. The Bible Concordance lists the words "fast," "fasts," and "fasting" 143 times! During Lent, Bible stories about events involving fasting should be discussed. It was fasting which caused Nineveh to be saved from the wrath of God, a lesson we in America need to remember. Do not let anyone tell you fasting is not an integral part of the practice of our Catholic Faith. Like the Bible itself, fasting will never be outdated!

Lent

During Lent, explain the sacrifices we need to make, why they are so important, and how we are joined with Christ and others in the Mystical Body of Christ to make reparation for sin. Read about how saints celebrated Lent. Read the fantastic words of Jesus to Sister Josefa in *The Way of Divine Love* (available from TAN), as He relates His thoughts during the events leading up to His Crucifixion.

Lent is a time when families could look into the Catholic customs of their ethnic culture. The Catholic cultural traditions, especially in the type of foods for Lent and for Easter, can become a cultural religious experience for the family, which can be handed on to future generations. We may develop a new appreciation for our Faith as we look into our own and other cultural Catholic traditions in our community.

In the past, all the statues, stations, and paintings in the churches were covered with purple cloth during Passion Week and Holy Week. This was a sign of penance. It was a time when feasting and enjoying beautiful things were put aside. In some families, this tradition is kept alive, not by totally covering the statues in the domestic church, but by placing purple ribbons at the foot of each statue or holy picture. Sometimes a purple shawl or cloth is hung over the top and down the sides of religious paintings.

Feasts of March

On March 17, try to attend a St. Patrick's Day parade with your children, or have your own parade with another home schooling family.

Help your children to make shamrocks, and relate the story of St. Patrick and his explanation of the Trinity. Be sure to discuss the tremendous sacrifices and efforts of St. Patrick to convert the Irish. Try to develop a sensitivity in your children for the Irish Catholics who have suffered so much from the English Protestant government. Your children may not only wear green, but hand out little holy cards to friends in the neighborhood or home schooling group, explaining who St. Patrick is. This is a form of witnessing or evangelizing to our society, such as what St. Patrick did himself.

St. Joseph's feast day, on March 19, could be celebrated over several days, with stories about him read each day. Since he is the special protector of the home and family, Catholic home schooling families will want to have an annual novena to him, including the Litany to St. Joseph. In these days of economic problems, St. Joseph needs to be called on to help Father in his job situation. Some home schooling families pray to St. Joseph every day, and keep a candle lighted for him in the parish church representing a daily reminder of our petitions to him. St. Joseph is considered the most powerful intercessor with Jesus next to the Blessed Virgin Mary.

On March 25, for the Feast of the Annunciation, help your children to collect famous paintings of this marvelous event. Look on the Internet for paintings and statues. Take photographs or video pictures of stained glass windows which depict the Annunciation in your area churches. Consider visiting a Marian shrine on this feast day, and praying the Litany of the Blessed Virgin Mary.

Stations of the Cross

Lent is the most appropriate time to teach your children about the meaning and ritual of the Stations of the Cross. Prayers have been composed by several saints for meditation on the Stations, the most popular being "The Way of the Cross" by St. Alphonsus Liguori and another by St. Francis of Assisi, who originated the devotion of the Stations. Both are available from TAN.

While the Stations of the Cross can be made all year long, consider making them a practice for your family every Friday in Lent. A plenary indulgence is given to anyone making the Stations the same day on which the Holy Eucharist is received. This is a wonderful way to obtain graces for the souls in Purgatory.

When said privately, the plenary indulgence is granted for saying the Stations only if the person making them actually walks around to each Station. A plenary indulgence can be gained at a public recitation of the Stations without walking to each Station as long as the leader moves from Station to Station. Remember that for any plenary indulgence, one must go to Confession within several days, before or after, plus pray for the Holy Father's intentions.

To make the Stations more varied for the children, use several different meditations. If you are in a hurry, simply walk around to each Station, genuflect, and say, "We adore Thee, O Christ, and we bless Thee, because by Thy holy Cross Thou hast redeemed the world." Teach your children the *Stabat Mater* hymn to be sung with the Stations: "At the cross her station keeping, stood the mournful Mother weeping, close to Jesus to the last," and all the following verses.

Since the Stations can be said at any time of day, you could take your children to the local Catholic church and say them every Friday afternoon. Some Catholic families make it a practice to visit a Marian shrine on First Fridays, and make the Stations there. When you visit shrines, see if you can obtain a plenary indulgence for visiting and praying there, as many popes have given such blessings.

If you cannot say the Stations at a church or shrine, consider purchasing pictures of the Stations and putting them up in a room where you and your family can say them. If you cannot find any pictures, you may be able to have the children draw pictures. Your children may color the illustrations of the Stations, and then you can use them for making the Stations.

Palm Sunday

On Palm Sunday, explain the meaning of palms and then put them around the house, on your family altar, and around holy pictures and statues. Some children like to make crosses out of the palms, often braiding them, in order to put them up on the wall. Remind your children that palms are a blessed sacramental. If your parish church does not have a procession, you may want to find a Byzantine church which does, or have one in your domestic church or with your local Catholic home schooling support group. Read to your children the Bible account of the triumphal entry of Jesus into Jerusalem.

Holy Week

Holy Week should be a time for serious reflection on the meaning of Christ's suffering and death. The week can be filled with both liturgical prayer and private prayer. Attend Mass each day if possible, as well as all the church services for the week. Teach your children the Lenten songs, such as "O Sacred Head Surrounded." For older children and parents, a book could be chosen to meditate on Jesus and His sufferings, such as *The Way of Divine Love, Revelations of St. Bridget,* or *The Sermons of St. Francis de Sales for Lent,* all available from TAN publishers.

During Holy Week, EWTN often features visits to the Holy Land or documentaries about the Crucifixion or the miraculous Shroud in which Jesus was buried. You can rent videos about the life of Christ or other appropriate movies.

Look for a parish which includes the traditional Holy Week ceremonies. The Byzantine Rite is very elaborate and inspiring. Holy Week ceremonies will be remembered for a lifetime by your children. Consider that, if in the future they cannot attend such ceremonies, they will be able to carry them on in somewhat the same fashion in their own homes.

On Holy Thursday, explain the meaning of the services before the children attend so they can understand how the services relate to the first Holy Week events. For Good Friday, try to go to a parish church which has the Stations and services in the afternoon. Not only are children too tired to appreciate the service in the evening, but since Jesus hung on the Cross in the afternoon, an afternoon service is more appropriate and accurate.

If your family is in the house, rather than in your parish church, after twelve noon on Good Friday, you may want to follow the tradition of keeping silence between noon and three o'clock. With young children, this may not be completely possible, but certainly some attempt at this is possible. Children should be encouraged to meditate or to say private prayers. Consider showing a video on the Stations of the Cross or on the Sorrowful Mysteries of the Rosary, and having the family pray along.

Church services usually start at 2 o'clock. Some families try to spend some time in church beforehand, or go to Confession later in the afternoon. The Church requires fasting on Good Friday (ages 21-59) and abstaining from meat (from age 14). In some families, almost no food is eaten by teenagers and adults. In the Byzantine Rite, "The Great Fast" means abstaining from meat and dairy products. Many continue the fast on Holy Saturday, until after the Easter Mass.

Holy Saturday

If the children decorate Easter eggs, teach them the various Catholic symbols, such as the symbol of the Paschal Lamb for Christ. These Catholic symbols can be taught to very young children to help them understand the proper meaning of Easter. In the Byzantine Rite, the parish churches usually have classes to teach adults and children how to make *pysanky*, which are eggs decorated with religious symbols and elaborate designs.

If your children attend the Holy Saturday or Easter Vigil services, they will come to love them, and to look forward to them each year as they grow up. The lighting of the candles in the darkened church gives vivid meaning to "The Light of the World." The ceremony of the lighting of the New Fire and the Easter candle should be read and explained to the children before attending church.

Some families attend the Easter Vigil services in order to be present at the Resurrection, but attend Mass again on Easter Sunday morning to celebrate the events surrounding the finding of the empty tomb as Mary Magdalen meets the angel and then Jesus, as St. John and St. Peter run to the tomb, and as the two disciples meet Jesus on the road to Emmaus. Both at the Easter Vigil and during the Mass on Easter morning, baptismal promises are renewed. Review their importance in your home schooling family.

In Byzantine Rite churches, parishioners bring homemade breads and baked goods to be blessed after the services. You and your children might make bread to be blessed. Holy Communion may be received both at the Easter Vigil Mass as well as on Easter morning. (In fact, one may receive Holy Communion twice a day, any day of the year, as long as Mass is attended both times.)

Easter

Make sure the excitement of the Resurrection is conveyed in your home. You might rent a DVD about the first Easter Sunday. Tell the story of Peter and John as they ran to the Tomb and later to the Upper Room. Read the different accounts of the Resurrection from the four Gospels.

The message of the Resurrection is the center of our Faith. As Christ's apostles today, we want to spread the message. Have your children write "He is Risen" on different colored sheets of construction paper, and tape them all over the doors of your domestic church. Greet each other with "He is Risen!" answered by "Indeed, He is Risen." Teach your children some of the Easter hymns, or listen to them on tapes.

In many Catholic cultures, a lamb cake is made for Easter dinner dessert. This is a beautiful cake shaped like a lamb, with white frosting and covered with coconut. You might want to buy one the first year to get an idea of how to make one the following year. Usually around Easter time you can buy the special lamb-shaped pans. Ask at bakery shops if you cannot find one.

During the forty days between Easter and Ascension, try to convey the happiness of the Apostles as the risen Lord appears again and again in His risen Body. This is an opportunity for the children to display their best artwork as they draw pictures of the glorified and risen Lord. Study arts and crafts books for methods and materials, but encourage your children to colorfully illustrate or represent the glorious event of the Resurrection.

During this time, discuss Our Lord's institution of the Sacrament of Penance. Notice how many times Our Lord says, "It is I. Do not be afraid." Present the Sacrament of Penance as a calm, loving sacrament. When I took my boys to Confession on Saturday, it was a happy occasion. We sometimes took their friends with us when we went, and sometimes had a treat on the way home.

Ascension

Ascension Thursday! What an event to celebrate! Jesus leaves us, rising on a cloud as the Apostles stand looking up. But we have the promise that He will return. How we look forward to that now!

Review the Apostles' Creed with your children, and explain "He ascended into Heaven, sits at the right hand of God the Father Almighty; from thence He shall come to judge the living and the dead." Read the Gospel story of the Ascension.

If you read some of the accounts of the Ascension by saints, Doctors of the Church, or Catholic writers, you might retell some of the surrounding events. Teach your children about the angels and the Blessed Mother, about the sorrow and regret of the Apostles as He was about to leave them, the gathering of the one hundred twenty persons to be witnesses, the many risen saints who must have accompanied Him, the joyful yet sorrowful singing that must have come from His Apostles. Retell the story of the procession walking up the mountainside of Mount Olivet, the message of Jesus to His Apostles, His prediction of the coming of the Holy Spirit, the likelihood that the risen saints ascended with Him, the questions of the two angels standing by and their assurance that He would return, and the Apostles being filled with joy and returning to Jerusalem, constantly speaking the praises of God.

Your Catholic home schooling support group could gather on Ascension Thursday and have a re-enactment of the Ascension procession, with prayers, a reading of the event, and the singing of hymns. Since there were several occasions when Jesus ate fish with His Apostles during the forty days before He ascended to Heaven, perhaps this event could be concluded with a picnic with tuna fish sandwiches or tuna salad. Remind your children about the symbol of the fish as a secret sign for Christians for many years to come. Perhaps children could draw or cut out fish designs at the Ascension picnic.

Pentecost

Between Ascension Thursday and Pentecost, your family could say a novena to the Holy Spirit. During this time, the catechism questions about the Holy Spirit could be reviewed, especially the virtues, the gifts, and the fruits of the Holy Spirit. During the novena, the family could pray for one gift of the Holy Spirit each day.

On the Feast of Pentecost, the readings from the Bible, as well as from meditations about the descent of the Holy Spirit, could be read as a family. Like the disciples, Apostles, and the Blessed Mother, the family could be gathered around the family table, waiting in expectation. The imagination of the children might be encouraged to imitate the thunder and the wind and bright light filling the house. Remind the children that this event is considered the Birthday of the Church, as well as the institution of the Sacrament of Confirmation.

Three thousand persons were baptized after St. Peter gave his sermon on Pentecost. Some of your children might want to represent different cultures by wearing a hat or other clothing to signify a nationality. After the readings, and perhaps a song or two, the family can celebrate with a

Holy Spirit cake, with white frosting and bright red tongues of fire. Place settings or coasters could be made by the children, each one shaped like a red-tongue of fire.

If there is a Holy Spirit parish in your area, check to see if any particular celebrations will be going on there for your family to attend. Also, if you receive Eternal Word Television Network, your family might watch the Mass for Pentecost Sunday from the National Shrine of the Immaculate Conception.

The month of May

The Feast of St. Joseph the Worker, on May 1, should have special meaning for our home schooling children as we emphasize the importance and joy of work in our lives. The feast could be preceded by a novena to St. Joseph. It is common tradition that we ask for our intentions carefully as St. Joseph is well-known for fulfilling requests. Besides their regular work, this would be a good day to have the children do some woodworking project around the house, such as fixing the wooden railings, or building that much-needed bookcase for the classroom, or perhaps repairing the wooden screen door. Discuss these carpentry projects and tell the children to ask St. Joseph to pray for them as they do their work, especially their school work. Special prayers to St. Joseph should be included for Father and his work.

During the month of May, the month to honor the Blessed Virgin Mary, a few churches still have May processions. Perhaps your local home schooling support group could persuade a pastor to have one. If not, have one in someone's yard for the Catholic home schoolers in your area.

Traditionally, the May procession is composed of children dressed in their Sunday best, processing toward a statue of the Blessed Mother while singing a Marian hymn. The procession is led by a young girl, usually dressed in white, carrying a crown of flowers to be placed on the statue. She is accompanied by two little girls, usually in white, carrying flowers. When the statue is reached, the Blessed Mother is crowned to the singing of

> Bring flowers of the fairest, bring flowers of the rarest,
> From gardens and woodlands and hillsides and dale.
> Our full hearts are swelling, our glad voices telling,
> The praise of the loveliest Rose of the Vale.
> O Mary we crown thee with blossoms today,

Queen of the Angels, Queen of the May.
O Mary we crown thee with blossoms today,
Queen of the Angels, Queen of the May.

After the May crowning, the Litany of the Blessed Mother may be said, followed by Benediction if possible. Two or three Marian songs may be sung during the program. Afterwards there can be a small social gathering.

June and July

On the Feasts of the Sacred Heart of Jesus and the Immaculate Heart of Mary, Father Robert Fox sponsors an annual Marian Congress in South Dakota, in special honor of the apparitions of Fatima. If your family cannot make that, then consider having a mini-Marian Congress with other home schooling families in your area. Have a speaker on the Blessed Mother, and a Rosary procession, followed by a social for the families.

There are some wonderful saints' feast days we celebrate in July which can lead to art and music projects, such as those of Blessed Junipero Serra, Blessed Kateri Tekakwitha, Our Lady of Mt. Carmel, St. Bridget, St. Maria Goretti, and Sts. Joachim and Anne. Use your creativity to help celebrate these feasts. Ask the children to read the lives of these saints and then ask them for creative ideas for the family to celebrate the feast day. Seton sells two books which might be helpful for activities in relation to saints' days and holy days: *Religious Customs in the Family* by Father Weiser, who writes about the feast day celebrations in his home as he was growing up; and *Saints and Feast Days*, which contains activities for children to celebrate the saints' feasts on every day of the year.

Starting the school year

As the school year starts, be sure to have a home schooling event in relation to a feast day. In Front Royal, Virginia, the home schoolers often start the year with a Dedication for School Children to the Infant of Prague in the parish church. It includes benediction, prayers, the sprinkling of holy water, and songs in Latin. The children decorate a little program book for each person which includes the prayers and a drawing of the crown of the Infant Jesus, decorated with sequins. After the ceremony, the families enjoy a party with an appropriately decorated cake.

Eternal Word Television Network

Eternal Word Television Network, the national Catholic television network, brings you events appropriate for the liturgical year and can help you and your family celebrate each feast day. EWTN is available on cable or by satellite. If you cannot access it by cable, you might want to buy a satellite dish.

Relevant Radio

Relevant Radio is a Catholic radio network which is based in Wisconsin, but has stations in fourteen states around the country. Besides being available on these stations, the programs are available over the Internet. Programming includes popular lecturer and family counselor Dr. Ray Guarendi. Since the programs are audio only, they are a great resource for moms and kids to listen to while working around the house. www.relevantradio.com

Conclusion

If your family life revolves around the annual feasts and seasons of the liturgical year, each member of the family should increase in prayer, in study of the Bible, in the knowledge and love of Jesus, Mary, and Joseph, and of the Church. Each member of the family can grow in understanding the importance of living the virtuous life. For more ideas about how to celebrate the various feast days, look for books which give you information about the saint or the event, and then try to devise creative ideas with the children. Be alert for saints who were taught at home (most of them were) and for saints who taught their children at home (most who were parents did).

The key to successful Catholic home schooling is living the sacramental life. Utilize some of these ideas in your home schooling family. Trust in Jesus and Mary to help you in your home schooling undertaking, in your home schooling apostolate. As Cardinal Edouard Gagnon, former head of the Pontifical Council for the Family, stated to me, home schooling is simply evangelizing at home, which is where evangelizing should start.

Chapter 7:
The Father's Role in Home Schooling

The following are reflections by Dr. Mark Lowery, a professor of Theology and a home schooling father.

Introduction

My wife, Madeleine, and I have seven children ranging from 12 years old to a few months old (as of 1993). When we moved to Texas in 1988, we began home schooling, having been disappointed in the parochial school where our eldest son, David, had attended kindergarten and first grade. We are presently home schooling our four oldest children: David in 7th grade, Daniel in 5th, Benjamin in 2nd, Elizabeth in 1st. We are now using our own curriculum, assembled over the last several years from a variety of sources, but we must credit Seton Home Study School for helping us get organized and bolstering our confidence when we first started. We had made a rather uneven start, and without Seton it probably would have been a disaster.

As a father, I have learned only gradually the things I wish to talk about in this chapter, and I am sure a wealth of insight still awaits my discovery. The most important thing for home schooling families—and the father therein—is to be patient. You will not "get it right" instantly; indeed, you will never have everything perfect. Be patient, and be open to new insights and suggestions, a few of which I will offer here. One important caveat, though: the fact that I have some suggestions, some of which may be helpful to you, does not mean that my family and I carry these out to perfection. Much of what I present here consists of ideals for which we strive, and only attain imperfectly. We have our fair share of blundering, frustration, and failure. Just as in living out our Catholic Faith, we all must be patient. "For us there is only the trying" (T. S. Eliot).

While we must be patient, we must be constant in our efforts because so much is at stake; the family is *the* essential bedrock of society. According to the fathers of the Second Vatican Council, in the document *The Church in the Modern World:*

> The family is a kind of school of deeper humanity. But if it is to achieve the full flowering of its life and its mission, it needs the kindly communion of minds and the joint deliberation of spouses, as well as the painstaking cooperation of parents in the education of their children. (#52)

The very next line of the document says, "The active presence of the father is highly beneficial to their formation." This chapter, as a reflection on that line, is organized around six key themes that should be of special interest to fathers: conversion to his family, attitude toward his spouse, discipline in the family, discipline in his home school, his practical contribution to the home school, and his role in teaching religion.

Conversion to the family

The most important skill needed for home schooling has nothing to do in particular with intelligence or teaching skills, the things that first come to mind when a father contemplates the task of home schooling. Rather, success at home schooling is integrally related with his understanding of what it means to be a father. While he of course *is* a father at the conception of the first child, he must work to *become* who he is—just as a person baptized into the Christian community must work to become a true Christian. In each case, he must work at being faithful to the new kind of life he now possesses.

Many people who were raised as Catholics experience, as adults, a kind of conversion to the Faith they already possess, a whole-hearted affirmation of the Church and the sacramental life. A similar conversion occurs for many fathers. They, of course, are committed to their family, but a part of their heart—often a significant part—lies elsewhere. Writer George Gilder has described how men have a natural impulse to be free and unfettered, a tendency to be "barbarians," and how they must sacrifice this impulse to hearth and home—to the values of the family.

This task is made especially difficult in our own society for a whole host of reasons. Pope John Paul II, in his encyclical on the Role of the Family in the Modern World *(Familiaris Consortio,* hereafter *FC),* devotes a special section to fathers, in which he says:

> Above all, where social and cultural conditioning so easily encourage a father to be less concerned with his family, or at any rate

less involved in the work of education, efforts must be made to restore socially the conviction that the place and task of the father in and for the family is of unique and irreplaceable importance. (*FC*, #25)

Fathers need to convert fully to the gift they possess; as Pope John Paul II says, "the man is called upon to live his gift and role as husband and father" (*FC*, #25).

I remember a precise moment at which such a conversion happened in my own life. We had two children at the time. I have always enjoyed bicycling, and had spent considerable time on various bicycling adventures. Now, I had installed a child carrier on my 10-speed and enjoyed taking my two children on short rides around town. But I would still go on longer rides by myself, and I distinctly recall on the morning of one such ride being irritated that I had a childseat attached to my bike which would take some minutes to remove. I decided to just leave it on, even though it would cause wind resistance. About half-way through my ride, it suddenly occurred to me that I was only half-way dedicated to my family. It was with a real reluctance that I had been making the necessary sacrifices mandated by family life. I was quite attached to the part of myself represented by a childseat-free ten speed!

Before this experience, I simply had not thought seriously about the *need* to shift my attitude. Just the awareness of it had a powerful impact on me and I must honestly say that I returned home that morning a new man—converted to what I already possessed. In the years that followed, I still enjoyed my own interests but I developed much more of a proclivity to sub-order them to my primary task of being a husband and father. This included not feeling sorry for myself when my commitment to the family precluded some interest of my own. And on the positive side, it included developing new interests directly related to the needs of my family. For instance, I developed a fascination for playground equipment, and it became somewhat of a hobby to visit every playground in the surrounding area, and then to return to the ones the children loved best.

What impact does this idea of "conversion to the family" have on education? The education of one's children is no longer just one more item in a long string of exhausting duties. Education is so essential a part of the child's life that, regardless of what kind of schooling is chosen by the parents, the father becomes integrally involved in the whole process. As Pope John Paul II says:

... a man is called upon to ensure the harmonious and united development of all the members of the family; he will perform this task by exercising generous responsibility for the life conceived under the heart of the mother, by a more solicitous commitment to education, a task he shares with his wife.... (*FC*, #25)

If parents have chosen a public or parochial school, it is essential for both parents—not just the mother—to be integrally involved with the educational process. Parents we know who get the most out of a school system are the ones who are constantly involved in the whole process, both at home and at the school. (And it often occurs to such parents that if they are already so involved in education, why not home school and reap the additional benefits?)

The breadwinner's attitude toward the mother

Fathers—even those really committed to their families—may easily suppose that it is the wife's task to be most involved in the educational process of the children. Of course, she is going to be more involved as regards amount of time spent. But, I submit, both father and mother must be equally involved in the task itself.

Consider this analogy. In pregnancy and childbirth, the mother obviously spends the greatest *quantity* of time. But the *qualitative* aspect of the project itself requires an equal donation of energy and commitment from both parents. So too with education. It must be a primary commitment for both, even though that commitment will be lived out in different ways that involve different quantities of time. The father should never have to say, "My wife does most of the work when it comes to the education of the children."

Indeed, it is extraordinarily easy for the husband to fall into the mistaken way of thinking in which he considers himself to have the really important and challenging work and his wife who stays at home to have the easier job— even if home schooling. Husbands need to reverse this way of thinking! Wives and mothers have the more important role, as well as the more difficult role. As George Gilder has put it:

The woman assumes charge of what may be described as the domestic values of the community—its moral, aesthetic, religious, nurturant, social, and sexual concerns. In these values consist the ultimate goals of human life—all those matters that we consider of such extreme importance that we do not ascribe financial worth to them. Paramount is the worth of the human individual life, enshrined in the home, and in the connection between woman and child. These values transcend the marketplace. (*Men and Marriage*, p. 168)

Likewise, Pope John Paul II writes, "The true advancement of women requires that clear recognition be given to the value of their maternal and family role, by comparison with all other public roles and all other professions," and speaks of the "original and irreplaceable meaning of work in the home and in rearing children" (*FC*, #23). Add to this the task of being the primary moderator of the home school! In a word, a crucial contribution to the home school on the part of the father is his attitude toward his wife. Needless to say, children pick up very quickly on the quality of relationship between their two parents and are profoundly influenced by it.

Discipline in the family

Just as it is easy for the father to relegate much of the "schoolwork" to his spouse, so too with discipline. The old caricature of the heavy-handed and much-feared father had its obvious problems, but today I see all too many fathers, including very sincere and dedicated fathers, taking too laid-back an approach to discipline. This is dangerous enough in the family where children attend school outside the home, and it becomes all the more dangerous in a home schooled family. I have worked in various classroom settings for many years and have become somewhat of a fanatic about a well-ordered, disciplined classroom. It makes for a happier and more effective teacher, and it is what children really do want even though they appear to want just the opposite. That appearance is deceptive—they are begging for order. One of my main frustrations with various schools we tried was the kind (or better, the lack) of discipline used. All too often the classroom was inundated by unruly children, who then commanded most of the teacher's energy. Even an exceptionally competent and ordered teacher will soon become frustrated because classroom discipline problems are so deeply rooted in the uneven discipline of home life.

Hence, in the home school, as well as in the home in general, humane but solid discipline is essential. During the day, the mother will be disciplinarian from a quantitative point of view, but the father, once again, must be thoroughly involved in the unending, demanding, but very rewarding project of raising well-mannered children.

Perhaps the most important aspect of a good system of discipline is knowing what to expect from a child. Generally, the expectations of parents today are far too low (though ironically the expectations in terms of achievement, at ever earlier ages, are often far too high). Children are *capable* of being well-mannered. One ought never to look upon his children misbehaving in church, in a restaurant, or at the shopping center, and say, "They're just kids."

The child's capacity to be well-mannered is analogous to a key feature in the Catholic moral life. As an abiding result of the Fall, we all have a tendency to misuse our freedom (to sin), because of concupiscence and irascibility. But we have a capacity to resist this tendency. As moral theologian William May has put it, "We can do as we ought." Similarly, children have a capacity to resist the tendency to be unruly. In both cases, we are happier when we rise above our lower appetites. And interestingly, these two areas of our lives—manners and morals—affect and mutually condition one another. Of course, there can be well-mannered thieves just as there can be (perhaps) ill-mannered saints, but in general a well-mannered person has conquered the lower appetites and developed good habits, and hence is well-practiced when it comes to doing the same in a moral situation.

One particular method I have found quite effective—and an easy entrance into this area for fathers—is to develop very concrete and clearly written out sets of standards for various situations. For example, some standards one might put forth for one's children while attending Mass are: stand straight; do not fidget; fold your hands when kneeling—and the like. The father should remind the children of these standards on the way to church, and let the children know precisely the consequences of breaking the standards. I call this the "method of pre-emption." It anticipates problems in advance, which goes a long way toward avoiding them in the first place. Most parents work the other way around. They are not consistently clear about the standards to which they wish to hold their children, and then throw somewhat of a tantrum of their own when they see their children following their natural tendencies!

Other situations for which concrete standards can be developed are shopping, eating, and, of course, home schooling. One of the reasons I wish to stress these other areas, however, is that home schoolers need to portray themselves very attractively in public (and with extended family). A home schooling family must go the extra mile to demonstrate to skeptics that they really "have their act together"—which might make skeptics wonder whether home schooling might not be so bad after all. So fathers, take charge! Make your family the kind to which others will be attracted and will wish to emulate.

Perhaps the greatest threat to a good system of discipline is a noxious idea that has run rampant in our culture: that self-esteem is the most important goal to strive for in raising children. This is a rather deadly idea because it gets right in the way of discipline. When you must be firm with children, you simply do not feel as though you are helping their self-esteem, and so you will draw back (and be quite ineffective). Self-esteem is obviously an absolutely crucial component of a healthy human being, but here is the catch: it is not an end in itself. If you try hard to help someone (or to help yourself) have self-esteem, you will probably fail. Self-esteem is an *end-product*, something that comes about as a result of having done other things—like discipline—well. It is very much like happiness. Most people who try hard to be happy fail. Happiness comes about as the *result* of a well-lived life. It cannot be pursued in and of itself. Rather, if you lead an ordered life, you will simply find yourself to be happy. Likewise, if children are properly raised, which especially means being challenged to live up to good objective standards of conduct, they will simply find themselves to have high self-esteem. Another catch: they often will not tell you how happy they are!

Discipline in the home school

If the father is away most of the school day, how can he possibly play a major role in building a well-ordered home school? Again, although he is not present quantitatively, he can be qualitatively. The children need to know that Dad is behind Mom. Some possible methods: Have a list of very clear rules for the home school. The father can read these at the beginning of the day if possible, or the evening before the school day. I myself have found it helpful to call home at mid-day, when possible, and talk briefly with each home schooler. If discipline problems have arisen, they can at least be discussed on the phone. This method is a great preventative—the home schooler knows Dad will call, or can be called.

Each family, of course, has to work out its own system of consequences for misbehavior. There is a lot of trial and error involved. The important thing is not having a perfect system, but rather that a consistent program exists and is in a constant state of upgrading. Part of the constant upgrading in our family is the "family council meeting," held every Saturday after breakfast. This is a time when all the older children along with Mom and Dad can vent their complaints and problems (regarding the home school as well as any other facet of family life). Such a meeting serves the purpose of a "mini-retreat" where everyone can stand back and look at difficulties a bit more objectively. It is most helpful for children to know that they can voice a complaint, and that the complaint can be intelligently discussed (outside the context within which the complaint arose). When complaints arise during the week, we have our children write them out and put them in a special jar for the upcoming family council meeting.

The actual task of home schooling

Throughout the years that we have home schooled our children, I have discovered that I thoroughly enjoy teaching my own children. In teaching, you become "grafted" into your children's lives in a special way. Being integrally involved with one's children is immensely enriching, for a reason that Pope John Paul II hit upon perfectly:

> Concern for the child, even before birth, from the first moment of conception and then throughout the years of infancy and youth, is the primary and fundamental test of the relationship between one human being and another. (*FC*, #26)

As parents work to "pass" this test, they are rewarded in turn, for the children "offer their own precious contribution to building up the family community and even to the sanctification of their parents" (*FC*, #26).

The father should not just "help out" with the teaching work of the mother; he should have several subjects that are his own, that he teaches to the children. What subjects ought he to choose? The usual reply is, whatever subjects he is especially competent in. Certainly that is a good criterion, but I think that, especially in grade school, the criteria can be much broader, and can extend to whatever subjects he is *interested* in. One of my friends tells the story of being hired to teach English in a high school. When the freshman physics teacher was on extended sick leave, he was asked if he would fill in. He knew little about physics, but was interested in the subject. He did a fine job, keeping just ahead of the students. College students will report that some of their best classes are from new professors who have a great deal of energy and enthusiasm even though, being just out of school, they feel barely competent. So as long as you are motivated and willing to think, you will do fine and will enjoy expanding your own horizons alongside those of your children.

How can a father fit several subjects into an already crowded day? For one, you can give assignments for each day (write them out in an assignment book for the students to check off), but only do formal work with the children every other day. I have been able to arrange my schedule so as to spend several hours at home two mornings a week. When this is not possible, I reserve evening or weekend time. I use this special time to work on areas that require intensive one-on-one instruction.

Other areas require less intensive work. All sorts of techniques can be used to allow for quick daily accountability. For science, we recently had the two oldest boys read chapters from a book of fascinating facts (*The Big Book of Amazing Knowledge*, Creative Child Press) and report on their findings at dinner each night. With mathematics, they do their daily assignment on their own each day, getting help from Mom if necessary, and usually I quickly correct their work soon after coming home. When they were mastering the catechism, I had them greet me upon my return home each evening with the answer to the assigned question for the day— they would beam with pride, and my own homecoming was combined with an enjoyable method of accountability.

I have often been asked whether the task of being both a father and a teacher to my children causes conflict. I think it is far more difficult for a mother to keep her roles as mother and teacher distinct, and this makes it all the more important for the father to be closely involved in the actual task of home schooling. I have found it relatively easy to keep the roles distinct, partly because I outrightly tell the children that they must view me and treat me as a teacher during school time.

One of the best parts of home schooling is that you yourself learn a lot. This is a real blessing because it feeds your enthusiasm, thereby making it easier for the student as well. Permit me to wax enthusiastic about my own involvement for a moment. I have (gradually) taken on five subjects in our home school. While teaching music, I have mastered parts of music theory I never had understood before. I have been motivated to improve my own technical skills. I have learned those obscure third and fourth verses of various songs we are learning as a family. While teaching Latin, I have mastered various paradigms—especially for irregular verbs—that I had never quite mastered before. I have not learned much new in mathematics yet—though I'm sure that will come—but I have greatly enjoyed trying to explain aspects like fractions or the decimal system. It is especially fun to find aspects of practical life for the children to practice with. My son Daniel and I are fanatics over the game Yahtzee; having kept track of our scores, we average them monthly and graph our averages. And what could be better than teaching math vis-a-vis baseball statistics! Physical education—for this, my role as father and teacher merge completely! We have a special "sports banquet" every year where the students are rewarded for their accomplishments with a prize of some sort. And finally, I teach religion, a topic to which I wish to give special attention.

The father's role in teaching religion

Religion is my most difficult subject, which is ironic because I teach religion and theology as a profession. But my own difficulties aside, I think it is essential for the father to teach, or at least co-teach, this topic. Due to the inherent differences between male and female, women have a more natural proclivity to enter into an attitude of worship before God. Men have to surrender a hefty portion of their ego to do so—and this is no easy task. But it is absolutely crucial that the children see their father doing this. They must see their father pray and they must hear their father speak and teach with pride about that noblest possession of the Catholic home school—the One, Holy, Catholic, and Apostolic Faith. As Pope John Paul II says:

> The concrete example and living witness of parents is fundamental and irreplaceable in educating their children to pray. Only by praying together with their children can a father and mother—exercising their royal priesthood—penetrate the innermost depths of their children's hearts and leave an impression that the future events in their lives will not be able to efface. (*FC*, #60)

The pope then quotes Pope Paul VI's appeal to mothers, and then to fathers:

And you, fathers, do you pray with your children, with the whole domestic community, at least sometimes? Your example of honesty in thought and action, joined to some common prayer, is a lesson for life, an act of worship of singular value. In this way you bring peace to your homes: *Pax huic domui* [Peace be to this house]. Remember, it is thus that you build up the Church. (*FC*, #60)

(In this last sentence, we find a cardinal tenet of Catholic social thought: that the proper role of the laity is to build up the Church, not chiefly by doing "churchly" things in the parish, though in this regard the donations of those who have time are of inestimable value; rather, their role is to bring transcendent truths to bear in the home and in society at large.)

When children see their father taking his religion seriously, they learn that religion is not in "the woman's sphere"—it is in the sphere of all who acknowledge themselves to be *creatures* rather than their own gods. They learn that freedom is not "doing your own thing," being autonomous, but rather a gracious surrender to a higher truth. We are most free when we are bound to the truth.

On the practical side, as regards religion, I would suggest combining the catechism, the Bible, and good biographies of the saints. When my children learned the catechism, they memorized one or two questions per day. As noted above, they would greet me when I came home with the answer to their assigned question—a most successful technique. And an added bonus: the answers to the catechism are in finely crafted sentences, the memorization of which facilitates the child's knowledge of grammar and composition as well as of the Faith.

In the context of teaching religion, it is important to note the father's irreplaceable role in educating toward chastity. Pope John Paul II connects this role to one of the principles of Catholic social thought, the principle of subsidiarity, which, among other things, asks that tasks which belong to a particular rung of the societal ladder, such as at the family level, ought not be taken over by higher levels, such as the State. Rather, the higher levels should serve the family and give them help (*subsidium*) in carrying out their appointed task.

Sex education, which is a basic right and duty of parents, must always be carried out under their attentive guidance, whether at home or in educational centers chosen and controlled by them. In this regard, the Church reaffirms the law of subsidiarity, which the school is bound to observe when it cooperates in sex education, by entering into the same spirit that animates the parents. (*FC, #37*)

This quote all by itself is a fine argument for the home school! The pope goes on to note the central role of chastity in such formation:

> In this context *education for chastity* is absolutely essential, for it is a virtue that develops a person's authentic maturity and makes him or her capable of respecting and fostering the "nuptial meaning" of the body. Indeed, Christian parents, discerning the signs of God's call, will devote special attention and care to education in virginity or celibacy as the supreme form of that self-giving that constitutes the very meaning of human sexuality. (*FC, #37*, emphasis added)

What practical steps can the father take in his children's education to chastity? First, be a real man and "toss" the TV. Do this literally if you can, but if you are like me, at least put it on wheels and keep it in the closet most of the time (baseball is better on radio anyway). If there were only one thing you were allowed to do for your family, this would be the optimal choice. It will educate to chastity and to many other virtues as well.

More directly, talk to your children about the virtues, and keep chastity and purity in the front line. When teaching the Sixth Commandment, explain its meaning *for them*, namely, that God wants them to respect their bodies and to respect their sexual organs in a special way. You must be very concrete with your sons as they grow toward and through puberty. Define purity in clear terms. Talk about how to refrain from playing with themselves, with a language that is humane and that will not produce excessive guilt should they fail. Ask them at regular intervals, "How are you doing with purity?" Do not get mad at them if they are struggling with it, but encourage them, letting them know that God will be patient with them but also that God wants them to master their desires. No doubt this is a challenging task—but keep the lines of communication open. They will know that you are there, willing to answer big questions when they arise. In all of this, you will find yourself strengthened in chastity as well. Stress to your children (and to yourself) that being chaste is a truly heroic activity.

When your children become adolescents and start paying attention to members of the opposite sex, some have suggested that, after appropriate discussion, you give your sons (Mom can work with your daughters) a special ring—a ring of purity—as a sign or reminder that they have pledged to God that they will remain chaste.

Conclusion

I hope you have taken my suggestions just as that—mere suggestions. As long as you completely embrace the one *non*-negotiable central idea— being integrally involved—the rest will flow from there as you develop your own distinctive methods. Fathers, as heads of your families, you are performing the most important of all tasks in your life. For as the Holy Father tells us, "The future of humanity passes by way of the family" (*FC*, #86). And you may be sure that God will give you all the grace and strength necessary to carry through.

End of Dr. Lowery's work.

What mothers think

A friend of mine, a home schooling father who gave a talk for our Home Educators Association of Virginia some years ago, took a survey of the home schooling mothers in his very large northern Virginia home schooling support group. His question in the survey was "What do home schooling mothers see as the role of their husbands in the home schooling family?"

The number one overwhelming answer by home schooling mothers was that the husband be committed to home schooling and be supportive of it by giving encouragement—encouragement to their wives and encouragement to their children. It surprised everyone—including the home schooling fathers—to discover that the wives were asking for a supportive attitude and encouragement rather than asking them to take over some of the teaching.

Mothers made statements about the importance of fathers being patient when they get home in the evening, showing interest in the children's work, praising the home schooling commitment, and believing that it is God's Will that the family home school.

The second point most often mentioned by home schooling mothers was that the fathers be willing to accept a different kind of lifestyle. Mothers simply cannot keep up the housework and the cooking as they did before home schooling, especially if the children are still too young to help out.

Third, fathers need to understand that home schooling is difficult for mothers. It takes a great deal of time and energy, especially if the mother is home schooling a strong-willed child or a child with a learning problem. Mothers would like their husbands to attend local support group meetings once in a while to hear others talk about their home schooling situations.

Fourth, mothers surveyed said that fathers should have a high vision for their children. Fathers need to believe in their children and in their ability to do their best. Children need to feel the support and encouragement from their fathers to do their best. Fathers should praise the children's success and minimize their failures.

Fifth, mothers would like fathers to be available by phone during the day so that on occasion, when a child needs some verbal disciplining, Father is ready and available to do it. It is usually not the length of the call that is important, but for children to know that Father is concerned that children do their work and that he is only a phone call away from keeping informed about what is going on at home.

Some mothers have told me that being able to call their husbands when there is a discipline problem has kept the problems to a minimum. Steve Wood, a Catholic home schooling father of seven children, who gives talks on discipline, says that when the school year starts, if he gets a "discipline" call from his wife while at work, he goes home to administer the discipline. This sets the tone for the school year, and the children know their dad is serious about obedience to their mother.

Fathers must realize that home schooling mothers have some additional needs for the home. For instance, fathers should provide a room to be used for study purposes. It helps mothers to keep order and discipline to have a special place for home schooling, especially as the school materials increase over the years.

Fathers as well as mothers need to talk with the children about why the family is home schooling and to show support for the purpose. They should discuss the fact that home schooling is the family's way of living out the kind of Christian life that Jesus wants.

Fathers should be concerned about the proper socialization of the junior high and high school children, especially for the boys. They need to take time with their children, take them to controlled activities, or be involved with them in church activities.

In this survey, the majority of mothers did not ask for fathers to teach any subject. With the father's support, these mothers feel they can handle the teaching themselves.

Discipline

We have another chapter on discipline, but when the focus is on the father's role, disciplining the children always comes into the picture. It is natural that the father should discipline the children since he is the head of the family.

Steve Wood, mentioned above, has been an active leader in the pro-life movement. The more he became involved in pro-life action, the more he realized that even good people did not want to have more children because they could not discipline those they already had. Mr. Wood believes that if we hope to "sell" people on the idea of having as many children as God wants to send them, and to stop practicing contraception, then we need to help these parents solve the problems they have with their present children. And the biggest problem is discipline.

He believes the same is true about home schooling. Problems with disciplining children is one of the most common reasons why parents either do not home school or cease to home school.

The Book of Proverbs is a wonderful guide for parents to study, especially for fathers. It is a God-given guide for the training and disciplining of children. In fact, many of the verses refer to a son taking instruction from his father.

> "A wise son heareth the doctrine of his father." 13:1
> "He that spareth the rod hateth his son; but he that loveth him corrects him betimes." 13:24
> "A fool laughs at the instruction of his father; but he that regardeth reproofs shall become prudent." 15:5
> "A foolish son is the grief of his father." 19:13
> "Folly is bound up in the heart of a child, and the rod of correction shall drive it away." 22:15

St. Paul reminds the Hebrews in chapter 12 about the commands in Proverbs. He says that God, like all good fathers who love their children, disciplines us, His children. If children are without chastisement, then they are not treated as true sons, but as illegitimate children. St. Paul says that the "fathers of our flesh" are our instructors, "and we reverenced them."

In Ephesians, chapter 6, verses 1 to 4, St. Paul instructs fathers and sons:

> Children, obey your parents in the Lord, for this is just. Honor thy father and thy mother, which is the first commandment with a promise: That it may be well with thee, and thou mayest be long lived upon earth. And you, fathers, provoke not your children to anger, but bring them up in the discipline and correction of the Lord.

Some years ago, the Home Educators Association of Virginia convention focused on the role of the father in the home schooling family. They took as the theme Malachi 4:6: "And he shall turn the hearts of the fathers to the children, and the hearts of the children to their fathers." We truly believe that as fathers become more involved with their children, they will come to know them better and to love them more, and the children will respond in kind. And the children will be motivated to do well in their schoolwork.

One of the points that Steve Wood makes in the training and disciplining of children is the vital necessity for fathers to spend time with them. Children are made in the image and likeness of their fathers, just as we are made in the image and likeness of God. Children tend to imitate their fathers. If fathers give good examples of living the authentic Catholic family lifestyle, children will not be the discipline problems that so many are today. Most children today take their "instructions" from their peers, not their parents, because they spend so much time with their peers, and not with their families. One of Steve Wood's favorite comments is "Love is spelled T-I-M-E."

Additional helps

While the father's role is clear in many areas, nevertheless, we need to discuss some other ways fathers can be of help in the home schooling family. Fathers can help in the area of housekeeping. Mothers do the vast majority of the housework; nevertheless, we encourage fathers to help whenever possible. While children usually help their mother, it is certainly a good example for children to see that housework is not just "women's work," but that good housekeeping is in the best interest of the whole family.

Daily school reports

Many home schooling mothers believe in the importance of Father asking for daily school reports from Mother and the children. This is the best technique for keeping the children on track and focused on their daily work, because they know they will be reporting to Dad when he comes home.

In addition, Dad needs to ask for a daily report about the chores. Mother needs her children to help with the housework, but they often will not do so unless they know that Dad has a serious interest in their performance, and will inflict due punishment on the unwilling if necessary.

Fathers could work with the children to arrange a chore schedule just like a job supervisor would, as he could explain. The children will better understand the importance of work and being part of the household team when Dad is in charge.

Building projects

The physical needs of the home school are Dad's domain. Money is needed for books and supplemental materials. Additional bookshelves are required on a regular basis. Fathers, in conjunction with children, should plan on building new shelves as Mother adds to the family library. Dad should keep aware of sales of used books, computers, and other equipment. This will be of great help to Mom, who spends her days teaching.

It should be Dad's responsibility to help develop a classroom or space for home schooling—sometimes a recreation room or a garage or study, or a room in the basement. This can be an all-family project sometimes, but Father needs to provide the supervision. And the money!

Teaching

Teaching is usually the toughest part for most fathers to adjust to doing, but it is truly the most wonderful experience. We especially encourage fathers to teach math to their high school sons. Even if a class is only fifteen minutes each day or every other day, just to teach new concepts, it gives the children time with Dad. Children come to understand how smart Dad is! They develop a real respect for Dad as an authority in certain academic areas, or in all areas, as the case may be.

Fathers should consider teaching science, or at least helping the children in weekly science projects, perhaps on Saturday or Sunday afternoons. Trips could be taken to museums or local conservation parks or special exhibits. A father could become an authority on educational resource opportunities, such as historical statues or underground caverns or old Catholic churches in the state.

In most families, since fathers are away from the home during the day, no one expects them to be greatly involved with the day-to-day teaching. But this is the fault of our society. Fathers should be involved on a daily basis with the teaching. We encourage families to consider, if possible, changing their lifestyle so that Father can be home more often to spend more time with the family. No matter what career Father has, it eventually will come to an end. However, raising children has eternal consequences, and ultimately fathers understand, often too late, that this is their primary job in life.

Home schooling has been causing fathers to place more value on spending time with their family. Many fathers are looking for jobs closer to home, or for homes which are less expensive. Some families are trying to find jobs for Father, or for both Father and Mother, which can be done at home. In addition, cottage industries are popular among home schooling families, in which the whole family, including the children, develops a family business. Like the Holy Family, parents and children can learn together, work together, and pray together.

And play together.
And sacrifice together.
And grow together.
And love together.

Babysitting

Some fathers do not like babysitting, but it really helps the overworked home schooling mother to have perhaps an evening free to do something with her friends. Some mothers may not need it, but other mothers would certainly appreciate it.

Learning about home schooling

The American home schooling movement is a gentle and growing revolution, impacting both American family life and education. The reasons for home schooling, the teachings of the Church, Biblical passages relating to education and parents, the many ideas about individualized learning and how children learn, stimulating ideas in relation to developments in religion, history, science—all these things offer intriguing topics for reading, learning, studying, and discussing. Fathers should be challenged to learn more about home schooling and to become involved in this movement which is in the forefront of the educational revolution in this country.

The home schooling movement, as it grows and expands, as it matures among Catholics, is going to offer interesting and professional work, intellectually stimulating work, for home schooling fathers.

As Catholic home schooling support groups grow, as regional and statewide groups develop, as lobbying efforts progress, there is going to be room, even a need, for home schooling fathers to be involved.

St. Joseph

No discussion of the role of the father in the home schooling family would be complete without mention of St. Joseph. After all, Jesus was at home for thirty years before He entered public life, meaning that His relationship with Mary and Joseph was certainly continual and close.

Jesus made the statement in John 5:19-20 that

> the Son cannot do anything of himself, but what he seeth the Father doing; for what things soever he doth, these the Son also doth in like manner. For the Father loveth the Son, and sheweth him all things which himself doth.

Jesus is clear that because God the Father loves God the Son, God the Father shows Him all things which He does, and then God the Son does them also, imitating His Father.

Since that is true, it would seem logical that St. Joseph gave Jesus a good example, showing Him all the good things he did, and in regard to human things, Jesus imitated St. Joseph.

Though Jesus is the Second Person of the Blessed Trinity, nevertheless, God wanted to emphasize the importance of Joseph as head of the Holy Family. God sent an angel to Joseph in a dream to tell him that "that which is conceived in her is of the Holy Ghost." God sent an angel to Joseph to tell him to "fly into Egypt" to protect Jesus from Herod's soldiers. It was Joseph to whom the angel appeared to tell him to return the family to Nazareth. It would seem that God the Father was careful that the head of the Holy Family was being notified from Heaven, instead of Jesus giving His foster-father instructions. This demonstrates the profound respect which God wants wives and children to have for the head of the family.

St. Joseph, as head of the family, was responsible for taking Jesus and Mary to Jerusalem for Jewish feast days. Thus the importance of fathers being responsible for leading the family to religious services is clearly evident.

At the finding in the Temple, when Jesus answered, "Did you not know I must be about My Father's business," it would seem He might be starting His public life. But, on the contrary, He voluntarily, immediately, and completely subjected Himself to the authority of Joseph and Mary for the next eighteen years.

The very fact that Jesus subjected Himself to Mary and Joseph, though He certainly was not required to, showed He wants us, parents and children, to respect the authority of parents over children. More than that, He was declaring to all of us the importance of obedience on the part of children and the importance of authority on the part of parents. It is a strong message, delivered in an extraordinary way. God subjects Himself to the authority of human parents. And He does it for a long time—thirty years, as if to doubly emphasize the importance of obedience of children to the authority of parents. Jesus is really teaching us that a father's authority in the family is of supreme importance, of supreme value, and of supreme dignity.

The Holy Family in Nazareth can teach us another lesson, that while fathers need to provide good example, religious education, and honest work, fathers should not worry about providing more than is necessary.

We can be sure that St. Joseph led the family in prayer as well as in reverence to God, in self-sacrifice, in humility, in purity, and in holiness. We pray that our Catholic home schooling fathers will look to St. Joseph for guidance in leading their families to live the authentic Catholic family life.

Chapter 8:
Discipline in the Catholic
Home Schooling Family

"Discipline" must be one of the most rejected words in our society. With the advent of the "Do your own thing!" generation, the very concept of restraint seems a quaint, old-fashioned idea. For those wishing to live the Catholic life, however, discipline is paramount. "Discipline" and "disciple" come from the same root. If we want to be a true disciple of Jesus Christ, we need the discipline necessary to follow His commandments, and to teach and to train our children to follow His commandments, rather than our own selfish will.

The discipline drift has affected even good and holy Catholic families. The most common reason why Catholic families are afraid to start home schooling or do not succeed with their home schooling is lack of discipline.

This is a pretty tough indictment of the Catholic family, which, even while rejecting the prevailing cultural attitudes, is still affected by them. Without even realizing it, many Catholic parents have lost control of their own children.

Definition

What do we mean by discipline? Basically, discipline means training—training of the will. Before we can hope to teach the minds of our children academic subjects or even the Faith, we need to train ourselves and our children to do the Will of God.

Discipline is a way of life with rules. It means self-control. For the Catholic family, it means obedience to God's rules.

One of the definitions in the dictionary for the word *discipline* is "a system of practice or rules for members of a church." In the Second Vatican Council documents, the Catholic home is called a "domestic church," so it is appropriate that a home should be ruled by discipline.

Another definition of the word "discipline," found in *The Catholic Encyclopedia*, is the "whip or cord which the monks used in the monasteries for self-flagellation as a means of mortification." A mortification is an act of self-discipline. These are acts done to lessen our love for self and to increase our love for God and others, to increase our willingness to suffer in reparation for our own sins as well as for the sins of others.

Before we can expect our children's obedience in relation to schoolwork assignments, we need to teach our children obedience first to God's rules, and second to ourselves as God's representatives. Our children need to understand the positive reasons why Catholics believe in discipline.

In addition to training our children, we need to think about disciplining ourselves as mothers and fathers. If our children understand that we ourselves are striving for discipline, then they will be more likely to make such an effort.

Catholic philosophy as basis of discipline

The Catholic Church teaches that because of Original Sin, the individual's intellect, even after Baptism, is darkened and needs guidance to attain the truth. Man's will also has been weakened, and thus has an inclination to evil. Divine grace enlightens the intellect to know the good and guides the will to choose good through the use of the sacraments and prayer.

In the Old Testament, God directed His chosen people through the Jewish leaders, who represented God's authority. In the New Testament, Christ established His Church, the Catholic Church, as the spiritual authority in this world. By following the teachings of the Church on doctrine and morality, we can have the sure and certain knowledge of truth.

All Catholics have the responsibility to recognize and be obedient to our rightful authority on Earth, the Catholic Church. Catholic parents have the further responsibility to teach their children to obey *them* as the rightful authority delegated by God until they are old enough to follow the authority of the Church directly.

So the goal of parental discipline in the Catholic family is to bring children to understand the Will of God and to do His Will. God has given parents, as well as the Catholic Church, the necessary authority to command obedience from children. The ultimate goal is to help the individual child to act always in accordance with the Will of God, and thus become holy as God calls us to be.

While most parents find that there often must be an external compulsion for the child to do what he is told, the goal should always be to obtain an internal change or self-discipline in the mind and will. If a child can learn to do the right thing when forced to do so at first, the hope is that it will create a habit of doing good in the child that will last throughout life.

Discipline in the Catholic family aims for all members to act constantly in accordance with the Will of God. But at the same time there must be a recognition that there is a constant interior battle due to the darkened intellect and weakened will. Each member of the family needs to help the other members to see the truth more clearly and to do the right thing more faithfully.

Discipline: training of the will

For us Catholics, the training of the will to do good is more important than the training of the mind to know. It is useless for the mind to know, if the will chooses to act in an evil fashion. Those running our public schools believe that the more children know about things, the better it is for the children. But if the will is not trained to act correctly on knowledge, to pursue the good, what is the point of knowing?

In the schools, children are taught to choose to do whatever they want, after they supposedly are "informed" about their choices. The children in America know everything there is to know about sex and drugs, but they continue to make bad choices. The school policy is to give no training in doing good and avoiding evil. Children in the schools have no discipline because the schools have given them no training in choosing good.

A good example of this is the Drug Abuse Resistance Education (DARE) program that is in use in many school districts across the United States. When researchers study the effect of the program, they find that students who complete DARE have a more negative attitude toward drugs and alcohol than other students. But they also find that the program makes little or no difference in the actual *use* of drugs and alcohol by the students. In other words, the DARE program is effective in reaching the intellect (students know about drugs), but has no effect on the will (they use them anyway).

In the encyclical on Christian Education of Youth, Pope Pius XI wrote that the "subject of Christian education concerns man as a whole, soul united to body." Man fallen from his original state has problems in learning as well as in controlling his passions. The chief effects of Original Sin, in fact, are a weakness of the will and "disorderly inclinations."

These disorderly inclinations, according to the pope, must be corrected. "Good tendencies" must be encouraged and "regulated from the tender age of childhood." The will must be strengthened by supernatural truths and by grace. This is the kind of discipline we need in our Catholic families. Without it, there can be no real learning or true education.

The Bible on discipline

The Bible has a great deal to say to parents regarding the education and disciplining of children. God spoke to Moses about how the Commandments are to be taught to children by parents. This theme continues throughout the Old and New Testaments.

For instance, the Book of Proverbs says:

> The fear of the Lord is the beginning of wisdom. Fools despise wisdom and instruction. My son, hear the instruction of thy father, and forsake not the law of thy mother: that grace may be added to thy head, and a chain of gold to thy neck.

Some of the statements from the Book of Proverbs upon which we parents should reflect are the following:

Instruct thy son, and he shall refresh thee, and shall give delight to thy soul.

The rod and reproof give wisdom, but the child that is left to his own will bringeth his mother to shame.

It is a proverb: "Train up a child in the way that he should go, and when he is old he will not depart from it."

He that spareth the rod hateth his son; but he that loveth him correcteth him betimes [speedily].

Chasten thy son while there is hope, and let not thy soul spare for his crying.

Folly is bound up in the heart of a child, and the rod of correction shall drive it away.

Other Biblical quotes we should consider are Ephesians 6:4: "And you fathers, provoke not your children to anger, but bring them up in the discipline and correction of the Lord."

Exodus 20:12, Matthew 15:4, and Ephesians 6:2: "Honor thy father and thy mother."

Colossians 3:20: "Children, obey your parents in all things."

Deuteronomy 27:16: "Cursed be he that honoreth not his father and mother."

1 Kings 3:13: "For I have foretold unto him, that I will judge his house forever, for iniquity, because he knew that his sons did wickedly, and did not chastise them."

We need to remember the words of Jesus which point out the necessary spiritual emphasis in our disciplining: "Let the little children come unto Me, and forbid them not, for of such is the kingdom of God."

Infants

The disciplining of infants is especially difficult for us Catholic parents in this period of history. We are living in times when infants are murdered, before birth and after birth, and each precious innocent baby has an extra special meaning for God and for us. But it is important that we protect not only the sweet little bodies of our babies, but also that we protect their souls from evil inclinations. In fact, protecting their souls is the graver responsibility. The best way to protect our babies from physical and spiritual harm is to train them, to teach them, and to discipline them.

There is much discussion in home schooling groups about such topics as attachment parenting, family beds, ecological nursing, etc. Some parents believe that a crying baby should always be picked up and attended to. Others believe that if a baby is put down for a nap at a certain time, the baby will cry for a little while the first few days, but after that will become accustomed to nap time and will not cry anymore. On the other hand, a nursing mother may be able to establish a sleep time by lying down with the baby at a certain time every afternoon and having the baby fall asleep nursing.

In any case, you will need to find some way to be able to take care of the baby and still do schooling. Because each mother must find her own solution to each situation, I will not go into more detail, but do consider the fact that it is not good infant training for mothers never to say "no" to a child, even to a baby.

You know the phrase, "The hand that rocks the cradle rules the world." We should be sure that as we rock our babies, we are concerned about training them so that someday when they "rule" the world, it will be with justice and self-discipline.

Toddlers

The toddler years are the most important time to train your child, probably the most important period in your child's life. It is said that a child learns more during these years than during all the rest of his life put together. Although I would question that, certainly attitudes about love, obedience, and respect for authority are learned at this stage.

This is a time when a child, for his own physical safety, needs to learn to be instantly obedient to his parents. He must recognize their rightful authority, as well as accept the fact that his parents know what is best for him, and that obeying instantly, without question, is important.

Young parents should understand that it is their responsibility as parents to train their young child, even if they are tired or exhausted. Sometimes it is a matter of persistence and a battle of wills, but parents must persevere.

We parents should study the Church teaching about the Sacrament of Matrimony, which tells us that we parents have the graces to know what is best for our own children. We have the command from God in our vocation as parents to demand respect and obedience from our children, just as God demands respect and obedience from us, His children.

We parents need to have confidence in ourselves, confidence in the graces which God gave us, and confidence from our own life experiences and knowledge. We can know and must demand what is best for our children.

We parents should be convinced, in spite of the television, modern psychologists, and social service workers, that children absolutely do not know what is best for themselves. We parents do. Many Catholic documents teach that parents, under the Natural Law, have the *responsibility* to demand respect and obedience from their children.

Tough love

Training young children is very difficult. Training young children can be a daily conflict of wills. Our parental will is often in conflict with the will of a sweet little child whom we love more than we love ourselves. We would give our lives for our precious toddler, but what our toddler needs now, at this stage in his life, is not our life, but our own personal sacrifice to demand obedience. In the short run, demanding obedience is arduous, but in the long run, it will save untold trouble and heartbreak. Once I met with a group of older ladies who were not Catholic. When a young mother stated she was holding her eighth child, one mother said, "I had only one child, and that was enough for me." Another mother said, "Two was all I could handle." Discipline is the key to managing children.

This is no time for a soft personality. This is no time to say, "Well, Mary never spanked Jesus." True. He never defied her, either. Or scratched her coffee table on purpose. Or kept banging the glass on her counter after she told Him ten times not to do it.

Pray daily with your children, including your toddler, for the necessary graces, the strength, the energy to train them, and to give them the necessary discipline and self-control so that eventually they will be obedient to their heavenly Father. This is a primary duty in the vocation of motherhood.

House rules for toddlers

Determine your house rules and post them on the refrigerator or in an appropriate room. Verbally explain them to your toddler. Even though your toddler cannot read them, he can understand that you read rules and that reading rules leads you to follow rules. Show your young child how you read labels on the cans in the kitchen and recipes in the cookbook, and then act on what you read. Show him that if you follow the directions correctly, measuring the ingredients carefully, setting the oven to the correct temperature, the result will be a successful meal.

Teach your child that you read signs when you drive the car, and by following the signs and directions, you can arrive safely at your destination. Toddlers can understand that the rules on your refrigerator are for him to obey, that you are reading them to him, and telling him to obey them. Teach him that by obeying rules, the family can reach a goal: a nice, pleasant home. Teach that, by learning to follow the rules of God, we can all obtain the ultimate goal: happiness in Heaven with Jesus.

Your house rules could include

- putting toys away after playing with them
- picking up clothes
- helping Mother to pick up at the end of the day
- using a napkin to wipe up spills
- eating at the dining table and not in the living room
- not going into the bathroom without Mother
- not banging on the table
- playing the piano gently
- wearing shoes outside

Needless to say, you cannot have an endless list, but a few for each room or occasion would not be too much.

An area which is often neglected for toddlers, and even for older children, is courtesy. It is vital to a smoothly running home that children learn to speak and act in a courteous way. If they don't, then it will cause strife and contention, with each child feeling slighted by the others, and no one acting properly. You cannot have a happy home unless the family members are courteous to each other.

Toddlers can and should learn basic courtesy, such as saying "please" and "thank you." They should be taught to ask politely for what they want, and to wait a short period of time to receive it. Little children, even from good families, are often terribly rude, which gives a bad impression of the family and of home schooling in general. Manners are important, and should never be considered optional.

Toddler psychology

The inclinations left from Original Sin are very obvious in young children. Many toddlers will purposefully, every day, test Mother to see how far they can go before she will actually punish them. Mothers can become tired of this daily conflict, this daily training period for toddlers. Toddlers can and often do outlast mothers. That is why we mothers need to ask for the daily graces to persevere and to be consistent.

Boys and girls who are disobedient, disrespectful, and who talk back to their mothers at thirteen are boys and girls who were not trained to be obedient and respectful toddlers.

Be obedient to God yourself. Train your children.

Give your toddler a certain period of the day to sit still, at least for a few minutes, perhaps 15 minutes in the morning, and later in the afternoon. Give your toddler a book or a toy, but explain that this is sit-still time. When you take your toddler to church, insist on his sitting still for Mass.

When your toddler is sitting at the table for meals, insist that he not jump up and down, or get out of his chair. Teach him to sit for a reasonable time, fifteen minutes or so, during the meal.

Take the time and effort to have a practice session with your toddler about the rules. For instance, if you have a rule that your toddler is to come into the house immediately when you call him, practice it. Send him outside, and call him in. Do this several times to make him understand and remember the rule.

Preschool catechism

When children are very young, even before they begin to talk, parents should begin teaching about Jesus, about His love for all of us, and about the importance of pleasing Jesus by being obedient. Show your child holy pictures. Teach your child to pray the Sign of the Cross, the Our Father, the Hail Mary, the Guardian Angel prayer, and grace before meals.

Teach your child about the Child Jesus and how He obeyed His parents. Read stories about Jesus and other Bible stories.

Explain over and over to your child that you love him, no matter what he does wrong, but that because you love him, because you must be obedient in training him as God has commanded you, you must punish him whenever he behaves with disrespect or disobedience.

Have regular prayer times when all the children, including your toddler, are required to join in saying the Rosary and other prayers. Schedule these times when the children are refreshed, not after the evening meal when the children are too tired. Children—whether toddlers or teens—should not be excused from the family prayer time. Adapt the prayers and participation according to the child's age. However, even very young children can learn the Rosary quickly, and soon can be leading the prayers.

Before their fifth birthday, children should be able to genuflect before entering a pew and maintain a respectful posture at Mass.

Preschool home schooling

For the sake of discipline in the family, allow toddlers and pre-schoolers to be part of the home schooling program. If you use desks for the older children, obtain a small desk for your toddler so he can feel like a part of the family home schooling activities. Give your toddler coloring books and crayons, or a small chalkboard with colored chalk. Allow a toddler or preschooler to sit on your lap while you are teaching. Let him turn the pages of the book for you.

Try to have a little "formal" home schooling with your toddler, even for just a few minutes each day, if he or she appears interested. Girls are interested even at two or three years old. Toddlers can learn their letters and their numbers. You want to develop a good attitude toward learning, and during the toddler years is the best time to start. The more a toddler feels involved in the family activities, the fewer discipline problems you will have.

Usually toddlers pick up the memory work from their older brothers and sisters even while they are playing on the floor. They may not understand everything they have memorized just from hearing it, but they have memorized it nevertheless. When it comes time for them to understand concepts, such as two plus two is four, or "The Savior of all men is Jesus Christ," they already have many of the facts memorized and can easily apply understanding. Discipline problems lessen as concepts are learned quickly and easily.

If a toddler becomes cranky, an older brother or sister might like to help him learn his letters or numbers or preschool catechism; or the brother or sister might like to read stories to the toddler. This is a good experience for children to help each other, and for the toddler to accept help from an older sibling. Often spoiled children will insist on only Mother teaching. Encourage the development of a good attitude on the part of the toddler to accept learning from an older sister or brother.

Equality

If your children have been enrolled in a school before you decide to bring them home, you have your work cut out for you as you try to discipline. Our society is selling children the idea that each person has the right to choose whatever he wants for himself. No one, not parents or friends or society, has any authority over anyone else. This secular teaching of "liberty," which many children have accepted, makes it very difficult for parents to discipline their children.

The idea of individual freedom has become so perverted that many elementary children believe that their decisions are of the same value with any their parents might make, and consequently they have equal rights and authority. Modern family counselors have sold young parents on the idea that they should have family meetings where each child may express his or her own ideas. Family meetings can be helpful, but only if the children realize that Dad and Mom have the final say as heads of the family. Many parents are literally bullied, sometimes even frightened, first by family counselors, and then by their children.

Television programs portray families with children having equal decision-making authority in the family. Those with cable TV have it better by being able to tune in the older shows which portray Mother and Father "knowing best." The whole concept of family is being portrayed perversely today. Situation comedies portray several men raising children, or simply groups of people living together.

A line of authority

The Catholic Church has a line of authority which was established by Jesus Christ Himself when He named St. Peter as the first pope. When the pope speaks on faith and morals, there is no vote taken among the bishops (except at Church councils). The pope speaks with divine authority, directed by the Holy Spirit. Bishops are to obey the pope, priests are to obey bishops, lay people are to obey the priests. Of course, all of this assumes a faithfulness to the truths of the Church. This line of authority must continue in the Catholic family. Father is the head of the family, while Mother is the heart of the family. Children are to obey their parents.

Parents who do not enforce respect and authority from their children are not following Catholic teachings, and their children are not being obedient to the Commandment of God that children must honor and obey parents. This particular Commandment was repeated strongly and frequently in the Old Testament. The duty to discipline is directly related to the parental vocation of marriage: to educate their children, which means the training of the will as well as the training of the mind.

Do not accept the world's view that children are normal if they insist on making all their own decisions or go through periods of being rebellious. Do not accept disrespect as a "sign of growing up." Do not accept back talk as normal. Do not accept freaky popular haircuts and strange or immodest clothes as normal. These outward signs are evidence of an inner acceptance of the values of the world.

It is SO hard to be consistently strong. But do it while they are young and little. It can just about kill you if you wait until they are teenagers!

The Catholic Church is like a loving mother. Her directives will give you strength and courage for the discipline work ahead.

Talking to newlyweds, Pope Pius XII said:

> Children are like the "reed shaken by the wind." They are delicate flowers whose petals fall with the slightest breeze. They are virgin soil on which God has sown the seeds of goodness but which are stifled by ... the "concupiscence of the flesh and the concupiscence of the eyes, and the pride of life."
>
> Who will straighten the reed? Who is to protect these flowers? Who will cultivate this soil and make the seeds of goodness bear fruit against the snares of evil? In the first place, it will be the authority which governs the family and the children: namely, parental authority.
>
> Fathers and mothers today often bewail the fact that they can no longer get their children to obey them. Stubborn little children listen to nobody; growing children spurn all guidance; young men and women are exasperated by any advice given, are deaf to all warnings, and insist on following their own ideas because they are convinced that they alone are fully in a position to appreciate the needs of the modern way of life....
>
> And what is the cause of this insubordination? The reason generally given is that the children of today no longer possess the sense of submission and respect due to the commands of their parents.... Everything they perceive around them serves the sole purpose of increasing, exciting, and setting fire to their natural, untamed passion for independence, for mocking the past, and thirsting avidly for the future....
>
> The normal exercising of authority depends not only on those who have to obey, but also, and in large measure, on those who have to command. To put it more clearly: We must distinguish between

the right to possess authority and give orders on the one hand, and, on the other, that moral excellence which is the essence and spirit of an effective ... authority, which is able to impose itself on others and to exact obedience.

The former right is conferred on you by God in the very act of your parentage. The latter privilege must be acquired and preserved; it can be lost and it can be strengthened. Now the right to command your children will not be worth much if it is not accompanied by that control and personal authority over them which ensures that they really obey you....

This authority must be tempered ... with loving kindness and patient encouragement.

To temper authority with kindness is to triumph in the struggle which belongs to your duty as parents.... All those who would advantageously rule over others, must, as an essential element, first dominate themselves, their passions, their impressions. There is no real submission to and respect for any authority, unless those who obey feel that this authority is exercised with reason, faith, and a sense of duty, because then only do they realize that a similar duty binds them to obey.

If the orders you give your children and the punishment you inflict proceed from the impulse of the moment, or from outbursts of impatience or imagination or blind ill-considered sentiment, they will mostly be arbitrary or inconsistent, and perhaps even unjust and ill-suited.

But how are you going to rule over your children, when you do not know how to conquer your moods, to control your imagination, and to dominate yourselves? If on occasions you feel that you are not completely master of your feelings, then put off to a later and better time the correction you want to make or the punishment you think you must inflict. This quiet dignity with which you speak and correct will be far more effective, far more educative and authoritative ...

Do not forget that children, no matter how small they may be, have a very observant eye and will immediately be aware of the changes in your moods. From the cradle itself ... they soon become aware of the power their childish whims and fits of crying have over weak parents, and with innocent cunning, will not hesitate to exploit it to the full.

Avoid everything that may lessen your authority with them. Beware against ruining this authority by a non-stop series of recommendations and criticisms ... Avoid deceiving your children with fake reasons.... Never falsify the truth. It is far better to keep silent.... Take care that no sign of disagreement appear between you [parents].... Do not make the mistake of waiting till your children are grown up in order to make them feel the calm weight of your authority ...

Your authority must be devoid of weakness, yet it must be an authority which stems from love, and is steeped in love, and sustained by love.... If you really have this parental love ... in the commands you give your children, these commands will find an echo in the intimate depths of the hearts of your children, without there being need to say very much.

The language of love is more eloquent in the silence of labor than in much speech. A thousand little signs, an inflection of the voice, an almost imperceptible gesture, an expression of the face, a little hint of approval ... all these tell them, more than any protestations, how much affection there is in the prohibition that annoys them, how much kindness is hidden in the order they find troublesome. Then only will authority appear to them, not as a heavy weight, a hateful yoke to be cast off ... but as the supreme manifestation of your love.

Must not example go hand in hand with love? How can children, who, after all, are naturally inclined to imitate, learn to obey, if they see the mother paying no heed to the order of the father, or worse, quarreling with him; if the home is full of continual criticism of all forms of authority; if they see their parents are the first not to obey the commands of God and the Church?

You must give your children the example of parents whose manner of speaking and acting serves as a model of respect for legitimate authority, of faithfulness to duty. From this edifying sight, they will learn the true nature of Christian obedience and how they should practice it towards their parents, in a far more convincing manner than any sermon to that effect. Be firmly convinced that good example is the most precious heritage you can leave your children.

Pius XII, 1941, Speech to Newlyweds

Explanation of philosophy

Children of school age can understand your explanation of why you are home schooling. The children need to understand. Understanding motivates them to be obedient, to do the schoolwork, and to help with the housework.

Take the time, perhaps at the beginning of each quarter of the school year, to explain again why you are home schooling. Take a whole day and help the children to write it down for themselves, in their own words. Let them post it up in their study area. They can decorate it with crayons or colored pens around the margins, perhaps even frame it.

"I am home schooling because I love Jesus and want to learn more about Him from my parents." Let them phrase it for themselves, but the spiritual motivation is important.

Emphasize the spiritual reasons you are home schooling, the positive reasons and not the negative problems in the local schools. Do not talk about drugs or sex education or lack of discipline or poor academics. Talk about living the Catholic Faith, being able to say family prayers together during the day, and using sacramentals for liturgical feasts.

Talk about the virtues to your children, that you want your Catholic family to live the virtuous life. Explain to your children that after faith, hope, and charity, the most important virtue is obedience. Have the children look up the virtues in their catechism. Let them write down and discuss the virtues of faith, hope, and charity. Let them write down the moral virtues of prudence, justice, fortitude, and temperance. Let them write down and discuss the other virtues listed in their catechism: piety, patriotism, patience, humility. Let them discuss other virtues they can think of.

You *can* discipline your children, that is, train them to be obedient and follow rules and regulations. They need to understand the higher goal, what the "big picture" is, what the mission of the Catholic individual and the Catholic family is about.

Explain again and again to your children that if parents love God, they must obey Him. In obeying Him, you yourself must teach your children to behave according to His rules, to practice the virtues. In order to properly train children, parents often must use punishment as a consequence of disobedience to the rules.

Explain Purgatory and why God requires justice in reparation for sin, either in this world or in Purgatory. Bring stories of saints into your explanation. Many young saints prayed and offered their sacrifices and sufferings to Jesus in reparation for sin. Relate stories of young saints to your children as you explain the purpose of discipline, or submitting one's will as an act of reparation for sin.

Teach your children about Hell. For almost two thousand years, parents have taught their children about Hell and about the Last Judgment.

We should not hide the existence of Hell from our children due to some modern psychological opinion. Children need to know the consequence of sin, especially of mortal sin. After all, Jesus died on the Cross as a consequence of sin and the need to repair for such offenses to God the Father. Your discussion of Hell, and its horrors, can be shaped by your child's degree of maturity. The Blessed Mother revealed a vision of Hell to the three children at Fatima to remind them about the consequences of sin.

A benevolent dictatorship

Do not run your family like a democracy. Run your family like a benevolent dictatorship. Parents are the loving "dictators" because they are given the graces to know what is best for their children. One problem that parents often have is that they try to explain to their children over and over why they should not do something. Explain to your children once or twice why they should not do something. Do not continue the conversation endlessly. Try not to argue or raise your voice, try not to keep talking, try not to become emotional or upset as a child persists in asking the same question over and over again.

Practical rules

For children at the elementary level, it is important to be very clear about the rules and regulations you expect for your home and family. Take a day about four times a year to discuss these at length and help your children write them down and memorize them. If you do this at the beginning of each quarter of the school year, they can be revised as necessary. Have the children post them at their study area, in the bedroom, or in the kitchen.

Some of the rules might be: to rise at a specific time, to make the bed, no running in the house, and to keep the clothes off the floor. "Keeping the room clean" is not specific enough for children. Other rules or goals, based on the Commandments, would be: no talking back disrespectfully, no temper tantrums, no throwing things at people, and no teasing brothers and sisters. Some positive rules might be doing the schoolwork when it is assigned, doing it neatly, reviewing the work, and correcting the errors before handing it in to Mom. Of course, do not overwhelm your children with rules. You can work on a few at a time. Discussing these rules when everyone is calm will result in better understanding and a better attitude toward obeying.

One note of hope for young families who are having problems disciplining their two or three young ones: as your family grows, believe it or not, the disciplining becomes easier. This is because once the older children have learned your rules and are obeying them, they will not allow the younger ones to break them. Often older children will do some disciplining themselves, keeping the young ones in line when Mother is absent or busy with the baby. Have courage. It does get easier!

Some references

There are many books on disciplining children, but choose ones which are written by Catholics. I recommend *Family Bonding Through Discipline*. This book contains chapters written by Catholic parents in conjunction with Father Robert Fox. Father Fox worked with families and teens for many years as he took regular trips to Fatima. He chose several families who had disciplined children, and they wrote about their methods of discipline.

Two other good books are *Life Line: The Religious Upbringing of Your Children* and *Upbringing* by James Stenson. Mr. Stenson has been a school principal for many years, and asked several Catholic parents who have disciplined children to talk to him about their practical methods. Chapters include Standards and Rules, Responsibility, Courage, and Self-Mastery. Mr. Stenson has become a popular speaker at conferences for parents.

Steve Wood gives excellent talks on discipline based on Biblical principles. His audio tapes are available from Family Life Center, P.O. Box 6060, Port Charlotte, FL 33949, or from www.dads.org.

Dr. Ray Guarendi is a clinical psychologist and radio host who is a frequent speaker at home schooling conferences. He has written several books, including *Discipline that Lasts a Lifetime* and *You're a Better Parent Than You Think*. His website is www.drray.com.

There are some Protestant pastors who have written popular books on discipline, including Dr. Moore and Dr. Dobson. If you read these, be aware that Protestant ideas about discipline are influenced by a very dark understanding of fallen human nature that is not a Catholic view.

Punishment

One Christian child psychologist believes that when children do something they should not, or refuse to do something you have told them to do, you should count to three and then the child must go to his room for five minutes. If you tell your child to stop teasing his little brother, and he continues to do so, you tell him, "That's one." If he continues, the parent does not shout or argue, but says, "That's two." If the action still continues, the parent says, "That's three. Take five." Taking five means the child must go to his room for five minutes. Sometimes, of course, the child must be dragged to his room, but after about a week, the child understands that when you start the counting, if he does not stop his unacceptable behavior, he will end up in his room.

If you try this, you might want to choose another place than the bedroom. Some parents choose a place without distractions or toys available. Some suggestions are a basement or an area in the hallway or a walk-in closet. Some parents have a younger child stand in a corner, or sit by himself in a chair away from others in the family. The amount of time should be adjusted according to the age of the child and the seriousness of the misbehavior. This type of punishment is to make the child aware that since he or she is not acting in an acceptable manner, he has temporarily lost the privilege of being part of the family activities.

The key to success in disciplining your children is to explain the rules first, then to explain the punishment (counting and then a time away from the family, or a spanking), and then to keep control by not talking, not arguing, not becoming upset yourself. *It is important to be consistent in your punishments.*

The practice of corporal punishment (spanking) of children is hotly debated. While surveys have shown that virtually all parents use spanking at times, so-called "child experts" have told parents that spanking is emotionally harmful to children. However, recent studies, including a study by psychologists Diana Baumrind and Elizabeth Owens of the University of California at Berkeley, have found that spanking is not emotionally harmful. Whether or not spanking is harmful, there is also the question of whether it is effective, which seems to vary from child to child. So, again, this is a question for each family to decide.

Give children some decisions in home schooling

Older children will need less discipline and will be more motivated in their home schooling if they are allowed to have participation in some of the decisions regarding their home schooling. Let them help decide their schedule for chores and when they want to work on each school subject for the day. Let them write their daily schedule and post it on the wall where they study. Ask them for their ideas concerning projects for the science class, and creative ideas for history lessons.

Meals, study, and chores

Little tricks can help older children learn self-discipline. Relate the schoolwork schedule to meals and chores for the day. For instance, schedule a certain number of school work assignments before meals are allowed. Perhaps a math assignment would need to be finished before breakfast. Certain classes would have to be finished before lunch, and three or four more classes before dinner. This should be only for older children, about 10 or older. This emphasizes the relation of work to eating, which is Biblical, and teaches the child in a dramatic way the value of Dad's work for the family. Household chores could be scheduled in the same manner. This should cut down on the necessity of Mother constantly nagging at the children to keep working.

The trick is for Mother to remain firm. It will not hurt a child to miss a meal or two; results will be achieved by the third meal. Be realistic, of course, especially when you start. Require less work rather than more. For instance, you actually want little Joey in fifth grade to do two math pages in the half-hour before breakfast. However, require only one page the day you start the new "Math Before Breakfast" program. In a couple of days, require one and a half pages. A few days later, require two.

In addition, chores should be scheduled between classes. This gives your children an opportunity to be active periodically throughout the day. It will help in the area of discipline if children can have frequent but brief physically active periods throughout the school day. If chores are left to the end of the day, after classes, parents will find children resistant and difficult to discipline.

Some children lack self-discipline because they have no concept of time. They seem to dawdle over their assignments and let their minds wander. Obtain an alarm clock for such a child to place on his desk. Set the time and the alarm for the amount of time needed to do an assignment. As the child works each day with his clock, he begins to realize how much time a particular subject takes him. He is able to pace his work. This teaches discipline, self-control, and responsibility—and keeps Mom from nagging.

The "I'm Dumb" syndrome

In a large family, you are likely to have one. He may be very bright, but with all the family activity going on all around him, and his attraction for the outdoors, he cannot seem to keep pace academically, especially as compared with his siblings. So he complains and whines, "I'm dumb." He resists doing his work because the others are doing so well or moving along more quickly.

Emphasize the different gifts which each family member has been given by God. Talk about the gifts of Mother and Father, as well as the gifts of grandfathers and grandmothers. Talk to him about the gifts your child inherited from Mother or Father. Explain that God decided that in an efficient society, everything could not run smoothly unless each person has different strengths and skills and, consequently, can do different jobs.

Give this child an opportunity to spend more time on assignments at which he can feel successful. If he loves drawing, give him an opportunity to make birthday cards for cousins. If he has great coordination at basketball shots, see if other home schooling families might like to start a basketball team.

Emphasize the spiritual aspect. Tell him to ask his guardian angel to help him to do his best for his patron saint and for the Baby Jesus. There were plenty of saints who were not good in school or were considered "dumb" by other people. Thomas Aquinas—perhaps the greatest of all Doctors of the Church—was called the "Dumb Ox" by his classmates. The great parish priest Jean Vianney graduated last in his class at the seminary and needed private tutoring to pass the necessary exams to become a priest.

Learn how your children learn

Sometimes discipline problems arise because children are frustrated with the learning process. Young boys, for example, often learn better orally, by hearing stories read to them. Obviously, they need to learn to read eventually, but some may not be ready for reading until they are seven or eight. So be sensitive to how each child learns best, and be sure that the classes are geared to the appropriate learning style. Using the proper method for the child, subject by subject, will increase learning success, and decrease behavior problems.

Of course, you should not rely exclusively on one learning style. If your child is an auditory learner, it is still good to practice with written words and instructions. As the child grows and goes on to college and the workplace, a variety of skills is needed to succeed.

Discipline problems sometimes arise because of assignments related to writing. Most boys have a problem with handwriting because their small muscle development is slow. They can swing a bat, toss basketballs into a hoop, and bang a volleyball over the net, but putting little lines down in a tiny space between parallel lines on a piece of paper just does not come naturally to the young male.

Consider doing the assignments with your boys orally. They can record some assignments onto a tape recorder. (They love hearing their own voice.) Another popular option is for them to type assignments on a word processor. Boys do extremely well on these because they can make corrections without rewriting the whole book report or assignment.

Do not give up teaching your boys handwriting, but for longer essay-type assignments, or when the boys are frustrated and are on the verge of becoming a discipline problem, parents should consider the word processor. The final product will even be legible!

Work should be neither too difficult nor too easy

Discipline problems often arise if the schoolwork is too difficult, or too easy, or too boring, or too repetitious. In the home schooling situation, even with a program, materials should be adjusted to the abilities of the child. Most home school programs will customize the materials, so that, for example, a student may be in fifth grade, but be taking fourth grade math and sixth grade spelling.

Home school programs will send placement tests which will help parents and the home school to identify the proper grade level for their children in each individual subject. However, placement tests are just one factor. The best evaluation is really done by the parents as they work on a day-to-day basis with their children.

Memory work

Discipline problems can arise when children do not have basic concepts memorized. Children become frustrated as they work long hours over math problems because they never memorized their multiplication tables. They become frustrated over catechism memory work in Book Two when they never mastered the questions and answers in Book One.

One of the attitudes in today's society is that nothing needs to be memorized. "Everything is going to change anyway, so why bother memorizing anything today?" But many things do not change. Catholic teachings will not change; the Bible will not change. Mathematical concepts will not change; addition and subtraction facts will not change. It is important to memorize basic facts in each area of knowledge.

Most important to the present discussion of discipline is this: children are more disciplined about their studies if they have basic facts memorized. In addition, memory work itself is a discipline. It forces the mind to focus on learning facts in a logical manner.

If your child has been in a school

There is no question about it. Many home schooling mothers can testify to it. The longer a child has been in a school situation, the more difficult the disciplining and home schooling are, especially during the first year.

Not only are the children usually behind academically, but their attitudes and behavior, in regard to schoolwork and to parents and family, often have been shaped negatively by the school environment, by schoolmates, by the secular textbooks, and by their teachers.

Your Catholic philosophy, your attitude about the Catholic lifestyle, probably is contrary to what your child has been learning from the secular, politically-correct textbooks used in both public and Catholic schools. Your values are in conflict with what the children have learned from many of their classmates.

Your values about family are often in conflict with those of teachers who are promoting their own ideas or the National Education Association's ideas of a new world order where "family" is being redefined, a world in which fathers and mothers are simply viewed as possible caregivers and not as uniquely important to a child's development, both emotionally and spiritually.

The less time your children have attended a school, the fewer discipline problems you will have. I have a box of letters over a foot long from parents and grandparents giving examples of children and the difference in their behavior between the years they were in school and the years they were home schooling. One grandmother reported her granddaughter was a sweet girl during the years she was home schooled, but when they moved, they decided to put her in a little rural public school. The girl began to change immediately, and after four years, she was nasty, violent toward her little brother, lied directly in the face of truth, yelled at her grandmother statements about wishing her brother were dead. The grandmother realized that her granddaughter was acting out the frustrations and behavior she needed to survive and be accepted in the school which eliminated God from the school day. She wrote that she believed that a whole nation of children have and will be rejecting God, but she is going to start home schooling her granddaughter again in hopes of pulling her back to the Catholic Faith.

Some rules to help you keep control

Exclude anti-Christian worldly influences, such as certain kinds of music, playmates with conflicting values, certain styles of clothes and haircuts, vulgar words, phrases, or conversation, semi-violent or violent "friends." Encourage pictures, illustrations, movies, DVDs, books of teen saints. Do not allow posters of secular "heroes" on bedroom walls. Show videos of good Catholic or moral stories rather than allowing the children to attend movies. Do not allow your children to attend any local classes, such as sports or arts and crafts, unless you monitor them first. Many of these teachers cannot keep control. Undisciplined classmates, even in little neighborhood classes, may influence your child to adopt language, clothing, or behavior which is demanded by their classmates to be accepted by the group. Monitor even the CCD classes which, after all, are for the public school students.

Of course, there is the television. Many home schooling families do not have a television. If you do, be sure you monitor what the children watch. Most of the shows reflect the pagan values of our society. Even television cartoon shows portray sex and violence and promote occult and criminal activities. This is very specifically documented in a book titled *Saturday Morning Mind Control* by Phil Phillips.

Mr. Phillips has studied toys which generally promote aggression. He has researched the electronic video games, which portray blowing up people, places, and things as the goal. Heroes and villains act violently with maces and swords; they mug their enemies, throwing people on subway tracks, and generally invent horrible death traps. Computer games commonly portray evil spirits, demonic characters, and witchcraft. Many advertise they are for "those interested in astrology, magic, fortune telling, and ancient mysteries" (p. 151, Phillips).

Mr. Phillips continued his research to include comic books.

> Many comic books have viciously anti-Christian themes and plots. Some blatantly present reincarnation, spirit channeling, and the use of psychic powers and even crystals as means of gaining and exercising power. (p. 155, Phillips)

In his research on specific PG-rated movies for children, Mr. Phillips writes:

> In *Care Bear Movie II*, an evil spirit occupies the body of a fourteen-year-old boy. *Rainbow Brite and the Star Stealer* was a children's movie with almost everything in it that a parent doesn't want to teach children: greed, self-centeredness, violence, sexism, and all-around evil. (p. 159, Phillips)

Many more children's movies are documented by Mr. Phillips.

> We are living in a pagan society, and the only way to raise our children as Christians is to keep them from anti-Catholic, anti-family, anti-life influences. It is almost a guarantee that if children are constantly exposed to these influences, there will be a discipline problem at home.

Confraternity of Christian Doctrine (CCD) classes

Some home schooling parents ask about whether their children should attend religious education (CCD) classes at their parish church. Many CCD teachers are influenced by the world, and are not necessarily Catholic in their beliefs. Some CCD teachers do not even pretend to be Catholic. There have been cases of non-Catholic parents hired as CCD teachers and even as the Director of Religious Education (DRE) for parish CCD programs. We should not be surprised because non-Catholics and even non-Christians are teaching in "Catholic" schools, colleges, and seminaries.

The students in CCD classes are from public schools and are very affected by the pagan school curriculum and environment. The CCD program was set up specifically for children in non-Catholic schools, not for home schooling families teaching a Catholic curriculum. Sometimes, the CCD classes are going to present values conflicting with those of Catholic home schooling families, either because of the teacher, the students, or the textbook.

If you want to put your child in the CCD program, take the time to monitor the CCD class before you allow your child to attend. Check out the teacher, the discipline, the textbook, and the students. I once observed a religious education class for young children where the priest had no control over a boy who physically abused the other children with constant pushing, kicking, and shoving. Many teachers cannot maintain discipline, and innocent children are physically assaulted right in the classroom, in front of the teacher.

Integrate Catholicism

The very best way to maintain discipline in your home is to integrate the Catholic sacramental life into your family life. If you and your children are daily living the Catholic life by saying the Rosary, wearing the scapular, making Advent wreaths, decorating a May altar, and all the other year-round liturgical observances, your children are more likely to be good children. They will respond to your directions and instructions. The spiritual bond and the respect based on their understanding of spiritual authority will keep them from exhibiting discipline problems.

Just because neighbors are having such terrible discipline problems with their children does not mean that we will have terrible problems. It does not mean that we should expect discipline problems, nor accept discipline problems as normal.

Catholic home schooling families should not have serious discipline problems with their children. It is a matter of taking control when children are young, and keeping control. Discipline is not easy, but it is important in preventing rebellious children, and in home schooling successfully.

Junior high and high school levels

Discipline must be started with babies or, as the papal directives put it, from the cradle. It must be done consistently during the toddler stage, and continued up to about age twelve. By age twelve or thirteen, the children should be well-disciplined.

Some parents might laugh at the idea that teens can be self-disciplined because the teenagers of today seem to be the worst discipline problem of all. They talk back, wear outlandish or immodest clothes and haircuts, have body piercings all over, spend money foolishly, spend too much time with their friends, talk on the phone too much (even insist on their own cell phone or car), and are generally out of the control of their parents. Some parents think this is just part of growing up, the generation gap, or some other secular modern excuse.

In a Catholic home schooling family, where discipline starts when the children are young, we can almost guarantee that the common teenage problems will not exist. In fact, many home schooling parents can say that the teen years are the best age for home schooling because their teens are self-disciplined, self-motivated, and have their study skills developed. In addition, the teens help the younger children with their studies and with babysitting, help with taking care of the house, and also assist Father with his business. In addition, they are interesting people who have thoughtful discussions about important matters with Mom and Dad. Many start taking vocational courses or college courses early; they become involved in church activities, or begin helping at the local pregnancy center.

Home schooling parents who have teenagers taught and trained at home since they were babies will tell you that one of their greatest joys is their teenagers. These young adults are happy, mature, good students, good Catholics, and good citizens. They are concerned about the basic issues of our society. Unlike many teens, they are socially well-adjusted.

In the biographies of successful people, whether saints or American heroes, we read that most matured at a rather young age. Our schools today are keeping young people from maturing, especially from maturing spiritually. That is the key. With spiritual maturity comes maturity in many other ways. Mature home schooled teens are a great blessing for parents.

Discipline for the young adult

For the home schooling teenager who has not had the benefit of home schooling in the earlier grades, learning at home can be a difficult adjustment. Since many teenagers are not happy in a school where values conflict with their own family's values, parents will find they are anxious but willing to come home to learn. Though the academics may be difficult, they are willing to work hard to remain at home away from the hostile environment they have experienced at school.

Some teens, of course, resist home schooling. For some families, bringing the teens home can be a terrible experience. Some teens are resentful and rebellious, and cause serious family disruptions. They have accepted the pagan values and behavior, and resist change.

Nevertheless, parents must persist in the struggle to teach obedience to their teens. In fact, for the first year a teen is home for schooling, it may be necessary to give the teen only two or three academic courses. The main thrust of the first year at home will be to teach discipline; that is, respect for authority, the meaning of obedience, the virtues of charity, kindness, and humility. The teen needs to discover Jesus and Mary, to pray every day, to go to daily Mass if possible, to get back to regular Confession, and so on.

Do you remember the movie *The Miracle Worker*, about Helen Keller and her teacher Anne Sullivan? Anne literally fought with Helen to make her change. Mothers of autistic children have to physically keep touching and pulling and pushing their children to come out of themselves into reality. When mothers love their children, they can go to great lengths to help them overcome terrible handicaps. If a teenager has been in a school and has accepted many of the attitudes and behaviors typical of the schools, home schooling parents will need to take drastic action, requiring great physical and emotional perseverance, to save their child's soul.

When a teenager is brought home, the training of the will must take priority over the academics. With the grace of God and the love and patience of parents, a young person can be turned around to accept and live the authentic Catholic family life.

Father can help

For the best help in discipline, enlist Dad. God gave fathers a certain authoritative manner in their voices which seems to elicit quick obedience from their children. A father's interest and concern in the disciplining and home schooling is a strong factor in motivating children. Father is especially important in the disciplining of teens.

On the other hand, if Dad is not supportive or openly critical of the home schooling, it will be most difficult to be successful. Children, though often innocently, try to widen the conflict between parents, usually as a gesture of unhappiness more than any personal pleasure in fomenting trouble.

Dad needs to teach and to reinforce certain attitudes about work: that work is important, that God expects us to work, that work is commanded by God, that we can gain graces by doing our school work well, and that God teaches us through the Bible that if we do not work, we do not eat! If Dad works outside the home, perhaps he could take each child to work with him to help the child to understand the importance of his work for the family. The children need to see that work provides the food and shelter for the family, and that a job well done is a source of human happiness.

In the encyclical on Christian Education of Youth, Pope Pius XI quotes the practical instruction of St. Paul to the Ephesians: "And you, fathers, provoke not your children to anger." The pope explains that this fault of provoking the children to anger is the result

> not so much of excessive severity as of impatience and ignorance of the means best calculated to effect the desired correction. It is also due to the all-too-common relaxation of parental discipline which fails to check the growth of evil passions in the hearts of the younger generation.

Disciplining ourselves

We home schooling mothers and fathers need to learn how to discipline ourselves as well as our children. Mary Kay Ash of Mary Kay Cosmetics, in her autobiography, explains her very disciplined life. She writes about getting up before the rest of the family, saying her prayers, and doing an hour of work in the quiet of the morning. Of course, she takes the time to put on her Mary Kay makeup, making herself look and feel beautiful.

We need to do the same in a Catholic way.

The best way to keep yourself disciplined is to have a written schedule or plan for each day. A teacher's plan book, such as we use for our children's lessons, makes a great personal plan book. The local discount or stationery stores sell personal planning books. For many years, I have been using these to record what needs to be done day by day. Obtain one large enough to record everything you want. Keep it in the kitchen or wherever you can get to it easily and frequently throughout the day. It may be near your telephone or on your dresser. Attach a pen so you never are looking for something with which to write.

Start each day by referring to your plan book. Write in it as the day goes along, recording appointments set up, calls you need to make, special times with the children, times for Mass or other church events, and so on. You may want to put some items relating to your home schooling, but those may be recorded sufficiently in the children's plan books. Before you retire at night, check off what you accomplished, and move into the next day what you did not accomplish.

If you do not set daily goals for yourself, you will never accomplish very much, and you will feel distressed that you did not do anything. Do you frequently say to yourself, "Where did the day go?" With a plan book, you know beforehand where you are going, and at the end of the day you know where you have been.

Good example

In a speech in 1941, Pope Pius XII directed parents to be good examples to their children as the primary means of disciplining them. The pope asked:

> Would it be consistent to correct a child for the same faults that you commit daily in his presence? To want him to be obedient and submissive if, in his presence, you criticize ecclesiastical or civil superiors, if you disobey the commandments of God or the just laws?
>
> Would it be reasonable to want your children to be loyal when you are untruthful, patient if you are violent and ill-tempered? Example is always the best teacher.
>
> With love, guided by reason, and reason guided by faith, home education will not be subject to those deplorable extremes that so often imperil it: alternating weak indulgence with sharp severity, going from culpable acquiescence which leaves the child unguided, to severe correction that leaves him helpless. On the other hand, the affection shown by parents ... distributes due praise and merited correction with equal moderation, because it is master of itself, and with complete success because it has the child's love.

And in another speech in 1941, Pope Pius XII counseled parents about disciplining children:

> Raise them in the Faith and the fear and love of God. Imbue them with the knowledge of right living, which makes the Christian, sets

him on the path of virtue, and guides him amid the dangers of many insidious enemies of youth.

Be an example to them in the pursuit of whatever is good, always behave in such a manner that your children may only have to model their lives on yours ...

Let the light of their lives be to observe you, to imitate you, to remember, some day when you are no longer at their side, your admonitions, exemplified and confirmed by a perfect fulfilling of all the obligations of a Christian life, by a refined and strong sense of duty without compromise, by an unshakable faith and confidence in God in the midst of the severest trials, by mutual affection grown stronger with the passage of years, by a charitable attitude to every sort of suffering.

The Holy Family

As we teach our children to be obedient as Jesus was obedient to His parents, we parents must study the lives of Mary and Joseph. They were obedient to the law of Moses in presenting Jesus in the Temple, and in taking Jesus to the Temple in Jerusalem when He was twelve years old. The Holy Family took part in the Passover celebration for eight days. After Mary and Joseph spent three days looking for Jesus, He explained He was being obedient to His heavenly Father by being about His Father's business. Then Jesus went back home with Mary and Joseph and was subject to them and their commands for Him.

Our primary goals in home schooling are to present our children to God, teach them the Word of God, the prayers and celebrations of the liturgical feasts, and to teach our children to be obedient to us as parents because we are the representatives of God while they are growing up. Finally, we must discipline ourselves by following God's commands and by giving good example.

Chapter 9:
Home Management in the
Catholic Home Schooling Family

Mrs. Ginny Seuffert, the mother of twelve children, has been home schooling for many years, and is a frequent speaker at home schooling conferences.

I have a dear elderly friend, in poor health, who becomes frustrated when she is unable to remember some event that happened recently, or when she must search for a word she needs to express a thought. Yet she can remember, in vivid detail, events from her childhood in a loving home. These memories are fresh and alive eighty years later. What a gift her parents gave to her!

No matter what sadness our children may encounter later in life, memories of a happy, loving, well-ordered home will sustain them. It is the ideal setting to pass on to them our beautiful Catholic beliefs. Armed with the true Faith and their parents' values, our children will never be alone with the troubles that come in every person's life. They will always have their faith in Christ, their guardian angels, and the comfort of the Blessed Mother. A dependable schedule will allow little ones the time and opportunity to develop a regular prayer life. Finally, a smooth, well-run household fosters attitudes of serenity and confidence which aid our children in their educational development.

In light of all this, isn't it sad that modern American society seems to save its recognition and support for professional accomplishments which occur outside the home? We devalue the irreplaceable role of parents (mostly mothers) in making homes places from which the next generation of good citizens and holy saints will come. Should we not devote to our homes the energy and innovation we now reserve for the workplace?

The key to successful home management, then, is to restore each Catholic household, the domestic church, to its rightful place as the building block of society. We must apply the same goal-oriented principles and professional attitudes to the running of our homes that a CEO gives to directing a Fortune 500 company.

A typical routine

Treating our housework as valued professional work means thinking about how we do our work, not just carrying on the same routine that mother or grandmother may have had. The following daily routine, which I generally follow for our family, is offered as a starting point to get you and other members of your family thinking about how to operate your home in an efficient, thrifty, cheerful manner.

A good day actually has its start before evening prayers the night before. Take a few moments and straighten the bedrooms. Have the children pick up any toys, put away any laundry, and clear the tops of their dressers. Have them lay out their clothes for the next day. This way you can approve of their choices and deal with any problem ("Mom! I don't have clean socks!") before it becomes an emergency. You probably will not have to dust and vacuum, and this should take no more than ten minutes per room.

The next day, try to get up at least 30 minutes before the rest of the family. This will allow you to say a good Morning Offering and plan for the school day without having every thought interrupted by a child's voice. Get dressed and complete your grooming for the day (even if you're wearing sweat pants and a ponytail) right away. Try to make your bed before heading out to the kitchen.

I start home schooling with the younger children as soon as the breakfast dishes are cleared. Math or phonics is usually assigned so they can work, more or less on their own, at the kitchen table, while I wash up. My two older pupils work independently in other rooms. My four-year-old plays with the toddler.

After dishes, the rest of the morning is spent home schooling. I usually sit down and work on religion, reading, and English, subjects with which the younger children may need help. After the second and third graders have completed most of their work, they take a turn with the baby so I can give my preschooler a reading lesson. My two older daughters, seventh and fourth grade, pop in and out as they need help with something.

We usually take a long lunch break, an hour or more. The older girls make lunch for the younger children while I fold a load of laundry and put another one in the washer. The children have play time while I eat and then wash another set of dishes. Sometimes I go to noon Mass.

Before the children begin schoolwork again, I plan my supper. Anything that can be prepared in advance is begun now. A little thought will show that almost any meal can be started hours before. For example, you can mix and shape a meatloaf and wash baking potatoes at noon. It will be easy to put them in the oven at 4:30 for a 6:00 dinner. Salad greens can be washed and cut in the middle of the day, allowed to drain in a colander, and refrigerated until mealtime. This planning and preparation will really pay off as dinnertime approaches and Mom is running kids to after-school activities, Dad is coming in, the baby is fussing, and the phone is ringing off the wall.

We start school again around 1:00. The younger children might color a map or write their spelling words. Sometimes they do an art or science project. I give more attention to the older girls, correcting their morning work, drilling their spelling or vocabulary, or proofreading a writing assignment on the word processor. Hopefully, the baby is napping now.

Around 3:00 school is over. Now is the time to clean the main living area of your home. Have the children pick up the mess they made while you were teaching. Make sure the bathrooms, especially the sink and toilet, are cleaned, run the vacuum, sweep the floors, and generally straighten the living room or den and the kitchen. Fold the last of the laundry and distribute it to the appropriate bedrooms.

Next, have a child set the table. This is a great job for a preschooler because you are in the room to supervise, and once the dinner plates are set, it is easy to add the silverware, napkins, and drinking glasses. As you finish with a pot, pan, or utensil, wash it right away. Dinner will be more enjoyable if you do not have to look at a sinkful of dirty pots. After dinner, clean-up will be quicker, too.

In our house, Mom and Dad usually do the dishes with the oldest son while the two older girls give baths and get the preschoolers ready for bed. The middle children take care of themselves.

As the children prepare for bed, your home should be reasonably straightened, the kitchen and bathrooms clean, and the laundry done.

Weekend work

A daily routine, similar to the one I just outlined, will keep your home tidy, decent meals on the table, and clean clothes in the dressers. At the same time, your children will be receiving the best education available in America today. In most cases, however, especially with a large family, you will still have to catch up on weekends.

I use weekends to correct assignments, prepare lesson plans, and organize the children's work for the following week. This is especially important for the older students who complete much of their work on their own. Even self-motivated, experienced, home-educated pupils need to have their assignments reviewed and their progress monitored. This weekly overview makes the end of each quarter less stressful.

Saturday is also the time to tackle more time-consuming chores such as washing windows, mopping floors, scrubbing the tiles around the tub, ironing, and grocery shopping. Your children should help with this work. Reserve Sunday as a day of worship and visiting with family and friends. It is crucial that home-educated children be allowed to socialize with children from other observant Catholic families. Memories of these happy times, and even many friendships made, will last a lifetime.

This is also the time to point out a fact that many hard-working Christian women are hesitant to admit: there is no disgrace in hiring domestic help. The year I began home schooling, I used the money we had been spending on tuition and had a cleaning lady come in two or three times each week. I no longer have any cleaning help, but that got me over the "hump" and allowed me some time to gain confidence in my ability to teach my own children and develop my daily routine.

Home teaching, especially if you have several children or students in the upper grades, is not something that can be done in your spare time. I believe many families send the children back to institutional schools when it seems as though the burden is overwhelming, as can happen when a new baby arrives. Domestic help might get you over a rough spot. Before you pay to send your children to public schools, where they may lose their faith, try getting a cleaning service. Even once a month service (getting the cobwebs down before the place looks haunted) will be a real help.

If you cannot afford a cleaning service, be creative. Maybe you can swing getting your husband's shirts professionally laundered. You can probably hire neighborhood kids to shovel walks or mow the lawn. Sometimes you can get a local teenager to watch the children for a few hours each week, freeing you up for household chores. Ask relatives to give you a one-shot cleaning service as a Christmas, birthday, or anniversary gift.

Motivating the children

The keys to training your children to be responsible for household chores are starting early and being consistent. Pray to their guardian angels for help in this important task. Give them the example of the Holy Family and add the ejaculation, "Jesus, Mary, and Joseph, pray for us now and at the hour of our death, Amen," to your Morning Offering.

One home school leader suggests you keep a basket in the corner of your toddler's crib and have the baby put stuffed animals and other crib toys into it before you pick him up. That is about as early as anyone could hope to start! Certainly, sometime between the ages of one and two years, all children can be trained to follow simple instructions. "Get me your diaper" and "Put this in the hamper" are just two examples.

Most three-year-olds are anxious to please Mommy and are capable of performing many simple tasks. They can empty wastebaskets with help, wipe down the kitchen table and the seats of the chairs, and pick up laundry.

Four-year-olds should be responsible for putting their own clothes into the proper dresser drawer, setting the table for dinner, and feeding the family pet.

By five, most children can sweep or vacuum a floor (well, maybe not the best job!), dust furniture, and even fold laundry. As soon as you are sure your child will not try to taste a dangerous substance and can learn safety rules, he can be taught to clean the bathroom.

Now most parents will claim that the problem is not that their children are unable to help with chores, it is that they are unwilling. I would like to see them be cheerful as they work, but my husband claims that is impossible, and if they were that good at this age, they would not need parents at all. Still, I will pass on a few tips that might prove useful in your situation.

1. Do not allow your children to argue with you. Complaints like, "Why do I have to do this all the time?" should be met with, "The only answer I expect to hear is, 'Yes, Mom.'"

2. Give your children the good example of hard-working adults. I am grateful to my own parents who instilled this value in their children, mostly through their own actions. All of my siblings are hard workers who are not afraid to tackle any new job. My husband gives great example to our own children.

3. Remind a child to do a job, even if it is for the fifth time, in the same tone of voice that you used the first time. Comments like "How many times do I have to tell you …?" delivered in a high-pitched screech are understandable but ineffective. A courteous and reasonably quiet atmosphere is more difficult to maintain in a large family, but just as important.

4. Remember that your children owe you respect and prompt obedience. Remind them that deliberate disobedience is a sin against the Fourth Commandment and should be confessed.

5. Thank your children when they do a good job, and brag about them, in their hearing, to Dad and others.

An efficient laundry routine

I have been attending a series of lectures given by a woman who directs a school for those entering the field of hotel and hospital management. After twenty-one years of marriage and eleven children, I can finally clean up my act in the laundry room. As with everything else, thinking about how to do the job will allow you to streamline the operation. Here are some simple ideas that have worked for me.

1. Have your husband hang a clothes bar next to the washer so shirts and dress pants can be hung up as soon as they have dried.

2. Buy a package of large safety pins and have family members pin their socks together before they are put into the hampers.

3. Invest in three hampers and write one word, either "light," "dark," or "white," on the tops. The wearer places the garments in the appropriate bin. You will be able to put a load of wash on much more quickly if it has already been sorted.

4. Fold each individual load as it is finished. Do not let it pile up!

Not all of the ideas in this chapter can be applied to every situation, but a little thought will allow you to come up with your own solutions. Pray to the Blessed Mother for help in modeling your home after hers.

End of Ginny Seuffert's work.

Ginny Seuffert's ideas for home management are certainly good ones, and you would do well to implement many of them. As you continue home schooling, you will, of course, make adjustments and find your own ways of doing things.

Successful home schooling is dependent on successful home management. If a mother feels she cannot keep her house decent, her frustration will be reflected in her home teaching. Or lack of home teaching.

Mothers often call me to say they are afraid to start home schooling because they are so disorganized. They believe they cannot manage both the housework and the schoolwork. We need to establish priorities here. Are we going to allow our kids to be exposed to sex education classes, or have peers laugh at them because they wear a scapular, or have teachers tell them that their parents are "old-fashioned" and that they can choose their own values? Are we going to allow this because we are disorganized, or because we are afraid we will not have time for housekeeping? Let's get control of ourselves and our lives!

To organize means to put parts together so that they work as a whole. For us home schooling mothers, it means to be efficient enough in the parts, the day-to-day tasks, so that our home schooling works overall, and is successful in training our children to be educated Catholics living the Catholic lifestyle.

Home schooling mothers need organization for their home management for several reasons: for themselves to have control over their own lives; to be a good example to their children; to bring calm and stability to the household; to accomplish goals and not feel frustrated and unhappy; and to give their children the best Catholic environment for learning and living their faith.

Scheduling

The home schooling mother is a manager of a small business. She needs to keep control of what is happening in her little home schooling household. The first thing I recommend is that you obtain your own plan book. You can purchase a teacher's plan book from Seton or an office supply store, or even a businessman's plan book in the stationery section of a department store. If you are computer-oriented, you can keep a daily schedule on your computer. Most cell phones also have calendars, to-do lists, and alarms.

Before we can achieve order, we need to define order. Some mothers feel that order means that everything is in its proper place, things are done at certain times, and the house is straightened up daily. But order, like so many other things, can be an attitude more in the mind than in the things around you.

A busy executive has a desk piled high with work. To a stranger, his desk is disorderly. But if someone comes along and straightens up his desk, he has a fit. He has certain piles in certain places, certain types of things in certain piles, and he is familiar with the order in the "disorder." He is mentally comfortable with his desk situation.

We mothers need to pray for a proper understanding of what an orderly home means. We should be able to function, but that may not mean the floor needs to be mopped every day or that everything needs to be in its place every day. We need to come to an emotional peace within ourselves, accept a certain amount of imperfection, and realize that the daily home schooling lessons, encompassing spiritual values, are much more important than perfect physical order in the house.

This is not to say that we cannot do better with putting things in their place, and keeping the house clean and straightened. We need to keep trying, and as our family grows, we need to teach these values to our children. In fact, they need "hands-on" practice in this area!

Clean rooms

I have worked to keep the major areas of my house under control. Thus, if someone walks into my home, he will see that the living room, the dining room, and the front hall are clean. It makes me feel better to have the major living areas kept clean and orderly.

Years ago, when I was not working full-time, I would make the boys clean their rooms weekly. But I seldom got upset about their rooms. There were too many other important things, such as saying the daily Rosary.

I have kept an extra closet for kitchen utensils. There is nothing more wonderful than a whole closet with lots of shelves to put away the mixing bowls and extra pans, the sifter and the mixer. In a small house, you can keep these things on a shelf in the laundry room.

Here is a trick one mother gave me to keep shoes and boots for her large family: her husband built shelves in an entryway by the back door. All the shoes and boots are kept there and do not cause a constant mess by being all over the house or under beds.

In addition, I have a place to put things which are out of season, or which I just want out of sight for a while. This is usually a place in the basement, but could be an extra small bedroom, or large walk-in closet.

When cleaning a room, have your child carry a trash bag and pick up things to throw away. Items to go in other areas of the house should be put in a pile according to the area. Once the room is picked up, others can pick up a pile and deliver it to the proper room.

Scheduling the cleaning

We busy home schooling mothers need to develop a strong managerial personality as we train our children to be the helpers necessary to maintain our home. Dad should be involved to make sure, each evening, that the children have done their daily household chores as well as their schoolwork.

Schedule what you are going to do each hour, each day, each week. This can be done for your home schooling, for housework, for Mass, *and for prayer*. (Prayer will often, almost inevitably, take a back seat unless it is scheduled—but it has to be given the front seat!) Schedule chores for each child in your plan book. This should be written in your child's lesson plan book as well, or posted in the kitchen.

Keep everything on a schedule as closely as possible: meals, chores, bedtime, rising, school work. You and your children need a regular schedule. You will feel better emotionally and even physically if you eat, work, and sleep on a regular schedule.

Get the kids to help with housework. Schedule household chores within the schoolday schedule, between classes. Making their beds or putting on a load of laundry can be scheduled between history and science. Other chores are taking out the trash, sweeping the floor, vacuuming the carpet, dusting, mowing the lawn, bringing in the wood (if you have a wood stove), straightening up the classroom or recreation room, and so on.

One successful home schooling mother of ten children said her success was due in large part to the fact that she had a daily schedule and "stuck to it religiously." She told me her schedule was never off "by even five minutes."

The meals

Keep your meals organized. The regularity of family meals is very important to children. Give children different responsibilities for setting the table or helping prepare the meals. Establish regular times and regular procedures for meals: prayer before meals, rules of courtesy, proper dress at the table, and so on.

There are many little tricks for preparing meals. When making dinner, make enough for at least two nights. I always make two meatloaves, or a double recipe of chicken, or enough stew for two nights. I have a friend, a home schooling mother, who is also a midwife, with a large family of eight children, who takes one day each month and cooks, with her children helping, THIRTY meals! She freezes them and, for the next four weeks, has the basic main meal ready in minutes. This gives *"Semper Paratus!"* (always prepared) a new meaning!

Reduce the number of things you have in the kitchen or pantry. Give away extra glasses or dishes. Keep only what you actually want to wash. When I moved the last time, I evaluated each kitchen item as to how much I really needed it. I gave away tons of things. I really like having less to clean. I am a big believer in paper plates for breakfast and lunch, and for dinner during the week.

Your greatest help, your children

It is important to teach your children to help with the housework. A home schooling mother cannot do the home schooling properly and still do all the housework. Children should not only help because mothers need the help, but also because it is morally a matter of justice that children learn to work as part of the family team. In addition, God made us so that we need to work to be happy, and children should learn that.

Many teenagers and adults have not learned the joy and happiness that work can bring. Since Jesus was "subject" to His parents, we can surmise that Joseph taught Him his trade of carpentry. We need to remind our children that Jesus was thirty years old before He started His public preaching, and St. Joseph had died before that. So we know that Jesus worked to help His foster-father, and later to provide for Himself and Mary. He was known as "the carpenter's Son."

It has been found that men who have problems with keeping jobs often did not work when they were young. They either came from wealthy families, or were spoiled, or no one really cared whether they worked or not. When children are not required to do work around the home, it is difficult to have them do their schoolwork as well. They are being pampered.

Schoolwork is important for children, but housework is for the benefit of the whole family. Housework promotes team effort. If we are home schooling to strengthen our family life, or family bonds, we need to realize that housework actually helps more in this area than schoolwork.

Some jobs for personal care should be routinely done, such as taking care of one's own bedroom. Extra jobs could receive some small allowance if the parents wish, such as washing the kitchen floor, cleaning the basement, or doing yard work.

Teaching the chore

When teaching children to do a chore, you need to help the child with the work the first few times. That is the only way the child will do the job the way you want, or nearly the way you want. I have found that working alongside my children on a big cleaning project helps keep them moving and doing the work the way I want.

It is important to show your children very clearly how to do a job. Instead of just handing a child the cleanser and a rag, show him how you clean the sink. Explain as you go, pointing out the necessity of getting behind the faucet, and so on. When you check his work at first, and later randomly, check all those points you spoke about when you taught him.

Older children can help teach younger children to do chores. If a younger child and an older child are a team, the older will keep doing the work as he teaches, and the younger one will be kept moving by the older one. The two children should not be close in age as they will end up arguing with each other. There should be several years' age difference in the children on a work team.

Just as you encourage your children in the schoolwork, encourage them in their household chores. One of the things I tell my children is that they should clean as if Jesus Himself were going to visit that particular room. It is important that our children understand that they must do their very best even in seemingly small and unimportant things. I reminded my sons that when the Challenger exploded in the sky and several people were killed, it was because someone was careless in regard to the formation of ice on an "O ring." Little things can mean life and death in some cases!

Just as it is a serious responsibility to teach our children their reading and their math, so it is a serious responsibility to teach them to do household chores. Unfortunately, there are some adults who cannot take care of themselves or their homes in an orderly and reasonably clean fashion because they were not taught to do chores when they were young. And if a child does not do his chores, or his schoolwork, to the best of his ability, he will probably not do his best at his job or career later on.

Teaching children to work, both physically, as in doing household chores, and intellectually, as in doing schoolwork, is a serious parental responsibility.

Learn from others

Locate books at the library or Christian bookstore on home management and chores for children, such as: *401 Ways to Get Your Kids to Work at Home.* This book has "Techniques, tips, tricks, and strategies on how to get your kids to share the housework … and in the process become self-reliant, responsible adults." There are several books in Christian bookstores which can help you in home management also. The home schooling associations promote the books by Don Aslett: *Is There Life After Housework?*, *Clutter's Last Stand*, *It's Not Just a Woman's Job to Clean*, and *Make Your House Do the Housework.* Another book presenting interesting and time-saving ideas is *Once-a-Month Cooking* by Mimi Wilson.

One word of caution. Church activities are wonderful, but do not allow them, even though they are good religious activities, to cause you to neglect your home and children. Your first duty is to raise your children in the Catholic family lifestyle. Limit your church activities or charitable works to those in which your children can participate with you.

Conclusion

Adjust your lifestyle and your home for home education. Make your home a haven—a stable, comfortable, orderly place, not like the frantic, stress-filled, disorderly, chaotic, and confused outside world. Make your home a refuge, a protection from the outside problems; make it a pleasant, loving, prayerful home. When God told Moses that our homes were to be decorated with the Ten Commandments on our doors and doorposts, on our entryways inside our homes, I believe He meant that our home environment should reflect our faith. Keeping an orderly home should reflect our faith in a God of order and harmony.

Chapter 10:
Home Schooling in the
Single-Parent Family

by a Home Schooling Single Mother

"Suffer the little children to come unto me, and forbid them not …" (Mark 10:14). These words of Christ, the greatest Teacher Who ever was or ever will be, show the enormous responsibility that parents have of teaching their children about God from infancy, developing in them a steady, ever-increasing knowledge, love, and service of Our Lord.

The Catholic position is, and has always been, that "Parents have the most *grave* obligation and the *primary* duty to do *all* in their power to ensure their children's physical, social, cultural, moral, and religious upbringing" (1983 Code of Canon Law, 1136, emphasis added).

Pope Leo XIII in *Sapientiae Christianae* states:

> By nature parents have a right to the training of their children, but with this added duty: that the education and instruction of the child be in accord with the end for which by God's blessing it was begotten. Therefore it is the duty of the parents to make every effort to prevent any invasion of their rights in this matter, and to make absolutely sure that the education of their children *remain under their own control,* in keeping with their Christian duty, and above all to *refuse* to send them to those schools in which there is danger of imbibing the deadly poison of impiety.

The Second Vatican Council also reiterated this statement in its Declaration on Christian Education. In fact, the primary and *co-equal* purposes of the Sacrament of Matrimony are the procreation *and* education of children. Our Creator Himself has ordained that for this divine purpose of marriage to be a success, it is essential that the order and structure of a solid family life be preserved.

What can be done, though, when you find that the sacred structure is missing a key component—when one parent is no longer part of the picture? Is it possible for the remaining members to survive? Can a broken home go beyond mere survival and elevate itself to becoming a healed, stable, happy, and God-centered family? Yes, if the children are home schooled.

Does home schooling under these circumstances seem unrealistic— perhaps impossible? Well, the Church informs us that as parents we have "the right," "the duty," and "the grave obligation" to provide for our children's education.

In his encyclical on Christian Education of Youth, Pope Pius XI tells us:

> Since education consists essentially in preparing man for what he must be and for what he must do here below, in order to attain the sublime end for which he was created, it is clear that there can be no true education which is not wholly directed to man's last end.

With this in mind, there is no way that a true educational system can include a perverted sex education, drug awareness, death awareness, AIDS education, values clarification, or any other topic of instruction of the humanist agenda. Clearly, this is not what Our Lord intended when He gave the command, "Go forth and teach ye all nations."

If the Church's position on the importance of a truly Christian education is not a convincing factor to home school, perhaps the concerns for the emotional stability of a child coming from a broken home environment will be. The emotional jarring that these children undergo during the breakup of their families is something they will carry with them for the rest of their lives. Do we want to further scar them by separating them from the family they have left—sending them to a school outside of the home for six to eight hours each day? They will not find there the security and stability they need so desperately. Do you place the younger ones in a day care center, or perhaps an after-hours school program, so much the trend now, if the parent must seek outside employment? What about the adolescents or teenagers who must come home to an empty house? It will not be long before trouble finds them. Will any of these solutions help them?

We have already experienced a generation of children being raised by strangers: the babysitter or day-care provider is the one who discovers the first tooth or witnesses the first step, and sadly, the one who is very often even called "Mama." Will these children become the well-adjusted, family-oriented adults of tomorrow? How could they when there was no one around *just* for them, who would love them as no "caregiver" ever would, because no one can take the place of a parent? That was the way God intended it to be, and without either the order of a stable family life or the hierarchical structure of parenthood, children will lack the proper nurturing. Sadly, the child of today's broken marriage often loses not one, but both parents.

During such an emotional upheaval as the loss of a parent, would not the best place for these children be in their homes? Is it not important for them to be able to cry when they feel like it, to scream when they have to, to act out in any other way that they need to, but most importantly, to know that one parent is *still there* for them?

In the face of a broken family, which is better: to leave your children at the school bus stop each morning, or to pack them all up in the car, drive down to the parish church, and begin each and every day with the Holy Sacrifice of the Mass? Without doubt, neither you nor your children could possibly get through such a trial without God's *constant* grace and the nourishment and strength of His Precious Body and Blood.

Will the school day go smoothly? Probably not, especially in the beginning. But think of the alternative. In any event, it is far better to endure whatever comes, together, *as a family*, rather than each one suffering alone.

Trust and pray to the Holy Family often; never permit a day to go by without the family Rosary being said. Entrust your children to Our Lady's care, being confident that the Blessed Mother will guard them as her very own. Do this and Our Lord will be ever present in your home as King and Head of your family and your home school.

The Teaching

How does a single parent go about teaching the children without the benefit of a partner? Actually, in this regard, things are virtually the same as for home schools having both parents. In most households, it is the father who is the breadwinner, leaving the majority if not the entirety of the schooling up to the mother. There are also many families whose circumstances require that both parents be employed, and yet home schooling is still an integral part of their life. In this respect, the situations are similar because the schooling is usually one parent's job, and so the same standards for successful home schooling apply to all.

First, be organized. Have a schedule and streamline your day. Eliminate all the unnecessary errands, visits, and events that take up your precious time. Set a timetable for getting up, Mass, breakfast, and the beginning of class, and stick to it. Do not answer the phone during school hours. Set a certain time for ending the school day and do not go beyond it, especially if you must then prepare for an outside job. If something in class is unfinished, it can wait until the next day.

Next, be flexible. If your situation requires you to work outside the house for two days, then teach on the other three days. Teach on the weekends. Homeschooling easily adjusts to a working schedule.

Third, be motivated. Home schooling is *good* for your family. Look upon it as such, each and every day.

Fourth, acknowledge that it is a sacrifice and a commitment, but no different, really, from the entire sacrifice that responsible parenting requires.

Fifth, enlist the help of others. The children, however young, should have their share of responsibilities: one washes dishes, the other sweeps the floor, the little one can put away clothes, pick up toys, etc. They must understand that you cannot do it all. If relatives approve of what you are doing, then have them help in whatever way they can. If they are not supportive, however, it is usually best to stay clear of them.

Finally, and most importantly, we must be virtuous. Patience must be cultivated as well as self-discipline, which also means self-denial. Perseverance also is vital. Do not be so discouraged that you want to give up! If the day becomes impossible, then let your children read a book on the life of a saint. Fill your children's bookshelves with wholesome, entertaining books: classics and good spiritual reading. Or let them watch a good video: *The Song of Bernadette, A Man for All Seasons, The Day the Sun Danced.* The children *will learn* from these.

Console yourself with the knowledge that as long as your children are home with you, their souls are safe. Teach them their prayers, the Ten Commandments, prepare them for the sacraments, have them examine their conscience each and every night. In the end, being a whiz at science or math will be of little consequence. What Our Lord wants to see in our children is a pure heart.

One of the things you must come to understand to successfully raise well-adjusted, spiritually healthy, *good* children without the benefit of a traditional family unit is that it cannot be done without traditional family routines and values. It is especially important that meals be taken with all family members present. These should be quiet, relaxed, sit-down-at-the-table times, where "company" manners are always observed and the TV is *never* on. This ought to be a time for discussion of the day's events, telling jokes, in all, pleasant communication among the family members. Cook their favorites. Avoid the temptation to think it is too much trouble to make that special dish just because there is only one adult around now.

Make a big deal of special occasions, especially those holidays that are traditionally family oriented. Go out together as a family often. Splurge when you can for a breakfast out. A dish of ice cream at the local shop is always a treat and is one of those few extravagances that will not do too much damage (hopefully) to a single parent's budget. Make Sundays special by packing a lunch and visiting a museum (or other free place of interest). The goal is to make life at home happy and memorable despite the circumstances.

How do you go about all this if you need to earn money as well as home school your children? Ideally, try to find employment that can be done at home, perhaps by "telecommuting" a few days a week. The fact that you will always be there for your children will be a far greater wealth than any you could amass at an office. But if this just is not feasible, then work out of the house in the evenings or at nights. The thing to strive for is to be home for your children during the day, when they need you most.

Remind yourself of the words of the great Doctor of the Church, St. John Chrysostom, "What greater work is there than training the mind and forming the habits of the young?" Be sure that the children are under the care of a trusted relative or conscientious babysitter. Have the sitter come to your home. This, too, builds stability in the child. It is never fun to sleep in an unfamiliar place only to be roused out of a deep slumber a few hours later, brought out into the cold night air, and have to face a car ride before being in the comfort of your own bed.

Again, pray for a solution. This is one area where if you storm Heaven, Our Lord will provide in great measure. Teaching your children at home is what God *wills* for you to do, and if you are determined to overcome the obstacles, He will reward you abundantly by removing whatever stands in your way.

The main objective is to minimize the loss, as far as possible, of the missing parent. You have been given the graces through the Sacrament of Matrimony to raise and *educate* your children properly, even if it means you must do so alone.

Our Lord has blessed nature with a wonderful capacity for resiliency and adaptability. If one should have the great misfortune to lose something so necessary as an eye, the tragedy does lessen to some extent because the surviving eye grows stronger *primarily because of the loss* and so begins to compensate and take over for that member which is no longer there.

A true follower of Christ knows that in being less we are capable of more. When we recognize our nothingness, Christ will use us to accomplish great things. For the sake of our children, we must go to Him each day acknowledging our weaknesses, our limitations, our mistakes, our uncertainties as single parents and ask Him to do for us and through us all that we are incapable of doing ourselves.

A single home schooling mother of several children wrote the previous article. Over the years, I have heard from many single parents who are home schooling.

How do they manage work and home schooling? Most have jobs they can do at home, such as typing or computer work, or editing, or proofreading. Some work for a relative who is understanding of the situation and is willing to allow the mother to be flexible in her hours.

Some are nurses or work in nursing homes, or work as private duty nurses at night. Others work at night-time jobs, such as with the phone company. Some arrange for another home schooling mother to take their children in the afternoon. Some live with or near their mother or a sister so they have a babysitter when they need to work in the afternoon or evening.

Some single mothers take their children to work. One works at a bookstore and the children sit in the back room. One is a secretary and the child has a desk next to hers. One mother cleans homes and takes her children with her.

There are a few single fathers teaching their children. Most work at home. One is a writer. One is retired. One teaches in the morning, then goes to work in the afternoon. One lives with relatives who help.

We need to commend, and pray for, single parents who recognize their responsibilities and are willing to make extra sacrifices for the sake of their children.

Chapter 11:
Teaching Children Who Learn Differently

by Cathy Gould

Cathy Gould is a learning disability specialist. She earned her B.A. in Education from James Madison University in 1977, and her M.A. in Education with endorsements in Learning Disabilities and Emotional Disturbance from George Mason University in 1981. Cathy is fully certified for teaching special needs children. She has been teaching special needs children and advising parent groups for over twenty years, including working with Seton families for many years. Cathy is the mother of four children.

Learning Disabilities (LD), Hyperactivity Disorder, and Attention Deficit/Hyperactivity Disorder (AD/HD) are often referred to as the hidden handicaps. Identifying educational handicaps early may alleviate some problems that are typically seen in children with learning disabilities, such as low self-esteem, failure syndrome, and depression.

When parents school their children at home, they notice at an early age when a particular child is not progressing using the traditional methods. Then the search begins to discover exactly how the child learns differently.

Just what is a learning disability? There are four points that most professionals will accept as true of all individuals with learning disabilities:

The individual with a learning disability does not learn satisfactorily with standard methods of instruction.

- The basic cause of failure to learn is not a lack of intelligence.
- The basic cause is not a psychological problem.
- The basic cause is not a physical handicap.
- The Education for All Handicapped Children Act defines a learning disability as a disorder in one or more of the basic psychological processes involved in understanding or using language, spoken or written, which may manifest itself in an imperfect ability to listen, think, speak, read, write, spell, or do mathematical calculations. Learning disabilities include perceptual handicaps, minimal brain dysfunction, brain injury, dyslexia, and developmental aphasia;

however, they do not include disabilities due to vision, hearing, or motor handicaps, or to mental retardation, or to cultural or economic deprivation.

Identifying

Learning Disability (LD) is a broad term that includes such difficulties as processing problems, dyslexia, dysgraphia, dyscalculia, Asperger's Syndrome, and autism. In assessing a child to determine if a learning disability exists, the professionals look for a discrepancy between a child's potential, or IQ, and performance or achievement. Children with a learning disability usually have an average to above-average IQ. Listed below are characteristics that occur in individuals with learning disabilities. Be aware that some of these characteristics may occur in young children even without a learning disability.

1. *Mixed dominance and directional confusion.* Past the age of five or six, a child still seems confused about whether to use his right and/or his left hand for writing, picking up objects, and eating. Some children may have difficulty crossing the midline of the body. They may have a hard time picking up an object to the left of their body using their right hand.

2. *Poor concept of time.* They do not have that internal sense of time. They have difficulty staying on a schedule, or with scheduling projects. An example of this may be that when you give your child ten minutes to play outside, ten minutes come and go. In 30 minutes, you must find your child, who is totally oblivious to the amount of time which has passed.

3. *Unusual powers of observation.* Nothing escapes their view. They have a difficult time filtering out unnecessary things and focusing on what is important.

4. *Unusual creativity.* They are able to see things very differently from others, and to approach problems in a very unique way. They can be very mechanical, take things apart, and eventually put them back together. Often these individuals can be very gifted artists.

5. *Appear to be "misfits and loners."* They are often called "dumb" by the other students; the teachers often call them lazy; they may not pick up on body language or jokes; and they may have difficulty knowing what is acceptable behavior.

6. *Mental retrieval problems.* They may know the word "red," and may have known it for a long time, but when you are talking to them in a conversation, suddenly they cannot pull that word out of their vocabulary.

7. *Memory problems.* Many children with learning disabilities have a difficult time memorizing the addition, subtraction, multiplication, and division facts. They also may have difficulty memorizing lists of information, such as names of the planets.

8. *Reversals.* While this is normal in young children, it should not be continuing past age 10. Reversals are evident in the writing of words and numbers. The frequently reversed letters are b and d, p and q; sometimes numbers are reversed, such as 3, 7, and 9 being written backwards; sometimes 6 and 9 are reversed.

9. *Fine-motor problems.* This may be displayed through shaky writing, inappropriate formation of letters, difficulty finding the space on a paper, difficulty with spacing letters and words, or difficulty staying between the lines.

10. *Attention problems.* They may have difficulty focusing their attention on the task at hand, or they may be able to stay on task only for very short periods of time.

11. *Sequencing.* Many of these individuals have difficulty retelling something that happened to them in the correct sequence. They may go to a party, and come back and tell you everything that happened at the party; however, the sequence of events may be all out of order. They also may have difficulty sequencing information that is told to them. Consequently, they may find it difficult to follow directions in order. They may have difficulty with mathematical problems which require a sequence of steps.

Attention Deficit/Hyperactivity Disorder

Attention Deficit/Hyperactivity Disorder is a neurobehavioral disorder. The child with AD/HD may display mostly inattention, or mostly hyperactive-impulsive behavior, or a combination of inattention plus hyperactive-impulsive behavior. Some of the signs a child might display include lack of organization, difficulty following directions, lack of attention, forgetfulness, being easily distracted, difficulty sitting still, excessive activity, frequently interrupting others, difficulty waiting for others. Please remember that such children demonstrate these characteristics, or behaviors, in a variety of situations over a long period of time.

Learning materials

Developing a curriculum for a child with LD or AD/HD provides a unique challenge for parents. With the one-on-one approach in home schooling, many children with LD or AD/HD are able to use a standard grade-appropriate curriculum. Of course, modifications may be necessary.

Other children may need a curriculum totally adapted to their needs. They may need books with shorter chapters, though basically the material is grade-appropriate. Some children need materials with more pictures and color. Some children may need to review more frequently, and actively respond to the material by using worksheets, computer drills, flashcards, and hands-on experiments.

Several publishing companies carry materials that have been designed specifically for the child with LD or AD/HD. There are other companies that have designed "remedial" textbooks which may be appropriate also.

Globe Publishers produces a series of textbooks for the junior high student in science, American history, and geography. Steck-Vaughn publishes an appropriate science and social studies series for the elementary level. Educators Publishing Service offers quality materials in spelling, vocabulary, phonics, and primary language arts in general. None of these are Catholic, but they are seldom anti-Catholic or anti-family, though parents should be sure to read the books before giving them to their children.

The questions to ask when you are looking for materials for your child are: what is your child's basic learning style, and what is the teaching style of the material? For example, if your child is an auditory learner, he or she may do very well with a sing-song kind of approach to phonics, whereas, if your child is a visual learner, that approach, no matter how catchy it might be, may not work for your child.

There are some key points to consider when you are establishing a curriculum for your child. The most important aspects to look at are your child's strengths and weaknesses. You want to develop a program that is based on your child's strengths, and using those strengths, you can reinforce the weaker areas.

If your child has a particular weakness, the most important thing to do is to find a way to deal with the material successfully. For example, if you have a child who has memory problems with math, work on the memorization of facts by using a variety of other materials, such as hands-on items. At the same time, you could take a few minutes each day and teach other math concepts, such as time or measurement.

If your child does not know the multiplication facts (tables), but you are letting him go on to the three-digit by three-digit multiplication problems using a calculator, such as (324 x 436), instead of having your child punch in each entire number and multiply, have your child do the problem step by step, so that he actually multiplies as he would on paper. The only need he has for a calculator is for the basic multiplication facts. When your child learns the facts, he is still able to do that particular type of multiplication problem. If you let him punch in the entire three-digit number times the entire three-digit number, your child is not learning how to multiply such numbers manually.

Memory problems

For children who have memory problems, a good technique is to develop a cue card system. Purchase spiral-bound index cards that are 5 x 8 or 4 x 6, or you can punch holes in the individual index cards and hook them together with a single notebook ring. Present the lesson, then have your child repeat the lesson back to you in his own words. As he repeats it, put the key points on a piece of paper or a chalkboard, and color code the different parts of whatever it is he is working with. For example, when presenting the three-digit by three-digit multiplication problem (324 x 436), color code the "6" in one color; use arrows drawn in the same color to indicate what to multiply (6 x 4; 6 x 2; 6 x 3), and use the same color when writing out the directions for these steps. Next, write the "3" in another color and draw arrows using the same color to designate what to multiply: (3 x 4; 3 x 2; 3 x 3). Write any instructions pertaining to the "3" in the same color. Use the same process when multiplying by the "4." Remember to write the addition sign in yet a different color.

In division problems, have your child use colored pencils for the different operations. Thus, the result of division would be in one color, the result of multiplying in another color, the result of subtraction in a third color. The words telling what to do for each step would correspond in each color. You can use this for math, spelling words, grammar, or anything else. Some parents use cue cards in science or history to help the child memorize lists of information.

Writing problems

The computer is a valuable asset for students with written language and fine-motor problems. Some students have difficulty forming letters, or spacing letters and words on the paper. Most children enjoy working on the computer, and children who have fine motor problems find that it helps them to avoid something that is just inherently difficult for them. The computer has wonderful abilities. For instance, it allows children to move and rearrange information without rewriting it. Spellcheckers help children who have spelling problems.

A tape recorder is another asset for children with written language problems. Some children just cannot use the paper and pencil to write their words on paper. If you ask them to tell you a story, they are beautifully creative; they can give you imaginative stories, long, in-depth, with a wonderful vocabulary. However, put a pencil in their hands, and they cannot do it. For these children, giving them a tape recorder is a terrific way to get around the negative feelings associated with trying to write. Once a child puts his thoughts on a tape recorder, he can go back and write those thoughts on a computer.

Learning styles

Knowing your child's learning style is most important when you are designing a curriculum for a child with a learning disability. For example, if a child is mainly an auditory learner, rather than visual or tactile, he learns best by hearing. So use materials with which you can do more auditory teaching. Most people learn best through a multi-modality presentation, combining auditory, visual, and tactile.

Children with learning problems need repetition. Be repetitive. If a child is having trouble with his multiplication facts, go over and over his multiplication facts, a few minutes every day, maybe several times a day, using different techniques. Use flash cards one time, drill sheets another time, a game another time.

When I talk about being repetitive, I'm also talking about spiraling. If something has been presented previously in the year, and the child has shown mastery, do not drop it. Try to incorporate that information in future lessons, either as part of the lesson, or as a review. For example, if you have taught addition, subtraction, and multiplication facts and now you are working on division, each of those skills is included in division. You would not really have to do a specific review, so you move past the division to fractions, then you might want to have one, two, or three problems a day that would be considered review. Do not overdo the review problems; keep it limited to three to five problems, depending on the child.

Children with LD or AD/HD need structure. Many of these children, as mentioned before, have no concept of time, and usually need to be put on a schedule, and sometimes even on a timer. One of the benefits of home schooling is the ability to have flexibility. So when I say "Structure, structure, structure," some parents are going to grimace; however, that is what these children need. They need to wake up at the same time every morning, and have the same morning routine. They should start their school work at the same time every day, and should be expected to do the same subjects first, second, and third.

For the child who has difficulty staying on task for any length of time, you may need to try a timer for a while. Determine the average time range your child stays focused. If your child stays on task comfortably for seven minutes, then set the timer for seven minutes. Most children need concrete reinforcement. It may be beneficial to make a chart and break the school day down into seven-minute increments, and give a sticker or star for every seven-minute interval that your child stays on task. Let the child get up at the end of seven minutes and put a sticker on the chart, come back and start again. Generally, that is enough of a little break to allow the child to start back to work without getting too distracted.

Set your child up for success. Make sure that your child understands what you expect. When you give a presentation, have the child repeat back to you in his own words a summary of what he believes he is supposed to know. If you give directions, have the child repeat the directions back to you. If your child is supposed to do math problems, show an example, and then have him work one while you are watching. Make sure that your child can succeed independently at the task you give him.

For a child who may have difficulty with writing, consider having your child do the work orally. This will get the work completed and have your child feel successful, and you will still be getting a response to the material. If you need a written response, you can write what your child answers.

Testing

Testing can be a difficult area for children with special needs. As a home schooling parent, you can be more flexible than the teacher in a classroom. Testing may be done with audio tapes, video tapes, singing, or dramatic presentation. Use any method you believe will show your child has mastered the material.

If you are in a situation where you need to have traditional testing done, either to submit to your school system or because you are with a home school that asks for testing, adapt the testing environment. Waive time limits. Take short periods of testing time over several days.

When you are testing the skills presented in the test, and not the ability to read and to figure out what is being asked for in the question, then you may read the test and the answers to your child. If necessary, allow your child to give answers orally, then write the answers yourself.

Another way that you can change the testing format is to change the test from a short answer, or a fill-in-the-blank or an essay, to multiple choice. Many times children do well with multiple choice; they see the answer, and they know it. Then there are children who do not do well with multiple choice at all because there are too many choices. If your child is in that category, narrow the choices down to two. Maybe your child does better with an essay; let him tell you what he learned in the chapter. You may find that he actually gives you more information than the test asks for.

Having a child privately evaluated for learning disabilities is very expensive; therefore, you may want to go through your school system. Just keep in mind, if you do go through your school system, it will be a good idea to check with other local home schooling families to see what their experience has been with exposing themselves to the school system. Some of the school systems across the country feel that if you have a child with LD or AD/HD, they have a right to educate that child because they are the professionals. So, if you are going to pursue testing, be sure to check with other home schoolers as to the local school's philosophy about home schooling children with special needs.

Home schooling

Basically, there are several good reasons why you should home school a child with special needs. The schools TRY to give your children individualized instruction; you CAN give your child individualized instruction. You can set up a curriculum that is designed to meet your child's specific needs, and you can be there, one on one, to give your child the attention and help that he needs.

There are many resources out there that are available for you and your child. Sometimes it is to your advantage to have your child formally tested so you can have access to those resources. Some school systems will allow children to attend speech and language resource classes, or learning disabilities resource classes, if they have been formally identified as having a learning problem.

There are laws to protect the child with special needs, such as Public Law 94-142 and 504, which might make it possible for home schooling parents to place the child with LD or AD/HD in a school for one or two special services, such as occupational therapy, speech therapy, and resource classes. Of course, the decision to make any use of the public school should be approached with caution and prayer.

Home schooling releases your child from peer pressure. Many times, children in schools are teased and made fun of because they cannot follow directions, or they do not follow conversations. They often look socially different. By taking the child out of the school, you may be able to provide him more suitable socialization in other situations, like Boy Scouts, 4-H clubs, a choir, or music lessons.

Research shows that a substantial proportion of delinquency or juvenile crime that is committed in America is done by children with learning disabilities. The last thing you need is for a child who already has problems to become involved in a drug situation. Illegal drug use can destroy the child who has perceptual and attention problems.

You may want to keep a child at home to give him the incentive to learn. Children in a school situation often acquire a failure syndrome, but at home you can give positive reinforcement and provide successful learning situations.

Your child does have special needs, and you know your child better than anyone else. You have more invested in your child being successful and feeling good about himself than anyone else. You have the love and patience to be successful. It may not be the easiest job in the world, but you *can* home school a child with special needs. And your child needs the love and patience that only you, as a parent, can give.

Chapter 12:
Home Schooling the Special-Needs Child

by Cathy Rich

There are many dimensions involved in raising, as well as teaching, the child with special needs. These include spiritual, parenting, sibling, and teaching issues.

I am the mother of five children. The boys are 12, 8, and almost 4. The girls are 10 and 2. My 12-year-old has Attention Deficit Disorder (ADD), predominantly inattentive type. The eight-year-old has Attention Deficit/Hyperactivity Disorder (AD/HD), predominantly hyperactive-impulsive type, temporal lobe syndrome, visual/auditory perceptual problems, speech, and fine/gross motor difficulties. The four-year-old is delayed on speech. I suspect AD/HD, but it is not certain. My ten-year-old girl has processing and memory difficulties. The two-year-old so far appears to be "normal."

I have been home schooling for five years after finding out the hard way with my oldest that private education does not work educationally or spiritually with these children. Obviously, it is challenging educating these children. This is in addition to managing the extraordinary family dynamics that occur. AD/HD impacts every aspect of our lives.

Spiritual life

The first and by far the most important topic to address is spiritual. The children's spiritual life must take precedence over everything else. These children are especially vulnerable to temptation because of their difficulties with self-control and their tendency to manipulate others. We must provide them with every spiritual aid available in their battle against their disorders. When their spiritual life is in order, they are better equipped to be successful in their school work. Faith should be your child's fortress. Surround him with it.

The day should begin with prayer. When the children first wake up, we make the Morning Offering and say the Angel of God prayer. This is followed by an Our Father, Hail Mary, and seven Glory Be's. We try to see who the saint for the day is the night before so we can begin knowing what virtues to concentrate on the next morning. Otherwise, the next morning or at the noon Angelus we read about that saint. We often make novenas in honor of special saints, and practice monthly devotions such as to the Sacred Heart in June, and to Mary in May.

It is imperative that the Rosary be part of each day. My eight-year-old's attention span cannot handle a five-decade Rosary yet, so we have him join in for one decade each day. Before that, we would have him say the Our Father and/or Glory Be at the end of each decade. He started by doing the beginning and ending prayers to the Rosary. When it comes to long prayers such as the Rosary, we must remember that our goal is to cultivate their relationships with God, not turn them off to the Faith by overwhelming them.

Finally, each day should end with an examination of conscience, no matter how brief, and an act of contrition with a prayer for penance afterwards. How often, outside of Confession, do we make our act of contrition without assigning a penance to ourselves afterwards? Children pick up on these omissions.

This may seem like a lot, but it actually goes fairly quickly. Depending on the age of your child, you may want to use some of the morning prayers as a mid-morning break. But the Morning Offering, Angel of God, and Hail Mary at the beginning of each day, before breakfast, are a must for our family.

The sacraments are very important to these children. Because of their strong temptations, I have my children go to Confession at least every two weeks. Daily Mass is also very important. I realize managing these children at Mass can be very stressful. I bring along plastic statues of religious figures, or religious coloring books to keep their hands occupied. My rule is to make whatever they are playing with religious. This seems to work fairly well. I have noticed that my children do better in churches that have a lot of statues to look at. In fact, sometimes they are the most quiet in the front pew because they have a statue staring them in the face to absorb their interest. Up front, they can also follow the movements of the priest more closely. I encourage the children to light candles at church. Anything you can do to give them a more active part in the Mass will help. The less often we go to Mass during the week the harder it is to control the children on Sundays. Consistency is very important in learning proper behavior.

In preparing my eight-year-old for his first Confession and first Holy Communion, I had to keep his uniqueness in mind and avoid the temptation about when he would "normally" be receiving these sacraments. He must be mature enough to appreciate the gravity of these sacraments, not just know his catechism and be physically capable of going through the motions. This is an area in which the parent must look at each child individually and decide. It should not be just the priest's decision, but yours primarily. A child needs to have a good idea of what sin is in his own life first and want to eliminate it. Right now he is not fully aware of what it is in his own life due to his attention problem. The other issue is understanding what Holy Communion means. It is very hard to feel comfortable with your child receiving Holy Communion when he cannot keep still during Mass. Again, you have to discern which behaviors are intentional, and which ones they honestly cannot control and be held accountable for. There are no easy answers.

The blessings of establishing in your children a devotion to their guardian angel are without end. I have just finished reading a book called *All About the Angels* by Fr. Paul O'Sullivan, O.P. I encourage everyone to read it. My children have so much more confidence knowing their angel is with them. It also helps them to avoid sin when they realize that their angels do not want them to sin. We do our children a supreme injustice when we do not help them foster a devotion to their guardian angels. They *must* have every advantage possible if they are to succeed in learning and in serving God.

Next in importance to these everyday devotions comes your children's catechism. It must come second to their daily prayer life because actions speak louder than words. You can teach them all the catechism in the world, but they must see you practicing it, and you need to make them practice it. If not, first, it becomes a burdensome subject because of the memorization. Second, they will resist learning it. Third, they are going to resent you for making them learn it. Logically, why should they learn something that their parents do not even feel is important enough to use? To put catechism before their daily living of the Faith would, in fact, ultimately turn them away from God.

In teaching the young learning-disabled child the Faith, use as many hands-on teaching tools as you can. A felt board with Bible figures for teaching them Bible stories is a great tool. Do role playing of different situations for teaching the Ten Commandments. Use your imagination and be creative. Encourage your child to work on a religious project for the topic you are teaching. For instance, if you are teaching about the Sacrament of Penance, let him make a poster showing how to examine his conscience. Talk to him about the different steps while you and he are working. Seton sells DVDs of Fr. Pablo Straub explaining the *Baltimore Catechism* for intermediate grades. This is a jewel to have, particularly on a busy day. Seton also has Catholic songs on CD. These CDs include songs that teach prayers and even the Commandments. Keep your eyes open for new resources to assist you in teaching the Faith.

The older child needs a slightly different approach. When teaching the *Baltimore Catechism*, decide which questions are the most important. Which ones will assist him the most in life? Have him memorize these. Discuss all of them with your child, however. Keep reviewing these questions each week. Do not just drop them as soon as he passes the test on them. Keep it up. You can rotate around different ones so he does not end up with 100 questions every week by the end of the year. An alternative to the fill-in-the-blank study would be discussions with your child. Discussions catch the child's interest and make him want to learn more. Go over the chapter narratives with your child. Explore them from all sides. Be a devil's advocate to show him how worldly values do not make sense. Point out the differences between today's secular values and Christ's teachings. Show them the fallacies in humanism. If we do not help our children think of arguments against Catholicism and then think of the rebuttal to these arguments, you can be sure that they will have a hard time when someone challenges them. We must prepare them for these attacks. Also, children naturally question their faith as they reach puberty. If we can work with them now to reason these questions out, their faith will be strengthened. If we are not intimidated by these challenges, they will also realize how strong our faith is and that we are not afraid of these questions. It will give the Faith credibility. Go through this challenging phase hand in hand with your child. It will strengthen everyone's faith and relationships.

Parental humility

The next topic I want to address is the spiritual lives of the parents of a special-needs child. There are many facets to this. They include the sacraments, forgetting self and being God's instrument, suffering, and our obligation to God.

We must keep our faith central in our own lives as much as we do with our children. God must be our "rock" as well as theirs. Let us remember to pray to their guardian angels as well as Mary and St. Joseph. Only with God's help will the negative aspects of learning disorders be overcome, and the family remain intact spiritually.

Frequent reception of the sacraments is one of my "rocks" in avoiding sin and keeping my sanity. The frequent reception of Penance has more blessings than I can describe. Penance helps me to avoid the many temptations I have to become angry when things get crazy, or to see only myself when I am frustrated with a child's lack of understanding or compliance. It is easy to feel sorry for ourselves when we see others having such an easy time of teaching their children, or managing them so well. I think one of our strongest temptations is comparing our children to others. This sacrament helps me to die to myself and become God's instrument. How easy it is just to think of how the day is going for ourselves with our daily tasks instead of what our children are feeling about the day.

Daily Mass is one of my biggest blessings. It gives my day order and meaning. Sometimes I become frustrated at Mass because of the children's behavior and wonder why I bothered going. It is then that I remember that the Holy Sacrifice of the Mass is an act of praise for God, and is not meant primarily to make us feel good.

One of my most difficult crosses used to be public humiliation. But I remember that humility is a virtue. My children make sure I get a good dose of it! How many times I have wished I could crawl under a table (or a pew) at some of their behaviors. Or when you get the "What kind of mother are you that you can't control your child?" look. I would have an even greater problem with pride if it were not for these times.

I sometimes feel guilty because home schooled children on the whole are supposed to be so much better behaved than those in a private or public school. We are supposed to be the shining example for everyone else; yet here we are with the worst of them. This is when it hurts the most. Only those of us with these special needs children can appreciate what our days are like. Yet, we can take solace in the fact that we are very blessed to have these children. What an honor to know that Our Lord would not have given them to us if He thought we could not handle them with His grace. All things are possible with God on our side.

Teaching Methods

Let us now consider teaching the other subjects in the curriculum. First, no two children are the same, and each child's curriculum and management may vary even within the same household, from year to year and sometimes week to week. We must always be flexible. The only given is that a problem exists and what the general nature of that problem is. My eight-year-old is very cyclic in his degree of disability. We have never been able to figure out why or control it. Consequently, he has shorter lesson plans in the fall and spring until he is over this difficult phase.

Another problem involves retention. A child may spend weeks learning a concept, get it down, and then one morning wake up and have forgotten it all. We know how frustrating this is for us. Can you imagine how frustrating it is for a child? Try to have different ways of learning the same concept planned. This increases understanding of the concept, alleviates boredom, and fosters cooperation. Their learning must be in short sessions, concise, and interesting. In teaching your child, remember to stop before your child gets frustrated. Frustration impedes learning. Take a break and come back to the problem later.

In selecting your texts, try to choose ones that are both cumulative and sequential. This is an absolute must for my children. By cumulative I mean that one concept builds on another and there is a review of previously learned concepts. Saxon Math does this with their series. By sequential I mean that there is a logical order to the concepts. English texts that jump around have no place in your child's work. It is better to explore each topic thoroughly before starting a new one. My daughter was thoroughly confused and had almost no retention with a text that jumped around. As with religion, review of previously learned concepts is essential for long-term retention, particularly if you have to worry about standardized tests at the end of each year.

As you plan your day, you must decide what is the absolute minimum that you wish to accomplish. What are your "core" subjects? Mine are religion, math, phonics/reading, English, and handwriting. Handwriting may be incorporated into either my first grader's English or reading/phonics. Any other subjects are extras. If you do not set a minimum, you are going to be more frustrated at the end of the day if you do not accomplish your goals. Some days we only do math, reading, and religion. This is particularly true during my son's difficult seasons.

Be sure to allow time for fun learning, like art projects and science experiments. These can be done after your core subjects. If your child is having a rough day, provide art projects that are simpler or have relay races or some activity outside. Take a nature walk.

In teaching your child history, I encourage you to be as creative as you can. Look at the suggested activities at the end of each chapter. Have him do the map skill assignments. End of chapter questions turn my children completely off to history. There is simply too much work involved in finding the answers, and it is an exercise in frustration for them. Discuss the chapters with your child.

Another teaching tool I use involves my two oldest making diagrams. The chapters are usually divided into sections marked with boldface print. For each section they must put the main ideas in the center of a circle. What is the main point? In rays going out from this circle are pertinent supporting details. All of the information in their diagram must be in words or phrases. No complete sentences are allowed. It takes away from the exercise. Discuss the diagram with them afterwards. They like doing this. It also makes them think and increases their reading comprehension. This is active learning vs. passive learning.

As I have mentioned previously, learning must be fun, interesting, and concise. It should be in short sessions. Stop a session at the first sign of frustration. Little, if any, learning takes place when we are frustrated. It turns children off to the task at hand. If you are becoming frustrated, think of what your child is feeling! I know of an adult with ADD who turns away from any learning because of frustrations as a child. It has given him a distaste for reading anything, even novels for enjoyment. Is this what we want for our children? Find out what your child's interests are and develop them. For instance, if your son is a baseball card collector, have him find out what was happening in history during the life of his favorite players. Were the players Catholic? What saints or holy people lived in their day? All of these things will foster their desire to learn.

Try to be flexible with how assignments are done. With a young child, you could have your child use stickers to mark answers instead of drawing circles or making x's. This is particularly helpful for the child with fine motor problems. For some of the phonics work, can your child draw lines to the correct answer instead of writing all the words? How about doing them orally or into a tape recorder? Be creative to accommodate their frustration levels and their disabilities.

Scheduling and spontaneity are both important for learning with AD/HD children. They must have structure in their lives. Usually we have several short sessions, or small doses of each subject, no more than 30 minutes long. My pre-K to first graders achieve most of their learning in impromptu settings. These include cereal box labels, clothing labels, signposts, license plates, etc. Anything that catches their attention, we try to turn into a learning experience. Try to make the most of every learning situation during the day. This is especially true with impulsive children. Either initiate the learning as the opportunity arises, or pick up on your child's most subtle cues.

I usually start my older two children on their assignments before beginning with my eight-year-old. I may give him a learning toy to play with while I get the others started. Then I switch back and forth with the children as the day progresses. Having several activities ready for him to switch to is important in keeping his attention. Organization is vital for success when teaching this many and tending toddlers at the same time. We do not have short days of school in our home, but, though we may go to late afternoon, our learning is not compacted and intense. There are many breaks for various reasons. This may not be the norm, but it works for us.

Managing

One of my greatest trials is managing to teach and take care of my other children while keeping my child with AD/HD occupied or teaching him. Many home schooling families enjoy the luxury of having the older children teach the younger to some extent. This is not possible for me. Either the child needs me there with him or he resists their efforts entirely.

Pacing yourself and the child so that he does not fall behind in the year is an area of concern. This is particularly true where standardized testing is concerned.

The first step is looking at your state's Standard of Learning Objectives. Devise your core curriculum to meet these goals. Keep in mind that the history and science tests are not usually required, depending on the age of your child and the state in which you live. Difficult as it sounds, religion class must come before meeting the SOLs. We answer first to God.

Decide on your goals for the year, then supplement as you are able. Please do not get hung up on completing one grade a year, or having your child in the same grade for each subject. This totally negates one of home schooling's main advantages, that is, learning well and at the child's own pace. What is more important: quality learning at a slower-than-average pace, or staying on schedule? Staying on schedule just leads to anger and resentment for both parent and child. It makes learning very difficult and will eventually lead to burn-out. Do not even concern yourself about what point in the school year he is in for different subjects. What is important is that he is learning at his pace and that you are working with him.

If possible, I highly recommend that you use portfolios instead of the standardized tests to submit to your school board or for your own records. They are more accurate in evaluating your child's progress. Many of these children who learn differently simply do not do well on formal tests by the very nature of their disability, not because they do not know the answer. If you must use testing, be sure it is done in your own home, and ideally by you. Just as school children take their tests in a familiar school environment for accurate results, your children deserve the same allowance by taking tests in *their* own familiar environment.

Sometimes there is a question of whether or not to go through testing when AD/HD is suspected. We knew that our first grader was a candidate by the time he was two. We saw no value in testing then. In retrospect, a positive diagnosis might have been helpful, because we could have learned management techniques sooner, and had more realistic expectations of him. Testing at age five helped us because we finally knew what we were up against. We did not feel quite so much like failures, because we knew that there was a medical reason for the problem. We are more confident in our roles, though still overwhelmed. We are able to learn more about this disorder instead of searching in the dark.

Discipline

Misbehaviors are very common in children with AD/HD. A psychologist gave me a couple of excellent ideas in this area. First, she advised me to be exaggerated in my praise and correction. This does not mean severe punishments. AD/HD children have a hard time keeping messages straight. Give him 100% of your attention. PRAISE each accomplishment. Make a BIG DEAL of it. Stop what you are doing to let him know. Hug him. On the other hand, be equally clear when correcting him. Look STERN. Let him know you mean business and are upset with him. Equally important when doing this is not to mince words. Do not take this time for lengthy talks or explanations. The time for talks is after the appropriate consequence.

Social skills are usually an area of difficulty for children with learning problems. Large group settings should be postponed with these children until they can handle small group situations. Professionals have told me that my children need *more* social interaction than most so that they can develop their skills. I disagree. This simply overwhelms and frustrates them. Family life teaches these skills the best, and field trips, story hours at the library, and sports activities take care of the rest. Other home schoolers can provide small group interaction also. Surely Our Lord will give us parents the grace to teach these social skills without putting our children in a large classroom situation which encourages acting out misbehaviors by its sheer size and abundance of distractions!

Special joys

One of the many blessings we receive in raising our special children is the joy we experience over their accomplishments. What is an ordinary accomplishment for many children is frequently a struggle for ours. What a reward it is, then, to see our children's faces when they have finally mastered something. It is a joy that parents of "normal" children can never fully appreciate.

Having a special-needs child is hard on brothers and sisters as well as parents. Imagine having to love your brother, but hating his unpredictable behavior at the same time. Siblings are subject to the same emotions as we are in living with AD/HD. It is not easy for them. I cannot emphasize enough the importance of accepting their feelings without judging them. Feelings are neither right nor wrong. It is what we do with them that may be sinful. We must teach them how to turn to God, the saints, and their guardian angels with their problems so that they, too, may be comforted and gain insight. We need to foster open communication with them so that they may understand why parenting techniques are modified and expectations are different for different children. Otherwise, they will easily assume that favoritism is present, causing anger and resentment.

Raising a child with AD/HD is a formidable task. However, with God's grace, particularly with the help of the sacraments and prayer, it can be done. God has honored us by giving us special children to raise. We are truly blessed to have been exposed to home schooling so that our children will not have to suffer the humiliation and abuse they would receive in any school system. This knowledge is what keeps me going at the most trying times.

Chapter 13:
The Socialization Issue

Once all the positive reasons for home schooling have been explained, once the explanations about the family benefits have been made, both the educational benefits and the spiritual benefits, one question always remains:

"But what about socialization?"

It is a sad commentary on our times, not to mention on our educational institutions, that many people, even professionals, even Catholics, are more concerned about the socialization of children than they are about their academic or religious education.

The reason educators have invented this word, "socialization," is because they can no longer "sell" the schools for academic reasons. They have had to invent a different reason for the schools to exist.

If the truth be told, the main purpose behind public schools has never been education. Writings of the fathers of the modern school system in America make it clear that what we are seeing today is the fulfillment of the plan they had from the beginning. "Mere learning" was never considered the goal, but rather "social efficiency, civic virtue, and character." (Ellwood P. Cubberley, *The History of Education*, p. 690. Also, Rousas John Rushdoony, *The Messianic Character of American Education*, passim.)

Of course, if schools were using the Bible as the guideline for social efficiency, civic virtue, and character development, we could not complain too much. Instead, since the 1960s, prayer is not allowed in schools, religious books and materials may not be used, and now books such as *Gloria Goes to Gay Pride* and *Heather Has Two Mommies* are being mandated in the schools of New York, New Jersey, and Connecticut. With homosexual "marriages" now becoming legal, this will be taught to the children in schools as an alternative lifestyle.

Wherever people congregate, there is going to be interaction, or socialization. What Catholic parents need to consider is, what kind of socialization do we want for our children? Do we want our children socializing with classmates who are involved in the drug culture, in the free sex culture, in the "Me First" culture? Do we want our children to be indoctrinated with the politically correct New Age culture? Do we want the "Up with Owls and Down with Babies" culture propagandized to our children by school teachers and brainwashed classmates?

How many times on the phone do I hear from parents about the ridiculing by classmates of Catholic students who wear scapulars or who stand up against the pro-death teacher in defense of unborn life! One priest recounted the time when he visited a Catholic school where students laughed when he said that the Holy Eucharist is Jesus Christ, the Son of God. And there is Donna Steichen's experience (author of *Ungodly Rage*) when a student in her CCD class exclaimed, "Gosh, Mrs. Steichen, you talk about Jesus like He was God or something!"

One priest told a group of us that when he visited a Catholic high school to talk about the Faith, he taught them the Catholic teaching about adultery and fornication and mortal sin. The kids were not only amazed, but the teachers were angry with him for talking about mortal sin! What kind of companions do we want our children to socialize with? Do we want to teach them to "get along" with those who have anti-Catholic values, with those who would push our kids into early sex and use of condoms? Do we want to teach them to spend their childhood schooldays in misery, being always the one who is different, always the one who is ridiculed by peers and teachers alike? How much daily attack on Christian values can a child take, day after day, week after week, month after month, year after year?

"He that walketh with the wise, shall be wise; a friend of fools shall become like to them" (Proverbs 13:20).

Socialization in schools

I receive calls from heartbroken parents all the time. They want to try home schooling not because their children are receiving a poor education, but because their children have had terrible "socializing" experiences in the school. Parents call because their children's classmates, after reading stories in their readers, are actually practicing witchcraft on the other children. Some children have been abused by other children, physically, verbally, or sexually. In one school, two boys sexually attacked a girl in a restroom. In another school, classmates tried to hang a boy in seventh grade. The stories are endless. There is certainly little evidence of healthy socializing in the schools of America. You can see it on television on any day of the week, or on the Internet.

In April, 1992, ABC News aired a ten-minute story on sex education in the classroom. A group of fifth graders, with playful childish faces, were shown laughing and grinning as they literally frolicked, throwing around condoms and teasing each other with the birth control devices handed to them by their teachers supposedly to teach them "safe sex." Socialization, á la paganese!

The U.S. Department of Education published a report in the late seventies on violence in the schools, giving statistics on how many rapes, personal attacks, and robberies occur in the schools. It was surprising that they would put it in print, but the report declared that a school was one of the most dangerous places in America!

The television graphically demonstrated recently how wonderful is the socialization at schools as educators debated about which is better: a hand-held metal detector or a more expensive detector built into the door frame, to detect the guns and knives being brought into the school buildings.

In February of 1993, an eleven-year-old boy was found with a loaded gun in an upper-class school in northern Virginia. In an interview with the police who arrested the boy, the police reported that children are taking guns to school to protect themselves from other children with guns. *In fact, a study by the Department of Health and Human Services found that one in twenty public school students carries a firearm to school at least once a month!*

The school children and parents of America are quite aware of peer pressure to use drugs and begin sexual activity. Two girls in a small rural Catholic high school in the Midwest told me they were the only virgins in their class. Mary Elizabeth Podles, in the April 1993 issue of *Crisis*, writes that her confidence in her local Catholic school was shaken when the eighth-grade class was assigned to write to *Catholic Review* asserting that the students should be given condoms to prevent AIDS.

There are so many children who have serious problems in the schools today that normal children think they are abnormal. Schools are conducting classes or classroom clinics designed for children's problems.

After a suicide in a school, teachers will conduct clinical-type classes dealing with suicide. If a student's parent dies suddenly, the school faculty decides to conduct all-school classes on death and dying. Schools have regular classes dealing with drugs and early sex experiences. There are classes to help children with single-parent families, children with "a live-in roommate" for a parent, and children of one or more remarriages.

There are so many non-academic but clinical-type classes going on in the schools today that it affects normal, healthy children. It can actually cause stable Christian children to become disturbed, to wonder if maybe they are not normal because they are not having these problems. One mother called me and decided to pull her young son out of school when he was laughed at because he had only two parents, the same two he started with!

One book I read exposes the terrible hypocrisy of socialization in schools. *Family Matters*, by public high school teacher David Guterson, who is also a home schooling father, tells about the obsession among high school students to be accepted by their peers. There is a constant battle for group status, and peer cliques keep teens from integrating into multi-age groups in the community. Their obsession to conform to the group regarding clothes, hair styles, values, and attitudes keeps them from emotional growth and adult socialization.

Some child psychologists are recognizing the social damage being done to children because of the schools. Dr. Raymond Moore reported in *Home Grown Kids* that Dr. Urie Bronfenbrenner of Cornell University conducted a study of 766 sixth graders, and concluded that most children are not carriers of sound social values. Dr. Moore believes that peer dependency is the social cancer of our times.

In this day and age, when children are spending more time with their peers than with their parents, both of whom are working outside the home for long hours, the children adopt the values of the peer group. Hence, we end up with the so-called "generation gap." This "gap" is being caused by the schools, and it is certainly not healthy socialization.

Catholic schools

Many Catholic parents are aware of these situations but hope that Catholic schools are safer. These Catholics may be ignoring the facts. Problems may not be as common in the Catholic schools, but Catholic schools today rarely employ firm discipline and teach positive Catholic values; rather, there is clear evidence that the level of immorality and loss of Faith is steadily climbing.

In January 1993, Father Kevin McBrien of the Brooklyn, New York, Office of Catholic Education was interviewed by Mother Angelica on EWTN. When asked why there is a need for the new Universal Catholic Catechism, he declared that each year for the past eleven years, 100,000 eighth graders were surveyed about their knowledge of Catholic Faith and morality. Father McBrien said that the results had grown more appalling year after year. The Vatican hopes the *Catechism of the Catholic Church* will stop the terrible loss of faith and stop the practice of immorality among young people, said Father McBrien.

Father Mitch Pacwa on EWTN in May of 2004, made the statement, along with Father John Connor, that the Faith is not being taught in the Catholic schools, and they both recommended home schooling. Father Pacwa said that when he was a professor in a large Catholic university, the first day of class he would ask the Catholic students to write the Ten Commandments and the seven sacraments, and they could not do it.

Healthy "socialization" means practicing Christian virtues. It means loving our neighbors as ourselves. It means wanting what is best for others, especially desiring their salvation. But if children are not reading the lives of the saints, they do not have the heroes or the saintly role models they need. If children are not taught the Ten Commandments, or the Beatitudes, and do not understand the principles that they imply, they cannot practice the selfless love for others which is the basis of all true and great friendships. They need to learn about Jesus and His self-sacrifice and love for us, so they will practice good socialization habits of kindness, generosity, and charity.

Would we do it?

Sometimes parents claim that they want to keep their children in a school in order to help the other children. They feel that the good example their children give will show others how one ought to behave. Perhaps in this way, they think, the other children will change.

What such parents fail to realize is that it may be their own children who will change for the worse. Evil is often well-disguised and holds a certain temptation. That is why good companions are so important and bad companions are so dangerous. In fact, our catechism teaches that after receiving the Sacrament of Penance, we should have a firm resolve of sinning no more, which means "not only to avoid sin but to avoid as far as possible the near occasions of sin." We are to avoid persons who are likely to lead us into sin.

Is it emotionally or spiritually good for children to be trying to convert their classmates, especially when the authority figures are themselves promoting anti-Catholic values or attitudes? How long can children stand against books put in front of them, which they are required to read, yet which attack the Catholic values they have learned from their parents? How long can children stand against teachers in positions over them, people to whom they ordinarily should be obedient, who laugh at and ridicule their Catholic beliefs?

Can we expect our children to stand firm for thirteen years? And keep their Catholic Faith? And continue to live the Catholic life? Is that what we expect our children to do, from kindergarten through grade twelve, when we send them to schools which actively, daily, promote an anti-Catholic world view?

Much is made in the news media these days about sexual harassment on the job. It is said that sexual harassment creates a "hostile environment" in which women cannot be expected to function. Well, if a few lewd comments here and there constitute a hostile environment for an adult, then we would have to conclude that, to the average Christian child, a public school is a war zone. And, sorry to say, too many Catholic schools as well.

The premise put forward by the educators is that somehow socialization with classmates is going to help children "fit in" to society. Of course, the irony is that they are right! After thirteen years of morally indifferent indoctrination and socialization, they will be properly accepting of the society's pagan values, properly socialized into being passive adult citizens of our American society. It is questionable after such socialization, however, whether they will ever be fine, mature citizens of the heavenly society.

The Catholic perspective

As Catholics, we need to approach the socialization issue from a Catholic perspective. "Socialization" is a word and concept invented by our modern educators. There is no mention in any good Catholic catechism, or the Bible, about "socialization." In the 1989 Webster's dictionary, "socialization" is defined as "socializing or being socialized." Socialize means "to be active in social affairs." Probably educators mean children should be able to adjust or to relate to others, usually peers of the same age, in various social situations.

If more Christians were not practicing birth control, most families would have a good many more children. Historically, in times past, families were quite large. And grandparents used to live with the family. In times past, an argument for "socialization" outside the family would have been ridiculous. It is largely because families have become so small that American parents have been so easily brainwashed into thinking that "socialization" in the school is so important.

Many educators, of course, are concerned about maintaining the school community, over which they have strong control in forming children's values. Many educators want our children to be accepting of modern secular ideas which they present in the classroom. They want to shape the attitudes and values of children in a way they think is best for society. The Catholic children who are socialized in public schools, and in some Catholic schools, end up rejecting Catholic attitudes and values.

If you have any doubt about the efficacy of campaigns to change people's values, just consider the anti-smoking campaign that has gone on for the last thirty years. Smoking used to be considered "cool." If you watch old movies or old shows from the 1950s, people smoked regularly. That attitude has completely turned around. If the anti-smoking campaign can turn around a whole society like it has, will not thirteen years of secular indoctrination have a profound impact on most children?

Teachings from Jesus

Catholic parents need to ask, "What has Jesus taught in the Bible? Is there any indication that we are to learn social virtues from a peer group situation?"

Jesus speaks often about how to treat others. Basically, he repeats the Ten Commandments, the last seven giving us specifics about how to act towards others: to be obedient and respect parents and those in authority; to not kill; to not commit adultery; to not steal; to not tell lies or bear false witness; to not covet another's wife; to not covet another's goods. These

Commandments seem simple enough to state in a paragraph, but unless they are taught in the first place, backed up by the example of parents, teachers, and other role models, they will surely not be followed.

Jesus taught that charity is the most important "social" virtue. He told the rich young man to go and sell what he had and give to the poor. Jesus told the parable of the man who lay hurt in the road while passersby ignored him. The "majority" did not choose to help the victim. The Good Samaritan who finally did help him was the true neighbor. Jesus teaches that true socialization often means going against the crowd, thinking not of our own business first, but of helping another individual. Christ's teaching is unflinching in calling us to sacrifice for Him and for others.

An important command was given to us by Jesus after He washed the feet of the Apostles:

> You call me Master and Lord. And you say well, for so I am. If then I being your Lord and Master have washed your feet, you also ought to wash one another's feet. For I have given you an example, that as I have done to you, so you do also. (John 13:13-15)

While we have constant teachings from Our Lord concerning how we should treat other people, the Bible is also clear that *children* are to be *taught* Christian values. We should not hinder children from learning of Him, Jesus explained to His Apostles on a particular occasion as the children crowded around Him. Yet in a public school, directives from the State Department of Education forbid the teaching of "religion." Children are not allowed to learn about Jesus and His "religious" teachings.

There is no indication in the Bible that Jesus attended a school. In fact, when He was twelve years old and visited the Temple in Jerusalem, the Jewish priests did not know Him, and were amazed at His understanding of the Scriptures. When Jesus went back home with Joseph and Mary, He was subject to them. During the time He was subject to them, He grew in wisdom and age and grace. There is no indication elsewhere in the Gospels that He received schooling, or that He received wisdom, age, and grace from anywhere other than at home, nor could I find in the writings of any of the Church Fathers that Christ attended a school of any kind.

Church documents

When looking over the Catholic Church documents on education, we cannot find the word "socialization." Obviously the Catholic Church does not agree that being "active in social affairs" is a goal in itself.

In *Familiaris Consortio* (Encyclical on the Role of the Christian Family in the Modern World), in paragraph 37, Pope John Paul II states the following:

> In a society shaken and split by tensions and conflicts caused by the violent clash of various kinds of individualism and selfishness, children must be enriched not only with a sense of true justice, which alone leads to respect for the personal dignity of each individual, but also and more powerfully by a sense of true love, understood as sincere solicitude and disinterested service with regard to others, especially the poorest and those in most need.
>
> The family is the first and fundamental school of social living: as a community of love, it finds in self-giving the law that guides it and makes it grow.
>
> The self-giving that inspires the love of husband and wife for each other is the model and norm for the self-giving that must be practiced in relationships between brothers and sisters, and the different generations living together in the family.
>
> And the communion and sharing that are part of everyday life in the home, at times of joy and at times of difficulty, are the most concrete and effective pedagogy for the active, responsible, and fruitful inclusion of children in the wider horizon of society.

Lives of the saints

In reading the lives of the saints, I cannot recall a single saint who benefited by going along with the crowd, or who became a saint because he was so adept at his socializing skills. On the contrary, if there is one thing in common among the saints it would seem to be their lack of acceptance of the values of their society.

In the study of any saint, we find that he or she stood against the values of the society. They refused to be "socialized" to accept the current social norms. It was by teaching and living the values of God rather than of men that they became saints.

Many of the saints lived as hermits or semi-hermits. St. Anthony of Egypt visited various holy men, learned about the virtuous life, and then lived as a hermit for twenty years. However, several men visited him to learn more about living the holy life, and he eventually started a monastery, the first one in existence. Christ appeared to him, and he worked many miracles. St. Athanasius, who wrote a biography about Anthony, says that "the mere knowledge of how St. Anthony lived is a good guide to virtue."

Other saints spent long hours or even days alone. St. Catherine of Siena spent several years in prayer before she worked in the hospitals and visited the pope. St. Jerome lived as a hermit for thirty years and produced the Latin Bible. St. Rose of Lima prayed daily in her little hermitage, but came out to help at the hospital or to lead her town in prayer against an impending calamity.

Our Lord did not start His public life until He was thirty. Even then, after being baptized, He took time away from people and made a forty-day retreat in the desert for prayer and fasting. On several occasions during the next three years, He retreated from the crowds and even from the Apostles to spend time in prayer. Certainly, we Christians can find many examples showing that in silence, in solitude, away from social situations, we can more easily find God. As is often said, God speaks in silence. Sadly, for many people, the virtue of silence has been lost.

The lives of many saints give us and our children specific ways to carry out the social virtues in practice. The saints helped their friends and those around them in need. They worked in hospitals, caring for the sick and the poor. They aided minorities and those suffering from diseases. They cared for babies and the elderly. In short, they sacrificed themselves for others.

If we are truly called to holiness, and to be saints, how can we be so concerned about socializing with our peers? Are we not rather called to evangelize our society with Christ's values? Are we not called to be Christian witnesses to others who have been "socialized" to accept society's values? Are we not called to live the authentically Christian lifestyle, and show our pagan society that such a lifestyle can lead to eternal happiness?

Home schooling

Home schooling children can practice social virtues in their own homes while relating to others in their family community. They can practice social virtues when helping at church or at the youth center, at local homes for the aged, at the local pregnancy center, at day care centers for children or for the elderly or for the mentally handicapped. They can help elderly neighbors who cannot go out, or visit families in spiritual or physical need due to a death or illness in the family, or read to the blind, or visit elderly nuns.

The opportunities for Catholic children to develop "social" virtues are almost limitless. It takes little time to think of opportunities with the family, with the church, and with community activities. There are always people around us who are in need. Socialization does not need to be in the institution called school.

So the question comes up: Do we not socialize with others from our parish who think differently than we do? Should we not allow our children to attend the parish school so they can be witnesses to the Catholic Faith and lifestyle?

There are two different issues here. One is regarding our children; the other is regarding ourselves. Young children do not yet have the foundation to be doing battle against the complex, sometimes subtle, ideas being promoted in our society, on TV, in the textbooks, by teachers, and by peers. We cannot expose our children daily to anti-Catholic and anti-family values, for hours each day, and expect them to remain true to Catholic values. Can any parent take the equal amount of time after school to counteract what is being taught each day in school? Even to know the issues which come up each day would be impossible. The children are not even necessarily aware that Mom and Dad would like to know what the teacher said about overpopulation! Children need to be nurtured carefully, consistently, in a Christian fashion in the security and stability of the home.

Parents, on the other hand, firm in their Catholic Faith and in their beliefs, MAY expose themselves to the evils of our society, for the purpose of witnessing or evangelizing. However, even parents need to be careful lest they fall. Exposing ourselves to evil ideas or practices on a regular basis can lead to subtle acceptance of such ideas. Many a mother working in the battle against pornography or sex education has found herself becoming desensitized to the evils herself.

What about socializing with the local parishioners? It depends on the parish. As I travel around the country, the differences in the churches are like night and day. One usher explained that the church and Mass did not look Catholic, "because we do things differently here." However, he was quick to reassure visitors that it was indeed a Catholic church.

Several mothers have called to tell me that after every Mass, they have a long discussion with their children to explain that various aberrations are not permitted, but they cannot explain why Father is doing them anyway. One mother was permitting her daughter to be an altar girl (when it was still forbidden) because the daughter saw so many other girls doing it. Obviously, social pressure was too much for mother as well as daughter.

In some situations, parents could choose to attend a good church at some distance, taking their children with them, and pointing out the blessings of the Mass. (This has the added benefit of bringing parents into contact with like-minded Catholics.) Perhaps at a later Mass, a parent could attend the local parish, without the children, and do a certain amount of witnessing or evangelizing.

Socialization, or destruction of personality?

Dr. Damian Fedoryka, former president of Christendom College and home schooling father of ten children, declared at a home schooling conference:

> I really didn't consider it proper for my child to spend a year of her life learning how to be an eleven-year-old, then another year of her life learning how to be a twelve-year-old, another year learning how to be a thirteen-year-old.... She has a mother at home. I'd rather she learn to be like her mother, and have plenty of time to do it.

Dr. Fedoryka is pointing out that the so-called social values being learned by children in school are constantly shifting values based on the collective immaturity of the group. On the other hand, the values learned from the mother are stable values which will be of use to the child all through life.

Instead of school socialization being simply an innocuous waste of time, Dr. Fedoryka claims that the kind of socialization which children are encountering in schools today is destructive of the child's personality, and consequently destructive of genuine society.

The child is like a precious, uncut, raw gem, Dr. Fedoryka says. The parent has the task of turning the gem into

> a brilliant diamond with facets that reflect the light of eternal values of truth and goodness. In contrast, today's system insists on grinding these stones smooth in such a way that each one is uniformly similar to the other.

Dr. Fedoryka warns us that educators use words such as freedom, responsibility, and morality, but that these have entirely different meanings outside of the Christian perspective. Freedom, to the educational secular humanists, means

> the loosening of all the moral and sexual inhibitions. Responsibility means making sure that you use a contraceptive. Morality means that you do not impose your opinions on somebody else.
>
> What is commonly called socialization is, in fact, a process which destroys the child's personal center, his capacity to be a free individual who is truly responsible for his character and destiny. It promotes the child's centering or focusing on satisfaction or on what is often called the human need, and teaches him to function effectively in whatever system of values his society holds.

The social behavior being promoted in the schools involves "a non-judgmental acceptance of the rights of others to their values, and an ability to function in a pluralistic values system," says Dr. Fedoryka. To be socially correct, children are taught that everyone has a right to his own values, and one set of values is as good as another.

Simultaneously, children are taught that their own opinions, their own values, are of primary importance. "Your parents have values, and they are fine values for them. But you are developing your own values. You are not bound by the values of your parents, or by the values of the past, or by the values of a church." In their interaction or socialization with state-certified teachers, with counselors or "agents of social change," with state-approved textbook authors, with inexperienced but easily manipulated peers, children are to develop their own set of values.

No matter what Hillary Rodham Clinton says about the "rights of children" and their "emancipation," the teachers, textbook authors, and counselors are pushing aggressively to manipulate children to make decisions according to THEIR values. The issue is not about children's choices, but about who chooses for them.

The current self-esteem programs teach children to focus on themselves and their own desires and wants. At the same time, they are taught not to be critical of others who focus on *themselves* and do whatever *they* want in order to obtain *their* wants and desires. With its emphasis on personal wants and desires, the whole public school system is an exercise in the destruction of true society.

Objective truth versus personal opinion

Dr. Fedoryka believes that a parent should be concerned

> with bringing the child out into the world of *objective* values. He should be concerned with the moral and religious perfection of his child, with the crystallization of his personality in light of the eternal and absolute values. And secondly concerned with the eventual communion of his child with another human being [such as in marriage], but in all cases with the ultimate communion with God. These should be the basic concerns of education.

If you deny a child guidance or education in the world of objective values, the child soon centers only upon himself.

"Modern philosophy of education," declares Dr. Fedoryka,

> in insisting that the child becomes self-centered, teaches the child to focus on what is peripheral and superficial in his experience: on the satisfaction of his needs.... There is a loss of a sense of identity of who one is.... The modern school system panders to that, teaches the child to turn inwards and, because of this, it is anti-personal. Because of this, every true communion is impossible, a genuine society is impossible.

Dr. Fedoryka's main thesis is that the modern secular humanist philosophy dominating the schools and seducing a nation of children rejects God as an authority, rejects God as our destiny, and sets up the individual person as a god.

> The philosophy of self-realization, self-affirmation, self-fulfillment, self-esteem is the dominant philosophy today, not only of our society and culture as a whole, but specifically of the schools. This is the predominant evil.
>
> Modern man is not atheistic by accident. Modern man rejects God as an obstacle to his own satisfaction. He must prove that he is superior to God. He does that by seducing the child, by getting, first of all, the child to deny God, and not give himself to God.
>
> Then modern man can show himself greater than God by saying, "God ... to whom does this child belong? Over whose heart are You Sovereign and Lord? Certainly not over the child's, because the child belongs to me, not to the parent." It belongs to Modern Man, the State, who cultivates a systematic warfare on innocence.

In claiming possession of the child, Modern Man thinks he is superior to God. The modern school system is essentially hostile to God.

Catholics believe, of course, that we are to reform and change society, to bring the Gospel of Christ to society. Why should we have our children spend thirteen years learning "how to fit into something which is not fitting?" as Dr. Fedoryka puts it.

Two world views

We are living in a society with two world views. The schools hold one world view, as promoted by the National Education Association, and we Catholics hold another world view, as promoted by Jesus Christ in the Bible and in His Catholic Church.

In our world view, socialization means we must try to be good, kind, loyal, truthful, obedient to authority, diligent, faithful, just, humble, and generous to others because others are children of God. Our idea of community or society is based on the fact that God is our Creator, the Creator of each individual human being, and we are all brothers and sisters in Christ.

In the secular humanist world view, students are encouraged to do whatever feels good. If it feels good to take drugs, or to lie, or to drive a car without permission, or to tease a classmate, or to trip someone in the classroom, or to join a gang and harass innocent people, or to vandalize a store, whatever; if it makes you feel good, then do it.

So the question your friends and relatives should be asking is not "What about socialization?" but "In whose world will your child be socialized—in the secular humanist world where personal satisfaction, personal values, and personal choice is primary, or in the Christian world, where serving others and ultimately serving God is the purpose of our existence?"

Service

The children in the schools today are not learning the basic Christian vocation which calls them to serve God and neighbor. Jesus said, "I am in the midst of you as He Who serves." And again, "I have given you an example, that as I have done to you, so you do also."

According to Dr. Fedoryka, the schools give evidence of

betrayal of the basic vocation of man as being created to serve another. That is, I claim, the crisis in our culture, the crisis in our educational system, and the most important reason to take your children out of a school, public or private, which betrays this basic destiny or vocation of man.

A genuine bond between people, genuine socialization, depends on giving of oneself. "If anyone wishes to come after Me, let him deny himself, and take up his cross, and follow Me." This does not sound like the current philosophy of self-esteem being sold to our schoolchildren! "For he who would save his life will lose it; but he who loses his life for My sake will find it." We know that it is required of us as Catholics to give up our lives in service to God and to God's children. In the past, we have considered as heroes those who have risked their lives in rescuing others from danger, and those who over several years have given their lives in service to others. Even our post-Christian society still admires those who follow this ideal. For example, Bob Hope was recognized and respected because he gave up his time every Christmas to uplift the morale of our servicemen. His priority was to serve the soldiers rather than to look for his own personal pleasure during the holidays.

Dr. Fedoryka believes that a genuine socialization, a genuine bond between people can only arise

> when one individual gives himself, surrenders himself, submits himself to the other. This will make a tremendous difference in the way we educate our children. If we recognize that each one of us has a destiny to forget about ourself and to serve the other, we also will recognize that the children who have been given to us must be shaped and educated in this attitude.
>
> The primary reason I am educating my children at home is that they learn to surrender to others, even if it costs them their happiness. They must be ready to give up, to negate themselves, in order to serve others. This should be the core, the heart, the spirit of Christian education.

Since our primary responsibility to our children is to direct them to Heaven, we need to have control over their social contacts, insisting that they be Christian and positive. The many deep and complex problems which children and young adults have today are, in part, the result of lack of parental control over their children's social contacts.

Social virtues are taught effectively primarily at home, within the family, as directed by papal documents. Additional social contacts can be with Catholic home schooling support groups, where families come together as families rather than children of just one age group, where older children learn to care for younger children and where younger children learn Christian values from older children and adults.

When parents take children to local clubs, such as Boy Scouts, or local sports activities or supplemental classes, such as drama or ballet, they should keep a watchful eye for lack of discipline, cursing, drinking, drugs, sexual aggressiveness, and so on. This is parent-controlled social activity, protecting the child from spiritually dangerous situations.

During children's formative years, parental control is a serious responsibility. Once the solid foundation is laid during childhood, like the house built upon the rock, the winds of society's pagan values may blow, but our children will be able to stand firm in the face of the hurricanes to come. They will choose a spouse of like formation, they will choose self-sacrifice for the sake of their spouse and children, and will raise another generation of virtuous Catholic children.

The pagan agenda for schools

Some educators are promoting specific agendas which ruin social relations between people. One of the most common agendas currently being promoted is that of the homosexuals, which is guaranteed to warp a child's view of sexuality.

In December 1992, when the city of New York decided to implement the *Children of the Rainbow* program to teach children to respect homosexuality as an alternative life style, many parents objected. The program was to begin in first grade, and the little ones were to be given books with illustrations, one depicting two men in bed. The children were to learn to respect "families" with "parents" who were homosexual or lesbian. Of course, in the process, children were being taught that such "families" are morally acceptable.

The agenda is being promoted by the National Education Association and other liberal groups. These groups supposedly support the ideals of democracy. However, when a majority of parents, who, through taxes, pay the salaries of these school educators, objected to the agenda, democratic ideals were thrown out.

In Virginia, meetings for a proposed sex education program were held around the state. Large groups of parents showed up at meeting after meeting to object, but the program was adopted anyway. The same situation happened in Michigan. Interestingly, the Michigan Senate held hearings with parents who complained about the situation. The Senate reported:

> Listening to hundreds of parents testify at our hearings, it became obvious that the desires of the curriculum writers in the Departments of Education, Public Health, and Mental Health rode roughshod over the wants and wishes of families…. Communities around the state were forced into accepting the state of Michigan's view of how and what their children should be taught about some of the most important and most intimate questions they will ever face.

In New York City, after a local school board supported the parents in their objection to the proposed homosexual-lesbian alternative lifestyle program, the duly elected school board was dismissed by the Central School Board. The local board was later re-instated, and this time the city school Chancellor, Joseph Fernandez, was dismissed. He was not dismissed because anyone in the New York State bureaucracy thought he was wrong. He was dismissed because of the way he handled the situation. In February 1993, ABC News "honored" Mr. Fernandez by featuring him in most laudable terms on their Person of the Week segment.

Right here in rural Front Royal, Virginia, 240 parents petitioned the school board to choose other books for the Reading List which would not present children with street language, vulgarity, and violence, nor with the idea that they should develop their own moral values. The school board rejected the parents' pleas. The board members are sure they know what is best for other people's children. (As an aside, home schooling parents need to be involved with electing and monitoring their local school boards. Home schoolers still pay taxes to support the schools, so they have just as much right as anyone to voice their opinions. Remember, too, that what the children learn in public schools will have a large impact on your children, your family, and your community.)

The fact is that Christian parents believing in absolute values cannot win this battle with logical presentations, because the idea of absolute values is so unacceptable to the school boards and educators. We cannot win this battle based on democratic values, such as that majority opinion should rule, because their agenda is of more concern to them than "democracy."

Catholics need to face the fact that good, healthy Christian socialization can be found only in good, healthy, authentically Christian homes.

Homosexual marriage

Now that a Massachusetts court has decreed that that state must endorse homosexual marriage, it is really only a matter of time before homosexual marriage becomes the law for the entire United States. The eminent jurist Robert Bork wrote in the August/September 2004 issue of *First Things*, "Within the next two or three years, the Supreme Court will almost certainly climax a series of state court rulings by creating a national constitutional right to homosexual marriage." With the appointments of Justices Roberts and Alito, perhaps this process will be delayed. While there is always hope, the trend is clearly against traditional marriage.

There will be profound implications in this change in the societal understanding of marriage. For children in public schools, there is simply no getting around the fact that homosexual sex education will be mandated. If many parents are upset over heterosexual sex education, one wonders what the reaction will be to homosexual sex education. Will this be too much for parents to bear, or will they bear this as they have borne so much else?

In an article in January 2004, the *Washington Post* reported that more and more high-school age girls are experimenting with homosexual relationships. The *Post* reports, "You can see them in the hallways of high schools like South Lakes in Reston, Magruder in Rockville or Coolidge in the District. In 2002 at Coolidge, a teacher got so fed up with girls nuzzling each other in class and other public places that he threatened to send any he saw to the principal's office." We have been told for years that sexual orientation is decided at birth and that people have no choice, but these girls are proving that wrong. According to the *Post*, "Try this on, Mr. and Mrs. America: These girls say they don't know what they are and don't need to know. Adolescence and young adulthood is a time for exploration and they should feel free to love a same-sex partner without assuming that is how they'll spend the rest of their lives."

These girls have already accepted the idea that sexuality has no inherent purpose or end, and that homosexual or heterosexual relationships are equally valuable. How much more of this will there be once their teachers start pushing it as the official position of the school? What will be the impact on society and child-rearing?

A pro-life view

In the Christian world view, each person has dignity. This includes both the unborn and the elderly. It also includes each child of school age. As we teach each of our children how important he or she is in God's eyes, and how each of our actions has importance to God, we are teaching the dignity of the individual.

In the secular humanist world view, which the children are learning at school, the group is what is important. While each child supposedly is to develop his own personal value system, if it does not fit into the group's values, the child is ostracized. Children in the schools often measure their worth by their acceptance by the group.

The reason why home schooling parents have difficulties teaching children at home when they pull them out of school in the later grades is that the children have replaced their parental image of themselves with the peer-group image of themselves. They have become peer-dependent.

Other home schoolers

Healthy socialization is a matter of importance to many home schooling parents. Much has been written about healthy socialization in many home schooling magazines. The following are a few points made by home schooling parents:

1. While many people seem to think that interacting with peers will help develop confidence and self-esteem, exactly the opposite is often true. With stress, rivalry, competition, and comparison with peers, children come to view themselves as their peers see them. They are not able to evaluate themselves objectively, and are often convinced they are inadequate in some way.

2. Mass education is proving that children are not learning good, positive social behavior in school. Children need personal, close associations with individuals, persons who love them and who can teach and train positive behavior, mainly through good example.

3. Children are too immature to have strong convictions and moral strength to develop positive social relationships when daily pressured by negative or immature social behavior. Children need to develop strong self-discipline, character, and strength before they can develop true friendships. This cannot be left to the result of interaction among others at the same level of immaturity, but should be directed by loving adults through daily good example.

4. The effects of peer group evaluation may inhibit creative expression and attempts to develop intellectually. In many schools, children purposely do not achieve because it is "cool" to be average with the group and not to appear "smart" (although in some schools the reverse could be true).

Peer-group evaluation is especially detrimental to girls of junior and high school levels in co-educational schools, as they want to be attractive to boys and so often purposely do not work to their full potential. Research and experience have shown that at these levels, girls achieve much higher when in all-girl classes.

Boys, who are not as mature as girls in the younger grades, tend to ask fewer questions or work less, since girls are more aggressive in achieving academically.

5. The peer group is becoming a replacement provider of family security for the individual child. The peer group, however, can offer neither the stability nor the love a child needs to grow emotionally and spiritually. The "generation gap" has been a phrase used to show the incompatibility of values between the peer group and the family. Children end up leaving the family at some point, but they usually carry away peer group values and not family values.

6. Children do not need to experience the teasing and cruelty of other children to learn about "the real world." There is a certain amount of give and take in a family, whose members ultimately care about the individual. And in a neighborhood, a child can walk away. In a school situation, where children are forced to interact with their classmates day after day, week after week, month after month, year after year, personalities can be almost totally destroyed.

Parents should realize simply by reading the newspaper, by seeing what is on television, and by talking with other parents that the schools are not doing a good job of teaching proper social attitudes and behavior. They should rely on their own common sense in raising their own children.

7. We need to remember that having a large number of friends is not a measure of a person's worth. Most adults have only a few good friends, while most other people are acquaintances. Parents will find that, if they concentrate on their children's development, encouraging each child daily, their children will be independent and self-confident.

8. Schools, run by professional educators with higher degrees, tend to set up a class status in the high schools, probably unconsciously. But as a result, those going into vocational areas are really looked down upon as not fully making it. Interestingly enough, even years later, while someone with a vocational degree or business degree might be very successful in various areas of leadership, he continues to believe he is of a lower status than the professional educator with loads of degrees and years of schooling but few Christian values.

9. While there are many positive reasons for home schooling, many parents who turn to home schooling are doing so precisely because of the problems related to socializing with children at school. Most parents want to keep their children away from the many, many social problems in the schools, most related to sex, drugs, and violence. Parents also want to be involved in selecting good companions for their children.

Some think that children should learn to live with different people in the world because for the rest of their lives they will have to live with people with different values. The fact is that as adults, we can control where we live and work and with whom we socialize. We can associate with good Catholic people if we try. Children should not be forced to associate with people who do not reflect Catholic values. After thirteen years, they will be so desensitized to the evil around them that they will accept this kind of living as part of their own lives.

There is a prevalent attitude that children should not be sheltered, but need to be out in the "real world." Well, what is the real world? Is the real world the world in which people know, love, and serve God, and acknowledge the permanent truths of the universe? Or is the real world the world in which everyone denies the reality of God and of moral responsibility? Clearly, the loving Catholic home is the real world, the world in touch with reality. The world in which children are taught they can indulge in every vice without consequence is a fantasy world.

Ostracism

On December 19, 1985, there appeared an article in the *Chicago Tribune* by columnist Bob Greene. It was entitled "Successful Adults Haunted by Ostracism." It was a real eye-opener for some of us, and perhaps not surprising for some others. Every parent who is afraid his child might miss out on socialization in school should read it.

Bob Greene starts his article by saying, "There seem to be so many grown people walking around still feeling the hurts inflicted upon them when they were children." In a previous article, Mr. Greene had written the story of a boy who was devastated when his fellow classmates gave him a "Most Unpopular Student Award." After the article was published, Mr. Greene received many letters from adults who related their personal stories of ostracism by classmates.

"What I'm hearing," wrote Mr. Greene,

> ...is that this never really goes away. A man may be a successful executive now; a woman may be a well-paid attorney. But if, in their youth, they were picked on and put down because they weren't as popular as their classmates, this sticks with them.

One man wrote:

> I feel for that boy in your column. I know exactly what he's going through. It has been 35 years since I was in his position, but I remember clearly sitting home all by myself after school and on weekends, because no one wanted to be my friend. It hurt so deeply that I never even talked to my parents about it, although I'm sure that they knew. It didn't seem like life was even worth living.

And another man wrote:

> That boy could be me when I was a child. It's the most intense pain in the world—knowing that even though it's not your fault, the other children don't want you to be part of what they're doing. There's no one to blame, so you end up blaming yourself. You even end up believing that the other children must be right—that there must be something wrong with you. Why else would you be treated that way?

Bob Greene quoted other similar letters, and concluded:

I am finding that there are so many who went through it, and who
remember. The hurt never seems to completely go away.... From what
I can tell, there are so many people who will never forget what it felt
like to be left out, and to be told that they weren't wanted.

When parents talk about the positive values of socialization in the
schools, they never think about the anti-social activities that hurt many
children. I have spoken with parents whose children hated school because
of the way they were treated, because they did not "fit in," or because they
were afraid of others who bullied them. Other mothers complain that their
children are so determined to fit in with a group that they turn to bad
influences. Several mothers have called with pregnant daughters. Another
mother told of her boy who used foul language because he wanted to be
accepted by the other boys. One junior high girl actually told her mother
she was turning bad because of her peer group and begged her mother to
teach her at home. These stories could go on endlessly.

Home schooling support

Home schooled children associate with all age groups, within their
family mainly, and within the home schooling support groups. If Catholic
parents are having large families, or if they have extended families with
grandparents and uncles and aunts and cousins, the children will be
interacting and socializing with all ages.

Home school support groups plan family activities, not just activities
for a certain age level. This encourages healthy social development
among all age groups as children adapt to children and adults of all ages.
Grandparents often join the families on these outings.

Home schooled children mature faster, though they are not as "street
wise" as public or parochial school children.

Home schooled children are better able to relate to all age groups
because they are not limited to several hours a day in a closed environment
with children the same age. Nor are they pressured by textbooks, school
movies, teachers, and peers to conform to the peer group. Their best friends
are family members, brothers and sisters who are loyal, supportive, and
not viciously competitive.

Because of better self-esteem based on a daily caring and loving family
support system, a home schooled child is better able to deal with social
setbacks or the group pressures of later life. A home schooled student tends

to be a leader rather than a follower, more able to make decisions based on what *he* believes or what he has been taught by his family rather than on what social change agents want him to think. Since a home schooled student is better educated and more secure in his value system, in a peer group he is generally admired and respected by those looking for answers in their lives.

When home schooled children meet other children, they are not tense or afraid of being called names or labeled. They do not feel pressured to dress in the same name-brand jeans, or wear the latest hair style. They are not pressured into wearing make-up or having a boyfriend by fourth grade.

Home schooled students are free to be involved in community activities or to be active in hobbies or sports. Seton has students who are ballet dancers, ice skaters, actors, musicians, models, tennis players, gymnasts, swimmers, and so on.

Home schooled students are spared the confused role-models being presented in the secular textbooks and classrooms of America. With the feminist and homosexual, gender-neutral ideology now infiltrating the schools, students are being taught to reject traditional Christian roles as mothers and fathers.

In *Familiaris Consortio*, His Holiness Pope John Paul II repeats Catholic Church teachings when he declares in paragraph 36: "Social virtues are best learned in the home."

Why are social virtues best learned at home?

Mother stays home and home schools. She protects the children, says the prayers with the children, teaches them the Faith, and tries to be a good example, like Mary, the Blessed Mother.

The socializing which children need today is with their parents and others who hold good Christian values. Their parents need to be role models, need to instruct both by words and by example, to follow the authentic Catholic lifestyle. All the negatives which we hear about the schools, all the positives which we see in the lives of the saints, the teachings of the Catholic Church and the Biblical teachings point to the fact that social virtues are best learned at home. According to the Second Vatican Council:

The family then is the first school of those social virtues that every society needs. But it is most important in the Christian family, enriched by the grace and the obligations of the sacrament of matrimony, that children must be taught right from infancy to know and worship God.

If we are really followers of Jesus Christ, we should not overly concern ourselves with "socialization" or the need for our children to socialize with other children their age. This has never been mentioned in the Bible, in the Church documents, in our catechisms, nor in the lives of the saints. When it comes to relating to other people, this is what we Catholics are directed to do:

To feed the hungry.
To give drink to the thirsty.
To clothe the naked.
To visit the imprisoned.
To shelter the homeless.
To visit the sick.
To bury the dead.
To admonish the sinner.
To instruct the ignorant.
To counsel the doubtful.
To comfort the sorrowful.
To bear wrongs patiently.
To forgive all injuries.
To pray for the living and the dead.

Chapter 14:
Catholic Support Groups

Why do home schooling parents need Catholic support groups? Most of our home schooling mothers can answer that quickly: because they desire the moral support of other Catholic parents, usually mothers, who are facing the same stresses and who can share their home schooling experience. It is clear from the writings of the pope and from many outstanding priests, such as Father Robert Fox and the late Father John Hardon, that Catholic families should join together to help each other persevere in virtue, particularly in a hostile anti-Christian culture.

We Catholics approach our problems and find our solutions through the Catholic Church, through our Catholic Faith, through our Catholic culture. Our Catholic beliefs about reparation for sin, about suffering and sacrifice, are distinctly Catholic. Our attitude about children, contraception, and marriage is distinctly Catholic. Most of us are Marian Mothers, who want to be like Our Blessed Mother in our approach to marriage, family, and home schooling. Therefore, when we Catholic home schooling mothers approach any kind of marriage, family, or home schooling problems, we want to confer with other Catholics.

When Father John Hardon gave a seminar on marriage at Christendom College, he concluded his presentation by reminding us that "No less than the members of a family are to be channels of grace to one another, so Catholic marriages and families are to be the means of grace to the world in which we live." While we want to evangelize others to be Christ-like, we need to associate frequently with those who help us become stronger in our faith. A Catholic home schooling support group can help mothers, fathers, and children to better understand and to better live the authentic Catholic life.

Women whose children are grown and who are no longer home schooling should continue to take seriously the call to evangelize. While their primary obligation as mothers at this point is to serve their children and grandchildren, these home school grandmas should be willing to help the young mothers coming along who yearn to hear the words of experienced Catholic mothers.

Reaching out

Once we decide that having a local Catholic home schooling support group is important, we need to reach out to find other Catholic home schoolers. If you cannot find a Catholic home schooling group in your area, the following suggestions may help you. You may feel shy to undertake them, but have trust in God, not yourself. Look to Him to help you to be an instrument of grace to others. Do not worry about what you will say or how you will do. God will give what you need.

First, find out if there is already a Catholic support group at your parish or in your area. If you are in a new parish, and don't know many people, look for a family with many children, and ask them about home schooling support groups at the parish.

If there is no Catholic group available, then attend the local area home schooling support group, which is probably Protestant. Let it be known that you are Catholic and would like to share ideas with other Catholics. Ask the members if any of them are Catholic or if they know any Catholics who are home schooling or who might be interested in home schooling. Give out a "business" card or 3 x 5 card with your name, address, and phone number, and ask them to pass it along to someone Catholic. Put on your card something similar to: "Looking for Catholic home schoolers to form a Catholic support group." If you feel there might be some antagonism, simply put on the card: "Catholic Home Schoolers Network."

Pass around your cards at the local and state home schooling conferences. If there is a possibility of having a table at a local or state home schooling convention, have a "Catholic Home Schooling" table. You could display your books and lesson plans or other Catholic materials.

Seton Home Study School's website (www.setonhome.org) lists Catholic home schooling conferences. These listings have contact information for the conference organizers. Call or write the organizers for the conference nearest your home and ask if you can display a sign, with a sign-up sheet for a new support group forming in your area. Attend and make sure you write the name of your hometown on your nametag for others to see.

Go to your pastor and ask if you could have a display on Sunday morning between Masses in the cafeteria. One mother in California gave us this idea. The pastor put it in his bulletin, and it was announced at Mass that Mrs. Smith was a home schooling mother who was displaying materials and would answer questions between Masses about Catholic home schooling. Be sure to bring your husband and children (assuming the children are well behaved). Do not worry if you do not know all the answers to all the questions. Tell them you will find out. Take down names and addresses. This personal approach goes a long way. It gives you an opportunity to be an instrument of grace to others, and it gives others a chance to respond to God's grace.

Consider putting an ad in your community newspaper, or ask for a notice under "Community Events." You may not wish to use the diocesan newspaper or the large city daily paper. You want the people to be local. And you want to find just a few people at first. An advertisement could read: "Catholic home schoolers meeting on First Friday after 9 A.M. Mass on June 7 at St. Matthew's Catholic Church. Catholic home schoolers and Catholics interested in home schooling are invited." Ask Father to let you serve refreshments in the social hall.

If you cannot rent the space in a local Catholic church, consider using the library meeting room, usually available free of charge. Post a notice stating that you will display Catholic home schooling materials and will answer questions. Advertise in your community newspaper that you and your husband will answer questions and display materials. It can be informal, and need not last more than an hour.

If you have a Catholic bookstore in your area, ask if you can put your 3 x 5 cards on their counter. You may want to put out a nice flyer inviting them to a Mass and meeting for Catholics interested in home schooling.

Forming the support group

Once you have made contact with Catholic families who would like to join your support group, you have a variety of things to consider. If you have only one or two other families, keep it simple, meet once or twice a month, let the kids play while you discuss home schooling and mutual family situations in a Catholic framework. Try to attend Mass together before your meeting. Continue with the reaching out activities at your local parish.

If you become a larger group of more than five families, you may wish to have a meeting once a month with just mothers, or mothers and fathers, for the purpose of adult discussion of home schooling and Catholic family life. This could be in the evening. Some groups schedule a Saturday morning breakfast at a reasonably priced restaurant so no one has to clean or prepare food.

In addition, mothers and children may want to meet regularly for a Play Day. This gives children time with other Catholic home schooling children, but should not be a time for mothers to conduct serious discussions.

You may be fortunate enough to have a sympathetic priest. If so, ask him to be the chaplain for your group. When you have your adult discussion meetings, he can help to present the authentic teachings of the Church. He need not come to every meeting, especially meetings which may be sharing ideas about disciplining and home management.

Maintaining

Some support groups start a monthly newsletter. This can be a simple list of upcoming local Catholic home schooling events, with perhaps a paragraph of commentary. Pro-life and Marian events could be featured. It could be a longer newsletter with one or more articles, but this takes precious time and money away from family and home schooling. As more and more families use the Internet, support groups are using electronic newsletters, news groups, and home schooling chat rooms to communicate. You can set these services up for free on several websites, including yahoo.com and msn.com.

Home schooling meetings usually begin with prayer. Many start with Mass; others with the Rosary. Some home schooling groups are also arranging Confessions before or after the Mass on First Fridays. Whatever it is, it should be done regularly. There is a real advantage for the group if it is general knowledge that on the First Friday of each month, you can find a group of home schoolers at the 9 A.M. Mass at St. Mary's.

Some other activities for a home school support group to consider include a Mass of the Holy Spirit to open the school year, a May Crowning, or a graduation for eighth and twelfth graders. In some support groups, mothers bring curricula or home school materials to the meetings for other home schooling mothers to look over.

Catholic Action or acts of charity should be encouraged as activities for the children in the Catholic support group. Children could volunteer at a local nursing home. Some groups help provide food or clothes for the poor or unwed mothers at a local crisis pregnancy center. However, any charitable work should be limited, based on just what families are really able to do without infringing on family life.

Often, the first thing a new home schooling mom wants to discover about a support group is what field trips they offer. An important service that support groups can provide is information about local attractions, especially Catholic sites. Some museums and other places of educational interest offer desirable programs to large groups only, so planning a support group outing might allow families access to programs that are being designed with traditional schools in mind.

However, support group field trips might not work for your family. Unlike schools, which plan trips for a particular grade level, home schooling families usually have students in a wide range of grades. This may not be what you want. Don't feel that you have to be a part of every scheduled activity. You may not want your high school students to miss a full day of school to pick pumpkins with preschoolers, and you may not feel comfortable leaving them at home alone. Planning and coordinating group field trips can use up precious time that might be better spent actually home schooling your children. Parents have also found that not all parents expect the same standard of behavior from children during these trips, leading to some stressful situations.

Because many parents have a background in institutional schools, they associate zoos and museums with group trips. As parents make the transition to family-based education, they frequently find that fewer children often brings a more relaxed and educational atmosphere. Many Catholic support groups "publish," either electronically or by print, a list of families home schooling in the geographic area, with the children's birth dates. It's a good idea to make friends with one or two other families who have children close in age to your own, and who share the same philosophy about behavior. You may find that planning some field trips with just one or two families will be less disruptive to your school week.

Since libraries are so important to home schoolers, you might take on supporting the local library. Catholic support groups should try to promote and praise good books to the librarian, and criticize the spending of tax money for anti-Christian materials. One Catholic support group donates good books to their library. As a matter of policy, libraries do not purchase books considered textbooks, but with the numbers of home schoolers, libraries should be changing their policy. Another Catholic support group met with the librarian and persuaded her to purchase good textbooks and supplemental materials for home schoolers' curriculums.

One Catholic support group in a large city found that the librarian was unfriendly toward home schoolers, and the group started their own library. They asked for book donations from older citizens who have excellent Catholic and other educational books now out of print.

The local parish should be a place where the pastor and members of the parish support home schooling families in various ways. Home school families tend to congregate at the same parish. When they become active in the church, as altar boys, as daily communicants, and as members of parish organizations, the pastor necessarily will take a second look. He eventually may be pleased. Hopefully, support groups will start meeting at the parish church, with priests helping out with talks, or with religion books, or offering space for a speaker.

The Catholic support group should maintain contact with the state home schooling association so that Catholic families can be kept aware of important statewide events or legislative activity. Most state home schooling organizations publish a state manual as well as a monthly newsletter.

Catholic home schooling support group discussions often focus on good Catholic literature, specifically on that which pertains to Catholic family life and home schooling. Each family might buy one book a month or subscribe to a good Catholic magazine or newspaper which can be shared with others. Perhaps the support group could have a revolving library so that parents may borrow books each month.

As the group grows, be sure that several parents share the leadership. The support group will be stronger if more parents are involved in arranging the meetings, not simply attending the meetings. Children, by the way, can be very helpful in the business of the support group. They can fold meeting notices, address and seal envelopes, print from the computer, and input names and addresses into the computer. They might even want to start their own children's newsletter.

Networking

The purpose of the local Catholic support group is to provide fellowship and help Catholic families on a day-by-day basis as family or home schooling problems and questions arise. This is the main purpose, and sometimes it should be the only purpose.

However, some small groups, particularly those in rural communities, may find a networking system helpful for arranging an annual regional conference and/or curriculum fair. Such gatherings can be very encouraging to the parents as well as provide an opportunity to meet a large group of people who are all home schooling. This convinces some husbands and other relatives that other people in their area think home schooling is great.

A statewide or regional conference is not necessary, but with wide publicity, it can attract new families to consider home schooling. A statewide conference or curriculum fair need not be an all-day event. It could be a Saturday morning event involving two or three speakers as well as a few vendors to sell home schooling materials. Keep in mind that, for people traveling a good distance, an all-day event is more of an attraction.

Smaller local support groups should do what they can to advertise a statewide Catholic home schooling conference. Catholic support groups need to help other Catholic parents to find help and encouragement, which they can find at a statewide conference with speakers, often priests, offering encouragement and spiritual help. The state organization vitally needs the support and advertising which the local groups can provide. Without the help of the smaller local groups, the statewide group cannot be successful in a statewide convention.

As for exhibiting curriculum materials, it is better to have fewer materials, which are Catholic, than to have an abundance of tables with possibly questionable materials. Inexperienced mothers trust that the support group is providing accurate and authentically Catholic materials. Do not be careless with that trust.

Consider leadership

More than two decades of experience with Catholic home school support groups has taught us some important lessons about what works and what does not. Support groups are intended to do just that—support. When a group's activities are too frequent, or parents feel pressured to participate in a large number of activities, the primary job of teaching our children is disrupted. Parents must carefully evaluate the level of support group activity that is right for their own family. This is especially crucial in the area of support group leadership.

Before a teaching parent undertakes a leadership role in a support group, parents should consider the possibility of sharing leadership. We are all extremely busy teaching our own children, raising our families, managing a household, and trying to be good parents and spouses while we are at it. Be honest before God, pray about what your responsibilities can and should be, and move into leadership cautiously. Look around for a mother who has finished home schooling her children and see if she might become an active leader. Younger mothers need to be careful not to jeopardize their own home schooling.

It does seem that for many support groups, there is a small core of committed families who repeatedly take the leadership roles. This can be necessary from time to time for the support group to survive, but it is not healthy long-term. When the leadership group is small, there is a greater chance for burnout. In addition, when leadership is shared widely, there is less chance that one or two people leaving the group will mean the end of the group.

Examples of support group activities

A Catholic home schooling group in New Jersey had a Rosary-making field trip at a monastery, and the children donated their rosaries to different Catholic charities. They planned a birthday party for the Blessed Mother in September, and an All Saints' Day party on October 31. For the latter, the children were to dress up as saints.

A parish priest in Florida agreed to have a blessing for the children and their parents in a Catholic home schooling support group. He also agreed to bless their school materials. The pastor has become more responsive, and the parents had a joint meeting with the Religious Education Director to show Catholic home schooling materials. The group meets on First Fridays for Mass and fellowship.

In Oregon, a Catholic home schooling support group meets for discussions on self-discipline, organization, scheduling, testing children, ideas for Lent and Holy Week, a review of a "hands-on chemistry book for the home," and the importance of prayer and practicing Christian virtues. The group meets at a Catholic church where the priest built an additional room for the use of the home schooling families.

A group in Virginia publishes a Catholic home school support newsletter. They report on their field trips, such as their visit to a monastery and to a home for retired nuns. They also meet for First Friday Mass, pray the Rosary, and have activities for the children. The group has a priest come to recite the Rosary with them. A field trip is planned for visiting the National Shrine of St. Elizabeth Ann Seton in Emmitsburg. The group also plans an All Saints' Day party at a local parish. They have started three small clubs for the children: a math club, a writing club, and a geography club.

A Catholic home school group in the Philadelphia area scheduled a retreat for home schooled boys at a local seminary. A group in Ohio visits a convent weekly where the nuns help the home schooled children learn Catholic music. The priest gives the children talks each week.

Here in Front Royal, Virginia, one of the mothers arranged for our pastor to have Benediction and a ceremony in honor of the Infant of Prague for the purpose of blessing the children and parents before the new school year started. The church was half full of home schooling families. Father brought out his most ornate candelabra. After saying the prayers to the Infant, he led the Benediction songs in Latin. He ended the ceremony by blessing us all with holy water.

Conclusion

The examples of activities of Catholic home school support groups as noted above represent just a tiny fraction of the reports we receive regularly from Catholic families. Catholic home schooling support groups are growing in importance for the Catholic home schooling families. They are supplying religious and social opportunities as well as moral support. We consider support groups very important for the success of home schooling in Catholic families.

Chapter 15:
Responding to Authorities

by Kenneth Clark, JD, MA

When I first began dealing with home schooling law many years ago, there were far more contacts by education authorities than there are today. In the last several years, fewer than ten people have contacted me to report they were having a meeting with their superintendent about their home schooling. These meetings went well.

In other "contact" situations in which Seton has been involved (every year there are about 200 of these), Seton is usually able to resolve the issue by sending a letter to verify enrollment. Sometimes authorities want proof of enrollment or a copy of our accreditation. In these cases, the families never meet with the superintendent or public school authorities. In most cases, these are routine requests for paperwork, for which we are happy to send parents the confirmation papers. If parents are enrolled in a program, they should contact the home study program for help in quickly resolving any issue with authorities that arises.

Even though it is very unlikely you will have any contention with school authorities or social workers, the following is offered to give you some help in dealing with authorities. When dealing with government authorities, you must consider two things. First, what are your legal rights? Second, how should a Christian respond to requests or demands from the government?

The first section of this chapter deals with the legislative and judicial system in our country to serve as a background for the second section, which gives Catholic home schooling parents practical hints on dealing with educational, social, and legal authorities.

The U.S. Constitution

The supreme law of our land is the United States Constitution. All laws—local, state, and federal, as well as all decisions of courts— must comply and be in agreement with the federal Constitution. Any law which the U.S. Supreme Court declares unconstitutional is considered not to be a law. Thus, when either the federal Congress or state legislatures pass laws, they must be written so that they pass "constitutional muster." Because of this, the United States Supreme Court is the most powerful group of people in the United States, since they must agree that any law passed by Congress or by the states is legal.

For home schoolers, this means that even if a president, or a governor, or state legislature is hostile to home schooling, we are still guaranteed certain protections under the federal Constitution. Thankfully, as of this writing, January 2014, the Supreme Court has ruled, based on the Constitution, that parents have a "fundamental right" to choose the kind of education they want for their children. The only way to change the Constitution is to amend it. This is a very difficult process, as is witnessed by the fact that in nearly 225, the Constitution has been amended only seventeen times since the passage of the Bill of Rights. Most important, then, is the federal Constitution and the rights it guarantees to all Americans.

Federal statutes

After the U.S. Constitution, federal statutes are the most important laws. Federal statutes are those passed by the United States Congress and apply equally in every state. Most federal legislation deals with issues that involve the whole country. Thus, Congress passes statutes dealing with interstate commerce and federal taxation. Education historically has been the primary responsibility of the individual states, not the federal government.

However, the U.S. Department of Education greatly influences the schools and educational situation throughout the country, though it can make no laws. This department researches and studies various aspects of education and of the schools. In addition, it is involved in the distribution of federal funds to the states. For instance, it has pressured Congress to allot funds to the states for schools to carry out certain programs. Congress sometimes passes laws stating that local schools will receive money only if they follow certain regulations. The schools are not required *under law* to follow these regulations, but most schools want whatever money they can get, so they tend to comply. The *No Child Left Behind* and the *Core* programs are an example of this.

While the people working at the U.S. Department of Education are not elected, they, along with the private but powerful National Education Association, greatly influence what is happening in the schools of the nation. Nevertheless, state legislators must pass final legislation regarding schools in a state.

State statutes

Most important after federal statutes are the state constitutions and statutes. State statutes apply only in those states in which they are passed. This is where we find home schooling laws. There are fifty states and fifty different state home schooling statutes (not counting Washington, D.C., plus the several U.S. territories). No two states have identical state home schooling laws. State statutes, however, must be in conformity with both the federal and the state constitutions.

Each state has a constitution, and those differ as widely from state to state as do the home schooling laws. The protections granted by the state constitutions, however, can sometimes be greater than those granted by the federal Constitution. It often has been said that the federal Constitution provides a "floor" of protection, not a "ceiling." In other words, the federal Constitution grants a minimum of protection, over and above which the states can grant more. In some states, the right to home school is guaranteed, even if not specifically, by the state constitution.

The state constitution is interpreted by the state supreme court, as by our United States Supreme Court interprets the U.S. Constitution. Thus, we have our federal Constitution and federal statutes, and the state constitutions and state statutes. State constitutions are somewhat easier to amend than the federal Constitution, but they too are difficult to amend.

State administrative regulations

After the state statutes, we have what are called "administrative regulations." Administrative regulations are adopted by various state agencies, such as the state Department of Education and the state Department of Transportation. These state administrative agencies usually work out the details for people to fulfill the requirements generally mandated by state statutes. In other words, if the state legislature passes a statute dealing with home education, the statute might read that home education is legal in the state, and that the state Department of Education will promulgate regulations governing it. These regulations might deal with such things as testing and parent-teacher qualifications.

Two examples of states that have home schooling laws that are procedurally explained and administered by state Department of Education regulations are Hawaii and Nevada. The administrative rules of both states further implement a state statute. Using Hawaii as an example, the statute would be worded something like, "A child is exempt from compulsory attendance when enrolled in an appropriate alternative education program as approved by the superintendent." This, of course, is very general. What does "approved by the superintendent" mean exactly? Approved how? As to teachers, curriculum, test scores, what? According to the Hawaii administrative rules, this means parents must provide a notice, the parent automatically is deemed a qualified instructor, and so on.

Administrative regulations, while not laws or statutes themselves, do have the force of law, because the state legislature has empowered the administrative agency with some of its legislative power. It has delegated some of its authority in a certain area—in the case of the Department of Education, only over the education of the state citizens—to pass these regulations. Although administrative regulations have the force of law, there is no penalty within them. Rather the penalty is in the law passed by the state that authorizes the passage of the administrative regulations.

However, administrative regulations must comply with both the federal Constitution and the applicable state constitution. Regrettably, many state agency regulations do not comply with the state or the federal Constitution, partly because the regulations are less formal and are implemented with less care than laws. Fortunately, administrative regulations are much easier to change than laws. It is at this level that state home schooling associations or even individual home schooling parents have the best opportunity to make changes.

Pronouncements by local school district

The last form of regulation that home schoolers often have to deal with is pronouncements handed down either by a local superintendent or by a local school board. These do not have the force of law, and parents are not required to follow these local "regulations." For instance, a superintendent might declare that children in his school district should take a standardized test, even though the state law says nothing about it and there are no administrative regulations on the subject.

Local school district pronouncements have no force of law. However, sometimes superintendents or school boards feel that the power of their authority comes from their position. A person may believe sincerely that by the mere virtue of his or her being on a school board, or being a superintendent, he or she has some legal authority. This authority is limited, however, to those areas where it has been granted specifically by the state legislature through a statute or through administrative regulation.

It is very important to realize that superintendents may make pronouncements, but whether or not they actually have the lawful authority to back them up is something else entirely. Parents need to be exceedingly cautious when dealing with such a situation. They must realize that the question of whether the superintendent's "requirement" is good or bad is immaterial. *If he does not have the authority granted him by the state, his "requirements" are no more than suggestions, and the parents are not obliged to comply with them.*

We urge parents to be very, very careful about complying with "regulations" from a superintendent. Even if it is something that is not particularly burdensome, we must seriously consider whether to comply with local pronouncements because it would set a precedent which could affect future legislation. For example, the superintendent may well inform the state legislature or the state Department of Education that he has been requiring students to take standardized tests in his school district for the last couple of years. If the parents have not objected to this or have complied even while objecting, he may suggest to the Department of Education that testing should now be an administrative regulation, or even a state law. The further up the chain a law or regulation goes, the more difficult it is to change.

Summary

To summarize: the most important and powerful law in the land is the Constitution of the United States. This is followed by federal statutes, followed by state statutes and the state constitution, with which the state statutes may not be in conflict. This is followed by administrative regulations from the various state agencies, and finally by pronouncements from a local government figure.

Parents should not be afraid to home school, as we have many decisions by the United States Supreme Court, as well as by state supreme courts, upholding the right of parents to educate their children. This parental right has even been called a "fundamental right." The list of Supreme Court cases supporting such parental rights goes back to the 1920s, with *Meyer vs. Nebraska, Pierce vs. Society of Sisters, Prince vs. Massachusetts*, and other cases, all the way up to the present, where we are steadily winning victories in the state courts and in the federal courts, protecting the rights of parents to teach their children at home.

Please note that while all the state laws and regulations *should* conform to the federal and state constitutions, this does not necessarily mean they do in fact. Some state laws and regulations do not conform to the Constitution. The problem is that it takes money and time for a person or a group to go to court claiming that a law is unconstitutional. Christians often interpret a law as just or unjust based on the Bible or Church teachings or the Natural Law, but with judges who are not Christian, or who are not approaching the law from a Christian viewpoint, such time and money is often wasted. In court, it is only the law, not eternal truths, which carries the day.

Some tips to make your home school experience safer and easier:

1. Home School Legal Defense Association

Consider joining the Home School Legal Defense Association. Their number is (540) 338-5600, or you can write to them at P.O. Box 3000, Purcellville, VA 20134-9000. Their website is www.hslda.org. It is the most effective legal protection for home schoolers. If you are a member, and you do run into a legal problem, they will provide you with an attorney and go into court. In fact, they will take the case to the United States Supreme Court if that is necessary.

The annual fee becomes very small when you consider that some HSLDA cases have cost $50,000 to $100,000. The main reason they are able to charge so little is that they are able to avoid most legal problems by talking to superintendents and persuading them not to follow through on a threat of prosecution or the like. While there are many families in the HSLDA organization, very few ever have legal difficulty. Statistically speaking, only one home schooling family in a hundred will ever be contacted in any sort of negative way, and only one in one hundred of that group will have any kind of serious legal trouble such as a trial or charges filed against them. That means that only about one in every ten thousand families will have a serious legal problem. However, this can only continue if parents keep themselves informed, and join HSLDA.

Superintendents know the reputation of HSLDA, and if you let them know that you are with HSLDA, local authorities often will back down just for that reason. They know that HSLDA is very aggressive and will fight to the finish.

Please note that HSLDA is like an insurance policy. You need to sign up for their services before you have problems. Although they may accept your membership after you have had a negative contact, they reserve the right to refuse membership in such cases.

2. Enrollment in a program

Consider enrolling in a home study program. The fact is that home schooling families enrolled in a program have fewer problems with local or state authorities.

When considering a program, you need to consider whether accreditation is important to you. Seton is accredited by the Southern Association of Colleges and Schools, which is a member of the Commission on International and Transregional Accreditation. These organizations are recognized as accreditation agencies by the U.S. Department of Education. There are six regional accrediting agencies:

- Southern Association of Colleges and Schools
- New England Association of Schools and Colleges
- North Central Association of Colleges and Schools
- Middle States Association of Colleges and Schools
- Northwest Association of Schools and Colleges
- Western Association of Schools and Colleges

Seton became accredited because we believed that our families would have less trouble with local and state superintendents, and that high school credits would transfer more easily and be more accepted by colleges. This has proved to be true.

Not all accreditation is equal. The agencies listed above are recognized accrediting agencies. If a school claims to be accredited, but is not accredited by one of the above agencies, then state and local authorities may not accept the accreditation.

There are other accrediting agencies, such as National Association of Private Catholic and Independent Schools or Association of Christian Schools International. While accreditation from a group such as these may be helpful in determining the educational quality of a particular school, the accreditation may not be any help legally.

Accreditation is important to school superintendents. We are pleased that the very fact that Seton is an accredited school has made superintendents back down from harassment. Often they will not even look at the curriculum, but are satisfied that an objective professional organization has evaluated and accredited our program.

In general, we have found that superintendents are more cooperative when a family is enrolled in a program. They like it when there is a third party involved in the home schooling. They also are much more impressed with a professionally prepared curriculum than one which is done by the family themselves. They like the idea that the family can phone a counselor for assistance in their home schooling venture.

Many times a problem with the local superintendent can be easily resolved by the home study school through a letter or telephone call. Often the superintendent merely wants to see an outline of the curriculum. At Seton, we call this a "scope and sequence." Probably nine out of ten "problems" we have ever had with superintendents have been resolved by sending them a scope and sequence of our courses for the student involved.

3. Statement of philosophy

Compose a written statement of philosophy or religious belief, that is, the reasons you are home schooling, especially if it is for religious reasons. Even though states do not require that you explain why you are home schooling when you notify the superintendent or the school board, we suggest that you do. In our experience, those who are home schooling for religious reasons are stronger in their commitment than those who are home schooling for any other reason. Superintendents realize this as well, and tend not to harass home schoolers who are religiously committed to their decision to home school.

Your statement of philosophy is basically a declaration that this is a tenet of your faith, and that you are commanded by God to teach your children. Although you may not include everything in a letter to the superintendent, you should have all your reasons for Catholic home schooling in a written statement for yourself and your family. It is better to have it as a reminder and as a frequent review. Hopefully, you will not need it.

How to handle an official contact

In this section, we will deal with two topics: first, how to handle a contact from a government authority regarding your children's education; and second, some hints on how to avoid legal troubles.

How should a Catholic home schooling parent handle a contact by educational authorities? There are two very important rules which should govern not only how you handle contacts, but are also good rules for almost any social situation. The first rule in handling any contact, whether by phone, letter, or in person, is to be polite. Be friendly, be a good Christian. "A soft answer turneth away wrath." In many situations, the contact person is someone just doing a job. He has nothing personal against you and probably no axe to grind against home schooling. He has been informed that you are home schooling, or perhaps has been told that your children are in some sort of school or perhaps not in school. He is merely doing his job in coming out to investigate a complaint and knows nothing about home schooling. You will be the one to make a first impression on him regarding home schooling and what it is. Try to give a good Christian impression.

The second rule is this: while being friendly and polite, **do not do anything that makes you feel uncomfortable**. Whether it is answering a particular question, letting a person into your house, letting him see your children, or whatever, follow your instincts. If the person wants information you do not want to give him, you are probably correct in wanting to withhold it. If you are uncomfortable with his coming into your house, you are right not to let him in. Be polite, be friendly, but do not do anything which makes you feel uncomfortable. Trust in your instincts. God will not allow you to go wrong when you trust in Him.

Telephone contact

With those two general rules in mind, let us address the different types of contacts. The first is a contact by telephone. Always ask the caller to put a request in writing and send it to you on business stationery. You need to do this for a number of reasons. First, you do not absolutely know to whom you are speaking. If someone calls up saying that he is from the state Department of Education, or from the local superintendent's office, or from the principal's office, you really do not have any way to verify that over the telephone. Unless you know the voice of the person who is calling, it could be anyone calling up to get information. There have been occasions when unauthorized persons have called home schooling families and asked some very personal questions about their home schooling and their lives. *Never give personal information over the phone to a stranger.* The person on the end of the phone is a stranger if you cannot verify who he is.

Also, do not promise to answer the questions that may be sent to you in writing. After talking with your spouse, or a home school lawyer, or a local attorney, you may find you are not required to answer the questions. In Virginia, parents can easily claim the religious exemption, but because the local superintendents send forms in the mail to home schooling families, never mentioning the exemption, many parents just fill out the forms and subject themselves to the unnecessary regulations.

The second reason you want the request to be put in writing is that it might not be mailed to you. Many of these officials are very busy; it is easier for them to pick up a telephone and ask a couple of questions than it is to sit down and type or dictate a letter. As a result, there have been many occasions where parents have received telephone calls requesting information and when parents ask for the request to be put in writing, for one reason or another, they never receive a written request.

Someone at your door

All this is fine, but what if someone comes to the door? Again, be polite, but do not do anything that makes you feel uncomfortable. The most important rule, and the one which cannot be over-emphasized, is that if someone comes to your door, you do not have to let him into your house unless the person has a search warrant. *Let me repeat: if someone comes to your door, anyone at all, you do not have to let him into your home unless the person has a search warrant.*

On a couple of occasions, someone came to our door when I was being home schooled, asking questions about the school we attended. Mother, even though not dressed completely appropriately for the outside weather, stepped out onto the porch, closing the door behind her. The visitors were never asked to sit down on the porch, nor allowed in, and Mother's hand remained on the doorknob. Identification was asked and given before any questions were answered. Not all questions were answered, either.

When you are meeting with a government official, such as a principal or superintendent, or someone from their office, he represents the government. You do not have to allow government representatives into your home without a search warrant. This applies to the police, the FBI, anyone from Social Services, the school district, or any other governmental agent.

The Fourth Amendment

You have a very important Constitutional right, the Fourth Amendment right, which protects you against unlawful searches and seizures. This means that a person's home is his or her castle. You are not required to let anyone into your castle unless the person has a search warrant.

Obtaining a search warrant is not simple. It requires the person who wishes to search to go to a judge and present that judge with probable cause that some crime is being committed. In other words, the police, social service worker, or superintendent must go to a judge and claim, "Your Honor, I have reason to believe, based upon testimony from an informant, that Mr. and Mrs. Smith are committing a crime because they are home schooling." But home schooling is not a crime. A judge will not grant a search warrant unless there is truly evidence of a crime. In many cases, when unfounded accusations are made about "child abuse," there was no search warrant but the mother allowed herself to be intimidated and allowed officials into her home.

Sometimes mothers or fathers unwittingly call Social Services for help, and find that Social Services are not really there to help, but to control. One Catholic father was at work while his wife was sick in bed when he called Social Services to see if someone would pick up his children and take them home. The Social Services people decided to place the children in foster homes. Though the mother does have chronic problems, she is able to walk around the house and take care of herself and could take care of the children. However, the parents are not allowed to see their children except on weekends, and they will have to fight the local social service bureaucracy to have their children returned to them. The lesson to be learned: *do not assume that social agencies exist to help you or your children!*

Short of exigent circumstances (that is, short of hearing the children screaming and yelling in pain), short of imminent physical danger to the children, no one is allowed to enter your home without a search warrant.

If you have heard of cases where social workers or police have entered the home of a home schooler with a search warrant, it is likely that an unfriendly neighbor gave an anonymous "tip" about possible child abuse. If you have a sudden problem at your door, call your attorney, or any nearby attorney, immediately. Have that attorney come to your house immediately. Do not answer any questions until an attorney is present. If necessary, have the person at the door talk to your attorney on the phone. Hand him the phone through the door, and make him talk to your attorney outside on your porch or front yard. (Just as you need to know the number of your doctor in case of emergency, you should also know the number of your attorney.)

Obtaining a search warrant is a very difficult and time-consuming process, except in a child abuse charge. *Do not be intimidated into allowing people into your house* simply because they tell you they CAN obtain a search warrant or will bring the police. If they say that, tell them you are very sorry, but you will not allow them in, and if they want to get a search warrant, it is up to them. If they want to call the police, that is also up to them. This gives you TIME to contact an attorney or your state or local home schooling organization.

How to proceed at the door

When someone comes to your door asking questions, the first thing to do is ask for identification. If he is unable or unwilling to provide it, do not speak with him. Stay in your house, close the door, and lock it. If he continues to stay on your property, call the police. Anyone who really is from the superintendent's office or from Social Services should provide you with identification. There is no reason not to, and in fact, in most states, government representatives are required by law to provide identification, which is usually a badge with a photograph.

In addition to seeing identification, ask for a business card. If you have a business card with the person's name, address, and phone number, there is less chance that he will be rude when speaking with you, because he knows that you would be able to report him. Also, you will want to contact an attorney after the conversation. Your attorney must know with whom you spoke, and thus whom to call at the Department of Education or Social Services.

Remember that anyone coming to your door from Social Services is probably overworked. Local Social Services agencies may have a staff of forty or fifty people, and it is virtually impossible to find someone if you do not have a name and that means a business card. Many parents, after such an encounter at their door, are too upset and cannot remember the name. So please obtain the business card, or write down the name, address, and phone number.

Whether or not to answer questions

After you have the identification and business card, the person at the door will probably want to ask you some questions about your home schooling. At this point, you will have to decide whether to talk with the person or not. Nothing requires you to answer the questions.

You have a Fifth Amendment right not to answer any questions, the right against self-incrimination. Even if you have not broken the law, the person at your door is asking questions that might lead him to believe that you have broken the law. Therefore, whatever answer you give, no matter how proper, could be self-incriminating in the eyes of the official. Thus, you have a perfect right not to answer on the grounds of possible self-incrimination. However, do not use those words to your visitor. Simply say, "I would rather have legal counsel before answering your questions."

If you feel comfortable talking with the person at your door, fine. Remember, however, that if you have no third party witness, anything you say may be written down, either accurately or inaccurately. It would be the word of the government agent against yours if any future proceedings should follow.

If you decide not to talk with the person, just say that you are busy, that you do not have time right now, but if he will put the request for information in writing, you will get back to him. This gives you time to contact your spouse, think about what you want to do, pray about it, contact an attorney, or contact your local or state home schooling support group.

If you decide to answer the questions, I strongly urge you to speak with the person *outside* the house. Step outside, close the door behind you, and talk with the person outside—no matter what the weather is. Whether you are in sunny southern California or in a blizzard in North Dakota, I would say to the person, "I'll step outside and we can talk for a few minutes." Keep your children away from sight if at all possible. You would be surprised how a social worker can use an inconsequential item, like a child without his shoes on, as evidence for child neglect.

Outside the door

Once outside, you should not answer any question that makes you feel uncomfortable. Even if the person asks you something he might be entitled to know, politely ask which law gives him permission to ask for test scores, for your teacher's credentials, or whatever. In fact, ask him to cite the law so that you or an attorney can look it up. Tell him you want to write down the State Code number so you can look it up later. And then do look it up.

You may be familiar with the law yourself, sometimes more so than the person at the door. You must decide whether you will show that you know the law, or simply to let the person speak without adding your comments.

If you know what the home schooling law is in your state, you may or may not want to quote it to them. If your visitor says, "It's the compulsory educational law," you could respond, "But isn't it true, according to the statute section such-and-such of the educational code, that I don't have to be a certified teacher? And isn't it also true that I don't need to administer an achievement test?" However, this kind of a discussion is usually not too productive. Authority figures do not like to be informed by the person they are supposed to be informing.

Some parents feel "called" to have a discussion with the government representative. If so, keep in mind that God will be with you, say a prayer, and rely on God to help you through and to help you give the best possible answers, so as to convince the person not only that what you are doing is right, but that what other home schoolers are doing is right. Next time he receives a call about home schooling, he may have a better understanding of it, know the type of people who are doing it, and treat parents' concerns for their children as real and legitimate.

If you have a copy of the law, you might want to keep it available so that you can produce it and say, "This is what the law says; I have a copy." Normally, having things in writing is better than quoting something.

Hints to avoid trouble

There are many practical hints to avoid legal trouble. Some are more important than others, and I will try to emphasize the hints which I think are very important that you do, as opposed to those I only suggest you consider.

The first hint is one that I emphasize very strongly. I give it first because it is extremely important. It is to keep good records. Many states require that you keep records such as standardized test scores, or grades, or attendance records. Some elementary schools and all high schools require transcripts if you transfer. Records should be kept for two or three years, or until your child graduates from high school. Transcripts for all four years of high school should be kept for a few years. These records should be handy and easily available. Even if your children are enrolled in a home study program, keep a copy of the records for yourself.

If you are planning to send your children to college, you are going to need records, especially a high school transcript, or diploma. Every college in the country requests the prospective student's high school transcript.

Attendance records are very important, and most states consider this the most important school document. The compulsory laws are for attendance, not for education. Attendance records prove to the state or school district which days your children have been in school, and how many days. Even if you think you may never need them, keep attendance records.

Report cards are required by schools if you ever transfer back into a school. Though only a few states require them by law, it is a protection against future problems. Grades should be given quarterly. They do not necessarily have to be numerical grades.

About half the states now require nationally standardized tests, such as the SRA, Iowa, CAT, or Stanford. They usually are required to be given to home schooled students each year. The standardized test scores show in an objective way that education is taking place. If you can show that your child has scored in a high percentile on his standardized tests for the last four years, it would be very difficult for someone to step in and claim that he is not learning anything, or is being educationally deprived.

Keep samples of work

The records we have been talking about are just one page each, but I also recommend that samples of schoolwork be kept. Some states call this a "portfolio," and it includes samples of papers the children have done, sample quizzes they have taken, sample workbooks, or whatever. Ideally, all the children's work for a particular year should be put in a box, stored, and kept for a year or two. It does not need to be kept as long as academic records. You probably will never need this, and it can be stored away in an attic. However, it will be important if there is ever a problem. It also is nice to have for your children when they get older. They like to look back at what they did when they were young and show their old school papers to their own children.

Keeping records and samples of work is important because it proves that education is taking place. If a home schooling family has trouble, it is often because they have been unable to demonstrate that education is taking place. There is no finer evidence that can be presented to a judge than samples of books and papers with your child's handwriting on them. Parents get into trouble when they cannot show that education is taking place!

If you are using a home study program that grades work, then keep copies of returned graded work. This shows not only that the child did the work, but that an outside evaluator saw the work.

Be organized

Be organized in your home schooling, and look organized. **You should have a class schedule**. You may not follow the schedule exactly each day, but you should be able to demonstrate how a typical day goes. I know of one particular case that parents lost because they could not show that they had a daily plan for their home schooling. At the beginning of the year, make a class schedule. **You should have a daily schedule and a weekly schedule.** Try to keep the schedule and not fall behind. Put the date that the children complete work on their papers, workbook pages, and tests.

There is much discussion among home schoolers about structure and non-structure. Legally speaking, if parents are ever asked by authorities, they need to produce some sort of organized plan showing classes at certain times of the day. It is not unusual for parents to be asked to explain a typical home schooling day. Remember, the people you may have to defend your homeschool to are used to a structured schooling approach – the public school.

Know the law

Read, study, and learn your state's home schooling law. Keep a copy easily available for quick reference. Knowledge is power. If someone comes to your door claiming that the law says one thing when you know it says something else, it gives you confidence and a comforting peace. It is amazing how often superintendents, or people from their offices, will mislead home schoolers, whether through ignorance of the law or merely for the sake of trying to gain an advantage. Whatever the reason, if you know the law, you are able to respond without fear, in whatever way you believe is best.

You can find a copy of the State Code or state laws at your local library, or on the Internet. Look under "Education," and you can find all the laws in your state relating to education, as well as references to legal cases. State home schooling associations publish an information packet with the current state home schooling laws. Every lawyer has a copy of the state laws also. Copies of each state's home schooling laws are available at Seton. The quickest way to find out about your state home schooling law is to go to the HSLDA website at www.hslda.org. All the state laws are there, and the lawyers have put the laws in an easy to follow chart.

Always double-check anything anyone tells you about the law that does not sound correct. Remember that the U.S. Supreme Court has ruled that no state may outlaw home schooling, nor may a state make regulations which would, in effect, make home schooling impossible. Although a few states, e.g. New York and Pennsylvania, have laws that require a lot of paperwork for example, there is no state that does not allow parents to home school. In almost thirty years, I have never encountered a situation where a family who truly wished to home school was unable to do so because of the state law.

Join the state association

Join your state home schooling association. State organizations are not Catholic because approximately 95% of the home schoolers in this country are Evangelical Christians. While we have some doctrinal differences, I can say, having met thousands of them, that the Christian home schooling families in these groups agree with us on the moral issues of the day. These are good, pro-life, pro-family people.

The state association can help home schooling families with information and support. Every state organization publishes a monthly or quarterly newsletter. They keep you up-to-date with proposed legislation in your state. They monitor state legislation and lobby for better home schooling laws. Catholics should be willing to help their state association fight for better legislation for home schooling families.

Home schoolers should not be satisfied holding onto the victories that we have won, we also should be working to increase our freedom to home school and ensure that hard won freedoms are not rolled back. The state organizations are in the forefront of these efforts.

Know your own school district

Know where your local school district stands on home schooling. Although the superintendent does not have any legal authority to pass home schooling regulations, he may make some pronouncements. Knowing the "politics" of your local school district is very beneficial, because many times this will give you an indication of how you wish to proceed when and if you notify your superintendent.

Learn your local district's position on home schooling by contacting your state or local support group. Local and state organizations are very knowledgeable about the local politics, because they are very involved in them, and have gone through experiences with the superintendent already. They know what is going on, and they can give you some good insight as to how to proceed.

If you feel so inclined, consider becoming involved in local politics, and encourage other home schoolers to do so as well. It is much harder for local politicians to harass home schoolers when home schoolers have political influence. Running for the school board or the town council or even minor town or county positions, or joining a county political organization is not that hard to do.

A letter

In the state of Virginia, parents are given a religious exemption from attendance at school and from the home schooling regulations. While the details of the following letter may not exactly meet your own state regulations, it may give you ideas about how you might write your local superintendent when declaring that you cannot follow a certain regulation.

In addition, such a letter is a good idea if you decide to follow a certain regulation for prudential reasons, but philosophically you believe you have the right not to follow the regulation. Your letter might start: "As a matter of courtesy, we are enclosing the following form (or test scores, or whatever). However, we (name of mother and name of father) are teaching our children at home because of our religious convictions."

Dr. Clark sent the following notarized letter to the local superintendent, and to all the school board members, by certified mail. She sent it only after her name had appeared so frequently in the newspapers regarding her home schooling lobbying efforts at the state capitol, that she received a phone call from the local school district. Otherwise, she would never have made any contact with the local school district. Many home school attorneys recommend not contacting any school district authorities until and unless you are first contacted. If your children have been enrolled in the public schools, this would not be possible. Obviously, a decision not to notify when called for by law must be made with careful thought, prayer, and prudence.

Here is Dr. Clark's letter:

Dear Dr. D.,

According to the Code of Virginia, 22.1-256-A: The provisions of this article (22.1-254, Compulsory Attendance) shall not apply to: 4. Children excused under 22.1-256 of this article.

The section 22.1-256 lists the groups of children excused from school attendance. It states that "A. A school board: ... 2. Shall excuse from attendance at school any pupil who, together with his parents, by reason of bona fide religious training or belief, is conscientiously opposed to attendance at school."

The section further states that "C. As used in paragraph A 2 of this section, the term 'bona fide religious training or belief' does not include essentially political, sociological, or philosophical views, or a personal moral code."

The Code does not elaborate on the procedure for parents to notify the school board members of their religious convictions. Therefore, we wish to use this notarized letter to inform each Warren County School Board member of the following:

We, Bruce and Mary Kay Clark, are teaching our children at home because of our religious convictions or bona fide religious beliefs. These are not essentially political, sociological, or philosophical views, or a merely personal moral code.

Though we realize our rights are a natural right of all parents, nevertheless we are also following the principles of our church, as outlined in the Charter of the Rights of the Family. Pope John Paul II states that a) Parents have the right to educate their children in conformity with their moral and religious convictions. b) Parents have the right to choose freely schools or other means necessary to educate their children in keeping with their convictions. c) Parents have the right to ensure that their children are not compelled to attend classes which are not in agreement with their own moral and religious convictions.

In conclusion, we note that our excuse from the 22.1-254 article includes the specifics of the home schooling regulations, such as up-front qualifications, curriculum approval, and annual testing.

Sincerely,

(Note: This letter uses wording in conformity to the Virginia home schooling law. However, the law is unconstitutional. In fact, it is so blatantly unconstitutional that a home schooling attorney once said of it: "You could drive a constitutional Mack truck through this one!" According to the U.S. Supreme Court, parents have the right to teach their children at home for *any* reason!)

Be not afraid

Each one of us must decide exactly where we are going to stand and which laws we believe we can obey. Just where you believe your position should be is between you and God. No home schooling parent should presume to judge the decisions of other home schooling parents. We each need to follow the graces God gives us to make decisions for our own family.

Be not afraid to home school, but be prudent in the way you run your home schooling. Home schooling is legal, and you should not hide your children or yourself from the world, but you should be prudent. Do not be secretive as you teach your children. You are more likely to get into trouble by acting strangely. If you act as if you are doing something wrong, your children will get the impression that what they are doing is wrong. We do not want them to believe that their parents are being deceptive or doing something illegal, because then the children will become fearful, which is certainly not what home schooling is about.

In 32 AD, the Church was so small that all its members could fit into one room. Yet like the tiny mustard seed, it grew. Thirty-five years ago, when Dr. Clark began home schooling my brothers and me, there were probably fewer than 100,000 children being home schooled in the United States. Today, January 2014, between two and three million children are being home schooled in the United States. [Three to five percent of these children are Catholic.] This is a greater number than ever in our history. This means that we are stronger now than we have ever been before. Of course, the opponents of home education have not raised the white flag and surrendered. The battle for the minds and souls of a nation begins with its children. Lenin once said, "Give me four years to teach the children and the seed I have sown will never be uprooted." Despite the hardships and struggles that home schoolers endure, the number of home schoolers grows every year. For hundreds of years the Roman Empire, the most powerful empire the world has ever known, tried to destroy Christianity. Christianity not only survived, but thrived!

Be not afraid.

A brief point for Catholics

Other chapters in this book show that our right to home school comes from God. This is clearly taught in the Bible and in Catholic Church documents. While we need to be aware of the state laws, actually they have little relation to the reality that God gives parents the right to teach their own children. Therefore, no matter how you deal with local authorities, remain firm in your beliefs and convictions based on the Bible and the teachings of the Catholic Church. No laws or regulations made by man can take away your God-given rights. Nor should they stop you, because they are God-given responsibilities as well.

Catholics and Christians are law-abiding citizens. We have a difficult time even considering breaking a "law" which may not be legal or constitutional or morally correct. Yet we know from our own history that sometimes civil disobedience is not only a valid form of expression but a persuasive one as well. We need to recall the African–Americans who sat in the front of the bus or at lunch counters in the early days of their fight for their civil rights. While we hope that such things will never happen in America, there may be a dark future, in which laws and regulations are passed that limit our rights to have children as well as how to educate our children. We need to understand now, before such dreadful laws are made, how we intend to respond, both spiritually and legally.

Chapter 16:
Home Schooling and Catechesis

Editor's Note: Much of the following is based upon the pamphlet "Responsibilities and Rights of Parents in Religious Education," published by the Catholic Home School Network of America.

Based upon many documents from the Church, it is clear that parents have the right and responsibility to be teachers to their children.

There has been some controversy, though, in trying to define the rights of parents and rights of the Church regarding sacramental preparation. Put another way, the question arises whether it is up to the parents or the Church to provide systematic teaching about the Faith.

Soon after a birth, parents seek out the Church in order to have their child baptized. This is perhaps the first catechesis of children, with the parents and Church cooperating in this important work of grace.

After Baptism, when a child is young, it is primarily up to the parents to teach the basics of making the Sign of the Cross, learning simple prayers, asking for help from a guardian angel. It is primarily up to the parents to teach proper behavior, by both word and deed.

At the same time that family catechesis occurs, parents make possible a second form of catechesis that extends beyond the family and into the parish. This second form is parents providing their children with the experience of the Church's liturgy in the parish with their family and other parishioners.

The children are instructed through the proclamation of the stories of the patriarchs, the prophets, and kings in the Old Testament and of the story of Jesus and the Apostles in the New Testament during the readings at Mass. The children also are instructed through the explanations and exhortations of the priest or deacon in his homily, through the directions and words the priest or deacon gives in celebrating the liturgy, and through the architecture, decoration, furnishings, vestments, and vessels of liturgy. Finally, the children are "instructed" by the supernatural realities of the Mass: The Real Presence of Jesus, the Sacrifice of Calvary, and Holy Communion.

However, when children reach school age, they commonly begin a series of systematic catechesis, in which the truths of the Church are explained and presented formally. Just as parents traditionally relied upon schools to teach history and science, parents traditionally have relied upon the Catholic schools or upon CCD classes at church for this systematic presentation of the Faith.

Parents who have decided to take upon themselves the duty of teaching their children science and history have naturally also taken upon themselves the duty of catechesis. This has brought parents and Church authorities, if not into conflict, at least into an area of contention.

Parents can prepare their children for First Communion or Confession at home, but obviously the sacraments themselves are celebrated in church. So when parents bring their children to the parish church and ask for the sacraments, parish priests may raise questions. And when enough of these parents come and enough priests ask questions, the matter may be bumped up the chain of command and produce a diocesan policy regarding home schooled children and the reception of the sacraments.

In previous chapters, we have gone over Church documents. These documents were mainly stated so that parents, pastors, and other authorities will understand the right and duty of Catholic parents to educate their children and how this right supersedes that of secular authorities who oversee educational efforts of civil governments and of private schools. However, these principles apply as well to parents' right to evangelize, catechize, and prepare their children for the sacraments and how this right relates to the Church authorities who provide systematic catechesis and the administration of the sacraments in parishes.

As a consequence, bishops and priests, and their representatives, must accept and respect the truth of the following assertions as much as civil authorities do: parents have the primordial and inalienable, and, therefore, the prevailing right and duty to educate their children, especially to religiously educate them; parents have a fundamental competence to educate their children because they are parents; and parents have the freedom to choose the means and institutions by which they educate their children generally and in systematic catechesis for the sacraments as long as it is according to the teaching of the Church.

It is true that there is not a strict likeness between the proper relations of the faithful and the hierarchy in the church and the proper relations of citizens and civil government in the state. The "freedom" and "rights" that order the relations between the faithful and the pastors in the Church are not going to be the same as the "freedom" and "rights" that order the relations between citizens and their government regarding religion and education. For example, the faithful do not have the "freedom" or the "right" in the Church to dissent from doctrine set forth by the Magisterium of the Church. Also, the faithful do not have the "freedom" or the "right" to say their opinions are the teaching of the Church on questions which are still open to various opinions (on both points see *Code of Canon Law* 227).

Nevertheless, the 1983 *Code of Canon Law* points out that the faithful of the Church do have a certain freedom and certain rights in the Church and not just in the state (see *CCL* 208-231). It is in its section on "The Obligations and Rights of the Lay Faithful" that the 1983 Code first mentions the right of parents to educate their children as we have seen above (*CCL* 226, art.2).

The 1983 Code contains language about "freedom" and "rights" as a result of the Second Vatican Council's call for updating in the Church. A shift from emphasis on obligations and duties to a more balanced emphasis on obligations and freedom, and on duties and rights, was part of the Council's call that the lay faithful take more personal responsibility for their Faith and rely less on having the pastors of the Church spell out every application and obligation of the doctrine and discipline of the Church. Thus, it would seem incontrovertible that pastors and catechists should respect the freedom and rights of parents to catechize their children even in relation to preparation for the first reception of sacraments in light of the teaching and emphasis in the cited documents of the Second Vatican Council, the Code, and the Catechism that parents are their children's principal educators.

All three authorities—the 1965 Council documents, the 1983 Code, and the 1992 Catechism—are concerned to point out when they say or imply parents are "principal educators," that they especially mean that parents are the principal religious educators of their children. We must reiterate the evidence again because of its extreme importance. Following immediately upon its statement that parents must be recognized as the primary and principal educators of their children, the Council's

declaration on education says, "it is above all in the Christian family …
that children should be taught to know and worship God and to love their
neighbor" (*Gravissimus Educationis* 3). The Council's decree on the laity
says married persons, "are to assert with vigor the right and duty of parents
to give the children a Christian upbringing" (*Apostolicam Actuositatem*
11). The Council's Constitution on the Church in the Modern World
says spouses, "will eagerly carry out their duties of education, especially
religious education, which primarily devolves on them" (*Gaudium et
Spes,* 48). After it says, "parents have a most serious obligation and enjoy
the right to educate [their children]," the Code says, "therefore Christian
parents are especially to care for the Christian education of their children"
(*CCL* 226, art. 2). Finally, the Catechism teaches in the same paragraph:
"the right and duty of parents to educate their children are primordial
and inalienable" and "the fecundity of conjugal love … must extend to
their [children's] moral education and spiritual formation" (*CCC* 2221).

Nevertheless, not all pastors and catechists accord full recognition to
the freedom and rights of parents in sacramental catechesis. This may be in
part because pastors have serious obligations according to the 1983 Code
to provide catechesis and to administer the sacraments rightly, or because
pastors may be unaware of these teachings of the Church. Therefore,
we have to investigate more specifically what the Code says and implies
about the proper relations between pastors and parents in systematic
catechesis, especially the catechesis associated with the preparation for
the first reception of sacraments.

Canon 773 in the Code's section on catechetical instruction gives
a special charge to pastors to provide catechesis in general to the faithful:
"There is a proper and serious duty, especially on the part of pastors of
souls, to provide for the catechesis of the Christian people.…"

The Code also says:

In virtue of his office the pastor is bound to provide for the catechetical
formation of adults, young people and children.… (*CCL* 776)

But then the Code asserts:

Under the supervision of legitimate ecclesiastical authority this concern
for catechesis pertains to all the members of the Church in proportion
to each one's role. (*CCL* 774, art. 1)

The Code then immediately declares that parents have the greatest role and the greatest concern for catechesis:

> Parents above others are obliged to form their children in the faith and practice of the Christian life by word and example. (*CCL* 774, art. 2)

And Canon 776 states, "The pastor is to promote and foster the role of parents in the family catechesis mentioned in Can. 774, article 2."

Regarding catechesis in relation to the sacraments, the section of the Code on catechetical instruction says:

> In accord with the norms established by the diocesan bishop, the pastor is to make particular provision:
> 1. that suitable catechesis is given for the celebration of the sacraments.
> 2. that children are properly prepared for the first reception of the sacraments of penance and Most Holy Eucharist and the sacrament of confirmation by means of catechetical formation given over an appropriate period of time ... (*CCL* 777).

In its section on the sacraments, the Code teaches:

> Pastors of souls and the rest of the Christian faithful, according to their ecclesial function, have the duty to see that those who seek the sacraments are prepared to receive them by the necessary evangelization and catechetical formation, taking into account the norms published by competent authority (*CCL* 843, article 2).

In the same section, the Code also says, speaking of preparation for First Holy Communion:

> It is the responsibility, in the first place, of parents and those who take the place of parents as well as of the pastor to see that children who have reached the use of reason are correctly prepared and are nourished by the divine food as early as possible (*CCL* 914).

In the same canon it also says:

> [I]t is ... for the pastor to be vigilant lest any children come to the Holy Banquet who have not reached the use of reason or whom he judges are not sufficiently disposed (*CCL* 914).

Finally, the sacramental section of the Code speaks about preparation for the Sacrament of Confirmation:

[P]arents and shepherds of souls, especially pastors, are to see to it that the faithful are properly instructed to receive it and approach the sacrament at the appropriate time (*CCL* 890).

In reviewing these canons on the role of pastors in catechesis, we would have to admit that, at first glance, the Code seems to support the customary situation in the United States today: Pastors provide catechetical programs and parents send their children to them. This view would seem especially plausible if one had not reviewed all that was said previously in this chapter about the foundation of parental rights in the new articulation of the Second Vatican Council and subsequent documents. Thus, the fact that little recognition is given to parental freedom in systematic catechesis is understandable if still quite unfortunate—hence the current controversy over authority and freedom in catechesis.

Nevertheless, upon closer inspection, none of what is said above about pastors' roles in catechesis takes away from the authority, autonomy, and freedom that parents have as principal religious educators of their children. The Code itself is clear about this. In its section on ecclesiastical laws, the Code says:

Laws which establish a penalty or restrict the free exercise of rights or which contain an exception to the law are subject to a strict interpretation. (*CCL* 18)

Parents not only have "a most serious obligation" to educate their children, but they also "enjoy the right to educate them" (*CCL* 226, art. 2). The Code says, "Catholic parents also have the duty and right to select those means and institutions through which they can provide more suitably for the Catholic education of the children …"(*CCL* 793, art. 1). Finally, in its section on the effects of the sacrament of marriage, the Code says, "Parents have the most serious duty and the primary right to do all in their power" to educate their children (*CCL* 1136).

Thus, what may appear restrictive of these rights of parents, such as the pastor's duties in catechesis, is to be more strictly interpreted. Pastors do not have the "right" to provide catechesis in the same way as parents; pastors are simply bound to provide it. It seems that the canons above are simply emphasizing that the pastor provide those aids parents may use to properly form their children. The pastor has a subsidiary obligation to the parents' principal obligation to catechize their children.

The serious duty of pastors in catechesis is emphasized in the Code, not because pastors are to supervise parents who undertake systematic catechesis with their own children, but because the pastor must provide catechesis for all of "the Christian people," not just children (*CCL* 773). In the case of adults, the duty of the pastor to provide catechesis is more direct. The pastor is to catechize adults either himself or delegate the task to catechists, who would be under his immediate supervision since they do not have a "right" to the task in the same way as parents do.

(It probably would be admirable, in light of the emphasis in the Second Vatican Council on greater personal appropriation and maturity of faith, if parishes spent more time on adult catechesis. One of the major tasks of adult catechesis should be to exhort parents to catechize their own children and provide parents with programs and materials to help them teach their own children. Indeed, we often hear from parents that they themselves never learned the Faith until they started teaching their children. With that in mind, it may be that the average parish has as much a need for adult catechesis as it does for catechesis of children.)

When the Code speaks of the duties of pastors in catechesis, it also speaks of the duty of others in catechesis, especially parents. Canon 843, article 2, says, "Pastors of souls and the rest of the Christian faithful have the duty to see that those who seek the sacraments are prepared ..." In Canon 773, the Code says pastors have a serious duty to provide catechesis, but in the very next canon it says the "concern for catechesis pertains to all members of the Church in proportion to each one's role" (*CCL* 774, art. 1). Then in the same canon, it says "parents above others" are responsible for catechesis of their children (*CCL* 774, art. 2). Canon 776 says the pastor, "is to promote and foster the role of parents" in catechesis. Finally, Canons 890 and 914 on Confirmation and the Eucharist, say that parents, first, and then pastors, are to see to proper instruction before children receive these sacraments.

Thus, while the Code speaks of the duty of all pastors and members of the Church to provide catechesis, it never speaks of their "right" to do this. All pastors and all the other members of the Church have an obligation to provide catechesis in some way (the Code even says all members of the Church "are not to refuse to furnish their services [for catechesis] willingly unless they are legitimately impeded" [*CCL* 776]). Pastors are to play a subsidiary role when it comes to children and their parents. The "prevailing right" (see *Letter to Families*, 16) and, therefore, the freedom of decision over means of catechesis, belongs to parents in the catechesis of their own children.

One might say that there is a certain parallel or analogy between parents and pastors: what parents are to children, pastors are to sacraments. As parents are the principal educators of their children, so pastors (bishops and priests) are the principal stewards of the sacraments. In regard to children first receiving the sacraments, parents, as principal educators of their children, have the larger say in how their children are prepared or educated for the first reception of a sacrament. However, pastors as principal stewards of the sacraments, have the larger say in judging the eligibility and disposition of those who want to receive a sacrament and setting the time, place, and manner for the reception of the sacrament.

Eligibility has to do with *who* may approach and receive a sacrament. Such issues as the age of the child, previous reception of certain sacraments, the Christian practice of the parents, and the presence of extraordinary conditions enter into a pastor's judgments of eligibility. To take an obvious example, someone who has not been baptized cannot receive any of the other sacraments because the Code says, "One who has not received baptism cannot be validly admitted to the other sacraments" (*CCL* 842, article 1). If a non-baptized person asked for any sacrament besides Baptism, a pastor must refuse the request. Such a person is *ineligible*. Another example is that those baptized children who have not reached the age of reason are not to receive Confirmation and First Holy Communion in the Roman Rite (cf. *CCL* 891 and 914). (While priests in the Eastern Rites of the Church may give the Eucharist to infants, priests in the Roman Rite may not.)

Pastors also determine whether a child has the readiness or proper disposition to receive a sacrament, such as the Eucharist or Confirmation. Disposition has to do with whether a child has sufficient understanding of the sacrament and sufficient willingness to respect and receive it with a reverence appropriate to his age. The need to have sufficient understanding and willingness usually requires that a child be instructed in the Faith in general and about a sacrament in particular before receiving it.

In order to judge the dispositions of a child who has reached the age of reason, a pastor should require that parents inculcate in the child a basic knowledge of the whole Faith and of the sacrament to be received.

Thus, the pastor, as a consequence of his own primary responsibility for the proper administration of the sacraments, has the right to promulgate reasonable standards about what knowledge a child must possess to be properly disposed for the first reception of a sacrament. Additionally, the pastor has the right to test or interview the child to determine whether a child has the prerequisite knowledge necessary for a proper disposition. Such standards should be according to the teaching of the Church, accommodated to the age of the child, and should be capable of being inculcated in a variety of ways by the parents or by parish programs if parents choose to use them. "Parents should not be subjected directly or indirectly to unjust burdens because of this freedom of choice" *(Dignitatis Humanae,* 5).

However, the eligibility and the proper disposition for the child to receive a sacrament should not include a requirement that the child's parents *must* enroll the child in a formal parish sacramental preparation program. Eligibility and proper disposition also should not include a requirement that parents be certified by the diocese, follow the regulations that other catechists must follow, or use catechetical material suited to the classroom or on the approved list of a diocese. For the pastor to ascertain the eligibility of a child for a sacrament, it should be sufficient that the parents provide the relevant information about the child and themselves through an interview or written communication.

For the pastor to determine the disposition of a child, that is, the child's understanding and willingness, it should be sufficient for the pastor or his representative to tell the parents how he will evaluate their child's disposition. Upon completion of parental catechesis that is directed to the pastor's standards, parents should allow the pastor or his representative to interview or test the child for the proper disposition toward the sacrament to be received.

The pastor provides religion programs in the parish as a means of assistance to parents who want to use them, but the parents are not obliged to accept the pastor's assistance. Parents may choose to provide the systematic catechesis for their children because parents have the prevailing right in educating their children. As the first and principal educators of their children, parents can choose to undertake the systematic catechesis themselves or choose other means of catechesis as long as such undertakings or means are in accord with the teachings of the Church.

The duty of a pastor to provide catechesis can not entail forcing the parents to accept his assistance. Pope John Paul II said in his *Letter to Families*:

> Certainly one area in which the family has an irreplaceable role is that of *religious education*, which enables the family to grow as a "domestic church." Religious education and the catechesis of children make the family a *true subject of evangelization and the apostolate* within the Church. We are speaking of a right intrinsically linked to *the principle of religious liberty.* Families, and more specifically parents, are free to choose for their children a particular kind of religious and moral education consonant with their own convictions. Even when they entrust these responsibilities to ecclesiastical institutions or to schools administered by religious personnel, their educational presence ought to continue to be *constant and active.* (*Letter to Families*, 16; emphasis in the original)

This recent teaching of Pope John Paul II makes explicit what was already implicit in Canon 797 ("It is necessary that parents enjoy true freedom in selecting schools") and in the Charter of the Rights of the Family ("Parents have the right to choose freely schools or other means necessary to educate their children in keeping with their convictions"): parents enjoy true freedom not only in choosing schools for the general education of their children but also in choosing the means of religious education for their children, provided such means are in accord with the teachings of the Church (cf. *CCL* 226, article 2).

Therefore, pastors should accept reasonable decisions that parents make as to how parents prepare their children for the reception of a sacrament. If a pastor requires parents to use a parish program as a condition for eligibility or for having the proper disposition of their child to receive a sacrament, then the pastor is not respecting the principal responsibility of the parents in the catechesis of their children, a role they have by Natural Law and Canon Law, and re-affirmed by recent papal teaching. Thus, a pastor violates the religious liberty of parents if he makes participation of their children in a parish catechetical program a condition and requirement for the reception of a sacrament.

In the mid-1990s, there was a trend around the country for dioceses to promulgate rules or guidelines regarding home schooled children and the reception of the sacraments. Among the dioceses affected were Monterey, Chicago, Peoria, Los Angeles, Atlanta, Pittsburgh, and Cincinnati.

The motivation for promulgating guidelines seems to have varied from a desire to control home schoolers to a desire to give real help to home schoolers. Sometimes the rules were developed in consultation with local home schooling groups. When this happened, as in Pittsburgh, the guidelines tended to include strong statements of parental rights and responsibilities and probably helped parents in case there was any dispute about sacramental preparation.

However, the guidelines in other dioceses tended to place the parish CCD program as the main source of religious education for children and reduced the parents to mere agents of the CCD program. For example, several guidelines included provisions that parents could use only teaching materials approved by the diocese. For example, the Los Angeles guidelines state: "Approved textbooks and other appropriate materials must be used in all sessions." Another common provision was that students must attend CCD classes in order to receive First Communion and Confirmation.

As is clear from the previously cited documents of the Church, regulations which severely restrict parental choice in education are contrary to Church teaching and regulation. Although guidelines tended to cite certain canons in their formulation, it was clear that the dioceses had no real authority to promulgate many of the rules which they devised.

Besides lacking authority, many of the rules were simply unenforceable. For example, a diocese may have a rule that only approved materials can be used, but children and parents are free to read non-approved books. The most a parish or diocese could do in this regard would be to give approved materials to the parents. Other restrictive provisions, such as for home visits or for extensive supervision by pastors, were probably not welcomed by either pastors or parents.

It appears that many diocesan guidelines were either not enforced, or were withdrawn, or were said to be merely suggestions. For example, Lesley Payne wrote in *San Diego News Notes*, "The Monterey guidelines were never enforced. Monterey's religious education director, Sister Dolores Fenzel, was quoted a year ago [1997] as saying the guidelines were a mistake, and that the intention had been to help parents, not to prevent them from teaching their children as they saw fit."

Regarding the Los Angeles guidelines, Sandra Guzman reported in *San Francisco Faith*, "Sister Edith Prendergrast, director of religious education for the Los Angeles Archdiocese, admitted that these guidelines are just that—guidelines. When asked how the archdiocese would enforce them, Prendergrast admitted that the guidelines could not be enforced. Prendergrast said that the archdiocese's intention is to say, 'here are some ways that we would like you to know how you can connect with your parish. The kids are being initiated into the parish community. We are saying these are ways to connect ... come to the parent meetings.'"

Whether any particular set of guidelines is actually being enforced probably depends as much on the parish priest as on the diocesan guidelines themselves. In parishes where the priest is either favorably or negatively disposed to home schooling, the presence of guidelines does not really matter. In parishes where the priest is neutral, or simply has no experience with home schooling, the priest may look to diocesan guidelines for help. The irony of guidelines is that, while they were supposed to give priests and parents more certainty about diocesan rules, they often raised more questions than they answered.

There is the matter, though, of whether parents are obligated to follow diocesan guidelines if they exist. That is a complex question. The first answer is that if a diocese has a set of guidelines which the diocese does not make any attempt to enforce, then those guidelines are probably merely suggestions and not commands, so there is no moral obligation to comply.

If a diocese does make an effort to enforce its guidelines, then a parent would have to take a look at the guidelines themselves. Some of the guidelines, such as requirements that children attend parish classes or use only certain materials, are clearly and obviously contrary to Canon Law and even to Natural Law and are de facto void. In such a case, a parent would not be obligated to comply with the law, although they could choose to comply. The only exception would be when a parent believes that it would be morally wrong to comply with the law.

In other cases, a parish or diocese clearly has the authority to promulgate rules. For example, a parish priest clearly has the authority to determine if a child is prepared to receive the sacraments. Therefore, if a diocese has a rule that a parish priest must test a home schooled child on his knowledge of a sacrament before its reception, a parent would be obligated to follow this rule.

Some points of the guidelines are simply good ideas that every family ought to follow anyway. For example, many of the guidelines state that families should be active in the life of their parish. Obviously, that is good advice. It is particularly good advice for home schooling families because their relationship with their pastor is especially important when it comes time for their children to receive the sacraments.

Chapter 17:
Catholic Home Schooling in Our American Democracy

Anyone who favors real school choice is eventually accused of being un-American.

American public schools, from the very beginning, have been devoted to preparing a certain kind of citizen for this country, rather than giving students a good general education. From the beginning, anyone who questioned the value of these temples of democracy was reviled by educrats. Horace Mann, the father of public schools, wrote long ago what he thought of public school detractors:

> Anything which tends to lessen the value of our free schools is hostile to the designs of our pious ancestors. Any man, who through pride or parsimony permits these schools to decline, can hardly be regarded as a friend to his country. I speak with plainness, for I am pleading the cause of humanity and of God. And I say that any man who designs the destruction of our free schools is a traitor to the cause of liberty and equality, and would, if it were in his power, reduce us to a state of vassalhood.

Even though the educrats have stopped talking about being on God's side, they still view the public schools as essential to the continuing democracy of this country. Albert Shanker, former head of the American Federation of Teachers, said:

> The purpose of education in our schools is to get all kids in our country to learn to live with and respect each other.... [To support private schools is to] destroy something that is extremely important as the glue of the United States of America.

More extreme is the head of the California Teachers Association, Del Weber, who wrote regarding a private school choice initiative in California, "There are some proposals which are so evil that they should never even be presented to the voters."

The view of the public school as the temple of democracy traces its roots back to the Puritans who came to this country about 400 years ago. They saw America as the promised land in which they could build the Biblical "shining city on a hill." America was to be the earthly reflection of the coming life in Heaven.

Indeed, this idea of America being a radically different and singularly special place on Earth has not lessened, despite the rejection of God by many Americans. In 1992, a Republican Party draft platform reflected this view by calling America the "last, best hope for mankind." Ironically, it was Christians, separating themselves from the Puritan tradition, who objected to this language on the platform committee, saying that Jesus Christ is the last, best hope for mankind.

Unfortunately, Catholics have not been immune from the idea that American democracy is somehow God-ordained. Along with this idea, many Catholics have come to believe the central democratic idea that all authority, as well as concepts of right and wrong, come from the majority vote of the people.

It is interesting to note that the first bishop of the United States, John Carroll, was not appointed by the pope, but was elected by the clergy of the United States. The pope reluctantly agreed to this election after being warned by Carroll that an appointment of a bishop by Rome would "shock the political prejudices of this Country." The unwillingness of the leading colonial Catholics in the United States to submit to the authority of Rome shows how deeply they accepted the principle of democratic rule even in matters of Church governance.

The Holy Father, Pope Leo XIII, wrote an apostolic letter, *Testem Benevolentiae*, to Cardinal Gibbons in 1899, specifically to warn against the heresy commonly called "Americanism." The basic principle of Americanism, as defined by the pope, is that the Catholic Church should "adapt herself somewhat" and "relaxing her ancient rigor, show some indulgence to modern popular theories." This is understood not only in regard to rules of life but also in regard to doctrines. The pope explains that Church doctrines are not theories, but a divine deposit to be carefully guarded and infallibly declared.

While certain rules of life, said the pope, can be modified according to the diversity of time and place, it is up to the Church, not to individuals, to judge how to adapt itself. Pope Leo XIII further points out that the

Church is of divine right, while other associations exist by the free will of men. Public prosperity, he wrote, "should thrive without setting aside the authority and wisdom of the Church." The Natural Law and the natural virtues need supernatural and divine help. The holy men of the past, "by humbleness of spirit, by obedience and abstinence, were powerful in word and work, were of the greatest help not only to religion but to the State and society."

The very concept of separation of Church and State, as we have come to know it in America, implies that eternal truths cannot be used as a basis for public laws. In this country, abortion is not considered evil because it is a horrible crime which God has condemned. It is evil only if one can convince 51% of the voters that it is evil. Such a situation implies that no real moral law exists, and any principle can be changed simply by holding another election. The concept of separation of God and State has come to mean separation of Truth and State. How can it be that such a fundamentally wrong principle could be a central tenet of a great and powerful nation?

To understand why moral principles based on God's laws are so anathema to American government, we have to go back to the early history of this country. In the founding days of the Republic, when all the documents guaranteeing religious liberty were written, separation of Church and State really was meant to guarantee that no one religion could get control of the government. There was to be no established national religion similar to the established national religions in England and European countries, nor were the constitutional laws to be dictated by any power other than by the governed people themselves.

But Protestantism was the underlying faith of this country's new leaders, and there was precious little separation between Protestantism and government.

Even if the Protestants had really meant what they said about separation of Church and State, this concept would have been radically un-Catholic. The Catholic Church has always taught that the State has an obligation to acknowledge that its authority comes from God. Pope Boniface VIII's *Unam Sanctam* in 1302 made clear the Church's teaching on the relationship of Church and State:

> We learn from the words of the Gospel that in this Church and
> in her power are two swords, the spiritual and the temporal.... Both

of these, that is, the spiritual and the temporal swords, are under the control of the Church. The first is wielded by the Church; the second is wielded on behalf of the Church. The first is wielded by the hand of the priest, the second by the hand of the kings and soldiers but at the wish and by the permissions of the priests. Sword must be subordinated to sword, and it is only fitting that the temporal authority should be subject to the spiritual.

As you recall, King Saul was reprimanded severely by the priests for going to war before consulting them and making sacrifices at the altar. Throughout Christendom, until the Protestant Revolt, kings and nations submitted to the authority of the pope, recognizing his authority as the Vicar of Christ. Henry VIII, defying the Church in the laws regarding marriage, drew his whole nation into a conflict with the Church.

Of course, it is easy to understand why the early Catholics in colonial America were only too happy to support separation of Church and State. The colonies at the time had established state churches, and they were, of course, Protestant. Many of the colonies, even after the Revolution, actively persecuted Catholics. The Catholics in the colonies realized that if any church were to be recognized as the official church of the country, it would not be the Catholic Church.

Most of the Catholics in the American colonies were Irish, and most of them either knew firsthand of the terrible persecution of Catholics going on in Ireland at the time, or they heard of them from others. Most Americans today, even those of Irish heritage, know little about the extent of the persecution that Catholics suffered in Ireland. This persecution, however, was extensive and brutal. Legally, Irish Catholics were not permitted to buy land, or to inherit property, or to educate their children in the Catholic Faith, or to send children to Catholic schools overseas, or to have Catholic churches, and could not even live in some towns. The great legislator Edmund Burke said that the Penal Laws in Ireland were "as well fitted for the oppression, impoverishment, and degradation of a feeble people ... as ever proceeded from the perverted ingenuity of man."

The legal persecution of Catholics in the American colonies was generally not nearly as bad as it was in Ireland or England. Thankfully, some of the laws passed against Catholics went largely un-enforced. The anti-Catholicism which existed manifested itself mainly in not permitting Catholics to vote. The anti-Catholicism at the time of the conversion of

Elizabeth Ann Seton in Philadelphia was so great, however, that Catholic men had to keep her surrounded to protect her from Protestant neighbors who aimed to verbally and physically abuse her.

Despite the nominal ban on establishment of religion, the public schools in this country started out as thoroughly Protestant institutions. Indeed, when public schools were first instituted, they were simply Protestant schools paid for with public funds.

The mass immigrations of the Irish began in the 1840s, just about the time that compulsory education was instituted. This brought about the problem of Catholic children being forced to attend schools which were instituted to teach against the Catholic religion. For this reason, the bishops of the United States determined to set up a Catholic school system which exists to this day.

Although the strict separation of morality from the state was never envisioned by the Protestant founding fathers, the language of the Constitution came to be used to enforce this separation starting in the 1950s, when prayer was first banned from public schools. Beginning with that ill-fated decision, there have been many anti-Christian rulings, such as that Christmas cannot be acknowledged with crèches on government property, that abortion must be allowed, that contraception and homosexuality are basic human rights, and that prayer may not be allowed at public school graduations. God has been forced from the public square, and the minions of Satan have hastily sought to erect shrines to the dragon in place of the lamb.

We see now that indifferentism, if not hostility, to eternal truth is not only enshrined in legislative halls, but also in the public schools. In New York State a new curriculum mandates that children as young as first grade be introduced to favorable presentations of homosexual "families." This curriculum is said to teach "tolerance" and "respect" for homosexuals, just as we need to respect racial minorities, say the proponents. What it really teaches is that homosexuality and homosexual "families" are good, that those who oppose them are un-American, and that it is un-American not to tolerate evil in our diverse and pluralistic American society.

The Catholic Church in America is not immune to erroneous ideas about the necessity of democracy to learn truth. How many times have we heard that the Church should change its teaching on birth control because polls show Catholics do not like it? The very idea that public opinion polls should determine Church teaching is ludicrous and insane; yet, this is a popular idea among some theologians and Church "leaders."

In a sense, it is true that Catholicism is un-American, if being American is believing that majority rule, or a Supreme Court decision, determines truth. But in a larger sense, it is true that being a good Catholic is the most patriotic of acts. To do what is right and good is always to do what is best, both in one's personal life, and in the life of nations. John F. Kennedy once stated that if he felt that the interests of the nation were in conflict with his Catholic Faith, he would resign the presidency. But, properly understood, such a situation is impossible, because a wrong act is never best.

When the people of our country are saying that it is all right to kill babies, the patriotic thing to do is to remind them that babies are the future of the nation. When the people of our country are saying that homosexuality is a good thing, it is the patriotic thing to tell them that homosexuality breeds contempt for families and encourages the use of others, even children, for personal lust. When the people of our country tell us that the old and infirm must be disposed of, it is the patriotic thing to tell them that unless we respect the life of each human being, no one will be safe in our nation.

Home schooling is in the best interests of America because it can only be good to raise up a new generation committed to living in harmony with God's Will. Home schooling is intensely patriotic because it trains future leaders of this country who will not be afraid to proclaim that the eternal laws of the universe must also guide the laws of our land. In the end, the glue which holds our country together is not the public schools, but the civic virtue which leads each citizen to care for his fellow man. Our social problems, whether low test scores or abortion or homelessness, can never be solved until the people in this country live by the Christian rule:

> Thou shalt love the Lord thy God with thy whole heart and with thy whole soul and with thy whole mind and with thy whole strength. This is the first commandment. And the second is like to it: Thou shalt love thy neighbor as thyself. There is no other commandment greater than these.

Alexis de Tocqueville, in his work *Democracy in America*, wrote many years ago, "America is great because she is good. If she ever ceases to be good, she will cease to be great."

Chapter 18:
The Future of Catholic Home Schooling

Those of us in the home schooling apostolate know we need to be concerned about what is happening in the schools, do what we can to influence legislators, and pray that God will protect the rights of home schooling families. As we pray, we need to have trust in Him for the future of Catholic home schooling because He works in ways we may not be thinking about at all. From what little we see on the horizon, we believe that Catholic home schooling will continue to be an educational choice among Catholic families for many years to come.

There is no question that home schooling is becoming more and more accepted in society. In any discussion of educational alternatives, home schooling is almost always brought up. In many ways, home schooling has ceased to be revolutionary. Now that everyone has a friend or a relative who home schools, it is thought of more as a mainstream choice than as a radical departure.

Home schooling continues to grow at a good rate. In August 2004, the U.S. Department of Education released a study reporting that the number of home schooled children in the United States was 1.1 million. As of spring 2010, Home school researcher Dr. Brian Ray estimates the actual number is between 1.73 and 2.1 million. Studies indicate that the home schooling population is growing somewhere between 2% and 8% each year.

Although we cannot predict the future, certain developments in this country are affecting Catholic home schooling positively and are ensuring that Catholic home schooling will continue to grow and succeed. These factors include advancements in technology, continued problems with public school systems, home school graduates, and support from Catholic clergy.

Advancements in technology

The Internet has become a household staple, and certainly has had an incredible impact on home education. You can find information on almost any topic on the Internet, and the benefit of this for home schooling families is noteworthy. "Google" makes it possible for students to easily research information on any subject. It used to be that home schooled students had to make frequent trips to the library for materials. Now students are able to find more information than would fit in many libraries right from their computer. Currently, Google is partnering with several libraries, such as Harvard University Library, the New York Public Library, and the University of Michigan, to scan their books and make them available online. One day, we may even see the entire contents of the Library of Congress available online.

There are many sites online that are of particular interest to Catholics. Perhaps surprisingly for an institution famed for moving slowly, the Vatican has a very good website, available at www.vatican.va. EWTN has a searchable library on their website containing archives of religious articles and church documents. There are also sites that offer everything from the entire contents of *The Catholic Encyclopedia* to the "Saint of the Day."

A major change in the internet, and one that is ongoing, is the move to broadband technology. This technology, such as DSL and cable, allows for extremely high speed transmission. Broadband usually allows for internet transmissions at least ten times faster than the old dial-up modem internet access. By mid-2004, more than half of all home internet users had broadband access. As of May 2013, the Pew Research Center estimated that this had increased to around 70 % of all home users. The much greater speed of broadband means that just about any data source, even full-motion video, can be downloaded over the internet. (In fact, internet video is so popular, that in May 2013, Netflix and YouTube accounted for just over half of all data downloaded in the United States.) The uses of the internet in education seem limited only by our imaginations.

Cell phones are also making an extraordinary impact on the world and can potentially affect the home schooling movement. According to industry marketing group Cellular Telecommunications and Internet Association (CTIA), as of June 2013, there were over 327 million cell phones in use in the United States. Throughout the world, there are nearly 7 billion cell phones in use, or almost one phone for every person on the earth. It used to be that employees had to be at their desks to answer their phones, but more and more people are using cell phones as their primary phone, meaning they do not have to be "in the office."

Over the last several years, tablets have been ever more popular. As the popularity of tablets has risen, many cell phones have become larger, to the point where some phones are really tablets with phones built in.

But perhaps both the cellphone and tablet are a transitional technology. One of the most interesting technologies being developed is called Google Glass. Moving away from the growing screen size trend, it puts a tiny screen right up by your eye. The built-in computer is hands free, and is operated via voice commands.

All of these new technologies have freed people from needing to be in a certain place to work or to access information. Historically, members of a family have lived and worked together. Children learned skills from their parents. With the Industrial Revolution and the rise of large cities, fathers left their families for work. In the past fifty years, mothers also have been leaving their families for work. With father and mother gone, children spend practically no time at home. However, with the new technology, parents can work at home on their computers and send their work into the office via the Internet. More and more people are working at home, or are using the home as a base for service jobs. Many home schooling parents are looking for "cottage industries" so they can be at home to raise their children and to help them with their education. The more parents work at home, the more families will be considering home schooling.

Continued problems with public school systems

Obviously, those who are promoting the current secular humanistic culture do not want home schooling and are opposed to parents influencing their own children. They want to continue the control that schools have over children, and to continue influencing them to accept the homosexual and contraceptive mentality. In general, the schools are promoting low standards in art, music, and entertainment, as well as low standards in educational achievements and social relationships. In recent years, in the name of "separating church and state," the public school systems have forbidden students from praying publicly or speaking about their faith. Christians in public schools are being persecuted, which can be damaging to the formation of our children. The culture war is raging stronger than ever in the public schools.

Common Core will be the next battle in schools. Common Core is a series of curriculum goals which were developed by the states, as a way of raising the level of education in public schools. While that is a laudatory goal, Common Core has essentially become a national curriculum, which takes more and more control away from local authorities and from parents. Even if a national curriculum were good in itself—and many critics say that Common Core is not good—the idea of a national curriculum is antithetical to many parents. As more parents find out about the Common Core, we can expect a new surge of home schooling.

Currently, the impact of Common Core is mostly limited to public schools. There are concerns, however, that as Common Core is implemented over the coming years, textbooks and standardized tests will be tailored to the Common Core requirements. If that happens, then home schoolers who purchase books or take standardized tests would be impacted, if only tangentially. There is also a concern that states may try to enforce Common Core standards on home schoolers, even though trends in recent years have generally been toward less regulation. Vigilance for student and parental rights has always been necessary to defend home schooling, and that will continue to be the case.

As if the amount of money spent on public education is not enough already, advocacy groups have been trying to use the courts in recent years to drastically increase school funding. These groups have pointed to provisions in state constitutions about providing public education in order to claim that states must increase their level of spending. The plaintiffs generally argue that the public education being provided is not "adequate" under the state constitution. The courts are then asked to order the legislatures to increase funding. The question is never brought up as to whether the whole system of public education is fundamentally flawed or whether throwing more money at the problem will help.

Perhaps the greatest threat to education in the United States is the National Education Association (NEA). The NEA has long been in the forefront of ensuring that schools spend more money for less educational return. The NEA has officially opposed home education for many years. It also opposes any real education reform and any true accountability. Despite a rather dismal track record, the influence of the NEA in the political arena is huge. It has been reported that as many as 1/3 of all the delegates to the national Democratic Convention in 2000 were either NEA members or the spouse of an NEA member. In 2012, approximately 95% of political contributions from the NEA went to Democrats.

Despite the power of the NEA, some Democratic office holders have made real attempts to reform public schools. For example, in 2007, Washington DC Mayor Adrian Fenty and DC Public School Chancellor Michelle Rhee started implementing a reform agenda. Although the reforms seemed to be bringing some improvements, Mayor Fenty was soon voted out of office, and Chancellor Rhee went with him.

The most important trend in the public school arena that is affecting home education is charter schools. Charter schools are public schools that are run outside of the normal system of control. Because they are outside the normal controls of the bureaucrats, charter schools have more freedom to try new ideas than traditional schools. According to the National Center for Education Statistics, there were 5,300 public charter schools operating the 2010-2011 school year. These schools served nearly two million students, with over 360,000 in California alone.

For home schooling families, charter schools are something of a mixed blessing. On the one hand, it can only help home schooling families when the range of educational options is expanded. As more options are available, the idea of choosing educational alternatives, rather than simply using the closest public school, becomes more acceptable. Also, choosing among the alternatives actively involves parents in their children's education. And, given a choice between a traditional public school and a charter school that actively works to satisfy the needs of parents and students, charter schools are probably a good alternative.

Some charter schools are now specifically targeting home schoolers, and that is where the difficulties come in. These home school charter schools, sometimes called "virtual academies," are public schools, so they offer free tuition. But the inducements often do not stop there. Because public schools receive so much money per child from state and federal sources, and because home schooling is so inexpensive, charter schools can offer all kinds of "free" extras to families who sign up. School districts often receive $5000 or more per year per child. If they pay out $1000 per year per home schooled child, they have turned a profit of $4000 per child. If they use part of that $4000 on recruitment incentives, they are still coming out way ahead.

A common incentive offered is a free home computer and free Internet access, but incentives often go far beyond this. One mother from California reports that she was told at a charter school recruitment meeting that her family would receive $100 per month per child. She was later told that the $100 would not be in cash, but in education-related goods or services. But even so, $100 per child per month worth of books, software, videos, technology, etc., is quite a bit. For a family with five children, that would be $500 per month, or $6000 per year. Instead of paying out money from their own pockets for educational materials, the family could be receiving a nice monthly stipend.

Several school districts in Alaska have started statewide programs for home schoolers. These school districts now enroll as many as 70% of all Alaska home schoolers, mainly because they offer as much as $1400 per child per year in financial incentives.

The problem with charter home schools is that they are public schools run by public authorities. They are not home schools where parents are in control. If the choice is between putting a child full-time in a traditional public school and the parents teaching the child at home in a virtual academy, then by all means we should support the option with more parental involvement. But charter home schools seem to be aimed more at parents already teaching at home, and the choice is between true Catholic home education versus public education taught at home by parents. There is an adage in government: "With money comes control." In other words, if the government is giving you money, they expect to control what you do. If the government is giving you money to educate your child, they expect to tell you how to do it. This has been very evident in the Alaska program. At first families could use the money to buy just about any education-related materials or service. Now, among several other rules, the state has told them they can't buy any religious educational materials with the money.

It's hard to say that parents are wrong to take the money and give up some of their freedom and control. After all, it is up to parents to decide what is best for their children. Perhaps parents feel that they can simply supplement the state materials they receive with Catholic materials. And having several thousand dollars extra per year to spend on education can be handy for buying technology or dance lessons or any number of other things.

But what families are giving up to get the money is quite a lot. In the early chapters of this book, we discussed how Catholic home education is first about faith and family. It is about passing on Catholic culture through a Christ-centered family life. But if the schooling must be pervasively secular in order to receive the state funds, then how can a family carry out true Catholic home education? If the family must spend hours per day satisfying the secular requirements of the oversight authority, what time is left for spiritual pursuits?

In the chapter on getting started, we also discussed the importance of having goals and a mission statement. That mission statement probably included many spiritual goals and objectives. It probably did not include a goal to receive state funds in exchange for using state-mandated materials. It probably did not include a goal of having a teacher come every quarter and interview you and your children to determine if their progress is sufficient (as is required in Alaska). It probably did not include using all secular books and materials in your home school. So, whether or not to join a charter school really comes down to why you are home schooling and what is important to you and your family.

Home schooled graduates

At Seton, we are now beginning to enroll the children of graduates of Seton Home Study School. These educated young parents are choosing home education for *their* children. Each year, more and more home educated students are graduating and getting married. These young people are open to life and will choose home schooling for their children.

In addition, our young home schooling graduates are taking up the banner to fight for the Catholic Church. Parents are taking their home schooling teens to various meetings and conferences, so they can see for themselves the feminist influences or the "arguments" for New Age positions. Recently, a New York mother phoned to tell me that she took her home schooled sixteen-year-old daughter to a meeting at the parish where all kinds of crazy and "nutty" anti-Catholic ideas were being promoted by a pro-feminist group. During the session, her daughter defended the Catholic Church position. "When I was sixteen," the mother said, "I certainly could not have defended my beliefs the way she did. And she spoke out in a public meeting with older adults." The mother was justifiably very proud of her daughter.

Employers are finding that home schooled students are serious workers, are more mature, are able to relate to different age groups, and are better educated. Home schoolers, interrelating with the elderly and the young, with clerks and gardeners, plumbers and electricians, professionals and non-professionals, interrelating with the community members almost daily, are more prepared for the larger society than those restricted to the classroom for so many hours a day for many years.

Joyce Swann of New Mexico, who home schooled ten children, was featured on national television in the spring of 1993 because two of her daughters, at 17 years old, not only graduated from college, but were hired by a local college as teachers! Alexandra Swann earned a master's degree at age 16 from the University of California external degree program. She wrote a book about her experiences called *No Regrets*.

Although the Swann family is obviously not an average case, home school graduates are achieving a high level of acceptance from colleges. Recent studies of college admissions officers have shown generally very favorable attitudes toward home schoolers. For example, a survey of 34 college admissions officers in Ohio reported that about 1/3 of them said home schoolers were more academically successful than average, 1/3 said they were about average, and 1/3 had no opinion. Significantly, not a single admissions officer said home schoolers were academically worse than average.

Anecdotally, home school graduates seem to believe that the emphasis on self-motivation given them from home schooling greatly helps them in college. While most students must learn self-motivation and time management after they get to college, many home schoolers have already developed these skills.

In 2004, Dr. Brian Ray, of the National Home Education Research Institute (NHERI), released a study of adults who had been home schooled, detailing their further education and their current attitudes. The study, called *Home Educated and Now Adults*, has three key findings that are important to the future of home schooling. First, of home schooled graduates from 18 to 24 years old, 74.2% reported that they had taken at least some college courses. Of the general U.S. population, only 46.2% of that age range reports some college education. Second, regarding civic participation, 71% of the home school graduates reported involvement in ongoing community service activities, compared to only 39% of all adults in the U.S. Third, a very small percentage, only 4%, reported that "politics and government are too hard to understand," compared to 35% of the general adult population. So, as a group, home schoolers are better educated and more involved in the community than the general population.

Another interesting fact in the study is that 82% of respondents said that they would home school their children. So even if your children do not now appreciate the education they are receiving, the odds are pretty good that they will appreciate it when they are adults.

The future for Catholic home schooling is bright as our young people witness to the truth in their communities. Young people will be leaders, will be independent thinkers, will not be afraid to speak in front of civic or church leaders, and with God's grace, will lead our country back to being a great Christian nation.

The Catholic clergy

An encouraging sign for Catholic home schooling parents is the growing number of priests who are beginning to recognize the value of Catholic home schooling. Many priests have agreed to be chaplains for Catholic home schooling groups. Some priests are giving regular talks for home schooling groups; other priests are willing to have home schoolers meet in their parish hall or have an activity at the church. Catholic home schooled children are having a quiet influence on the hearts of pastors in the parish churches where they attend Mass or serve as altar boys. Priests are asking, "What can I do to help these families who are willing to make the personal sacrifice to teach their own children?"

Antagonism between clergy and home schoolers has broken down with a speed we never predicted. Just as increasing numbers of home schoolers has led to a certain "normalcy" of home schooling in the wider society, it has had a similar impact in the Church. In the early years, home schooling was new and unknown and was sometimes seen as a challenge to the authority of bishops and priests. But as the number of Catholic home schoolers has increased, home schooling is seen more and more as simply another educational option, not as something to be feared and controlled. For example, on the website of the Diocese of Colorado

Springs, "Catholic Homeschooling" is listed on the page related to educational matters, along with the diocesan school and other educational ministries. Several dioceses—including Colorado Springs, Toledo, Raleigh, and Manchester—host an annual diocesan home school Mass.

When a diocese or parish runs its own schools, homeschooling inevitably is seen as in some amount of competition with those schools. When pastors and bishops are struggling to maintain diocesan schools, we cannot realistically expect widespread public endorsements of home schooling from them. Even so, several bishops have publicly supported home schooling in various ways, such as speaking at home schooling conferences. For example, Cardinal Archbishop Emeritus William Keeler of Baltimore has been the keynote speaker at several home schooling conferences in the Washington-Baltimore area. Cardinal Edouard Gagnon, (now deceased), past president of the Pontifical Council for the Family, was long been a staunch supporter of home schooling.

The home schooling movement has been consistently blessed with the support of good and holy priests. The late Father Vincent Miceli, an outstanding moral theologian and author, was a chaplain for Seton Home Study School, and spoke at various conferences supporting home schooling. The late Father Robert Fox, internationally known for his tours for young people to Fatima and his Fatima Family Apostolate, endorsed home schooling for many years. Father Pablo Straub, also deceased, had regular programs on EWTN and spoke at Catholic home schooling conferences. He also produced a series of video tapes on catechetics, especially for home schooling families. Father George Rutler, after a speech at Christendom College, gave parents an endorsement of home schooling. The priests of the Institute of the Fathers of Mercy speak frequently at home schooling conferences.

The most public priest to support Catholic home schooling parents was the renowned theologian Father John Hardon, now deceased. He was the author of numerous books including *The Catholic Catechism*, *Modern Catholic Dictionary*, *Question and Answer Catholic Catechism*, *The Treasury of Catholic Wisdom*, and *The Catholic Lifetime Reading Plan*. Father visited the Vatican several times a year, worked directly with the Vatican on a variety of American projects, and was for several years the religious support behind the Catholic home schooling conferences sponsored in Washington, D.C.

There are no current statistics on the rate of vocations coming from home schooling families, but at Seton we often hear of our graduates who are entering the priesthood or religious life. In fact, one of the readings at the installation Mass for Pope Benedict XVI was done by a former Seton student and seminarian, Justin Ferguson. In the future, we can look forward not only to priests who support home schooling, but also priests who are the product of home schooling. And, eventually, perhaps, we will have home schooled bishops.

A hopeful future

Catholic home schooling is a movement started by parents. It has come from Catholic families. It continues to grow as parents reject the latest fads and false agendas, and dedicate themselves to teaching their own children. We must constantly pray for these heroic parents, who often suffer persecution from friends and neighbors. God is working in many diverse ways to help Catholic parents. It is an important mission we have, and, as we have seen, many factors are helping us.

Father John Hardon believed that the difficult times we are having in the modern world is simply the persecution before a Golden Age of Christianity. If he is correct, we home schooling parents need to prepare our children to be leaders in that Golden Age to come.

Appendix
John Paul II's *Letter to Families*

The following is the section on education from John Paul II's 1994 *Letter to Families*.

16. What is involved in raising children? In answering this question two fundamental truths should be kept in mind: first, that man is called to live in truth and love; and second, that everyone finds fulfillment through the sincere gift of self. This is true both for the educator and for the one being educated. Education is thus a unique process for which the mutual communion of persons has immense importance. The educator is a person who "begets" in a spiritual sense. From this point of view, raising children can be considered a genuine apostolate. It is a living means of communication, which not only creates a profound relationship between the educator and the one being educated, but also makes them both sharers in truth and love, that final goal to which everyone is called by God the Father, Son and Holy Spirit.

Fatherhood and motherhood presume the coexistence and interaction of autonomous subjects. This is quite evident in the case of the mother when she conceives a new human being. The first months of the child's presence in the mother's womb bring about a particular bond which already possesses an educational significance of its own. The mother, even before giving birth, does not only give shape to the child's body, but also, in an indirect way, to the child's whole personality. Even though we are speaking about a process in which the mother primarily affects the child, we should not overlook the unique influence that the unborn child has on its mother. In this mutual influence which will be revealed to the outside world following the birth of the child, the father does not have a direct part to play. But he should be responsibly committed to providing attention and support throughout the pregnancy and, if possible, at the moment of birth.

For the "civilization of love" it is essential that the husband should recognize that the motherhood of his wife is a gift: this is enormously important for the entire process of raising children. Much will depend on his willingness to take his own part in this first stage of the gift of humanity, and to become willingly involved as a husband and father in the motherhood of his wife.

Education then is before all else a reciprocal "offering" on the part of both parents: together they communicate their own mature humanity to the newborn child, who gives them in turn the newness and freshness of the humanity which it has brought into the world. This is the case even when children are born with mental or physical disabilities. Here, the situation of the children can enhance the very special courage needed to raise them.

With good reason, then, the Church asks during the Rite of Marriage: "Will you accept children lovingly from God, and bring them up according to the law of Christ and his Church"? In the raising of children conjugal love is expressed as authentic parental love. The "communion of persons", expressed as conjugal love at the beginning of the family, is thus completed and brought to fulfillment in the raising of children. Every individual born and raised in a family constitutes a potential treasure which must be responsibly accepted, so that it will not be diminished or lost, but will rather come to an ever more mature humanity. This too is a process of exchange in which the parents-educators are in turn to a certain degree educated themselves. While they are teachers of humanity for their own children, they learn humanity from them. All this clearly brings out the organic structure of the family, and reveals the fundamental meaning of the fourth commandment.

In rearing children, the "we" of the parents, of husband and wife, develops into the "we" of the family, which is grafted on to earlier generations, and is open to gradual expansion. In this regard both grandparents and grandchildren play their own individual roles.

If it is true that by giving life parents share in God's creative work, it is also true that by raising their children they become sharers in his paternal and at the same time maternal way of teaching. According to Saint Paul, God's fatherhood is the primordial model of all fatherhood and motherhood in the universe (cf. Eph 3:14-15), and of human motherhood and fatherhood in particular. We have been completely instructed in God's own way of teaching by the eternal Word of the Father who, by becoming man, revealed to man the authentic and integral greatness of his humanity, that is, being a child of God. In this way he also revealed the true meaning of human education. Through Christ all education, within the family and outside of it, becomes part of God's own saving pedagogy, which is addressed to individuals and families and culminates in the Paschal Mystery of the Lord's Death and Resurrection. The "heart" of our redemption is the starting-point of every process of Christian education, which is likewise always an education to a full humanity.

Parents are the first and most important educators of their own children, and they also possess a fundamental competence in this area: they are educators because they are parents. They share their educational mission with other individuals or institutions, such as the Church and the State. But the mission of education must always be carried out in accordance with a proper application of the principle of subsidiarity. This implies the legitimacy and indeed the need of giving assistance to the parents, but finds its intrinsic and absolute limit in their prevailing right and their actual capabilities. The principle of subsidiarity is thus at the service of parental love, meeting the good of the family unit. For parents by themselves are not capable of satisfying every requirement of the whole process of raising children, especially in matters concerning their schooling and the entire gamut of socialization. Subsidiarity thus complements paternal and maternal love and confirms its fundamental nature, inasmuch as all other participants in the process of education are only able to carry out their responsibilities in the name of the parents, with their consent and, to a certain degree, with their authorization.

The process of education ultimately leads to the phase of self-education, which occurs when the individual, after attaining an appropriate level of psycho-physical maturity, begins to "educate himself on his own". In time, self-education goes beyond the earlier results achieved by the educational process, in which it continues to be rooted. An adolescent is exposed to new people and new surroundings, particularly teachers and classmates, who exercise an influence over his life which can be either helpful or harmful. At this stage he distances himself somewhat from the education received in the family, assuming at times a critical attitude with regard to his parents. Even so, the process of self-education cannot fail to be marked by the educational influence which the family and school have on children and adolescents. Even when they grow up and set out on their own path, young people remain intimately linked to their existential roots.

Against this background, we can see the meaning of the fourth commandment, "Honour your father and your mother" (Ex 20:12) in a new way. It is closely linked to the whole process of education. Fatherhood and motherhood, this first and basic fact in the gift of humanity, open up before both parents and children new and profound perspectives. To give birth according to the flesh means to set in motion a further "birth", one which is gradual and complex and which continues in the whole process of education. The commandment of the Decalogue calls for a child to honor its father and mother. But, as we saw above, that same commandment enjoins upon parents a kind of corresponding or "symmetrical" duty. Parents are also called to "honor" their children, whether they are young or old. This attitude is needed throughout the process of their education, including the time of their schooling. The "principle of giving honor", the recognition and respect due to man precisely because he is a man, is the basic condition for every authentic educational process.

In the sphere of education the Church has a specific role to play. In the light of Tradition and the teaching of the Council, it can be said that it is not only a matter of entrusting the Church with the person's religious and moral education, but of promoting the entire process of the person's education "together with" the Church. The family is called to carry out its task of education in the Church, thus sharing in her life and mission. The Church wishes to carry out her educational mission above all through families who are made capable of undertaking this task by the Sacrament of Matrimony, through the "grace of state" which follows from it and the specific "charism" proper to the entire family community.

Certainly one area in which the family has an irreplaceable role is that of religious education, which enables the family to grow as a "domestic church". Religious education and the catechesis of children make the family a true subject of evangelization and the apostolate within the Church. We are speaking of a right intrinsically linked to the principle of religious liberty. Families, and more specifically parents, are free to choose for their children a particular kind of religious and moral education consonant with their own convictions. Even when they entrust these responsibilities to ecclesiastical institutions or to schools administered by religious personnel, their educational presence ought to continue to be constant and active.

Within the context of education, due attention must be paid to the essential question of choosing a vocation, and here in particular that of preparing for marriage. The Church has made notable efforts to promote marriage preparation, for example by offering courses for engaged couples. All this is worthwhile and necessary. But it must not be forgotten that preparing for future life as a couple is above all the task of the family. To be sure, only spiritually mature families can adequately assume that responsibility. Hence we should point out the need for a special solidarity among families. This can be expressed in various practical ways, as for example by associations of families for families. The institution of the family is strengthened by such expressions of solidarity, which bring together not only individuals but also communities, with a commitment to pray together and to seek together the answers to life's essential questions. Is this not an invaluable expression of the apostolate of families to one another? It is important that families attempt to build bonds of solidarity among themselves. This allows them to assist each other in the educational enterprise: parents are educated by other parents, and children by other children. Thus a particular tradition of education is created, which draws strength from the character of the "domestic church" proper to the family.

The gospel of love is the inexhaustible source of all that nourishes the human family as a "communion of persons". In love the whole educational process finds its support and definitive meaning as the mature fruit of the parents' mutual gift. Through the efforts, sufferings and disappointments which are part of every person's education, love is constantly being put to the test. To pass the test, a source of spiritual strength is necessary. This is only found in the One who "loved to the end" (Jn 13:1). Thus education is fully a part of the "civilization of love". It depends on the civilization of love and, in great measure, contributes to its upbuilding.

The Church's constant and trusting prayer during the Year of the Family is for the education of man, so that families will persevere in their task of education with courage, trust and hope, in spite of difficulties occasionally so serious as to appear insuperable. The Church prays that the forces of the "civilization of love", which have their source in the love of God, will be triumphant. These are forces which the Church ceaselessly expends for the good of the whole human family.

Selected Bibliography

Cover Story

Dias, Joao S. Cla. *The Mother of Good Counsel of Genazzano*. Sunbury, PA: Western Hemisphere Cultural Society, 1992.

Chapter One

Eakman, B. K. *Educating for the New World Order*. Portland, Oregon: Halcyon House, 1991.

Engel, Randy. *Sex Education: The Final Plague*. Gaithersburg, MD: Human Life International, 1989; TAN, 1993.

Flesch, Rudolf. *Why Johnny Still Can't Read: A New Look at the Scandal of our Schools*. New York: Harper & Row, 1981.

Kilpatrick, William. *Why Johnny Can't Tell Right from Wrong*. New York: Simon & Schuster, 1992.

Morris, Barbara M. *Change Agents in the Schools*. Upland, CA: Barbara M. Morris Report, 1979.

Parker, Star. *Uncle Sam's Plantation: How Big Government Enslaves America's Poor and What We Can Do About It*. Nashville, TN: WND Books, 2003.

Schlafly, Phyllis, Editor. *Child Abuse in the Classroom*. Alton, IL: Pere Marquette Press, 1984.

Wrenn, Msgr. Michael J. *Catechisms and Controversies: Religious Education in the Postconciliar Years*. San Francisco: Ignatius Press, 1991.

Chapter Two

The Catholic Hearth. Monthly Catholic family magazine for children. Long Prairie, MN: The Neumann Press.

Chapter Three

Encyclicals:

Casti Connubii, or On Christian Marriage.
Humanae Vitae, or Of Human Life.
Sapientiae Christianae
Militantis Ecclesiae
Divini Illius Magistri, or On Christian Education of Youth.

Other Vatican Documents:

Catechesi Tradendae, or Catechesis in Our Time
Charter of the Rights of the Family
Declaration on Christian Education, Second Vatican Council
Familiaris Consortio, or The Role of the Christian Family in the
 Modern World.
Canon Law Society. *Code of Canon Law*. Washington, DC: Canon Law
 Society of America, 1983.

Other Books:

Daughters of St. Paul. *The Family, Center of Love and Life*. Boston:
 Daughters of St. Paul, 1981. [Selection of documents of Pope
 Paul VI, Pope John Paul I, Pope John Paul II]

Hardon, Rev. John. *The Catholic Family in the Modern World*. St. Paul,
 MN: Leaflet Missal Company, 1991.

Krason, Stephen M., editor. *Parental Rights*. Front Royal, VA:
 Christendom College Press, 1988.

Peters, Dr. Edward. *Home Schooling and the New Code of Canon Law*.
 Front Royal, VA: Christendom College Press, 1988.

Chapters Four and Five

Home School Legal Defense Association. *Home Schooling: A
 Foundation for Excellence*. VHS. Paeonian Springs, VA:
 HSLDA, 1992. 30 minutes.

Seton Home Study School, editor. *Bringing the Children Home*. VHS.
 Front Royal, VA: Seton, 1992. 6 hours.

Seton Home Study School, editor. *Keeping the Children Home*. VHS.
 Front Royal, VA: Seton, 1993. 6 hours.

Chapter Six

Ball, Ann. *A Handbook of Catholic Sacramentals*. Huntington, IN: Our Sunday Visitor, 1991.

Eternal Word Television Network, Irondale, AL 35210.

Isaacs, David. *Character Building*. Great Britain: Four Courts Press, 1993. Available from Sceptre Press, Princeton, NJ.

TAN Books and Publishers, Inc., Rockford, IL.

Chapter Eight

Dobson, Dr. James. *The Strong-Willed Child*. Wheaton, IL: Tyndale House, 1978. (Christian)

Phillips, Phil. *Saturday Morning Mind Control*. Nashville, TN: Oliver Nelson Books, 1991.

Walsh, Marion. *The Christian Family Coping*. Omaha, NE: Help of Christians Publications, 1986.

Wood, Steve. *The Training and Discipline of Children*. Audio tapes. Family Life Center, 2130 Wade Hampton Blvd., Greenville, SC 29615

Chapter Eleven

Barkley, Russell A. *Attention Deficit Hyperactivity Disorder: A Handbook for Diagnosis and Treatment*. New York: The Guilford Press, 1990.

Lidden, Craig B., Roberta L. Newman, and Jane R. Zalenski. *Pay Attention!!! Answers to Common Questions about the Diagnosis and Treatment of Attention Deficit Disorder*. Monroeville, PA: Transact Health Systems, Inc., 1989.

Martin, David L. *Handbook for Creative Teaching*. Crockett, KY: Rod and Staff Publishers, 1986.

Stevens, Suzanne. *Classroom Success for the Learning Disabled*. Winston-Salem, NC: Blair Publishers, 1984.

————. *The Learning Disabled Child: Ways That Parents Can Help*. Winston-Salem, NC: Blair Publishers, 1980.

Chapter Sixteen

Catholic Home School Network of America. *Responsibilities and Rights of Parents in Religious Education.* Available from Seton Home Study School.

Chapter Seventeen

Carthy, M.P. "Catholicism in English-Speaking Lands." *The Twentieth Century Encyclopedia of Catholicism.* Vol. 92. New York: Hawthorn, 1964.

Davies, Michael. *The Reign of Christ the King,* Rockford, IL: TAN Book and Publishers, 1992.

McAvoy, Thomas. *The Great Crisis in American Catholic History, 1895 - 1900.* Chicago: Regnery, 1957.

Pope Pius XII. *Summi Pontificatus.* Rome: Vatican, 1939.

Woodruff, Douglas. "Church and State." *The Twentieth Century Encyclopedia of Catholicism.* Vol. 89. New York: Hawthorn, 1961.

Chapter Eighteen

Ray, Brian D. *Home Educated and Now Adults.* Salem, OR: National Home Education Research Institute, 2004.

U.S. Department of Commerce, National Telecommunications and Information Administration. *A Nation Online: Internet Use in America.* Washington, DC, 2002.

Index

The Clark Family, July 4, 2008

The Clark Grandchildren, July 4, 2008